DATE DUE			
OCT 06 1995			

THE SOCIOLOGICAL TRADITION

ROBERT A. NISBET

THE SOCIOLOGICAL TRADITION

BASIC BOOKS, INC., PUBLISHERS

 NEW YORK

© 1966 by Basic Books, Inc.
Library of Congress Catalog Card Number: 66-28636
Cloth: SBN 465-07953-9
Paper: SBN 465-07952-0
Manufactured in the United States of America
Designed by Florence D. Silverman

20 19 18 17 16 15 14 13

To
E. P. N.

PREFACE

This book is an effort to set forth what is conceptually fundamental and historically distinctive in the sociological tradition. Although it covers some of the same ground that one would find in a history of sociological thought, it is far from that. What I have written is at once narrower and broader: narrower in that I have excluded more than a few names that would ordinarily be dealt with in a formal history of sociology; broader in that I have not hesitated to emphasize individuals who were not, either nominally or substantively, sociologists but whose relation to the sociological tradition seems to me vital.

Central to any intellectual tradition is the nucleus or core of ideas that gives the tradition its continuity from generation to generation and its identity amid all the other disciplines that make up the humanistic and scientific study of man. For reasons set forth generally in the first chapter and explicitly in the main body of the book, I have chosen five ideas as the constitutive elements of sociology: *community, authority, status,* the *sacred,* and *alienation.* These, I believe, are the ideas which, in their functional relation to one another, form the nucleus of the sociological tradition.

It is unnecessary to state that I do not for a moment suppose that these five ideas, far-ranging and magnetic though they be, represent the entirety of modern sociology: its manifold empirical interests, methodologies, and concepts. I argue only that these ideas form the nucleus of the sociological tradition, giving it the continuity and coherence it has had for more than a century. Changing our figure, the five ideas may be likened, in their union, to an alembic which distills into sociological essence those more general and encompassing ideas that are the common province of *all* the social sciences: structure, culture, individuality, process, development, function, and so on. In the great formative period

1830–1900 it was the coalescence of these five ideas that marked the increasingly distinct emergence of sociology from the matrix of moral philosophy that had once contained the elements of all the modern social sciences.

The towering roles of Tocqueville and Marx will not be missed in the chapters that follow. In every respect relevant to this book Tocqueville and Marx are at opposite theoretical extremes. The sociological tradition may indeed be seen as a kind of magnetic field with Tocqueville and Marx as the two poles of attraction. In the long run the influence of Tocqueville on the sociological tradition has been the greater. Even before the nineteenth century had run its course, the works of Tönnies, Weber, Durkheim, and Simmel—the four men who, by common assent, did the most to give systematic shape to modern sociological theory—reflected, on the whole, the triumph of the Tocquevillian over the Marxian image of society and its course of development.

To say this is in no way to join in the chorus of depreciation of Marx that today fills the atmosphere of Western thought. Marx remains, along with Tocqueville, one of the two most creative and influential minds in the social thought of the nineteenth century. Apart from the intellectual tension created by the immense and opposite power of Marx, the true heir of the Enlightenment, it is unlikely that the Tocquevillian vision of society could have attained the shaping influence that it did. In the history of ideas, influences always demand counter-influences for their nourishment. And, in any event, who is to say that the writ of Marx (after all, still magisterial in many non-Western parts of the world) will not, in the decades and generations ahead in the West, supersede the present ascendance of Tocqueville? The rhythms of ideas and values in history permit no easy generalizations.

Paralleling in significance the contrasting roles of Tocqueville and Marx are the conflicting themes of traditionalism and modernism. Of all the contemporary social sciences, sociology is the one in which tension between traditional and modern values is most evident in its conceptual structure and its underlying assumptions.

Sociology, above any other scholarly discipline, has taken the conflicts between traditionalism and modernism in European culture and converted them into a set of analytical and interpretative concepts. To label Weber or Tönnies or Durkheim or Simmel traditionalist (even more, politically conservative) would be absurd. But it is not absurd to suggest that their writings, more surely than those of any other major social scientists in the nineteenth century, exemplify—are indeed founded upon—

tensions of value and perspective that, in the writings of the more polemically minded, loom up as the constituent elements of nineteenth- and twentieth-century ideologies.

It is surely plain today that the most fundamental ideological conflicts of the past century and a half have been between, on the one hand, values of *community, moral authority, hierarchy,* and the *sacred* and, on the other hand, *individualism, equality, moral release,* and *rationalist techniques of organization and power.* What sociology, at its best and most creative, has done is to lift these conflicts from the currents of ideological controversy in which they made their appearance during the age of the industrial and democratic revolutions and to convert and refine them—in a host of theoretical, empirical, and methodological ways— into the problems and concepts that today give sociology its unique position in the understanding of not only the development of modern Europe but of the new nations that are now undergoing some of the same kinds of social change that were still vivid in Europe and the United States two generations ago.

So long as these conflicts continue, will the sociological tradition remain the evocative and relevant tradition that has been for more than a century.

I wish to thank the University of California for sabbatical leave, the John Simon Guggenheim Foundation for generous financial assistance, and Princeton University for hospitable fellowship-residence in which to write this book. It is a pleasure, finally, to thank Irving Kristol for deeply valued stimulus and suggestion and Carolyn Kirkpatrick for indispensable assistance in every phase of preparation of the manuscript.

Robert A. Nisbet

University of California, Riverside
June, 1966

CONTENTS

PART ONE

IDEAS AND CONTEXTS

1 THE UNIT-IDEAS OF SOCIOLOGY

IDEAS AND ANTITHESES

The history of thought is commonly dealt with in one of two ways. The first, and oldest, is to begin with the *dramatis personae,* the thinkers themselves, whose writings furnish the bibliographic substance of the history of thought. There is much to be said for this way. It is indispensable if what we desire is understanding of the motive forces of intellectual history: the perceptions, insights, and discoveries that come only from individuals. Nevertheless, this approach has its disadvantages. Chief among them is the ease with which the history of thought becomes merely the biography of thought. Ideas are treated as extensions or shadows of single individuals rather than as the distinguishable structures of meaning, perspective, and allegiance that major ideas so plainly are in the history of civilization. Like institutions, ideas have independent relationships and continuities, and it is only too easy to lose sight of these when we focus attention on biographies.

A second approach directs itself not to the man, but to the system, the school, or the ism. Not the Benthams and the Mills but utilitarianism, not the Hegels and the Bradleys but idealism, not the Marxes and the Proudhons but socialism is here the prime object of attention. This approach is valuable; the history of thought is indubitably a history of systems: as true of sociology as of metaphysics. Presuppositions, ideas, and corollaries congeal into systems which often develop the same power over their followers that religions do. Systems can be likened to the psychologist's *Gestalten;* we acquire ideas and facts, not atomistically, but within the *patterns* of thought that form so large a part of our environment. But the pitfalls of this approach are well known. Too often systems are taken as irreducible rather than as the constellations of distin-

3

guishable, even separable, assumptions and ideas that they are in fact: all decomposable, all capable of being regrouped into different systems. Systems moreover tend to become lifeless; what excites one generation or century becomes only antiquarian in the next. One need think only of socialism, pragmatism, utilitarianism, and, long before them, nominalism and realism. Yet each of these systems has component elements that are as viable today, though in different ways, as when these systems were being formed. To lose sight of the elements would be unfortunate.

This leads us to a third approach, one that begins with neither the man nor the system, but with the ideas which are the elements of systems. No one has more lucidly or authoritatively described this approach than the late Arthur O. Lovejoy, and I cannot do better than quote the passage in which he introduces it.

"By the history of ideas," wrote Lovejoy, "I mean something at once more specific and less restricted than the history of philosophy. It is differentiated primarily by the character of the units with which it concerns itself. Though it deals in great part with the same material as the other branches of the history of thought and depends greatly upon their prior labors, it divides the materials in a special way, brings the parts of it into new groupings and relations, reviews it from the standpoint of a distinctive purpose. Its initial procedure may be said—though the parallel has its dangers—to be somewhat analogous to that of analytical chemistry. In dealing with the history of philosophical doctrines, for example, it cuts into the hard-and-fast individual systems, and, for its own purposes, breaks them up into their component elements, into what may be called their unit-ideas." [1]

In Lovejoy's *The Great Chain of Being* we see how it is possible to cut into systems as complex and unlike one another as Platonic idealism, medieval scholasticism, secular rationalism, and romanticism, and to lay bare such powerful, wide-ranging unit-ideas as *continuity* and *plenitude,* and to do this in such a way as to throw new light on the systems and also on the philosophers, from Plato to the Enlightenment, who produced the systems. We see not only the component elements, the unit-ideas, but also new groupings and relationships of men and ideas; we see affinities, but also oppositions, that we should not have supposed to exist.

The canvas of my own book is, of course, a much smaller one than Professor Lovejoy's and I cannot claim, in any event, to have followed his approach in all its brilliant suggestiveness. But like Lovejoy's, this book is concerned with unit-ideas: specifically, with certain unit-ideas of European sociology in its great formative period, 1830–1900, when the foundations of contemporary sociological thought were being laid by such men as Tocquevi'le, Marx, Weber, and Durkheim.

I stress this, for the reader should be clearly warned of what he may, and may not, expect to find in this book. He will find, for example, no effort to unfold the meaning of Marx, the essence of Tocqueville, or the unity of Durkheim. Such a task, invaluable though it be, is left to others. Nor is there effort to deal here with any of the overt systems that may be found in the writings of nineteenth-century sociologists: dialectical materialism, functionalism, or utilitarianism. Our concern will be with unit-ideas which seem to me to provide fundamental, constitutive substance to sociology amid all the manifest differences among its authors, ideas which persist throughout the classical age of modern sociology, extending indeed to the present moment.

And the present *is* our point of departure. History, it has been well said, yields her secrets only to those who begin with the present. The present is, in Alfred North Whitehead's phrase, holy ground. All of the unit-ideas considered in this book are as visible and as directive of intellectual effort today as they were when the works of Tocqueville, Weber, Durkheim, and Simmel made these ideas the foundation stones of modern sociology. We live, and we should not forget it, in a late phase of the classical age of sociology. Strip from present-day sociology the perspectives and frameworks provided by men like Weber and Durkheim, and little would be left but lifeless heaps of data and stray hypotheses.

What are the criteria by which we select the unit-ideas of an intellectual discipline? Four, at least, are governing. Such ideas must have *generality:* that is, all must be discernible in the works of a considerable number of the towering minds of an age, not be limited to the works of a single individual or coterie. Second, they must have *continuity:* they must be observable in the early as well as late phases of the period, as relevant indeed to present as to past. Third, such ideas must be *distinctive:* they must participate in what it is that makes a discipline significantly different from other disciplines. Ideas like "individual," "society," "order" are useless here—however valuable they may be in more general contexts—for these are elements of *all* the disciplines of social thought. Fourth, they must be ideas in the full sense: that is, more than wraithlike "influences," more than peripheral aspects of methodology. They must be ideas in the ancient and lasting Western sense of the word, a sense, indeed, in which Plato and John Dewey could find common meaning. An idea is a *perspective,* a framework, a category (in the Kantian sense) within which vision and fact unite, within which insight and observation are brought together. An idea is, in Whitehead's word, a searchlight; it lights up a part of the landscape, leaving other parts in shadow or darkness. It does not matter whether our ultimate conception of idea is Platonist or pragmatist, for idea, in the sense in which I shall use the word in this book, may be described as either archetype or plan of action.

What are the essential unit-ideas of sociology, those which, above any others, give distinctiveness to sociology in its juxtaposition to the other social sciences? There are, I believe, five: *community, authority, status,* the *sacred,* and *alienation.* Detailed exposition of these ideas is, of course, the subject of the chapters which follow. All that is necessary here is their brief identification. *Community* includes but goes beyond local community to encompass religion, work, family, and culture; it refers to social bonds characterized by emotional cohesion, depth, continuity, and fullness. *Authority* is the structure or the inner order of an association, whether this be political, religious, or cultural, and is given legitimacy by its roots in social function, tradition, or allegiance. *Status* is the individual's position in the hierarchy of prestige and influence that characterizes every community or association. The *sacred* includes the mores, the non-rational, the religious and ritualistic ways of behavior that are valued beyond whatever utility they may possess. *Alienation* is a historical perspective within which man is seen as estranged, anomic, and rootless when cut off from the ties of community and moral purpose.

Each of these ideas is commonly linked to a conceptual opposite, to a kind of antithesis, from which it derives much of its continuing meaning in the sociological tradition. Thus, opposed to the idea of community is the idea of society (*Gesellschaft,* in Tönnies' usage) in which reference is to the large-scale, impersonal, contractual ties that were proliferating in the modern age, often, as it seemed, at the expense of community. The conceptual opposite of authority in sociological thought is *power,* which is commonly identified with military or political force or with administrative bureaucracy and which, unlike the authority that arises directly from social function and association, raises the problem of legitimacy. Status has for its conceptual opposite in sociology not the popular idea of equality but the novel and sophisticated idea of *class,* at once more specialized and collective. The opposite of the idea of the sacred is the utilitarian, the profane (in Durkheim's momentous wording), or the *secular.* And, finally, alienation—considered at least as a sociological perspective—is best seen as an inversion of *progress.* From precisely the same assumptions regarding the nature of historical development in modern Europe—industrialization, secularization, equality, popular democracy, and so on—such minds as Tocqueville and Weber drew, not the conclusion of social and moral progress, but the more morbid conclusion of man's alienation from man, from values, and from self; an alienation caused by the very forces that others in the century were hailing as progressive.

Community-society, authority-power, status-class, sacred-secular, alienation-progress: these are rich themes in nineteenth-century thought. Considered as linked antitheses, they form the very warp of the sociological tradition. Quite apart from their conceptual significance in sociology, they may be regarded as epitomizations of the conflict between tradition and modernism, between the old order, made moribund by the industrial and democratic revolutions, and the new order, its outlines still unclear and as often the cause of anxiety as of elation or hope.

THE REVOLT AGAINST INDIVIDUALISM

Obviously, these ideas and antitheses did not arise in the first instance in the nineteenth century. In one form or another they are old. They may be seen in the ancient world: in, for example, Plato's Athens, when Greece, like Europe two thousand years later, was searching for new foundations of order to replace those that had seemingly been destroyed by the ravages of war, revolution, and *stasis*. Plato's concern with community, alienation, authority, hierarchy, the sacred, and with social generation and degeneration is, of course, profound, and it is hardly extreme to say that all the essential elements of subsequent Western social thought are to be found in, first, Plato's development of these ideas and, second, in Aristotle's responses to them. The same ideas are to be seen, though in modified form, in the writings of the Roman moral philosophers in the first century B.C. when once again a traditional social order appeared doomed, the consequence of prolonged war, of social revolution, of moral decay, and, spectacularly, by the overthrow of the Republic and its replacement by the military imperium of Augustus. We see these ideas again, four centuries later, in the works of the Christian philosophers, who were preoccupied, as were so many of their pagan contemporaries, by man's alienation, man's search for the blessed community, for sanctity of authority, and by his proper place in the hierarchical chain of being that culminated in the City of God.

But while these ideas are indeed timeless and universal, they have, like all major ideas of man and society, their periods of ebb as well as flow, of dearth as well as abundance. There are other ages in which these ideas have only small significance, ages when they are placed in the shadow of strikingly different ideas and attitudes regarding man's fate and man's hope. Thus, none of the ideas we are concerned with in this book was especially notable in the Age of Reason that so brilliantly lighted up the seventeenth and eighteenth centuries, reaching its high point in the Enlightenment in France and England.

Then, a different set of words and ideas encompassed moral and political aspiration: ideas like *individual, progress, contract, nature, reason*. The dominant objectives of the whole age, from Bacon's *Novum Organum* to Condorcet's *Sketch of a Historical Picture of the Human Mind,* were those of release: release of the individual from ancient social ties and of the mind from fettering traditions. Towering over the whole period was the universally held belief in the natural individual—in his reason, his innate character, and self-sustaining stability.

The ideas and values of seventeenth- and eighteenth-century individualistic rationalism did not, of course, disappear with the coming of the nineteenth century. Far from it. In critical rationalism, in philosophic liberalism, in classical economics, and in utilitarian politics, the ethos of individualism is continued—together with the vision of a social order founded on rational interest.

But despite a once common and widely expressed point of view among historians of the age, individualism is far from the whole story of nineteenth-century thought. There is much reason indeed for regarding it as the fading, if still rosy, blush of an individualism that had attained its true zenith in the preceding century. And, as we have come only slowly to realize in our histories, what is distinctive and intellectually most fertile in nineteenth-century thought is not individualism but the reaction to individualism: a reaction expressed in no way more strikingly than by the ideas that form the central subject of this book.

These ideas—*community, authority, status,* the *sacred,* and *alienation*—taken together constitute a reorientation of European thought quite as momentous, I believe, as that very different, even opposite, reorientation of thought that had marked the waning of the Middle Ages three centuries earlier and the rise of the Age of Reason. Then it had been individualistic rationalism asserting itself against medieval corporatism and authority. Now, in the early nineteenth century, it is the reverse: the reaction of traditionalism against analytic reason; of communalism against individualism; and of the non-rational against the purely rational.

The reaction is widespread; it is to be found in literature, in philosophy and theology, as well as in jurisprudence, historiography, and, most systematically, in sociology. In widening areas of thought in the nineteenth century we see rationalist individualism (kept alive, of course, most impressively by the utilitarians, whose doctrines provide negative relief for so many sociological concepts) assailed by theories resting upon a reassertion of tradition, theories that would have been as repugnant to a Descartes or a Bacon as to a Locke or a Rousseau. We see the historic premise of the innate stability of the individual challenged by a new social psychology that derived personality from the close contexts of society and that made alienation the price of man's release from these contexts. Instead of the Age of Reason's cherished natural order, it is now the institutional order—community, kinship, social class—that forms the point of departure for social philosophers as widely separated in their views as Coleridge, Marx, and Tocqueville. From the eighteenth century's generally optimistic vision of popular sovereignty we pass to nineteenth-century premonitions of the tyranny that may lie in popular democracy when its institutional and traditional limits are broken through. And, finally, even the idea of progress is given a new statement: one resting not upon release from community and tradition but upon a kind of craving for new forms of moral and social community.

LIBERALISM, RADICALISM, CONSERVATISM

This reorientation of social thought, of which the rise of sociology is so important a phase, is not, let us emphasize, the result of purely intellectual, much less "scientific," currents in the age. As Sir Isaiah Berlin has stated, and as his own historical studies so superbly illustrate, ideas never beget ideas as butterflies beget butterflies. The genetic fallacy has too often made histories of thought into abstracted sequences of "begats." Especially in political and social thought do we need constantly to see the ideas of each age as responses to crises of events and to the challenges formed by major changes in the social order.

The ideas we are concerned with are incomprehensible save in terms of the ideological contexts in which they first arose. The major sociologists of the century, from Comte and Tocqueville to Weber and Durkheim, were caught up in the currents of the three great ideologies of the nineteenth and early twentieth centuries: liberalism, radicalism, and conservatism. In the next chapter we shall deal with the two revolutions —industrial and democratic—that shaped the ideologies and also the fundamental ideas of sociology. Here it is important, first, to identify the three ideologies.

The hallmark of liberalism is devotion to the individual; especially to his political, civil, and then, increasingly, his social rights. What tradition is to the conservative and use of power is to the radical, individual autonomy is to the liberal. There are, to be sure, striking differences between the liberals of Manchester, for whom freedom meant chiefly release of economic productivity from the fetters of law and custom, and the liberals of Paris in 1830, for whom liberation of thought from clericalism loomed up as the major objective. But granted the differences, what liberals had in common was, first, acceptance of the basic structure of state and economy (they did not, like the radicals, see revolution as the indispensable basis of freedom, though they could on occasion join in support of revolution) and, second, a belief that progress lay in the emancipation of man's mind and spirit from the religious and traditional bonds of the old order. Liberals in the nineteenth century continued the Enlightenment's faith in the self-sustaining nature of individuality once given its release from corrupting and fettering institutions. There are, admittedly, those such as Tocqueville, John Stuart Mill, and Lord Acton—who must certainly be counted, even as they counted themselves, among liberals—for whom institutions and traditions could take on something of the importance that conservatives granted them, but this was only to the degree that these entities offered reinforcement to individuality. The touchstone was individual freedom, not social authority. Utilitarian liberalism—which stretches from Jeremy Bentham to Herbert Spencer—held to a view of church, state, parish, guild, family, and moral tradition that did not differ in any significant respect from earlier views of the Enlightenment. In the writings of Macaulay, Buckle, and Spencer the notion of the discrete, self-motivating, and self-stabilizing individual is primary. Institutions and traditions are secondary: at best, his shadows; at worst, barriers to self-assertion.

In radicalism—which often draws from and is not infrequently aligned with liberalism—a very different state of mind is to be found. If there is any one element that gives distinction to radicalism of the nineteenth and twentieth centuries it is, I believe, the sense of the redemptive possibilities which lie in political power: its capture, its purification, and its unlimited, even terroristic, use in the rehabilitation of man and institutions. Coupled with power is almost limitless faith in reason in the fashioning of a new social order.

Prior to the eighteenth century, revolts against the social order—

and they were not infrequent, even in the Middle Ages—were set in the framework of religion. The objectives of Hussites, Anabaptists, Levelers, Shakers, and others who from time to time rose up against constituted authority were religious. Social and economic conditions obviously contributed to the igniting of these revolts and there were indeed references to poverty and suffering in the tracts and manifestoes that were on occasion drawn up. But the important point is that these references were couched in religious terms, and it was the appeal to the lost purity of apostolic Christianity or to the hope of Christ's second coming that was fundamental.

The main line of nineteenth-century radicalism is unqualifiedly secular. The torch of revolt passed to those who saw the hope of Europe and mankind not in the religious but the political arm of society. Millennialism did not disappear, only its Christian content. What we have in nineteenth-century radicalism, with Jacobinism, the Committee of Public Safety, and perhaps, above all the *coup d'état* of 18 Brumaire, for firm models was a revolutionary chiliasm that sprang from faith in absolute power; not power for its own sake but for the sake of rationalist and humanitarian liberation of man from the tyrannies and inequalities (including those of religion) that had plagued him for millennia.

When we come to conservatism, the matter is more complex. Since it is the least dealt with of the three ideologies and since there is an unusually close relation between the principal tenets of philosophical conservatism and the unit-ideas of sociology, we must go into more detail.

Modern conservatism is, in its philosophical form at least, the child of the Industrial and French revolutions: unintended, unwanted, hated by the protagonists of each, but the child nevertheless. What the two revolutions attacked, the conservatism of such men as Burke, Bonald, Haller, and Coleridge defended. And what the two revolutions engendered—in the way of popular democracy, technology, secularism, and so on—conservatism attacked. If the central ethos of liberalism is individual emancipation, and that of radicalism the expansion of political power in the service of social and moral zeal, the ethos of conservatism is tradition, essentially medieval tradition. From conservatism's defense of social tradition sprang its emphasis on the values of community, kinship, hierarchy, authority, and religion, and also its premonitions of social chaos surmounted by absolute power once individuals had become wrenched from the contexts of these values by the forces of liberalism and radicalism.

Unlike the philosophers of the Enlightenment, the conservatives began with the absolute reality of the institutional order as they found it, the order bequeathed by history. For them, the "natural" order, the order revealed by pure reason, the order on which the *philosophes* had mounted their devastating attacks upon traditional society, had no reality whatsoever. The matter is indeed reversed in conservative thought. For it is on the claimed priority of society and its traditional institutions to the individual that the conservatives based their onslaught against the Enlightenment's ideas of natural right, natural law, and independent reason.

The conservatives at the beginning of the nineteenth century form an Anti-Enlightenment. There is not a work, not a major idea indeed, in the conservative renaissance that does not seek to refute ideas of the *philosophes*. Some, such as Chateaubriand, delighted in seeming occasionally to espouse one of the Enlighteners as the means of mounting attack on another—usually on Voltaire, whose brilliant attacks on Christianity were vitriol for the deeply Christian conservatives. Even in Burke there are kind words occasionally where these will serve to promote a sense of inconsistency and division within the Enlightenment. But hatred of the Enlightenment and especially of Rousseau is fundamental in philosophical conservatism.

Prophets of the past, the conservatives have been well called, scarcely likely to affect the main currents of European life and thought. Yet it would be fatal to an understanding of much that we now know to be significant and profound in the nineteenth century if we were to dismiss the conservatives as of but antiquarian significance. That Burke, and especially Hegel, had great influence is, of course, sufficiently attested in all histories of the thought. But both tend to be dealt with as individuals rather than as figures in a movement of ideas that went far beyond them in scope. They must be seen, just as Voltaire and Diderot are seen within the Enlightenment, as individuals, yes, but also as two among a considerable number of minds that had enough in common to form, incontestably, an age, a pattern of ideas.

The French conservatives are perhaps the most neglected among them all. Bonald, Maistre, and Chateaubriand are commonly dealt with as odd, somewhat gothic figures in the history of "romanticism," a categorization that must have the first two at least turning in their graves; the brilliant Lamennais' conservative youth is generally forgotten in the luminescence of his later, radical, activities. But the influence of the French conservatives on social thought was substantial. We need only glance at some of the sociologists to be clear on this. Thus, Saint-Simon and Comte were lavish in praise of what the latter called "the retrograde school." This "immortal group, under the leadership of Maistre," wrote Comte, "will long deserve the gratitude of Positivists." [2] Saint-Simon attributed to Bonald the inspiration of his interest in "critical" and "organic" periods of history and also in the beginnings of his proposals for "stabilizing" industrialism and democracy. Le Play, a generation later, was but giving scientific expression, in his *European Working Classes,* to Bonald's early, polemical work on the family. Of the influence of conservatism on Tocqueville's mind there can be no question; it is the immediate source of his troubled and oblique appreciation of democracy. And, at the end of the century, in the writings of the non-religious and politically liberal Durkheim we find ideas of French conservatism converted into some of the essential theories of his systematic sociology: the collective conscience, the functional character of institutions and ideas, intermediate associations, as well as his whole attack on individualism.

What was conservatism against? The Revolution foremost, of course, but by no means exclusively. I believe we can best understand conservatism as the first broad-gauged attack on modernism and its political, economic, and cultural elements. The Revolution provided the point of departure, but for all of the conservatives the chief significance of the Revolution was historic and symbolic. They saw it as the iron culmination of tendencies that lay deep in modern European history; tendencies that were now indicated by their awful consequence. Few went as far as Bonald in referring to the Terror as God's proper punishment of Europe for its secular and individualistic heresies, but, without exception among the conservatives, there was a deeply fixed belief that what was most distinctive and "modern" in history after the Reformation was either evil or the prelude to evil.

As the conservatives reconstructed European history, they saw first the Protestant wrenching of individual faith from the discipline of the Church, leading to the inevitability of perpetual dissent. From this violation it was but a short step to Baconian and Cartesian arrogation to individual, finite man of intellectual powers and certainties that belonged to God and society. Given the heresy of secular individualism, did it not follow that men would look upon society as they did upon physical landscape, as something on which inventive faculties could tinker endlessly, remaking, refashioning as impulse suggested? And, finally, there could not help but emerge from all this the dangerous romantic image of man as the creature of inherently good, ineffaceably stable, instincts on which institutions and government sat repressively and needlessly. Such, in its essentials, was the conservative view of what had preceded the Revolution and modernism.

There are other elements in the conservative picture of modernism, elements proceeding directly from the Revolution in France. Equalitarianism and centralized power based on the people are perhaps the leading elements of the picture, but they arc closely joined with others: the substitution of feeling and passion—in religion and politics and art—for the disciplined restraints of tradition and piety; the replacement of non-rational, sacred values by impersonal and ephemeral norms of contract and utility; the decline of authority, religious and social as well as political; the loss of liberty—which the conservatives chose to define in the medieval sense of this word, as connoting not so much freedom, which signified disengagement and license, as principled *right* within divine law and tradition; the debasement of culture, the consequence of its mass dissemination; and, finally, governing all of these, the whole progressive-deterministic mentality that insisted upon regarding past, present, and future as iron categories of the ethically bad, better, and best.

This is the constellation of elements that emerges from conservatism's general view of the modern world, the world that the Reformation, capitalism, nationalism, and reason had engendered and that the Revolution had now given birth to. We have no difficulty in finding all of these elements in Burke's reaction to the French Revolution, and they remain vivid in the writings of other conservatives in Europe and also America. If conservative ideas never really took root in America, it was not because a few minds of genius such as John Randolph of Roanoke, James Fenimore Cooper, and John C. Calhoun, among others, did not try to inseminate them in American political thought. It was because the United States, lacking the persisting reality of a medieval institutional past, had little with which to nourish them, to give them urgency and relevance to the American scene. But in Europe this medieval past became, very suddenly after the French Revolution, an evocative set of symbols.

The rediscovery of medievalism—its institutions, values, themes, and structures—is one of the significant events in the intellectual history of the nineteenth century.[3] Although its first and lasting significance is to European conservatism, forming the model, so to speak, of the conservative image of the good society, it has a good deal of significance also to sociological thought, forming the conceptual stuff of much of its own response to modernism. As much as any single event, this rediscovery of the Middle Ages accounts for the sharp difference between what had been the Enlightenment's typical reconstruction of European history and that which becomes standard in so much nineteenth-century historical writing. For the French *philosophes* and also for such English rationalists as Gibbon, Adam Smith, and Bentham, there was categorical disdain for the Dark Ages, a period universally taken to cover the more than thousand years that intervened between the fall of Rome and the beginning of the Age of Reason.

Now, of a sudden, the Middle Ages are restored to humanist regard: first in the writings of such men as Haller, Savigny, Bonald, and Chateaubriand, for whom the period is unconcealedly inspirational; then, in constantly widening compass, in the works of jurists, historians, theologians, novelists, and others. The Middle Ages furnished theme and atmosphere in the nineteenth century much as classical thought had in the Renaissance. The rise of what was known generally as the historical school in the social sciences was based on the utilization of historical and institutional materials that were preponderantly medieval. It was medieval society that came more and more to provide a comparative offset to modernism for the critics of the latter. Just as the eighteenth century had popularized the use of primitive materials—the whole vogue of "exoticism," for example, which so strongly undergirded natural law models— for purposes of contrast with the present, so, now, the nineteenth century began to utilize medieval materials for comparative purposes. There was more than comparison in it, of course. As the monumental studies of von Gierke, Fustel de Coulanges, Rashdall, and Maitland make clear, interest in the Middle Ages was harnessed to scholarly search for the institutional origins of European economy, polity, and culture. The Middle Ages could be the basis of idealization and utopia for the nineteenth century—as in the writings of Chateaubriand, Sir Walter Scott, and others down to William Morris—but it could also be a mine for some remarkable researches in history and the social sciences.

The relation of medievalism to sociology is particularly close. We have noted Comte's admiration for the conservatives. Out of it flowed appreciation in almost equal degree of the Middle Ages. Few approached Comte's adulation; medievalism is beyond any question the real model for his sociological utopia in *The Positive Polity*. Into its veins Comte pumped the blood of Positivism, replacing Catholicism, but he leaves us in no doubt of his admiration of the *structure* of medieval society or of his desire to restore its essence, infused by "science." Medieval society, with its localism, hierarchy, and religious constitution, is the constant point of reference in Tocqueville's studies of both American democracy and the modern regime in Europe. Le Play frankly based his vaunted "stem family" on the medieval family, and declared the Middle Ages to be (rather than "irrelevant primitive and ancient societies") the proper object of attention in the "comparative study of social facts." Tönnies derived all of the substance of his typology of *Gemeinschaft* from medieval village, family, and clan. Durkheim based his celebrated proposal for intermediate occupational associations on medieval guilds, taking care, naturally, to specify the differences, for he had been all too often charged by critics with basing his science of society upon values of corporatism, organicism, and metaphysical realism.

All of this is not to suggest that the sociologists were medieval in temper. We should have to look far to find a mind more "modern" in social and political affiliation than Durkheim's. Even within the body of his social theory, Durkheim's overriding spirit is rationalist-positivist, derived in large part from Descartes, who, above any other philosopher of the seventeenth century, had put scholasticism to rout. The same, essentially, is true of Tönnies, Weber, and Simmel.

IDEOLOGY AND SOCIOLOGY

This brings us to the important matter of the personal ideologies of the sociologists we shall be concerned with. We have thus far been considering ideologies abstractly, taking them as seedbeds of doctrinal and conceptual issues in the century. The picture is not nearly so distinct or easily divided when we turn to individuals. It is easy enough to assign Le Play, Marx, and Spencer to their respective ideologies. Le Play was the conservative *par excellence,* Marx the very personification of radicalism in the nineteenth century. And, by any standard appropriate to that period, Spencer was a liberal. But it is not so easy with respect to some of the others. Comte, we may think of as radical when we look at the utopianism of his *Positive Polity* with its plan for the total reordering of Western society. But to a good many in the century, including, at first, John Stuart Mill, Comte's measured paeans to science, industry, and Positivism placed him among the liberals; and of the profoundly conservative cast of the actual concepts of his new science there can be no doubt— concepts indeed that led to the special place that Comte had in French conservative thought right down to the *Action Française* and also in the pre-Civil War thought of the American South. Tocqueville is perhaps a clearer picture: liberalism and conservatism coalesce. His personal associations were with the liberals of his time; he served in an influential role in the Revolution of 1848, and there are no illusions in Tocqueville about revival of the past. For him democracy is one of the irresistible, irreversible movements of history. Yet the special cast of his consideration and criticism of democracy is emphatically conservative.

The matter becomes more complex when we consider the other titans. Tönnies would be generally categorized, I suppose, as a conservative, if only because of his personal roots and obvious attachment to the *Gemeinshaft*-like conditions of his rearing. But Tönnies did not consider himself a conservative, and his political sympathies were incontestably liberal. Simmel, Weber, Durkheim: were they liberals? The closest answer would probably be yes. Radicals, no; not even Durkheim, who has occasionally been placed by the unwitting among the socialists. Conservatives? Not in any political sense that had currency in their day. One and all, Weber, Durkheim, and Simmel dissociated themselves from political and economic conservatives.

But to leave the matter there would be deceptive. There is conservatism of concept and of symbol, as well as conservatism of attitude. From the vantage point of the present day, it is possible to see deep currents of conservatism in the writings of all three men, currents running against the stream of overt political affiliation. In each man we can today see elements in almost tragic conflict with the central tendencies of liberalism and modernism. Throughout his life Weber's liberal propensities were at war with his realization of what modernism—in the form of rationalization of culture and thought—was doing to the values of European culture. This inner conflict goes far to explain the melancholy that spread itself over parts of Weber's thought and that actually immobilized him as a scholar for short periods. No such melancholy is to be seen in either Simmel or Durkheim, but neither can we miss in the works of each the same kind of tension between the values of political liberalism and the values of a humanistic or cultural conservatism, however reluctant this conservatism might be.

The paradox of sociology—and it is, as I argue in these pages, a creative paradox—lies in the fact that although it falls, in its objectives and in the political and scientific values of its principal figures, in the mainstream of modernism, its essential concepts and its implicit perspectives place it much closer, generally speaking, to philosophical conservatism. Community, authority, tradition, the sacred: these are primary conservative preoccupations in the age, to be seen vividly in the intellectual line that reaches from Bonald and Haller to Burckhardt and Taine. So are presentiments of alienation, of totalitarian power rising from mass democracy, and of cultural decay. One will look in vain for significant impact of these ideas and presentiments on the serious interests of economists, political scientists, psychologists, and ethnologists in the age. But in sociology they are—transfigured, of course, by rationalist or scientific *objectives* of the sociologists—at the very core of the discipline.

THE SOURCES OF SOCIOLOGICAL IMAGINATION

Two final points must be stressed: first, the *moral* basis of modern sociology and, second, the intuitive or artistic frame of thought in which the central ideas of sociology have been arrived at.

Major ideas in the social sciences invariably have roots in moral aspiration. However abstract the ideas may eventually become, however neutral they may come to seem to scientists and theorists, they do not ever really divest themselves of their moral origins. This is pre-eminently true of the ideas of this book. They did not arise out of the simple and morally uncommitted reasonings of pure science. There is no detraction from scientific greatness when we emphasize that such men as Weber and Durkheim were working with intellectual materials—values, concepts, and theories—that could never have come into their possession apart from persisting moral conflicts in the nineteenth century. Each of the ideas makes its first appearance in the undisguised, unambiguous terms of moral affirmation. Community begins as a moral value; only gradually does the secularization of this concept become apparent in sociological thought in the century. Precisely the same is true of alienation, authority, status, and the others. The moral texture of these ideas is never wholly lost. Even in the scientific writings of Weber and Durkheim, a full century after these ideas had made their first appearance, the moral element remains vivid. The great sociologists never ceased to be moral philosophers.

And never ceased to be artists! [4] It is important to keep in mind, if only as a prophylaxis against vulgar scientism, that not one of the ideas we are concerned with—ideas that remain, let it be emphasized, central in contemporary sociological thought—came into being as a consequence of what we are today pleased to call "problem solving" thought. Without exception, each of these ideas is a result of thought processes—imagination, vision, intuition—that bear as much relation to the artist as to the scientist. If I seem to stress this point it is only because we are living in an age when well-meaning and eloquent teachers of sociology, and of other social sciences as well, all too often insist that what is scientific (and therefore important!) in their discipline is the consequence solely of problem-defining, problem-solving thought.

Can anyone believe that Tönnies' typology of *Gemeinschaft* and *Gesellschaft*, Weber's vision of *rationalization*, Simmel's image of *metropolis*, and Durkheim's perspective of *anomie* came from logico-empirical analysis as this is understood today? Merely to ask the question is to know the answer. Plainly, these men were not working with finite and ordered problems in front of them. They were not problem-solving at all. Each was, with deep intuition, with profound imaginative grasp, reacting to the world around him, even as does the artist, and, also like the artist, objectifying internal and only partly conscious, states of mind.

Consider one example: the view of society and man that underlies Durkheim's great study of suicide. Basically, it is the view of the artist as much as that of the scientist. Background, detail, and characterization blend into something that is iconic in its grasp of an entire social order. How did Durkheim get his controlling idea? We may be sure of one thing: he did not get it, as the stork story of science might have it, from a preliminary examination of the vital registers of Europe, any more than Darwin got the idea of natural selection from his observations during the voyage of the *Beagle*. The idea, the plot, and the conclusion of *Suicide* were well in his mind before he examined the registers. Where, then, did he get the idea? We can only speculate. He might have got it from reading Tocqueville, who could certainly have got it from Lamennais, who could have got it from Bonald or Chateaubriand. Or, it could have come from personal experience—from a remembered fragment of the Talmud, from an intuition born of personal loneliness and marginality, a scrap of experience in Paris. Who can be sure? But one thing is certain. The creative blend of ideas behind *Suicide*—a blend from which we still draw in our scientific labors—was reached in ways more akin to those of the artist than to those of the data processor, the logician, or the technologist.

It is not different with the ideas and perspectives of Simmel, in many ways the most imaginative and intuitive of all the great sociologists. His treatments of fear, love, conventionality, power, and friendship show the mind of the artist-essayist, and it is no distortion of values to place him with such masters as Montaigne and Bacon. Remove the artist's vision from the treatments of the stranger, the dyad, and the role of secrecy, and you have removed all that gives life. In Simmel there is that wonderful tension between the esthetically concrete and the philosophically general that always lies in greatness. It is the esthetic element in Simmel's work that makes impossible the full absorption of his sociological substance by anonymous, systematic theory. One must go back to Simmel himself for the real insight. As with Darwin and Freud, it will always be possible to derive something of importance from the man directly that cannot be gleaned from impersonal statements in social theory.

Our dependence upon these ideas and their makers is akin to the artist's dependence upon the artists who precede him. In the same way that the novelist will always be able to learn from a study and restudy of Dostoevski or James—to learn a sense of development and form, as well as to draw inspiration from the creative source—so the sociologist can forever learn from a rereading of such men as Weber and Simmel.

It is this element that separates sociology from some of the physical sciences. There is, after all, a limit to what the young physicist can learn from even a Newton. Having once grasped the fundamental points of the *Principia,* he is not likely to draw very much as a physicist from rereadings (though he could as a historian of science). How different is the relation of the sociologist to a Simmel or Durkheim. Always there will be something to be gained from a direct reading, something that is informative, enlarging, and creative. This is precisely like the contemporary artist's return to the study of medieval architecture, the Elizabethan sonnet, or the paintings of Matisse. This is the essence of the history of art, and why the history of sociology is so different from the history of science.

2 THE TWO REVOLUTIONS

THE BREAKUP OF THE OLD ORDER

The fundamental ideas of European sociology are best understood as responses to the problem of order created at the beginning of the nineteenth century by the collapse of the old regime under the blows of industrialism and revolutionary democracy. This is the only conclusion one can reach when he looks at the character of the ideas, the nature of the works in which they appeared, and the relation of idea and work to age. The intellectual elements of sociology are refractions of exactly the same forces and tensions that also produced the outlines of modern liberalism, conservatism, and radicalism.

The breakup of the old order in Europe—an order that had rested on kinship, land, social class, religion, local community, and monarchy —set free, as it were, the varied elements of power, wealth, and status that had been consolidated, however precariously, ever since the Middle Ages. Dislocated by revolution, scrambled by industrialism and the forces of democracy, these elements can be seen tumbling across the political landscape of Europe throughout the nineteenth century in search of new and more viable contexts.

In the same way that the history of nineteenth-century politics is about the *practical* efforts of men to reconsolidate these elements, the history of social thought is about *theoretical* efforts to reconsolidate them: that is, put them in perspectives having philosophic and scientific relevance to the new age. The nature of community, the location of power, the stratification of wealth and privilege, the role of the individual in emerging mass society, the reconciliation of sacred values with political and economic realities, the direction of Western society—all of these are rich themes in the nineteenth-century science of man. They are equally rich as issues in market place, legislative chamber, and, not infrequently, on the barricades.

Two forces, monumental in their significance, gave urgency to these themes: the Industrial Revolution and the French Revolution. It would be hard to find any area of thought and writing in the century that was not affected by one or both of these events. The cataclysmic nature of each is plain enough if we look at the responses of those who lived through the revolutions and their immediate consequences. Today it is only too easy to submerge the identity of each revolution in long-term processes of change; we are prone to emphasize continuity rather than discontinuity, evolution rather than revolution. But to intellectuals of that age, radical and conservative alike, the changes were of almost millennial abruptness. Contrast between present and past seemed stark— terrifyingly or intoxicatingly, depending upon one's relation to the old order and to the forces at work on it.

We shall be concerned in this chapter less with the events and changes of the two revolutions than with the images and reflections that are to be found in the social thought of the nineteenth century. What either the Industrial or the French Revolution was in its historical actuality, in its concrete relation to what preceded and what followed, is not a matter for assessment here. Our interest is in ideas, and the relation between events and ideas is never direct; it is always mediated by *conceptions* of the events. The role of moral evaluation, of political ideology, is therefore crucial.

The Industrial Revolution, the power of the bourgeoisie, and the rise of the proletariat may or may not have been all that Marx thought them to be, but the fact remains that apart from his *conception* of them there is no way of accounting for perhaps the major intellectual and social movement in the subsequent history of the West. The same is true of the French Revolution. Alfred Cobban has recently referred to "the myth" of the French Revolution, by which he seems to mean that not only the suddenness but the significance of the Revolution have been exaggerated. But from the viewpoints of some of the founders of sociology—Comte, Tocqueville, Le Play—the French Revolution was myth in quite another sense, one rather that Sorel was to give to this word. To these minds—and to many others—the French Revolution appeared almost as an act of God in its cataclysmic immensity. With the possible exception of the Bolshevik Revolution in the twentieth century, no event since the fall of the city of Rome in the fifth century has aroused emotion so intense, thought so preoccupied, nor been the basis of as many dogmas and perspectives regarding man and his future.

Words, as E. J. Hobsbawm has written recently, are witnesses which often speak louder than documents. The period comprised by the last quarter of the eighteenth and the first half of the nineteenth century is, from the point of view of social thought, one of the richest periods of word-formation in history. Consider the following which were either invented during this period or—which is the same thing—modified to their present meanings: *industry, industrialist, democracy, class, middle class, ideology, intellectual, rationalism, humanitarian, atomistic, masses, commercialism, proletariat, collectivism, equalitarian, liberal, conservative, scientist, utilitarian, bureaucracy, capitalism, crisis.*[1] There were others, but these are the crucial ones for what we shall be concerned with in this chapter.

Plainly these words were not simple counters in a game of abstract reflection on society and its changes. One and all these words were saturated with moral interest and partisan identification. This was as true at the end of the nineteenth century as at the beginning, when the words first made their appearance. To say this is not to deny or cast shadow on their later efficacy in the objective study of society. All major ages of thought in the history of culture are characterized by the proliferation of new words and new meanings of words. How else can the bonds of intellectual conventionality be cut through except by the sharp edges of new words that alone can express new values and new forces struggling for expression? It is only too easy at the time of their first appearance to fling the epithets "jargon" and "linguistic barbarism" at the words— some of which indeed deserve the epithets and receive the just punishment of later oblivion—but the history of thought makes plain that few if any of the key words in the humanistic study of man and society do not begin as neologisms born of moral passion and ideological interest.

THE THEMES OF INDUSTRIALISM

Nowhere is this more plainly to be seen than in the impact of the Industrial Revolution on nineteenth-century thought. Although it is English thought and writing—literary as well as scholarly—that most plainly reveals the force of the Industrial Revolution, if only because this revolution is as distinctively English as the political revolution beginning in 1789 is French, the implications of industrialism were not lost upon French and German thinkers. The wide reading which Adam Smith's *Wealth of Nations,* published in 1776, had received throughout Europe gave even the most cloistered of scholars a forewarning of what the issues of the Industrial Revolution would be. Well before the phrase "Industrial Revolution" gained currency, the words, "English System" were used by German and French writers to describe the combined forces of legal individualism and economism which were transforming English society. As we shall repeatedly see in the chapters that follow, problems of community, status, and authority were dealt with by sociologists, from Comte to Weber, in the almost invariable contexts of the changes wrought on European society by the forces of division of labor, industrial capital, and the new roles of businessman and worker.

What were the aspects of the Industrial Revolution that were to prove most evocative of sociological response, most directive in the formation of sociological problem and concept? Five, we may judge, were crucial: the *condition of labor,* the *transformation of property,* the *industrial city, technology,* and the *factory system.* A great deal of sociology can be seen as response to the challenge of these conditions, its concepts as subtilizations of their impact upon the minds of such men as Tocqueville, Marx, and Weber.

Beyond question, the most striking and widely treated of these aspects was the condition of the working class. For the first time in the history of European thought, the working class (I distinguish "working class" from the poor, the downtrodden, the humble, which, of course, form timeless themes) becomes, in the nineteenth century, the subject of both moral and analytical concern. Some recent scholarship has suggested that the condition of the working class under even the first stages of industrialism was better than that which had prevailed for a couple of centuries before. This may be true. But it was rarely the view of independent observers in the early nineteenth century. For radical and conservative alike, it was the undoubted degradation of labor, the wrenching of work from the protective contexts of guild, village, and family, that was the most fundamental, and shocking, characteristic of the new order. The decline of the status of the common laborer, not to mention the skilled craftsman, is as much the subject of conservative indictment as it is of radical. On the Continent, both Bonald and Hegel referred with distaste to "the English system," noting the general instability to society that would be the necessary consequence of man's loss of the roots of his labor in family, parish, and community. In England, as early as 1807, Robert Southey based his criticism of the new manufacturing system in large part on its impoverishment of ever larger segments of the population. Nine years later, in his *Colloquies,* he wrote: "[A] people may be too rich; because it is the tendency of the commercial, and more especially of the manufacturing system, to collect wealth rather than to diffuse it . . . great capitalists become like pikes in a fish-pond, who devour the weaker fish; and it is but too certain that the poverty of one part of the people seems to increase in the same ratio as the riches of another." [2] The contrast between his own age and earlier times is stressed by Southey, as it is to be throughout the century. "Bad as feudal times were," Southey has his central spokesman Sir Thomas More say in the *Colloquies,* "they were less injurious than these commercial ones to the kindly and generous feelings of human nature." [3]

Turn now to the writings of the ablest of the English radicals in the same period, William Cobbett, hated and persecuted relentlessly by the forces in power. The basis of his criticism of the new economy is not very different from Southey's; it is precisely what he believes to be the dismal decline of the worker's status. The new system "has almost entirely extinguished the race of small farmers; from one end of England to the other, the houses which formerly contained little farmers and their happy families, are now seen sinking into ruins, all the windows except one or two stopped up, leaving just light enough for some labourer, whose father was, perhaps, the small farmer, to look back upon his half-naked and half-famished children. . . ." [4]

"I wish to see," Cobbett wrote, "the poor men of England what the poor men of England were when I was born; and from endeavouring to accomplish this wish, nothing but the want of means shall make me desist." All around him Cobbett could see traditional, security-giving relationships being ground into dust, craftsmen and farmers transformed into "hands," subject now to "Seigneurs of the Twist, sovereigns of the Spinning Jenny, great Yeomen of the Yarn . . . When *master* and *man* were the terms, everyone was in his place, and all were free. Now, in fact, it is an affair of *masters* and *slaves.*" [5]

The likeness between the conservative Southey and the radical Cobbett here is reflective of a certain affinity between conservatism and radicalism that was to last throughout the century. (I am referring, of course, to the evaluation of industrialism and its byproducts. There was little if any affinity when it came to political matters.) What conservatives such as Tocqueville, Taine, and the American Hawthorne were to write in horrified reaction to the scene presented in Manchester and other cities of the Midlands in England did not differ in descriptive character or emotional intensity from what Engels was to write. It was Manchester that became the "ideal type," so to speak, of conservative and radical reactions to the new industry and to the displacement of working class from rural confine.

Even Marx, whose distaste for ruralism was as boundless as his hatred of the past, found himself, in the *Communist Manifesto,* contrasting the "feudal, patriarchal, idyllic relations" of the past with those which have left no other "nexus between man and man than naked self-interest, than callous 'cash payment.' " Industrialism has drowned the "most heavenly ecstasies of religious fervor, of chivalrous enthusiasm, of philistine sentimentalism, in the icy waters of egotistical value." [6] To be sure, Marx took a cynical view of the patriarchalism of the past, seeing in it but a veil that hid real exploitation. But his terminology could have been accepted without demur by many a conservative of the time. Reference to "cash-nexus" is owing first, apparently, not to the radicals or liberals, but to Carlyle, whose *Signs of the Times,* written in 1829, dealt eloquently and passionately with the commercialism that Carlyle felt was despoiling European culture. [7] In France the conservative Balzac would write: "There is no kin but the thousand-franc note." And before him Bonald, in an essay on the rural and urban family, made commercialism the prime attribute of all that he hated about modernism.

This is why the indictment of capitalism that comes from the conservatives in the nineteenth century is often more severe than that of the socialists. Whereas the latter accepted capitalism at least to the point of regarding it as a necessary step from past to future, the traditionalists tended to reject it outright, seeing any development of its mass industrial nature—either within capitalism or a future socialism—as but a continued falling away from the superior virtues of Christian-feudal society. It was what the socialists *accepted* in capitalism—its technology, modes of organization, and urbanism—that the conservatives most despised. They saw in these forces causes of the disintegration of what Burke called the "inns and resting places" of the human spirit, Bonald, "les liens sociales," and Southey, "the bond of attachment."

The second of the themes to emerge from the Industrial Revolution has to do with property and its influence in the social order. As we shall note below, nothing in the French Revolution so outraged conservatives as its confiscation of property and its weakening of the institutional supports of property. Property, and its desired role in society, goes further than any other single symbol to separate conservative from radical in the nineteenth century. For conservatives, property was the indispensable basis of family, church, state, and all other major groups in society. For radicals, increasingly, the abolition of property, save as a vague collective sentiment, became the prime goal of their aspirations.

And yet there is here, as in the condition of the working class, a curious affinity between radical and conservative. In part it was interpretative. Marx and Le Play were perfectly agreed upon the unvarying economic basis of the family in history, and both could have agreed with some highly illuminating words that a twentieth-century conservative, Sir Lewis Namier, was to write: "The relations of groups of men to plots of land, of organized communities to units of territory, form the basic content of political history; social stratifications and convulsions, primarily arising from the relationship of men to land, make the greater, not always fully conscious, part of the domestic history of nations—and even under urban and industrial conditions ownership of land counts for far more than is usually supposed." [8] No conservative could have doubted the truth of these words; no more could a radical, though liberals might.

But the affinity between conservative and radical went further. It extended to hatred of a certain type of property: large-scale industrial property, but more especially the abstract and impersonal type of property that was represented by shares bought and sold on the market. The speculator, who best exemplified the new economic order in conservative eyes, is the special object of Burke's condemnation. The malign ascendancy of what Burke called "the new dealers"—speculators in land and property, buyers and sellers of shares of stock—figures prominently in his pages. Burke is forthright about the matter. It is the transfer of political power from the land to new forms of capital that he fears. But beyond this was Burke's deep-seated conviction that the whole order that he was so passionately committed to rested, at bottom, on landed property. In the new economic order he could see the fragmentation, the atomization, of property and its conversion into impersonal shares that would never inspire allegiance or lead to stability. And Burke was, of course, right. It was still another twentieth-century conservative, the economist Joseph Schumpeter, who made this point the very thesis of *Capitalism, Socialism, and Democracy,* concluding with the observation that a people in whom hard property has softened to possession of impersonal shares of stock will never even notice the transition, when it comes, from capitalism to socialism.

In the nineteenth-century conservative and radical alike distrusted industrial and finance capital. But whereas radicals tended more and more, after Marx, to see this mode of property an essential step in the evolution toward socialism and its capitalistic evils subject to the cure of revolutionary liquidation of the privateness of its ownership, conservatives thought that it was the very nature of such capital to create instability and alienation in a population, and that this was quite unaffected by the mere matter of public or private ownership. All that had made landed property the subject of entail and primogeniture in almost every country at one time or other—had led its peasantry and aristocracy alike for centuries to make preservation and continuity of property sovereign over all but religious values, to make it the object of boundless ambition, covetousness, and protectiveness—now made land the pillar of conservative ideology.

A third theme to emerge from the Industrial Revolution was urbanism. In the same way that the social condition of the working class became for the first time the subject of ideological passion, so did the social character of the city. Prior to the early nineteenth century the city, insofar as it was dealt with at all in humanistic writing, was seen as the repository of civilized graces and virtues. Now and then, as in Montaigne's *Essays* or Rousseau's *Confessions,* expressions of distaste might be found, but these were directed less at the nature of the city (even less at the poverty and squalor that might be found) than at the distractions its wealth and more active intellectual life sometimes caused. But actual revulsion for the city, fear of it as a force in culture, and forebodings with respect to the psychological conditions attending it—these are states of mind hardly known before the nineteenth century. It is, as we shall repeatedly see, the city that forms the context of most sociological propositions relating to disorganization, alienation, and mental isolation —all stigmata of loss of community and membership. There was, to be sure, much to shore up presentiments of evil. To take Manchester again: between 1801 and about 1850 the population shot up from some seventy thousand to slightly more than three hundred thousand. Accompanying the raw growth in numbers went, of course, increase in squalor—"illth," as Ruskin was to term it—beyond anything that European man's experience had prepared him for. Here, as in the two other themes we have noted, contrast was inevitable: contrast between the relatively simple, stable, and *walled* towns that could be seen in hundreds of extant prints of medieval urban life and the sprawling, planless, and unbounded aggregates that eyesight revealed in the new cities of the Midlands. English cities may have presented the worst of the spectacles of urbanism—so regarded by French and German as well as English humanists—but, as the novels of Balzac, Victor Hugo, and, later, Zola make plain, the phenomenon of Paris was sufficiently arresting to the imagination.

In the beginning, radicals and conservatives were largely united in their distaste for urbanism. There is as much nostalgia for the rural past in Cobbett as there is in Burke. But as the century progresses, one cannot but be struck by the increasingly "urban" character of radicalism. I mean by this not only the demographic roots in the city of almost all nineteenth-century radical movements but also the urban flavor of radicalism, the characteristically urban ordering of values that we see in radical thought.

Marx regarded the onset of urbanism as one of the blessings of capitalism, something to be spread even further in the future socialist order. The essentially "urban" character of modern radical thought (and therefore its theoretical and tactical unpreparedness for the twentieth-century role of peasant populations) derives largely from Marx and a view that made ruralism a recessive trait. Engels, it is interesting to note, whose study of the English working classes has more of the spirit of uplift in it, generally, than of strict Marxism, was, on the other hand, anguished by creeping urbanism. "We know well enough," he wrote, "that [the] isolation of the individual . . . is everywhere the fundamental principle of modern society. But nowhere is this selfish egotism so blatantly evident as in the frantic bustle of the great city." [9] His words can be set alongside these of Tocqueville, written after a visit to Manchester: "From this foul drain the greatest stream of human industry flows out to fertilize the whole world. From this filthy sewer pure gold flows. Here humanity attains its most complete development and its most brutish, here civilization works its miracles and civilized man is turned almost into a savage." [10] The conservatives emphasized the degree to which European culture—from its moral and spiritual ideals, to its crafts and songs and literature—was based on the rhythms of the countryside, the succession of seasons, the alternation of natural elements, and the deep relation between man and soil. Only rootlessness and alienation could be expected from a separation of man from these rhythms and his exposure to the artificial pressures of the city. If modern radicalism is urban in its mentality, conservatism is largely rural.

Two final themes, equally alive, equally freighted with ideological passion in nineteenth-century thought, must be mentioned: technology and the factory system. Under the impact of the former and within the confines of the latter, conservatives and radicals alike could see changes occurring that affected the historic relation between man and woman, that threatened (or promised) to make the traditional family obsolete, that would abolish the cultural separation between town and countryside, and that would make possible, for the first time in history, a liberation of man's productive energies from the restraints that both nature and traditional society had imposed.

Each theme, technology and factory, is the subject of countless tracts, sermons, and orations as well as scholarly works in the nineteenth century. Among the radicals there is a kind of ambivalence toward both. The worker's subjection to the machine, his anonymous incorporation into the regimentation enforced by factory bell and overseer, his proletarianization of status are, plainly, rich themes in radical writing. But here too the conservative response is the more fundamental. For while Marx could see a form of enslavement in the machine, and a manifestation of alienation of labor, he came increasingly to identify this enslavement and alienation with private property rather than with the machine as such. And as for the discipline of the factory, Engels' words, aroused by anarchist condemnation of the factory system, are reflective of what became nearly universal in radical writing by late century: "Wanting to abolish authority in large-scale industry is tantamount to wanting to abolish industry itself, to destroy the power loom in order to return to the spinning wheel." [11] From acceptance of the factory and its mechanically imposed division of labor as historically necessary, it was but a short step to the kind of idealization of factory and machine that we find in early twentieth-century radical writing and art.

The conservatives distrusted the factory and its mechanical division of labor as they did any system that seemed, by its nature, calculated to destroy the peasant, the artisan, as well as family and local community. It was easy to see in the workings of the rotary steam engine, the flying shuttle, or the spinning jenny a form of tyranny over the mind of man and an instrument in his moral degradation. Between man and machine there was occurring, it seemed, a transfer of, first, strength and dexterity and, then, intelligence that boded ill for creatures made in the image and likeness of God. In exactly the same way that the factory (which to Bentham had appeared the very model of what all human relationships should be) became to such men as Coleridge, Bonald, and Haller the archetype of an economic regimentation hitherto known only in barracks and prisons, so the machine became in their minds the perfect symbol of what was happening to men's minds and culture.

Carlyle spoke for conservatives and for humanists alike when he wrote: "Not the external and physical alone is now managed by machinery, but the internal and spiritual also. . . . The same habit regulates not our modes of action alone, but our modes of thought and feeling. Men are grown mechanical in head and in heart, as well as in hand. They have lost faith in individual endeavour, and in natural force of any kind. Not for internal perfection, but for external combinations and arrangements, for institutions, constitutions—for Mechanism of one sort or other, do they hope and struggle. Their whole efforts, attachments, opinions, turn on mechanism, and are of a mechanical character." [12] In the same spirit, Carlyle wrote: "Mechanism has struck its roots down into man's most intimate, primary sources of conviction; and is thence sending up, over his whole life and activity, innumerable stems—fruit-bearing and poison-bearing." [13] And Tocqueville saw in the machine and in the division of labor that accompanied it instruments of a degradation of man more awful than any that had befallen him under ancient tyrannies. All that was given to the machine in the way of skill and direction was, Tocqueville thought, taken out of man's essence, leaving him weak, narrow-minded, and dependent. "The art advances, the artisan recedes." [14]

DEMOCRACY AS REVOLUTION

The French Revolution was no less shattering in its impact upon cherished dogma and traditionalist feeling. And the political revolution in France had what the economic revolution largely lacked: dedicated emissaries and disciples who made of it the first great ideological revolution in Western history. Whether the political changes of the French Revolution proved more fateful in subsequent European—and world— history than the economic changes of the Industrial Revolution will always be debatable. But by its very nature the French Revolution was possessed of a suddenness and dramatic intensity that nothing in the Industrial Revolution could match. The stirring Declaration of the Rights of Man, the unprecedented nature of the laws that were passed between 1789 and 1795, laws touching literally every aspect of the social structure in France—not to emphasize the sanguinary aspects of the Revolution, especially those embodied in the Terror—were sufficient to guarantee to the Revolution a kind of millennial character that was to leave it for a whole century the most preoccupying event in French political and intellectual history. All that industrialism is to English letters, social movements, and legislation in the nineteenth century, the democratic revolution in France at the end of the eighteenth century is to French.

Today every schoolboy knows that the French Revolution did not *commence* the processes of centralization, equalitarianism, nationalist collectivism, secularism, and bureaucracy that partisans on both sides first thought it had. Before the nineteenth century was well under way, there were historians, the most notable among them being Tocqueville, who pointed to the deep roots these processes had in French history. But the Revolution gained its tenacious hold upon European consciousness before these roots had been made clear by historical analysis. In any event, quite apart from all that had happened prior to the Revolution in preparation of the way, nothing could detract from the exciting spectacle of a small number of men composed of liberal reformers, political intellectuals, financial speculators, economic visionaries, moral zealots—to name a few of the types who flourished together, or successively, during the course of the Revolution—who thought themselves, and who were thought by others on both sides of the Atlantic, to be engaged in the building of a new social order. Taine, whose scholarship and judgment may be questioned, but not his acumen, did not err in describing the Revolution as the most important single historical event in Europe's history after the fall of Rome.

We can do no more here than hint at the scope and intensity of the Revolution's influence on European thought. It will suffice to look at the sociologists. Without exception, from Comte to Durkheim, they gave the French Revolution a decisive role in the making of those social conditions with which they were immediately concerned. Thus, it was social disorder engendered by the Revolution that Comte specifically pointed to as the background of his own work. It was, Comte thought, the "false dogmas" of the Revolution—equalitarianism, popular sovereignty, and individualism—that, above even the new industrial system, were responsible for the spread of moral disorganization in Europe. Tocqueville was haunted by the Revolution; it is the real theme of his study of American democracy, and he planned a long work specifically on its effects. Le Play repeatedly attributes to the Revolution the chief causes of the distressed condition of the working classes in mid-century, as well as the secularization of education, the individualization of property, and the acceleration of bureaucracy that he so disliked. At the end of the century Durkheim is still concerned with what he calls the Revolution's replacement of "corporate egoism" by "individual egoism." The intellectual impact of the Revolution was hardly less general in Germany. Of Hegel's fascination with it there is ample record, and it was undoubtedly the dramatic rationalization of law undertaken by the revolutionaries that was the immediate impulse of Savigny's studies. Otto von Gierke found in the Revolution's destructive impact on such intermediate associations as monastery, guild, and commune the principal inspiration of his monumental study of state and association in European history. And Leo

Straus is undoubtedly correct in his statement that Max Weber's basic categories of authority—traditional and rational and charismatic—owe much to the Revolution and its impact on the old order.[15] Mosca, deeply impressed by his reading of Taine, took from the Revolution the essential elements of his theory of power. Michels was not less affected in the formulation of his "law of oligarchy" and his critique of "democratic centralism."

What is true of sociology is equally true of many other areas of thought in the century: historiography, jurisprudence, moral philosophy, political science. One and all, they found themselves dealing with the issues raised dramatically by the Revolution: tradition versus reason and law, religion versus state, the nature of property, the relation of social classes, administration, centralization, nationalism, and, perhaps above all others, equalitarianism. It was the word democracy that summed them up, and in its modern form, this word springs straight from the French Revolution. "It was not," E. Weekley writes, "until the French Revolution that *democracy* ceased to be a mere literary word, and became part of the political vocabulary." [16]

Why did the Revolution, as no revolution ever had before, seize the minds of men for a century after, dominating thought in so many areas, affecting the very categories of men's identification of themselves and their relation to politics and morality? The full answer is complex, but there is one important aspect that is relevant to our purposes here. The French Revolution was the first thoroughly *ideological* revolution. This is to take nothing away from the American Revolution, which had excited the mind of Europe with its Declaration of Independence. But the goals of the American Revolution were limited, limited almost wholly to independence from England, and at no point do we find any of its leaders —not even a Tom Paine—suggesting that the Revolution be the means of social and moral reconstruction which would involve church, family, property, and other institutions.

The French Revolution was a very different phenomenon. Within a few months after it had begun, moral principles became clamant and, as the Revolution progressed, very nearly total. We may say all we wish about the economic causes, the role of the non-ideological businessman or civil servant, the importance of purely administrative processes, and the internal effects of the foreign wars the Revolution found itself fighting. But all we need to do is examine the preambles of laws that began to appear by 1790, the debates that went on in Assembly and Convention, the tracts and pamphlets that were circulated throughout France, to make it apparent that, whatever the underlying forces were in the beginning, the power of moral utterance, of ideological affiliation, of sheer passionate political belief reached a point shortly that is without precedent in history, save possibly in religious wars or revolts. The ideological aspect is plain enough in the Declaration of the Rights of Man and in the early debates on the place of religion, but it reaches almost apocalyptic intensity by the time of the Committee of Public Safety ("Salvation," as Albert Guerard has suggested, is the more expressive translation of the French "Salut" here).

It was the conservatives, beginning with Burke, who first called attention to the ideological character of the French Revolution. Burke was bitterly attacked for suggesting in 1790 that the aims of the Revolution were fundamentally different from those of the American Revolution. He was accused of having betrayed the principles that had actuated his indictment of the East India Company and his defense of the American colonists. But Burke saw in the French Revolution a force compounded of political power, secular rationalism, and moralistic ideology that was, he believed, unique. And Burke was right. However prejudiced his account may be of actual events and laws, however sentimental his regard for French monarchy, however malicious his characterization of those in revolutionary power, there is a certain ironic humor in the reflection that by 1794 such men as Robespierre and Saint-Just would have had to find Burke's account of the implications of the Revolution far closer to reality than that of the liberal Richard Price which had, as we know, been the immediate impetus to Burke's *Reflections*. For, whereas Price saw no further than the announced political objectives of the Revolution, Burke saw the underlying oral, quasi-religious intensity of the political rationalism within which these objectives took form. What the philosophers of rationalism during the Revolution took away from the hated Christianity, they vested with truly missionary zeal in the work of the Revolution.

A generation later, Tocqueville was but giving new phrasing to Burke's assessment when he wrote: "No previous political upheaval, however violent, had aroused such passionate enthusiasm, for the ideal the French Revolution set before it was not merely a change in the French system but nothing short of a regeneration of the whole human race. It created an atmosphere of missionary fervor and, indeed, assumed all the aspects of a religious revival—much to the consternation of contemporary observers. It would perhaps be truer to say that it developed into a species of religion, if a singularly imperfect one, since it was without a God, without a ritual or promise of future life. Nevertheless, this strange religion has, like Islam, overrun the whole world with its apostles, militants, and martyrs." [17]

It was the ideological character of the Revolution that made it the obsession of intellectuals for decades afterward. Mere events, even those involving dethronement, expropriation, and beheading, do not captivate the hopes of romantics, idealists, and visionaries for generations, nor torment the apprehensions of traditionalists. Dogmas and heresies are required, and these the Revolution had in abundance. It was the Revolution that contributed to Western Europe states of mind about political good and evil that had previously been reserved to religion and demonology.

The whole character of politics and of the intellectual's role in politics changed with the structure of the state and its relation to social and economic interests. Politics now became an intellectual and moral way of life, one not unlike that which Rousseau had described in his *Confessions*. "I had come to see that everything was radically connected with politics, and that however one proceeded, no people would be other than the nature of his government made it." [18]

In his *Discourse on Political Economy*, Rousseau wrote: "If it is good to know how to deal with men as they are, it is much better to make them what there is need they should be. The most absolute authority is that which penetrates into a man's inmost being, and concerns itself no less with his will than with his actions . . . If you would have the General Will accomplished, bring all the particular wills into conformity with it; in other words, as virtue is nothing more than this conformity of the particular wills with the General Will, establish the reign of virtue." [19]

Rousseau's relation to the Revolution is an interesting one. To think of him as one of the "causes" of the Revolution is, of course, absurd. He was too little read, too little respected in France during the years that preceded the Revolution. Even in 1789, when the Revolution broke out, there is little evidence that his ideas mattered very much. But by 1791, thirteen years after his death, he had become the Gray Eminence of the Revolution: the most admired, most quoted, and most influential of all the *philosophes*. His exciting combination of individualistic equalitarianism (so vivid in the discourses on the arts and sciences and on the origin of inequality) and of a General Will that gave legitimacy to absolute political power (expounded in the *Discourse on Political Economy* and in *The Social Contract*) was made to order for revolutionary aspirations.

There was, to begin with, the majestic Declaration of the Rights of

Man which clearly specified that "the source of all sovereignty is essentially in the nation; no body, no individual can exercise any authority that does not proceed from it in plain terms." And further, "Law is the expression of the general will. All citizens have the right to take part, personally or by their representatives, in its formation. It must be the same for all whether it protects or punishes. All citizens, being equal in its eyes, are equally eligible to all public dignities, places and employments, according to their capacities, and without other distinctions than those of their virtues and talents."

Much of the specific legislation of the Revolution can be seen in these terms.[20] In a law of March 2–17, 1791, the hated guilds and trade corporations were abolished for once and all, inaugurating freedom of occupation (*liberté du travail*). This law was followed three months later by a more rigorous measure, the famous *Loi Le Chapelier* of June 14–17, which not only confirmed abolition of the guilds but forbade the establishment of any analogous form of new association. "There is no longer any corporation within the state; there is but the particular interest of each individual and the general interest . . ." At a stroke, democratic assemblies were thus able to present a magnitude of power that had eluded the efforts of supposedly absolute kings. Rousseau's dislike of "partial associations" within the state was now converted into legislative action. "Citizens of certain trades must not be permitted to assemble for their pretended interests." A state that is "truly free," one of the legislators said, "ought not to suffer within its bosom any corporation, not even such as, being dedicated to public instruction, have merited well of the country." Benevolent societies and mutual-aid associations were made illegal or at least suspect. "It is the business of the nation," Le Chapelier declared in an address before the Assembly, "it is the business of the public officers in the name of the nation, to furnish employment to those who need it and assistance to the infirm." If old corporations were unacceptable, on the ground of their corruption of general will, why should new ones be allowed? "Whereas the abolition of all kinds of corporations of citizens of the same estate and of the same trade is one of the fundamental bases of the French constitution, it is prohibited to re-establish them *de facto* under any pretext of form whatsoever."

Napoleon's later edicts respecting associations were but extensions and reinforcements of what the Revolution, in its democratic-liberal phase, had already begun, a fact sometimes overlooked by historians who stress Napoleon's "reactionary" relation to the Revolution. Admittedly his laws were more encompassing, and he had a police system for their enforcement that was lacking in 1791. But he did not originate them; he merely extended and systematized them. Thus, in 1810 new articles were appended to existing laws which forbade associations numbering more than twenty persons. Although popular protest led to a moderation of these restrictions in 1812, it was not until nearly the end of the nineteenth century that three generations of bitter political controversy on associations were terminated by final repeal of the laws forbidding or limiting them. We will find that Comte, Le Play, and Tocqueville, to name but three sociologists, were deeply concerned with the implications to society of restriction of the freedom of associations.

The family also underwent profound change in law during the Revolution.[21] Like the *philosophes,* the Revolutionary legislators found patriarchal customs and the indissolubility of the marriage tie "against nature and contrary to reason." In a law of 1792 marriage was designated a civil contract and several grounds for divorce were made available. The arguments for such measures invariably rested on natural law with frequent citation of philosophy. That the relaxation was not unwelcome in some quarters may be inferred from the fact that in the sixth year of the Republic the number of divorces in Paris exceeded the number of marriages. But there was more to follow in reform of the family. Strict limitations were placed upon the paternal power, and in all cases the authority of the father ceased when the children reached legal age. In 1793 the age of majority was fixed at twenty-one, and in the same year the government decreed the inclusion of illegitimate children in matters concerning family inheritance. The attitude of the legislators was plainly hostile to the customs governing the solidarity of the old family. Such men as Lepelletier and Robespierre, specifically appealing to the precepts of Rousseau (in his *Discourse on Political Economy*), insisted that the state should have primacy of claim upon the existence of the young. The legislators held that within the family, as elsewhere, the ideals of equality and individual rights must prevail. The family was conceived as a small republic (*une petite république*), and the father prevented from exercising "monarchical" authority. Relations between the family and its domestic dependents, such as servants, were put upon a contractual basis. The patriarchal unity of the family was thus dissolved, in law at least, in line with general policy toward all groups.

Property was no less thoroughly modified by the Revolutionary legislators.[22] Before the Revolution, custom and law had encouraged a system of inheritance under which estates, both large and small, tended to be preserved intact, and were passed on from generation to generation in the same families. It now became difficult for family property to perpetuate itself in the aggregate. The government, taking the view that property belongs to the individual members of the family, proclaimed the *partage forcé,* whereby the father was legally obliged to will to his children equal amounts of property. By limiting the testamentary freedom of the father and forcing an equal division of property, the economic solidarity of the family was weakened. This, as we shall note, above anything else the Revolution did, obsessed Le Play, leading indeed to a vast study of family and property.

As one more expression of its dedication to the liberation of individuals from ancient authorities, the government, in 1793, took from the family the control of education.[23] Previously, primary education had been the joint concern of family and church. Universities in France were semi-autonomous ecclesiastical institutions. The successive governments of the Revolution, believing with Danton that "after bread, education is the chief need of the people," passed numerous measures designed to centralize and broaden education simultaneously, making it not merely the right but the political duty of all citizens. This legislative design for centralization of education was given powerful effect by Napoleon, who avowedly regarded education as a machinery for the production of efficient subjects. "In the establishment of a teaching body," he remarked, "my principal aim is to have a means of directing political and moral opinions; for so long as people are not taught from their childhood whether they are to be Republicans or Monarchists, Catholics or freethinkers, the State will not form a nation." [24] Omitting the matter of motivation, the words could have come from either Rousseau or one of the Jacobins.

Religion also was deeply affected, and here the link between Enlightenment and Revolution is perhaps clearest of all. The Abbé Raynal, whose anti-ecclesiastical writings had earned him censure by the church, achieved belated revenge during the Convention, when his words were read aloud enthusiastically. "The state is not made for religion; religion is made for the state. The state is supreme in all things; any distinction between temporal power and spiritual power is a palpable absurdity, and there cannot be more than a sole and single jurisdiction throughout in matters where public utility has to be provided for or defended." [25] At the outbreak of the Revolution there was no manifest wish to abolish Christianity, but there was plainly desire to regulate it completely. If there was to be a church, it must reflect the character of the new political order. In the name of *liberté,* the Assembly suppressed all perpetual monastic vows and all religious orders. Educational and charitable functions held by the chu.ch and its various orders were transferred to the state. Bishops and parish priests were to be elected like ordinary officials. It was ruled that clerics must accept their living from the state, and in such capacity must take an oath of fidelity to the state. Those who refused to swear fidelity were declared enemies of the people.

But the most severe blow fell when the property belonging to the church was confiscated by the state. From the point of view of the nature of social groups and associations under the law, the chief interest of this act lies in the discussions which were precipitated concerning the corporate nature of the church. The question was raised by more than one member of the Assembly whether the church, by its corporate being, should not be indemnified for the expropriation. Older corporate ideas of jurisprudence still found expression, even in that body. But they were drowned out by the overwhelming flood of natural-law arguments that persons other than natural persons (that is, individuals) do not in fact exist, and any rights which the church might claim disappear before the sovereign rights of the state. Thouret declared, in a legislative address: "Individuals and corporations differ in their rights. Individuals exist before the law, and they hold rights drawn from nature that are imprescriptible, such as the right of property; all corporations, on the other hand, only exist by law, and their rights are dependent on the law." [26] He concluded with the pregnant observation: "The destruction of a corporate body is not a homicide."

In countless ways, then, the Revolution must be seen in fact for what it was in image to generations of intellectuals afterward: the combined work of liberation, of equality, and of rationalism. Tocqueville was to write that equalitarianism quickly became, after libertarianism's first excitement had waned, the compelling moral ethos of the Revolution. But we should not overlook its rationalism and the appeal that this rationalism had for all those who, following Plato, believed in the rational foundations of the just state. A passion for geometrical unity and symmetry in the minds of the Revolutionary legislators drove them beyond such relatively minor matters as reform of the currency system and standardization of weights and measures to the more exciting task of rationalization of the units of space and time within which men lived. The ancient provinces were to be abolished, to be replaced by geometrically perfect units and sub-units of political administration, all oriented ultimately toward their center, Paris. The calendar was reformed, with new names for the days and months in order to remind the people constantly of their separation from the old regime. For, if a people are to be both free and wise, they must be liberated from old memories and the prejudices embedded in traditional associations and symbols. Traditional centers of education having been abolished, new centers must be established, an office of propaganda formed, in order that the people might be emancipated, in Rousseau's words, from the "prejudices of their fathers."

The Revolution was also the work of power; not power simply in the mechanical sense of force applied to a people by external government in the pursuit of its own objectives, but power regarded as arising from the people, transmuted by libertarian, equalitarian, and rationalist ends so that it becomes, in effect, not power but only the exercise of the people's own will. This was Rousseau's dream and it was the dream of a great many during the Revolution.

What gave the Revolution epochal significance in the minds of its leaders and, even more, in the minds of nineteenth-century revolutionaries for whom the Revolution became an obsessive model, was its unique blend of power and freedom, of power and equality, of power and fraternity, and of power and reason. From a purely intellectual point of view these affinities come close to representing the successive phases of the development of the Revolution. How else than by the massed power of the people, represented first by Assembly and Convention, then by Committee, and finally by one man alone, could the freedom of the millions of suffering and oppressed be achieved from the hated authorities of church, aristocracy, guild, and monarchy? From power conceived as liberation it was but a short step to power conceived as equality, for if each citizen of France was by definition a participant in the new political order, did this not bring with it equality of power; the most basic form of equality? And in the structure of the nation, which had from the beginning been declared the only legitimate source of authority in the Republic, lay a form of fraternity that made all older forms seem obsolete and discriminatory. Finally, how else could the political, social, and economic confusion that was the legacy of feudalism be exterminated, and a new system of society inaugurated, save by the exercise of a power that would be as rational as it was limitless?

"The transition of an oppressed nation to democracy," the Committee of Public Safety declared, "is like the effort by which nature arose from nothingness to existence. You must entirely refashion a people whom you wish to make free, destroy its prejudices, alter its habits, limit its necessities, root up its vices, purify its desires." [27]

Nor can one miss in the Revolution the rising note of political moralism, sometimes total moralism, that is added to the themes of liberation, equality, reason, and power. Rousseau had shown the way in his *Discourse on Political Economy* and in *The Social Contract*. Power without morality is tyranny; morality without power is sterile. Hence, as the Revolution progressed, the increasing appeal to virtue in support of the most extreme measures taken by the government. With moralism went, inevitably, a new manifestation of religious consciousness. "How are you to know a Republican?" asked Barère de Vieuzac. His answer might have been taken directly from Rousseau's chapter on the civil religion in *The Social Contract*. You will know him, Barère declared, when he speaks of his country with "religious sentiment" and of the sovereign people with "religious devotion." With reason have historians of nationalism traced its modern origins directly to the Revolution. Political sentiment became a flame, melting all social relationships and symbols that stood between the citizen and the goal of France *une et indivisible*.

It was Jacobinism that came to appear, in later decades, most expressive of the Revolution's unique fusion of rationalism, moralism and absolute power. No matter what recent research has revealed of the middle-class origins, the merely economic objectives, and the debating-club techniques of a majority of the members of the Jacobin clubs, the image of Jacobinism that was ever after to inspire the radical and to torment the conservative was of something much closer to the reality of twentieth-century revolutionary politics than of anything to be found in liberal, bourgeois nineteenth-century society. The historian, Robert Palmer, has suggested something of this in the following words on the Jacobins:

"Their democratic Republic was to be unitary, solid, total, with the individual fused into society and the citizen into the nation. National sovereignty was to check individual rights, the general will prevail over private wishes. In the interest of the people the state was to be interventionist, offering social services; it was to plan and guide the institutions of the country, using legislation to lift up the common man. It was to resemble more closely the states of the twentieth century than those of the nineteenth . . . 'The function of government,' Robespierre had said on 5 Nivôse, 'is to direct the moral and physical forces of the nation.' " [28]

From power to terror is the final step. In a revolution worthy of the name this step must be taken. For, as Robespierre declared: "If the basis of popular government in time of peace is virtue, the basis of popular government in time of revolution is virtue and terror: virtue without which terror is murderous, terror without which virtue is powerless." [29] No doubt some of the fascination and sense of self-justification which Christian onlookers found in the burnings of religious non-believers and heretics during the Inquisition were found by Revolutionary onlookers of the guillotinings of political counter-revolutionaries and traitors in Paris in 1794. It was in the context of the Terror that the peculiarly modern connotations of treason and subversion had their origin: each connotation is as inseparable from the character of modern mass democracy as heresy is from the character of the medieval church. To a Saint-Just, inspired by the spiritualized, disciplined ferocity of a medieval inquisitor, terror could take on the properties of a cauterizing agent: indispensable, however painful, to the extermination of political infection. It was in these terms that nineteenth-century revolutionists, such as Bakunin, could justify the use of terror. It is a justification that continues in the twentieth century—in the works of Lenin and Trotsky, of Stalin, Hitler, and Mao. There is, to be sure, a vast difference between the reality of the French Revolution and the reality of twentieth-century totalitarianism, but there is, as such present-day scholars as J. L. Talmon and Hannah Arendt have stressed, following insights of Tocqueville, Burckhardt, and Taine, vital continuity nonetheless.

INDIVIDUALIZATION, ABSTRACTION, GENERALIZATION

If one looks at the two revolutions from the point of view of the most fundamental and widespread processes they embodied in common, three are especially striking. I shall call them *individualization, abstraction,* and *generalization.* Together these terms convey a great deal of what revolutionary change meant to philosophers and social scientists of the nineteenth century. And the relevance of each has lasted well into the twentieth century.

INDIVIDUALIZATION Everywhere in the modern world, the clear direction of history seemed to be toward the separation of individuals from communal or corporate structures: from guild, village community, historic church, caste or estate, and from patriarchal ties in general. Some, perhaps most, people saw this separation in the progressive terms of liberation, of emancipation from tradition grown oppressive. Others took a more somber view of the separation, seeing the rise of a new type of a society, one in which moral egoism and social atomism were the dominant qualities. But whether from the over-all point of view of progress or decline, there was a unanimity of recognition that covered philosophers as different as Bentham, Coleridge, Tocqueville, Marx, Spencer, and Taine. Not the group but the *individual* was the heir of historical development; not the guild but the *entrepreneur;* not class or estate but the *citizen;* not corporate or liturgical tradition but *individual reason.* More and more, society could be seen as a vast, impersonal, almost mechanical, aggregate of discrete voters, tradesmen, sellers, buyers, workers, worshipers: as, in short, separated units of a population rather than as parts of an organic system. To be sure there were those such as Marx who saw, along with the decomposition of old hierarchy and authority, the formation of a new type—that of the industrial system—but this did not prevent Marx from seeing the individual as nonetheless the beneficiary of the process and, when once separated from the tyranny of private ownership of industry, the recipient of final salvation.

ABSTRACTION   This is related to individualization, but refers primarily to moral values. What struck a great many minds in the century was not merely the tendency of historic values to become ever more secular, ever more utilitarian, but increasingly separated from the concrete and particular roots which for many centuries had given them both symbolic distinctness and means of realization. Honor—as Tocqueville was to show in a masterly chapter of *Democracy in America*—and loyalty and friendship and decorum had all begun, as values, in the highly particular contexts of locality and rank. Now, without their appeal as words, as symbols, becoming in any way lessened, the contexts through which their meaning and direction had for centuries been communicated to human thought and behavior were undergoing profound alteration. Many of these values had depended for their effect on man's direct experiencing of nature: of its rhythms and cycles of growth and decay, of cold and warmth, of light and dark. Now a technological system of thought and behavior was coming between man and the directness of natural habitat. Still other values had depended on the ties of patriarchalism, of close and primary association, and of a sense of the sacred that had rested upon a religious or enchanted view of the world. Now these values were becoming—through processes of technology, science, and political democracy—abstract; removed from the particular and the concrete. Here, again, this could represent progress to many, cultural decline to others.

GENERALIZATION   The nation and even the international sphere come to be seen more and more as essential areas of man's thought and allegiance. From family and local community to nation, to democracy, to visions of international order: this is the course of thought in the age. Loyalties become broadened, along with interests and functions. So do perceptions. Men saw their fellows less as particular individuals and more as members of a general aggregate or class. As Ostrogorski has written: "In decomposing the concrete, the logic of facts as well as that of ideas, opened the door to the general. Here, as elsewhere, industrialism gave the first impulse. In the eyes of the manufacturer the mass of human beings who toiled in the factory were only *workmen,* and the workman associated with the factory-owner only the idea of *capitalist* or *master.* Not being brought into immediate contact, they formed a conception of each other by mentally eliminating the special characteristics of the individual and retaining only what he had in common with the other members of his class." [30] What the Industrial Revolution accomplished in the economic sphere, revolutionary democracy did in the political. In each instance the particularism of the old order—the tendency to think in terms of the concrete, *identifiable* rich or powerful, poor or helpless— disappeared along with its localism. The same tendency to think now increasingly in terms of "the working class," "the poor," "the capitalists" expressed itself with equal force in the tendency to think in terms of "voters," "bureaucracy," the "citizenry," and so on.

In his *Reflections on the Revolution in France* Burke wrote: "Many parts of Europe are in open disorder. In many others there is a hollow murmuring underground; a confused movement is felt, that threatens a general earthquake in the political world." [31]

But not even Burke's prescience could have told him how general, how limitless, was the earthquake that began in Western Europe, spread to the rest of Europe and the Western hemisphere in the nineteenth century, and goes on unabatedly in the twentieth century in Far East, Middle East, Latin America, and Africa.

PART TWO

THE UNIT-IDEAS OF SOCIOLOGY

3 COMMUNITY

THE REDISCOVERY OF COMMUNITY

The most fundamental and far-reaching of sociology's unit-ideas is community. The rediscovery of community is unquestionably the most distinctive development in nineteenth-century social thought, a development that extends well beyond sociological theory to such areas as philosophy, history, and theology to become indeed one of the major themes of imaginative writing in the century. It is hard to think of any other idea that so clearly separates the social thought of the nineteenth century from that of the preceding age, the Age of Reason.

The idea of community holds the same pivotal importance in the nineteenth century that the idea of contract had held in the Age of Reason. Then, philosophers had used the rationale of contract to give legitimacy to social relationships. Contract provided the model of all that was good and defensible in society. In the nineteenth century, however, we find contract waning before the rediscovered symbolism of community. In many spheres of thought, the ties of community—real or imagined, traditional or contrived—come to form the image of the good society. Community becomes the means of denoting legitimacy in associations as diverse as state, church, trade unions, revolutionary movement, profession, and cooperative.

By community I mean something that goes far beyond mere local community. The word, as we find it in much nineteenth- and twentieth-century thought encompasses all forms of relationship which are characterized by a high degree of personal intimacy, emotional depth, moral commitment, social cohesion, and continuity in time. Community is founded on man conceived in his wholeness rather than in one or another of the roles, taken separately, that he may hold in a social order. It

47

draws its psychological strength from levels of motivation deeper than those of mere volition or interest, and it achieves its fulfillment in a submergence of individual will that is not possible in unions of mere convenience or rational assent. Community is a fusion of feeling and thought, of tradition and commitment, of membership and volition. It may be found in, or be given symbolic expression by, locality, religion, nation, race, occupation, or crusade. Its archetype, both historically and symbolically, is the family, and in almost every type of genuine community the nomenclature of family is prominent. Fundamental to the strength of the bond of community is the real or imagined antithesis formed in the same social setting by the non-communal relations of competition or conflict, utility or contractual assent. These, by their relative impersonality and anonymity, highlight the close personal ties of community.

In the sociological tradition, from Comte to Weber, the conceptual contrast formed by the communal and the non-communal is vivid and articulate. It was Tönnies, toward the end of the century, who gave it its lasting terminology of *Gemeinschaft* and *Gesellschaft,* but the contrast is hardly less real in the works of each of the other sociologists, before and after, with only Marx dissenting significantly from the value implications carried by the contrast.

It is neither sufficient nor accurate to say, as many historians have, that the most distinctive feature of the rise of sociology in the nineteenth century is the idea of "society." This says too much and too little. For, in one form or another, society as a concept had never ceased to be the object of philosophical regard—not even during the Age of Reason and the Enlightenment, when doctrines of individualism were rife. As Sir Ernest Barker has so illuminatingly emphasized, the whole secular theory of natural law from 1500 to 1800 was engaged in working out little else but a theory of society. But behind the rationalist image of society in this period there was always the prior image of naturally free individuals who had rationally bound themselves into a specified and limited mode of association. Man was primary; relationships were secondary. Institutions were but the projections of fixed, atom-like sentiments innate in man. Volition, assent, and contract—these were key terms in the natural-law view of society.

Groups and associations that could not be vindicated in these terms were cast into the lumber room of history. Few traditional communities survived examination by natural-law philosophers in the seventeenth and eighteenth centuries. The family was generally accepted, of course, though we find Hobbes using the idea of a tacit contract to justify the parent-child relationship and, a century later, Rousseau flirting with the idea of submergence of family in the General Will. A special case had to be made too for the church, but this case had worn increasingly thin by the end of the seventeenth century. When we turn to other associations, no mercy is shown. Guild, corporation, monastery, commune, kindred, village community—all of these were regarded as without foundation in natural law. Rational society must be, like rational knowledge, the very opposite of the traditional. It must rest on man not as guildsman, churchman, or peasant, but as *natural* man, and it must be conceived as a tissue of specific and *willed* relationships which men freely and rationally enter into with one another. This was the model of society that reached the French Enlightenment.

For the *philosophes* this model was made to order for their political objectives. The communal relationships of feudalism were repugnant to them on both moral and political grounds, and if it could be shown that such relationships lacked the sanction of natural law and reason, why, all the better. France, in their view, was surfeited with relationships of a corporate and communal character. What was required was a social order founded on reason and instinct, bound by the loosest and most impersonal of ties. The problem, as Rousseau posed it so momentously, was "to find a form of association which will defend and protect with the whole common force the person and goods of each associate, and in which each, while uniting himself with all, may still obey himself alone, and remain as free as before." [1] Such a state could not, however, come into being so long as the inherited structure of society was left undisturbed. Social evils had come into being in the first instance as the consequence of factitious interdependence. "From the moment one man began to stand in need of the help of another; from the moment it appeared advantageous to any one man to have enough provisions for two, equality disappeared, property was introduced, work became indispensable, and vast forests became smiling fields, which man had to water with the sweat of his brow, and where slavery and misery were soon seen to germinate and grow up with the crops." [2] Nothing less than the total destruction of evil institutions would permit the fresh start that the social compact called for. The fault of previous reform has been that "it was continually being patched up, when the first task should have been to get the site cleared and all the old materials removed, as was done by Lycurgus at Sparta. . . ." Not all the *philosophes* would have agreed with Rousseau, to be sure, in the implications he drew from his own radical combination of individualism and political absolutism, but there was no question, certainly, of the irrationality of most of the old order. Hence the uncompromising opposition in the Enlightenment to all forms of traditional and communal association. "No period was more impoverished," wrote W. H. Riehl, "than the eighteenth century in the development of a common community spirit; the medieval community was dissolved and the modern was not yet ready. . . . In the satirical literature of the time, whoever wanted to portray a blockhead represented him as a Burgomaster, and if he wished to describe a meeting of Jackasses, he described a meeting of Town Councillors." . . . The Enlightenment "was a period when people yearned for humanity and had no heart for their own people; when they philosophized about the state and forgot the community." [3]

Intellectual hostility to the traditional community and its ethos was given powerful impetus, as we have seen, by the two revolutions, in each of which the union of legislative and economic forces working toward the destruction of medieval-born groups and associations could be seen as the work of Progress, fulfilling what had been prescribed or foreseen by rationalist philosophers since Hobbes. In nineteenth-century thought the animus against the traditional community is reflected most powerfully in the writings (and practical works) of the Philosophical Radicals, led by the remarkable Jeremy Bentham. Bentham and his successors rejected the French Enlightenment's faith in natural rights and natural law, but as Halevy has emphasized, the consequence of their own doctrines of natural harmony and of rational self-interest was the same to the corporate communities which lay intermediate to man and the sovereign state. Bentham's loathing for traditional community extended to the common law, the jury system, the borough, and even to the ancient universities. Rationalism which, in its Cartesian form, had swept away superstition and revelation must also be made to sweep away the relics of communalism.[4] In the accomplishment of this radical goal, commerce, industrialism, and the administrative law of the state would be the instruments. Each would, in its own way, accomplish the social ends of rationalism.

Legislatures in the nineteenth century, increasingly responsive to the expressed desires of the new men of business and public administration, found much to be fascinated by in the tracts of the utilitarians, from Bentham to Herbert Spencer. It was not difficult to make the transition from the philosophical abstract to the needs of polity when the common enemy was persistence of communal traditions that had outlived their usefulness, that were as inimical to economic development as they were to administrative reform. It is no mere coincidence that, almost from the beginning of the Industrial Revolution, there was as much interest in political and administrative reform among the partisans of commerce and industry as there was in the spread of the new economic system.

There is thus to be found in Bentham's disciples the twin passion for economic individualism and political reform—the latter often taking the shape of proposed administrative centralization that was extreme for that day. The relation between industrialism and administrative centralization was a close one throughout the century. Clouds of Manchester rhetoric about laissez-faire have often covered the influence of political actions by legislatures, but the influence was there. Both economism and calculated politicization were required for the gigantic task of sweeping away the communal debris of the Middle Ages.

THE IMAGE OF COMMUNITY

So much is true, but what we also see in the nineteenth century is a sharp intellectual reaction to all of this. The conservatives began the reaction. In their dislike of modernism they were bound to seek out for emphasis those elements of the old regime on which modernism rested hardest. And high among these elements was the traditional community.

Burke paid his hostile respects to reformers who sought, he said, "to tear asunder the bonds of the subordinate community and to dissolve it into an unsocial, uncivil, unconnected chaos of elementary principles." [5] Burke's major contributions to political thought are based indeed upon what he regarded as the ethical priority of the historic community (whether in the Colonies, in India, or in France) either to the "asserted rights of non-existent individuals" or to the "geometric distribution and arithmetical arrangements" of political centralizers. "Corporate bodies are immortal for the good of their members, not for their punishment," he wrote in bitter response to the individualistic laws of Revolutionary leaders in France.[6]

In the works of all of the conservatives rediscovery of the traditional community and its virtues is central. So is the contrast between community and the impersonal individualism that conservatives could see springing up around them. In France Bonald declared the major requirement of the times to be the re-establishment of the communal securities of church, family, and other pre-Revolutionary solidarities, including guilds and communes. Contrast between the patriarchal security of these bodies and the insecurity of the new order is a recurrent theme in Bonald. Haller made the local community and its natural autonomy the pivot of his science of society. Carlyle's denunciations of "mechanism" were grounded at least in part on displacement of "modes of thought and feeling" from their historic communal contexts. No one stated the conservative view more eloquently than Disraeli. In *Sybil* he writes: "There is no community in England; there is aggregation, but aggregation under circumstances which make it rather a dissociating than a uniting principle. . . . It is a community of purpose that constitutes society . . . Without that, men may be drawn into contiguity, but they still continue virtually isolated." This condition of men is most intense and evil in cities. "In great cities men are brought together by the desire of gain. They are not in a state of co-operation, but of isolation, as to the making of fortunes; and for all the rest they are careless of neighbours. Christianity teaches us to love our neighbour as ourself; modern society acknowledges no neighbour." [7]

"Modern society acknowledges no neighbour." Disraeli's words could serve as the theme of a vast amount of nineteenth-century thought —radical as well as conservative, imaginative as well as empirical. Or hearken to the words of William Morris, whose celebration of medieval virtues was the primary basis of attack on modern individualism: "Fellowship is heaven, and the lack of fellowship is hell; fellowship is life, and the lack of fellowship is death; and the deeds that ye do upon the earth, it is for fellowship's sake that ye do them, and the life that is in it shall live on for ever, and each one of you part of it." [8]

It is fellowship, neighborhood, community, each in its special way, that forms the new pattern of *utopia*. What had been the dream of earlier utopian minds now became actuality—short-lived, often disillusioning, but actuality nonetheless—for more than a few in the century. Robert Owen's *New Lanark* did not, of course, affect the practical lives of many, but its theme was a heralded one. Involving more persons were the religious utopian communities of the century. Their motivations lay as much in repudiation of economic and political egoism as they did in efforts to regain for Christianity its apostolic or prophetic purity. Communalism, as an ethic, is a powerful force in nineteenth-century religion, as it is in many another area. In socialism, the Marxians turned resolutely away from any model based on localism and tradition, finding in "the vast association of the nation" and in the factory sufficient structure for mankind's ethical redemption. But there were others of different mind: Proudhon, whose defense of the patriarchal family, localism, regionalism, is the special element of his socialist thought; the anarchists, many of whom saw in extant village communities and rural co-operatives the very molecules of the new order—properly liberated from landlord and monarchy and class, of course. Much of the impetus of the co-operative and mutual-aid movements in the century came from the effort to restore to society something of what had been lost with village community and guild. In a great many tracts and pamphlets of the time, the vanished solidarities of village community and guild are held up against the egoism and avarice of the age. Sometimes these were radical in motive—bound to the abolition of private property and social class—sometimes conservative, resulting in the quaint efforts of such men as William Morris to restore or preserve the communal-handicraft past. Often communalism took a purely antiquarian form, resulting in clubs, journals, and amateur researches. Such efforts were by no means sterile, for the emerging movement of town planning and civic restoration in the age was based in part on the invidious contrasts that contemporary cities presented to prints and sketches of medieval village and town.

But community is a model in subtler and more strictly intellectual ways. Much of the reorientation of moral and social philosophy is the consequence of the impact of the rediscovery of the community in historical and sociological thought. A whole shift in perspective is involved.

We see the influence of the idea of community on a substantial vein of political thought in the century. The idea of the abstract, impersonal, and purely legal state is challenged by theories resting on the assumed priority of community, tradition, and status. The foundations of modern sovereignty, prescriptive law and citizenship are shown by such scholars as Sir Henry Maine, Otto von Gierke, and, at the very end of the century, the great F. W. Maitland, to derive not at all from individual will and assent, much less any mythical contract, but to be best understood as historical emergents from the breakup of the medieval community and corporation. The very image of the state is affected. Although in the works of John Austin the abstract, individualist view of the state and sovereignty received eloquent and powerful statement, it was nonetheless rivaled by views—some of them ominous—of the state as community, with the political nation held to be the just successor of the church in its claim upon individual loyalties.

So too are the radiations of community to be seen in the religious thought of the age. The religious individualism and rationalist theology of the eighteenth century—themselves lineal consequences of what Luther and Calvin had begun—are now challenged on a number of fronts: canonical, liturgical, moral, and political. Lamennais, in his influential *Essay on Indifference,* published in 1817, could see only atheistical despair for man once he had become separated from the communal and corporate character of religion. In the beginning, he tells us, is, not the word, but community: community of man and God and of man and man. So runs an increasingly powerful vein of thought in the century, one that was to touch theologians in every Western country and form perhaps the first significant reaction to Protestant individualism that Europe had seen since the Counter Reformation. A veritable renascence of liturgical and canonical themes takes place—themes that are, to be sure, intellectual or creedal in content, but are also vivid aspects of the communal temper that pervades so many nineteenth-century spheres of thought. The political manifestation of religious corporatism is to be seen most tellingly in the ideas of religious autonomy and pluralism of such men as Döllinger in Germany, Lacordaire in France, and Acton in England. If the church was in fact a community rather than a mere assemblage of individuals, then it deserved its just share of authority in society and the right to be considered coeval with the state in matters germane to its nature. The real roots of the political pluralism that the writings of F. W. Maitland, J. N. Figgis, and the young Harold Laski were later to embody are to be found in nineteenth-century religious communalism.

In philosophy the idea of community reveals itself in a host of ways: especially social and moral, but also epistemological, even metaphysical, for the attack that begins to be mounted on the sensationist and atomistic perspectives of reality by, first, Hegel and then such men as Bradley in England and Bergson in France—culminating for our purposes in what Durkheim was to write on the communal origins of man's conception of the universe and the categories of his knowledge—is a part of the same communal perspective that is only more obvious in the social and political areas of philosophy. Consider Coleridge and Hegel. The first, in his remarkable *Constitution of Church and State,* made the vision of community the essential basis of attack on utilitarian rationalism, religious individualism, and laissez-faire industrialism. As community is Coleridge's model of the good society, so tradition is the root of his attack upon intellectual and literary modernism.

In Hegel the influence of the idea of community is seen most strikingly in his *Philosophy of Right,* the work which, above any other single piece of writing in early nineteenth-century German philosophy, created the effective setting within which German sociology was later to arise. *Philosophy of Right* is an essay in rationalism, but it is a very different kind of rationalism from that of the Enlightenment—in either Germany or France. Hegel was a conservative, and the conservative cast of his social thought was shaped largely by the dominant role that the image of community held for him. His criticism of natural rights individualism, of direct and unmediated sovereignty, his rejection of the equalitarianism of the French Revolution, and his denunciation of contract as the model of human relationships are all predicated on a view of society that, like medieval society, is concentric: composed of interlocking circles of association—family, profession, local community, social class, church—each of which is autonomous to the limit of its functional significance, each of which is held to be the necessary source and reinforcement of individuality, and all of which, taken together, form the true state. The true state, for Hegel, is a *communitas communitatum* rather than the aggregate of individuals that the Enlightenment had held it to be.

Finally, we may note the influence of the rediscovery of community upon the whole area of nineteenth-century historiography. If there is any one aspect—apart perhaps from the increasingly scientific character of its objective—that separates history writing in the nineteenth century from that of the preceding century, it is the veritable eruption of scholarly interest in the communal and traditional past of Europe—manifest in countless works on the manor, the village community, guild, shire, borough, the hundred, and so on. In the same way that nineteenth-century historiography rejected the eighteenth century's pursuit of "natural," "conjectural," and "hypothetical" histories—founded, avowedly, on the light of reason rather than on historical archive—it rejected also the hostility toward the Middle Ages that had led Voltaire, Gibbon, and Condorcet to dismiss the entire period as one of barbaric interruption of progress. One need but mention the names of Stubbs, Freeman, Maitland, Fustel de Coulanges, Savigny, and von Gierke to suggest the degree to which historians of the first rank in the century gave themselves to the study of medieval communities and institutions. The nineteenth century remains unexcelled even today in its institutional histories, and these are a part of the same awakening of interest in the medieval community that also affected the rise of sociology. The largely adverse or hostile relationship that eighteenth-century historians had seen between medieval institutions and the modern electorates, assemblies, and liberties is now reversed; throughout the century we find historians searching for origins of democracy in the once despised contexts of folkmoot, manor, shire assembly, and estate.

THE MORAL COMMUNITY—COMTE

Our chief concern, however, is with sociology and the influence exerted upon it by the idea of community. This influence was vast. Community is not merely a dominating empirical interest of sociologists—manifest in studies of kinship, locality, and guild—but a perspective, a methodology, that lights up the study of religion, authority, law, language, personality, and gives a new scope to the age-old problem of organization and disorganization. Sociology, above any other discipline in the century, gave primacy to the concept of the social. The point to be emphasized here, however, is that the referent of "social" was almost invariably the communal. *Communitas,* not *societas* with its more impersonal connotations, is the real etymological source of the sociologist's use of the word "social" in his studies of personality, kinship, economy, and polity.

Nowhere was the vision of community more blinding at the beginning of the century than in the mind and works of Auguste Comte, who gave sociology its name, and who, more than any other single person in the century, gave sociology its footing in the world of philosophy and scholarship. We are prone to think, when Comte's name is mentioned, of "the law of three states," of the "hierarchy of the sciences," and vaguely, of Positivism, which Comte made synonomous with, first, science, and then, late in his life, with a new religion that would, he thought, replace Christianity. But Positivism is only a method, and the law of three states and the hierarchy of the sciences have little to do actually with the system of sociology that Comte conceived; they are preliminary to it; arguments, so to speak, for the necessity and inevitability of a new science of society. If we are interested in what Comte himself regarded as his systematic sociology, we will turn to, not the *Positive Philosophy* (admittedly the more influential, philosophically and generally, of his works) but to the *Positive Polity,* the subtitle of which is "A Treatise on Sociology." And here the ambience of community is overwhelming.

Community lost, community to be gained: these are the themes that give direction to both his social statics (the science of order) and social dynamics (the science of progress). Progress Comte defines simply as the achievement of order, and there is no doubt that by the time he reached the fullness of his thought, he regarded social statics as the more basic of the two divisions. Social dynamics, Comte tells us, rests upon insights regarding developmentalism which emanated from the "metaphysical" thinkers of the Enlightenment; social statics, on the other hand, rests upon ideas derived, he is frank to concede, from the "theological" or "retrograde" school of which Maistre, Bonald, and Chateaubriand were, in Comte's mind, the pre-eminent figures. In theory, Comte's repudiation of both schools is even-handed, but it is impossible to read his bitter words about such men as Voltaire and Rousseau ("doctors of the guillotine," he calls them in one angry ascription of the ideological origins of the Terror) and his gentler, even approving, words about the conservatives without realizing why the non-Catholic, supposedly republican and progress-oriented philosophy of Comte could, throughout the nineteenth century, appeal as it did to French traditionalists and reactionaries all the way down to the *Action Française*.

Comte's sociological interest in community was born of the same circumstances that produced conservatism: the breakdown or disorganization of traditional forms of association. This point must be emphasized, for it is often said that the rise of sociology was a direct response to, or reflection of, the proliferation of *new* forms of associative life in Western Europe, forms that industrialism and social democracy brought with them. Comte was interested in these (unlike the conservatives, he welcomed industry, science, and republicanism, at least in name), but it is not difficult to show that what led to his earliest sociological reflections was not perception of the new but, rather, an anguished sense of the breakdown of the old, and of "the anarchy which day by day envelops society," as the consequence. The ghost of traditional community hovers over all his sociology, as it does—though less obviously—over the work of Tocqueville, Le Play, and their successors.

For Comte, restoration of community is a matter of moral urgency. In his mind the Revolution was little else than social disorganization presided over by political tyranny. Comte shared the conservatives' repugnance for the Enlightenment as well as for the Revolution. Individual rights, freedom, equality are for Comte mere "metaphysical dogmas," [9] without substance to support a genuine social order. Only in his philosophy of history does Comte differ significantly from the conservatives. Veneration of the past does not reach categorical repudiation of modernism or a pessimistic view of the future as it does in the conservatives. Moreover, like Marx, he could see in the Enlightenment and the Revolution historically necessary steps toward the Positivist future. Just as Marx was to pay capitalism the compliment of being the historically necessary agent of the dissolution of feudalism and, more important, the means of shaping the technological and organizational contexts of socialism, Comte paid his respects to the Enlightenment for having "once and all put to burial the obsolete precepts of the theological-feudal system." Only through the doctrines of the *philosophes,* repugnant though they be, he writes, could the outmoded social system that had reached its height during the Middle Ages have been forever destroyed, thus clearing the way for the new social system that would proceed from the dissemination of the science of sociology.

When we turn, however, to the actual content and principles of the new science and to the meticulous description of the new order, both of which are detailed by Comte in *The Positive Polity,* we find something very different from the temper of mind that exists in Marx's work. For Marx, it is not unfair to say, socialism (in structure) is simply capitalism minus private property. Socialism is seen by Marx, however dimly, as consonant with and as emergent from the organizational categories of capitalism: the industrial city, factory, machine, working class, and so on. But when we look at the picture of future Positivist society that Comte gives us, we find an order that has a strikingly detailed analogy with, *not* the industrial-democratic scene around him, but on the contrary with the Christian-feudal system that had preceded it. It is not necessary to repeat here what was said in the first chapter about the appeal of medievalism to the makers of the sociological tradition. It need only be stressed that the further Comte went into the analytical elements of his sociology and into the structural details of his anticipated sociological utopia, the more compelling he found the ideas and values he had absorbed from Bonald and Maistre and, originally, from his devoutly Catholic-royalist parents. What we are given is the pouring of Positivist wine into medieval bottles. If socialism for Marx is capitalism minus private property, Positive society for Comte is simply medievalism minus Christianity. Over and over, in *The Positive Polity,* Comte tells us how Positivist principles, dogmas, rituals, and forms may properly rest upon the models presented by the Middle Ages.

In Positivist society, the business class replaces landed aristocracy, science replaces religion, republican forms those of monarchy; but with this done, the vision of Positivist society that we are given has far more in common with the spiritual and social categories of medieval society than with anything that comes after the Protestant Reformation (which, along with individualism, natural rights, and secularism, Comte condemned). Rarely has the outline of utopia been presented with more devotion to hierarchy, membership, duty, corporatism, liturgy and ritual, functional representation, and autonomy of the spiritual power. Even the vestments for his sociologist-priests, the nature of the altar, a new calendar of feast days, and modes of worship are prescribed or suggested. So too are the outlines of Positivist family, church, town, guild, and class presented. In them all, Comte's passion for moral community, at every level of the social pyramid, is vivid.

It would be, however, unfair to the name of one of the most learned and imaginative minds of the century if we left Comte's interest in community at the level of the utopian. There is in *The Positive Polity* (and also in some sections of the earlier *Positive Philosophy* and his still earlier essays) a view of community and its properties that is sociological in the sense that Durkheim was to give this word. Like Durkheim, Comte makes everything human above the level of the purely physiological derive from society, and, like Durkheim, Comte sees society as community written large. Not for Comte the Enlightenment's conception of society as a collection of individuals, with institutions merely projections of the intra-individual. Not for Comte, either, the view that Bentham and his followers made popular, of society likened to a vast arena of intersecting individual interests. For Comte society is substantive and primary; it precedes the individual logically and psychologically, and it shapes him. Apart from his roles in society, man, as we know him, is not even conceivable. Carried away by philosophical fervor, Comte makes society the "Supreme Being" of Positivist worship. But beneath this veil of religiosity lies a penetrating view of the social sources of personality, language, morality, law, and religion.

At the base of Comte's sociology lies his total rejection of individualism as a perspective. The individual, he writes, in terms drawn directly from Bonald, is an abstraction, a mere construction of metaphysical reasoning. "Society is no more decomposable into individuals than a geometric surface is into lines, or a line into points." Society is reducible only into elements which share the essence of society, that is, into social groups and communities. The most basic of these is, of course, the family.[10]

It would be possible to illustrate Comte's interest in community by reference to what he wrote on language and thought, on morality and religion, on economy and class, or on polity and law. But it is in his detailed treatment of the family—which we can only summarize briefly —that we see most clearly the power of his mind on an area of society that had been largely neglected by rationalists and utilitarians. The family, Comte writes, must be extricated from the negative contexts in which it has been placed by modern thought. Foremost among the obligations of the new sociology is the dissemination of a Positive or scientific view of the family to take the place of "the sophisms" uttered by rationalists since the sixteenth century.

What do we find in Comte's theory of the family? It is only too easy to forget the substance and to focus on some of the patently sentimental, nostalgic, and romantic observations which all too often adorn his more serious insights. To do so would be a mistake, however, for what Comte gives us, often distorted by utopian sentiment and Positivist jargon, is the first modern systematic and theoretical statement of the family as a unity of relationships and statuses.[11]

There are, Comte tells us, two perspectives through which the family must be studied: the *moral* (by which he means, as we shall see, the social) and the *political*. Under the first, we have reference to the whole process of socialization of the individual, his preparation for passage into the larger community. Under the moral, Comte treats of the constitutive relationships within the family: the filial, the fraternal, and the conjugal. Each of these he makes the subject of extended analysis, with emphasis constantly on the formation of personality within the medium provided by the three relationships together. From the filial relation derives the respect for superior authority, so vital to the contexts of morality; from the child's feeling for the authority of parent evolves his successive regards for the other authorities of society. From the fraternal relationship arises the earliest sense of social solidarity and of sympathy; this is the sense that the *philosophes* mistakenly had supposed to lie within individual nature, in the form of instinct. Third is the conjugal relation. For Comte (at least by the time he came to write the *Polity*) this is perhaps the most fundamental of all relationships. So crucial is it as a tissue of society that he denounces all those, from Luther to the *philosophes,* who had given approval to divorce. Divorce, we read, is one of the major manifestations of the "anarchical spirit" that pervades modern society. Under Positivism it will cease. There are other roles and relationships treated by Comte—among them the role of father and the master-servant relationship—all within the larger context of their socializing properties and all within the defense that Comte mounts against the atomizing, secularizing influences of his day.

Under the second, or political, perspective, Comte analyzes the internal structure of the family: first, its monogamous nature; and second, the authority that naturally flows from the father (Comte's medieval cast of mind shows in his advocacy of a restoration of the full patriarchal authority within the family that the Revolution had taken away). He is concerned also with the internal hierarchy of the family and with the "necessary" inequality of its membership; predictably, Comte addresses sharp words to the egalitarian reformers of the Revolution and to socialists who wish, he says, "to carry into the very bosom of the family their anarchic doctrines of leveling." He deals, finally, under the same perspective, with the relationship of the family to community, to school, and to government.

THE EMPIRICAL COMMUNITY—LE PLAY

It is not Comte, but Frédéric Le Play who introduces the substantive and empirical study of the community in the nineteenth century. Of all the major figures Le Play remains the least appreciated for the design and scope of his work. The thick folds of utopianism, romanticism, and sentimentality in which Comte concealed so many of his sociological insights are absent in Le Play. He began his career as a mining engineer, in which capacity he traveled over much of the Eurasian continent. Wherever he went he recorded observations of the peoples and social organizations he encountered. Gradually his interest in these superseded his mining interests, resulting finally in a determination to abandon his professional career and to devote the rest of his life to the scientific study of society. Le Play did not call himself a sociologist; that word, in his day, was still suffused by Comtean Positivism, which Le Play cared little for. But *The European Working Classes*[12] is a work squarely in the field of sociology, the first genuinely scientific sociological work in the century. Others, such as Fourier, Saint-Simon, and Comte, had used the terminology of science, had rung changes on the theme of a science of society. Still others, such as Quetelet, proceeding from eighteenth-century "political arithmetic," had compiled, or would compile, quantities of social statistics, pointing to correlations, or "patterns," and preening themselves on the quantitative exactitude of their handiwork. Le Play went much further, however, in that he set up a clear problem and, through a rigorous if sometimes extreme method, reached objective conclusions. Durkheim's *Suicide* is commonly regarded as the first "scientific" work in sociology, but it takes nothing away from Durkheim's achievement to observe that it was in Le Play's studies of kinship and community types in Europe that a much earlier effort is to be found in European sociology to combine empirical observation with the drawing of crucial inference —and to do this acknowledgedly within the criteria of science. Admittedly, Le Play allowed his politically conservative and Catholic presuppositions ("un Bonald rajeuni" Sainte-Beuve was to call him) to color later summarization of results, but if we restrict attention to his major work, *The European Working Classes,* published in some six volumes and based upon a staggering compilation of field data and case histories, the wonder remains how this work, despite its shortcomings, could be as neglected as it has been in the history of sociology.

The European Working Classes is, without any doubt, the supreme example in the nineteenth century of actual field study of the traditional community, its structure, relation to environment, component elements, and disorganization by the economic and political forces of modern history. Many others in the century were also concerned with the substantive community: Tocqueville, with the township in the United States and the village community in medieval Europe; von Maurer with German mark; von Gierke with the legal structure of the medieval community and its atomization under the buffets of modern natural-law individualism; Maine with the village community in India, Eastern Europe, and early England; Laveleye with the Russian and Swiss communities; Seebohm with the English rural community; and Weber with the medieval town. There were scores of others. But none approached Le Play's work either in scope of enterprise or in imaginativeness of method.

Le Play wrote: "the point of departure in my work, and the constant guide of my inductions, is a series of studies begun by me a half century ago, and since extended by younger friends to the whole of Europe, the adjoining regions of Asia, and more recently still to the rest of the world. Each study has for its object the working-class family, the locality it inhabits and the social constitution by which it is governed. . . . Populations consist not of individuals but of families. The task of observation would be vague, indefinite, and inconclusive, if in every locality it were required to extend it to individuals differing in age and sex. It becomes precise, definite, and conclusive when its subject is the family." [13]

No brief description can do justice to the contents of *The European Working Classes.* Its excellence lies in its combination of the intensive and extensive, of the micro- and macro-sociological. Every individual study within the larger work has for its essential subject a concrete, actual family. Using this group as his point of departure, Le Play deals systematically with the internal workings of the family, not neglecting its relation to the community around it—which he calls the social constitution. It is here that his famous budgetary technique is employed. What better and more exact means is there, he asked, of detailing what a family is and does than through examination of its income and its expenditures? More important, by using the family budget as the schema, it becomes possible to put family study on a comparative and a quantitative basis.[14]

Comparison is the essence of Le Play's method. "Observation of social facts" is the term he used to describe his method, but the important point is that it is *comparative* observation. Some forty-five families, drawn from all over Europe, are studied separately and intensively, ranging from a semi-nomadic Bashkir shepherd in Eastern Russia to a compositor and his family in Brussels. The studies fall into two groups. In the first, Le Play is interested in the family types characterized by a high degree of stability, commitment to tradition, and security of the individual. Examples he uses for study in this group are a peasant in Orenburg, an iron worker in the Urals, a cutler of Sheffield, a foundry worker of Derbyshire, a cottager of Lower Brittany, and a soap maker of Lower Provence. As is obvious from the range of these examples, Le Play does not confine himself to culturally backward areas to find stability and security.

In the two final volumes of the work Le Play deals with family systems undergoing disorganization. He uses cases drawn, to a large extent, from France, mostly Paris, for it is in France, chiefly, he argues, as a consequence of the Revolution, that the bases of tradition and communal security have been largely disintegrated. In his analyses of an agricultural laborer of Morvan, a carpenter of Paris, and a clockmaker of Geneva, we see the results of fragmentation of property, of the loss of legal paternal authority, and of the rupture of relation between family and tradition caused by modern individualism and secularism.

Le Play's studies of kinship led him to the conclusion that there are three basic types of family to be found in the world. His classification has become famous.[15] The first is the patriarchal family, found chiefly in steppe country where economic and political conditions make the large, patriarchally dominated family wholly functional. In such circumstances there is seldom any external form of political and social authority, and it is therefore the patriarchal family alone that must wield it. But although appropriate to pastoral conditions, this type of family would be, Le Play concludes, inappropriate to the modern political and economical order. Second, there is the "unstable" family type (*la famille instable*). This is most notably found in post-Revolutionary France, but examples of it are to be seen in other ages of history—in the Athens that followed the disastrous war with Sparta, Rome in the later Empire, and so on. The characteristic features of the unstable family are its extreme individualism, its contractual character, its lack of roots in property, and its generally unstable structure from generation to generation. It is this type of family, Le Play contends, that is largely responsible for the endemic insecurity and spiritual uncertainty of France. The third type of family Le Play calls the *stem family* (*la famille souche*). In its most vigorous and successful form, this is to be found in Scandinavia, Hanover, Northern Italy, and, to some extent, in England. It is also to be seen in modern China. The stem family does not hold the children together throughout their lives, as does the patriarchal; they are free to leave when they come of age. With a single exception, the children generally do leave and found "branch" families of their own. But whoever remains at home becomes the full heir; the family property is preserved intact and is represented legally by him alone. The stem family is always there to return to for those who need its security, but the system encourages personal autonomy and the development of new households, new enterprises, and new forms of property. It combines, in other words, the best of the patriarchal system with the individualism of the unstable type.

Le Play's interest in the community goes beyond simple analysis of family types. Each of these is a microcosm, each a key element of the community, but the important objective for Le Play is to relate the family to other types of institution in the community. It is the family's role in the social order that interests him the most. The ties uniting the family with other parts of the community—religion, employer, government, school, and so on—are Le Play's ultimate ends of study. He deals with the nature of the physical environment of each family, its surrounding religious and moral customs, its rank in the hierarchy of the community, its food, shelter, recreations, and, of course, occupation.

The last is crucial in Le Play's work. Not even his contemporary, Marx, could exceed the emphasis Le Play placed on the economic basis of family and community life. We study social life, Le Play tirelessly emphasized, in terms, first, of *place*—within which he includes natural resources as well as topography and climate—and, second, of *occupation,* through which alone environment becomes meaningful to man. Some students have treated Le Play as a geographic determinist. He was not a determinist at all (his strictures on determinism in the first volume of *The European Working Classes* are still worth reading), but if he were, it would be more accurate to call him an economic determinist.

He is concerned with levels of occupational status among working-

class families, and his classification along these lines is subtle and penetrating, and clearly the base of later studies in both Europe and America.[16]

Families may be differentiated in the status hierarchy of a community, Le Play tells us, in three ways: (1) by occupation or trade; (2) by
grade within this occupation; and (3) by the nature of the contract that
each worker has with his employer.

He divides occupations into some nine groups, ranging from peoples entirely dependent on the natural productions of the earth, through
pastoral, fishing, and extractive economies, to agriculture, manufacturing, commerce and, at the upper level, the liberal arts and professions.
Having in this way reached his economic picture of the working class, Le
Play turns to the matter of social grades accompanying these groups of
occupations.

In almost every occupational group six status-grades are to be
found. At the bottom are servants lodging in the master's household,
paid partly in kind, partly in wage. Next above are day laborers with
households of their own, sometimes paid in money, sometimes in kind,
or both. Third come pieceworkers who are paid a fixed price for a definite piece of work and whose status is generally regarded as higher than
that of labor based solely on time. Fourth are the tenants renting property from a landlord; this status is far from homogeneous, since it can
range from a household servant holding the right to pasture a few heads
of stock with his master's, to prosperous master workmen renting property on which to work for their own profit. Fifth are those who own
instead of renting property. They have no rent to deduct from their
profits and generally become disciplined by ownership into habits of
thrift and accumulation. Sixth, and socially highest in the working class,
is the status of master workmen, whether tenant or owner. Master workmen have their own customers, set their own standards and recompense,
and are often assisted by hired servants, which, of course, puts them on
the borderline separating working class from employer.

The third set of circumstances that differentiates one group of
workers from another is the contractual status held by the worker in
relation to his employer. This, Le Play says, depends less on the amount
of the wage paid than it does on the nature of the contract which binds
them. Where there is abundance of soil available to a population, compulsory permanent engagements are the rule, and this system (as in feudalism) works well provided proprietors feel a sense of responsibility to
dependents and the latter a sense of loyalty to proprietors. Frequently,

Le Play notes, the proprietors have more to gain in strictly economic terms by a dissolution of this permanent tie than the dependents—who would thus be thrown into the impersonal market. As available soil becomes scarcer, voluntary permanent engagements tend to replace the compulsory ones and, in time, to acquire higher social value in a population. These, finally, become outnumbered as available land diminishes, by relationships of a temporary, purely wage, nature. Under this system the old solidarity of master and dependent declines and, under the type of industrialism that is to be found so strikingly in France, strikes, lockouts, and other pathological symptoms of conflict occur.

Along with kinship and local community, Le Play was interested in other modes of communal association, especially those which the peasantry had founded for accomplishment of technical or economic ends that the family or local community was unable alone to meet. He was concerned, too, with such diverse social forms as the guild, the cooperative, and the monastery. To these and other units like them he gave the term *communautés*. They are, he writes, of economic value in traditional societies (as they were at one time in Europe) but of diminishing value in the European present. There are also the groups that he calls *corporations*. These he defines as associations separate from industry which perform for individuals in an industry functions of a social, moral, and intellectual nature. He refers to mutual-aid associations among the poor, to insurance societies, and to cultural associations for the preservation or development of arts and crafts. Le Play did not see as much value in these corporate associations as Durkheim was to later—from Le Play's point of view these associations would not be necessary if a stable family system were to come into existence—but he does not deny them importance. Le Play was keenly interested in intellectual and professional associations. These, he writes, are among the distinctive glories of England, and go far to explain English intellectual leadership, especially in the sciences.[17]

A Note on Le Play and Marx

There is both charm and novelty in comparing Le Play with Marx. For both men the principal object of thought and research was the working class—with emphasis on the rural in Le Play, on the industrial in Marx. Both saw the long-run affluence and dignity of society resulting from an elevation of the position of the working class. Each detested the bourgeois democracy that had emerged from the Revolution; each saw in it, not the liberation and prosperity that most liberals hailed, but modes of corruption and tyranny. Both looked forward to a social order that would be as free as possible from competition and strife. Le Play is sometimes referred to as "the Karl Marx of the bourgeoisie," but the play on words is deceptive. There is little more regard in Le Play than in Marx for the kind of society that the bourgeoisie was constructing in France. Each found Balzac's merciless limnings of that society perfectly to his taste. Economic individualism, status-striving, and mass electorates were as repugnant to Le Play as to Marx.

But the similarities are reduced greatly by the profound differences of historical perspective and ethical evaluation between Le Play and Marx. For Marx, the essence of historical method is the discovery of the iron law of development that will clarify the relation of past to present and to future. Marx is a determinist in the full sense of nineteenth-century historical determinism. Le Play repudiates historical determinism of any type. Historical materials are only to be used comparatively, with respect to specific problems; their purpose is the formulation of empirical conclusions like those which Le Play's early training as an engineer suggested. He criticizes all efforts to reduce history to unilinear direction, either "progressive" or "regressive."

Both Le Play and Marx were sensitive to the institutional component in history, but beyond this generic likeness there is only stark contrast. For Marx the key institution is social class. For Le Play it is kinship: the structure of society varies with the type of family that underlies it. Marx detested private property; Le Play declared it the indispensable basis of social order and freedom. Marx treated religion as something superfluous to an understanding of human behavior and, in its effects, an opiate. For Le Play religion is as essential to man's mental and moral life as the family is to his social organization. For Marx, the whole rural scheme of things is tantamount to idiocy as far as its impact on human thought is concerned. Le Play, for all his conscious acceptance of industry, plainly prefers rural society, seeing in it the haven of security that urban life, by its very nature, must destroy. Marx was socialist; Le Play put socialism, along with mass democracy, secularism, and equalitarianism, among the major evils of his time—all of them unmistakable signs of social degeneration.

There is, finally, the matter of community. Plainly, Marx was interested in community of a type, the type being, first and foremost, solidarity of the working classes in the world and, second (as a technique for advancing socialism once the revolution overthrew the power of private capital), the kind of community implicit in what he called "the vast association of the nation." [18] But this is not community in the sense that either Le Play or any other sociologist—or, for that matter, some of Marx's socialist contemporaries—emphasized. Marx's contempt for the past, for "kitchen recipes," and, above all, his insistence that major organizational problems must be solved by history, not by piecemeal reform, placed him completely outside of Le Play's universe of thought.

We acquire some insight into Marx's view of the traditional community from what he wrote in 1853 on the village community in India. He saw, just as clearly as Le Play or Maine, that the effect of English occupation had been to accomplish what "all the civil wars, invasions, revolutions, conquests, famines" had not done: that is, break down "the entire framework of Indian society, without any symptoms of reconstitution yet appearing." Marx writes, in some strikingly prescient words: "This loss of his old world, with no gain of a new one, imparts a particular kind of melancholy to the present misery of the Hindu, and separates Hindustan, ruled by Britain, from all its ancient traditions, and from the whole of its past history." [19]

But what is Marx's view of the nature of proper reconstitution? Not, certainly, any shoring up of these ancient traditions. Hear him specifically on the subject of the village community:

"Now, sickening as it must be to human feeling to witness those myriads of industrious, patriarchal and inoffensive social organizations disorganized and dissolved into their units, thrown into a sea of woes, and their individual members losing at the same time their ancient form of civilizations and their hereditary means of subsistence, we must not forget that these idyllic village communities, inoffensive though they may appear, had always been the solid foundation of Oriental despotism, that they restrained the human mind within the smallest possible compass, making it the unresisting tool of superstition, enslaving it beneath traditional rules, depriving it of all grandeur and historical energies. . . . We must not forget that these little communities were contaminated by distinctions of caste, and by slavery, that they subjugated man to external circumstances instead of elevating man into the sovereign of circumstances, that they transformed a self-developing social state into never changing natural destiny. . . ." [20]

Admittedly, Marx continues, England is actuated only by the "vilest interests" in what she does to India and its ancient social interdependences, and has been "stupid in her manner of enforcing them." But that, Marx goes on in a revealing glimpse into his distinction between short-run good and long-run, or "historical," good, "is not the question."

"The question is: Can mankind fulfill its destiny without a fundamental revolution in the social state of Asia? If not, whatever may have been the crimes of England, she is the unconscious tool of history in bringing about that revolution." [21]

What Marx writes on the village community in India is in perfect accord with a view of the European scene that had been stated with great analytical insight in his early essay, "The Jewish Question." There he wrote of the "political revolution" that had begun in the sixteenth century and had, for the first time, brought into being a clear sense of "the *general* concern of the people." "It [the political revolution] dissolved civil society into its basic elements, on the one hand *individuals,* and on the other hand the *material and cultural elements* which formed the life experience and the civil situation of these individuals. It set free the political spirit which had, so to speak, been dissolved, fragmented, and lost in the various culs-de-sac of feudal society. . . ." [22] Such culs-de-sac, as Marx makes clear, as family, types of occupation, caste, and guilds. It was in the light of Marx's distaste for all the communalism and corporatism bequeathed by history that he could refer approvingly to the "giant broom" of the French Revolution which had swept these into the dustbin of history.

Nor is there anything in Marx's writing to suggest that his view of community ever changed. There is a perfect line of continuity between what he wrote of the village community in India and the position that the Bolsheviks were to take—though only after considerable debate—on the subject of traditional communal institutions in Russia: such institutions as the *mir* and the peasant co-operative. Engels, to be sure, writing in 1875, foresaw the possibility of a socialist revolution working on the basis of, rather than on the destruction of, these groups.

"It is clear that communal ownership in Russia is long past its flourishing period and to all appearances is moving towards its dissolution. Nevertheless, the possibility undeniably exists of transforming this social form into a higher one, if it should last until circumstances are ripe for that, and if it shows itself capable of development in such a way that the peasants no longer cultivate the land separately, but collectively; and to transform it into this higher form, without it being necessary for the Russian peasants to go through the intermediate stage of bourgeois small ownership. This, however, can only happen if, before the complete breakup of communal ownership, a proletarian revolution is carried out in Western Europe, creating for the Russian peasant the preconditions necessary for such a transformation. . . . If anything can still save Russian communal ownership and give it a chance of growing into a new form really capable of life, it is a proletarian revolution in Western Europe. . . ." [23]

But Engels' words notwithstanding, it was the hard, "historical" line that was to prevail in the debates on peasant institutions that took place among the Russian revolutionaries after their conquest of power. There was, it was decided early by the Bolsheviks, no place for even a modified form of any group—village community, guild, or co-operative —that had formed under feudal despotism. The stage of bourgeois capitalism might be jumped over, but not on the basis of stilts provided by any such legacies of the past as the *mir*.

Not all European radicalism followed Marx's view of the obsoleteness of the local and kinship institutions. Far from it. If there is anything that differentiates Proudhon from Marx, and the two traditions which followed each man—decentralist, pluralist anarchism on the one hand and centralized, nationalist socialism on the other—it is in the contrasting attitudes that we find on the subject of these institutions. There is a clear strain of traditionalism in Proudhon despite his hatred of private property, church, social class, and state. And, unlike Marx, Proudhon does not hesitate to be a utopian: to provide, that is, detailed previews of the anarchist Europe he foresees and desires. It is to be a Europe resting upon localism, with the small community—rural and industrial—the essential element. Between Proudhon and Le Play there is an affinity that does not exist between either and Marx, and it is an affinity that extends even to the structure of the family. Here, indeed, Proudhon appears more traditionalist than Le Play, for it is the patriarchal family that Proudhon espouses.[24]

It was the Marxian tradition, however, that achieved power in European radicalism, especially after Prussia's defeat of France in 1870, and the main line of radicalism thereafter was as hostile to localism, community, and co-operation as was the line of utilitarian liberalism that reached from James Mill to Herbert Spencer.

COMMUNITY AS TYPOLOGY—TÖNNIES AND WEBER

From community as substance we pass to community as typology. Here the work of Tönnies is of greatest importance. Nowhere has sociology's contribution to modern social thought been more fertile, more often borrowed from by other social sciences, especially with reference to the contemporary study of undeveloped nations, than in the typological use of the idea of community. Through this typology, the momentous historical transition of nineteenth-century society from its largely communal and medieval character to its modern industrialized and politicized form has been taken from the single context of European history in which it arose and made into a more general framework of analysis applicable to analogous transitions in other ages and other areas of the world.

As I have noted, the outlines of the typological use of community are to be found in the writings of conservatives and radicals alike at the beginning of the century; they are a part of the wider contrast between modernism and traditionalism that figured so prominently in polemical as well as philosophical analysis. The very warp of Burke's *Reflections on the Revolution in France* (and of some of his other works as well, including his addresses on the American colonists and on India) is his constant contrast between "legitimate society," which is compounded of kinship, class, religion, and locality and cemented by tradition, and the new type of society that he could see growing up in England as well as on the Continent which was, he thought, the predictably unstable consequence of democratic leveling, unchecked commercialism, and rootless rationalism. Hegel's contrast between "family society" and "civic society" clearly embodies the typology; it is set moreover in a basically unpolemical context. And it is again appropriate to cite Bonald's essay, "The Agricultural and Industrial Family," written in 1818, in which he deals with the antithetical modes of thought, feeling, and social relationship in rural and urban society. Similarly, in the writings of Coleridge, Southey, Carlyle, and others, all of whom we have before noted in connection with the ethos of community, the same contrast is made central. To these writers the essence of the contrast lay in what had reached its communal height in the Middle Ages and what, as the result of atomization and secularism, was so lamentably to be seen in the modern world.

Ideological writings aside, there are three major scholarly works in the mid-nineteenth century which, above any others, I think, provided the effective background for the typological use of community that we find in Tönnies and the sociological tradition.

The first is Otto von Gierke's monumental *Das Deutsche Genossenschaftsrecht,* publication of which began in 1868 and continued through the next several decades. Given the constitutional situation in Germany at that time—with the conflict between "Romanist" and "Germanist" interpretations of law at the heart of much of the situation—it was perhaps inevitable that von Gierke's work, written from a pronouncedly Germanist point of view, would attract much attention not merely in the field of law but in the wider area of the study of society. For at the center of his thinking is the vivid contrast he draws between the *medieval social structure,* based upon ascribed status, membership, the organic unity of all communal and corporate groups before the law, upon legal decentralization and the fundamental distinction between state and society, and the *modern nation-state,* resting upon, first, the centralization of political power, and, second, the individual, with a consequent pulverization of all that had once lain in between. Fundamental is his contrast between *Genossenschaft* and *Herrschaft.* No one in the century explored more carefully than von Gierke the communal foundations of medieval society or etched more sharply the contrast between the medieval community and modern society. His work was widely read not only in Germany but in other parts of the world, and a section of it was translated by F. W. Maitland and, later, by Ernest Barker.

The second work is Maine's *Ancient Law,* published in 1861. Written in one of the finest prose styles of the nineteenth century, this small volume was almost immediately regarded as a classic, as important to politics and sociology as to the special field of jurisprudence within which Maine wrote it. The typology of community is phrased by Maine in terms of "status" versus "contract." Each is defined by Maine primarily with respect to law of persons, but the implications of both terms go plainly beyond—to the total contrast of types of society. The contrast between societies or ages resting primarily on ascribed status and tradition and those resting on contract and achieved status lights up not merely what Maine chose to call a principle of development (all societies, he wrote, tend to move from status to contract in their emphasis) but, of more current relevance, to classification of types. It proved, in Maine's hands, to be a tool for the understanding of existing societies: for example, Eastern Europe, India, and China in their contrasts with Western European society. It was also a tool applicable to previous periods of history—for example, in the history of the *patria potestas* in ancient Rome from the "status" society of the Republic to the "contract" society of the late Empire. The principal point of Maine's volume was to demonstrate the impossibility of understanding modern legal concepts except in the light of the transition from a social system based upon status to one based pre-eminently on contract, but the two terms have since been widely used—were used, indeed, by Maine himself—for categorization of societies in the world—underdeveloped and modern, as we would say today. Tönnies was well acquainted with Maine's work.

The third book, and of stylistic quality equal to Maine's, is *The Ancient City* by Fustel de Coulanges, published in 1864. I shall have much more to say of this book in a later chapter, for it is one of the key works in the formation of the perspective of the religio-sacred. Here it is enough to observe that this penetrating study of the ancient Greek and Roman city-state is also an account of the processes of community formation and of the processes of community disintegration. Fustel's contrast between the stable, closed community that characterized the earliest history of Athens and Rome and the individualized, open society that each became in its later history is made the basis of a sociological interpretation of classical culture and its changes that remains as fresh and evocative as when he wrote the book.

All three of these books, it will be noted, appeared during the 1860's, and their influence upon European thought was immediate. By the time Tönnies wrote his *Gemeinschaft und Gesellschaft* the ideas expressed in these three works were well known and could not but have had impact upon his mind. If we examine Tönnies' work, indeed, we find it to be in very considerable part a fusion, within his own distinctive typology of community, of the basic themes of von Gierke, Maine, and Fustel de Coulanges: (1) the transition of Western polity from the corporate and communal to the individualistic and rational; (2) of Western social organization from one of ascribed status to contract; and (3) of Western ideas from the sacred-communal to the secular-associational. Tönnies gave these three themes theoretical articulation, and although his materials are drawn also from the Western European transition from medievalism to modernism, his typological use of these materials permits universalized application.

It is not always realized that Tönnies' book was written when the author was only thirty-two and before any of the major works of Weber, Durkheim, and Simmel had been published, or that a long life of scholarship, extending into many areas of theory and history, followed the writing of this early work.

It has often been said that Tönnies sought, nostalgically, to celebrate the communal past when he wrote his book, and that he was hostile to the liberal tendencies of the modern age. That such charges left their impress on Tönnies' mind is shown by his preface to the final edition of *Gemeinschaft und Gesellschaft:* "By way or orientation, I would like to add that I neither had fifty years ago nor have now the intention of presenting in this volume an ethical or political treatise. In this connection I warned emphatically in my first preface against misinterpreting explanations and clever but misleading applications of my ideas." [25] There is pathos in this statement when we recall that it was written at a time when the Nazis were broadcasting to the world their vulgar doctrines of the sanctity of "community" based upon race and nation. That Tönnies' *Gemeinschaft und Gesellschaft* reflects a considerable degree of nostalgia for the communal forms of society in which he had himself been born, in Schleswig, is doubtless true, though it is questionable that it is any greater than what is to be seen in Weber and Durkheim. A degree of nostalgia is built into the very structure of nineteenth-century sociology. It is, in any event, a universe apart from the doctrines of Nazism.

Let us turn to the two concepts *Gemeinschaft* and *Gesellschaft*. The first translates easily enough into community—using the word in the full sense of this chapter. The second is more difficult. The commonest translation is "society," which says, on the face of it, almost nothing, for, after all, community is itself a part of society. *Gesellschaft* acquires its typological importance when we see it as a special type of human relationship: one characterized by a high degree of individualism, impersonality, contractualism, and proceeding from volition or sheer interest rather than from the complex of affective states, habits, and traditions that underlies *Gemeinschaft*.

The development of European society, Tönnies tells us, has been from *unions of Gemeinschaft* to *associations of Gemeinschaft,* thence to *associations of Gesellschaft* and, finally, to *unions of Gesellschaft*. This, in essence, is the summarization of European development that Tönnies converts into a classificatory typology for the analysis of any society, past or present, European or non-European. The first three phases of the development reflect a growing individualization of human relationships, with impersonality, competition, and egoism becoming gradually more dominant. The fourth phase represents modern society's effort to recover —through techniques of human relations, social security, and job insurance—within the context of the *Gesellschaft*-like private or public corporation some of the communal securities of earlier society. The fourth phase may thus be likened to *pseudo-Gemeinschaft* in its more extreme manifestations.

Given the historical outline, let us look more carefully at the terms themselves. We shall begin with *Gemeinschaft* and its two phases. "The prototype of all unions of *Gemeinschaft* is the family. By birth man enters these relationships: free rational will can determine his remaining within the family, but the very existence of the relationship itself is not dependent on his full rational will. The three pillars of *Gemeinschaft*—blood, place (land), and mind, or kinship, neighborhood, and friendship —are all encompassed in the family, but the first of them is the constituting element of it." Associations of *Gemeinschaft,* on the other hand, "are most perfectly interpreted as friendship, *Gemeinschaft* of spirit and mind based on common work or calling and thus on common beliefs." Among the numerous manifestations of *Gemeinschaft* association are guilds, fellowships of the arts and crafts, churches, and holy orders. "In all these the idea of the family persists. The prototype of the association in *Gemeinschaft* remains the relationship between master and servant or, better, between master and disciple . . ." Plainly, the combination of *Gemeinschaft* unions and associations that Tönnies sketches for us is nothing more nor less than a social sketch of Europe's Middle Ages, though its implications extend beyond Europe.

Conversely, *Gesellschaft,* in its two forms, association and union, reflects the modernization of European society. It is always important to bear in mind that *Gesellschaft* is process as well as substance. For Tönnies it epitomizes modern European history. In pure *Gesellschaft,* which for Tönnies is symbolized by the modern economic enterprise and the network of legal and moral relations in which it resides, we move to association that is no longer cast in the mold of either kinship or friendship. "The difference lies in the fact that all its activities are restricted to a definite end and definite means of attaining it, if it is to be valid, i.e., to conform to the will of its members." [26] The essence of *Gesellschaft* is rationality and calculation. The following passage is a perfect rendering of Tönnies' distinction between *Gesellschaft* and *Gemeinschaft:*

"The theory of the *Gesellschaft* deals with the artificial construction of an aggregate of human beings which superficially resembles the *Gemeinschaft* insofar as the individuals live and dwell together peacefully. *However, in Gemeinschaft they remain essentially united in spite of all separating factors, whereas in Gesellschaft they are essentially separated in spite of all uniting factors.* In the *Gesellschaft,* as contrasted with the *Gemeinschaft,* we find no actions that can be derived from an *a priori* and necessarily existing unity; no actions, therefore, which manifest the will and the spirit of the unity even if performed by the individual; no actions which, insofar as they are performed by the individual, take place on behalf of those united with him. In the *Gesellschaft* such actions do not exist. On the contrary, here everybody is by himself and isolated, and there exists a condition of tension against all others." [27]

It would be a mistake to suppose that Tönnies considers substantive, empirical contrasts of human relationships to be as sharp in contour as the two concepts of *Gemeinschaft* and *Gesellschaft* might imply. Although the sway of influence of each roughly corresponds to the two great phases of European history—traditional and modern—in his mind, he nevertheless uses each as a kind of ideal-type, and is thus able to show *Gesellschaft* elements in the traditional family as easily as he can *Gemeinschaft* elements in the modern corporation. This point is often overlooked in Tönnies. Weber was to expand it, make it more flexible, but it is present in Tönnies.

Always, everywhere, Tönnies notes, the moral element is strong in popular characterization of the two types of organization. *Gemeinschaft* and its various correlates tend to be "good": that is, one refers to someone as having fallen into bad "associations" or "society" but never "bad community." All of the cherished elemental states of mind of society—love, loyalty, honor, friendship, and so on—are emanations of *Gemeinschaft*. Simmel, as we shall see, makes a great deal of this, though without reference to Tönnies' own two terms. *Gemeinschaft* is the home of morality, the seat of virtue. It is also potent in its influence upon labor. "*Gemeinschaft*, to the extent that it is capable of doing so, transforms all labor into a kind of art, giving it style, dignity, and charm, and a rank in its order, denoted as a calling and an honor." It is *Gemeinschaft*, for Tönnies, when the worker—be he artist, artisan, or professional—gives himself limitlessly to his job without calculation of units of time and compensation. "However, through remuneration in money, just as through the holding of finished products for sale, there tends to be a reversal of this process, which makes the individual, along with this mental construct, into its sole personality. In *Gesellschaft* . . . such a personality is by nature and conscience the businessman or merchant." [28]

There is even, Tönnies tells us, a useful differentiation of the two sexes in terms of the typology. Woman is by nature more easily given to *Gemeinschaft* pursuits and values. "From this one understands how averse trade must be to the feminine mind and nature." That women can be, and have been, converted to *Gesellschaft* roles is, of course, clear enough in European history. It is bound up with the emancipation of women. But as the woman enters into the struggle of earning a living, "it is evident that trading and the freedom and independence of the female factory worker as contracting party and possessor of money will develop her rational will, enabling her to think in a calculating way, even though, in the case of factory work, the tasks themselves may not lead in this direction. The woman becomes enlightened, coldhearted, conscious. Nothing is more foreign and terrible to her original inborn nature, in spite of all later modifications. Possibly nothing is more characteristic and important in the process of formation of the *Gesellschaft* and the destruction of *Gemeinschaft*." [29] It is the *Gemeinschaft* element in the woman—and also in the child—Tönnies tells us that accounts for the ease with which women and children were exploited in the early factories. Both were inherently more vulnerable than the adult male.

Does all of this mean that there are no positive moral elements in *Gesellschaft*? By no means. Without *Gesellschaft* and its special constellation of social and intellectual elements, modern liberalism and many of the graces of modern culture could not have arisen. The city is the home of *Gesellschaft*. "The city is also the center of science and culture which go hand in hand with commerce and industry. Here the arts must make a living; they are exploited in a capitalistic way. Thoughts spread and change with astonishing rapidity. Speeches and books, through mass distribution, become stimuli of far-reaching importance." But with the advance of *Gesellschaft* and its cultural brilliance, must go the disintegration of *Gemeinschaft*. On this point Tönnies is clear and emphatic. I know of no single passage that so well exemplifies this and encapsulates the moral, the sociological, and historical arguments of his book as does the following. It is set in the specific context of Tönnies' application of his typology to Roman history and the birth of the Empire, but it might as easily have been placed in any other section of his work.

"In this new, revolutionary, disintegrating, and leveling sense, general and natural law is entirely an order characteristic of *Gesellschaft*, manifested in its purest form in commercial law. In its beginning it seems quite innocent, it means nothing but progress, refinement, improvement, and facilitations; it stands for fairness, reason, and enlightenment. This form persisted even in the moral decay of the Empire. Both trends, the elaboration, universalizing, and finally systematizing and codification of the law, on the one hand, and, on the other hand, the decay of life and mores along with brilliant political successes, capable administration, and an efficient and liberal jurisprudence, have often been described. But only a few seem to have realized the necessary connection between, and the unity and interdependence of, these two trends. Even the learned writers are seldom able to free themselves from prejudices and to arrive at an unbiased, strictly objective view of the physiology and pathology of social life. They admire the Roman Empire and the Roman Law; they abhor the decay of the family and of the mores. But they are unable to discuss the causal relationship between the two phenomena." [30]

Gemeinschaft and *Gesellschaft,* as concepts, thus embody or reflect many things: legal, economic, cultural, and intellectual; even, as we have seen, the division between the sexes. But at the heart of each concept is the image of a type of social relationship and of the affective and volitional elements of mind entering respectively into each. What aristocracy and democracy were, typologically, for Tocqueville; patriarchal and unstable family-types for Le Play; and feudal and capitalist modes of economic production were for Marx, *Gemeinschaft* and *Gesellschaft* are for Tönnies. In each case, a single aspect of the larger social order is abstracted, given dynamic significance, and made, so to speak, the *causa efficiens* of society's evolution.

The important point of Tönnies' work is not mere classificatory analysis; nor is it simple philosophy of history. The important point is that through his differentiation of *Gemeinschaft* and *Gesellschaft* as types of social organization, and through his historical and comparative use of these types, we are provided with a *sociological* explanation of the rise of capitalism, the modern state, and the whole modernist temper of mind. What others found in economic or technological or military areas of causality, Tönnies found in the strictly social area: the area of community and its sociological displacement by non-communal modes of organization, law, and polity. The rise of capitalism and the modern nation-state are both made aspects, by Tönnies, of the more fundamental social change that he identifies for us in the terms of *Gemeinschaft* and *Gesellschaft.* This is the major accomplishment of Tönnies' book. Whereas, for example, in Marx the loss of community is dealt with as the consequence of capitalism, in Tönnies capitalism is treated as the consequence of the loss of community—of the passage of *Gemeinschaft* into *Gesellschaft.* What Tönnies' thus does is to take community from the status of *dependent* variable that it had in the writings of the economists and classical individualists in general and give it *independent,* even causal, status. This is the essence of Tönnies' typological use of community. It is an essence that extended itself into the works of Durkheim, whose criticism of Tönnies and reversal of terminology cannot conceal the cognate relation that lies between his "mechanical" and "organic" types of solidarity and Tönnies' concepts. The same typological essence is to be seen in Simmel, for whom "metropolis" becomes the encapsulating term of modernism, and, at bottom, it is the essence of the American sociological distinction between the "primary" and "secondary" types of association for which Charles H. Cooley was primarily responsible.

Nowhere, however, did Tönnies' typology strike more deeply and creatively than in the works of Max Weber. We shall reserve for the next chapter treatment of Weber's seminal concepts of "traditional" and "rational" types of authority and society. It suffices to note here only that these two types have almost perfect correspondence with Tönnies' terms. I am more interested for the moment in Weber's direct use of the typology of community. Its empirical origins may well lie in Weber's interest (aroused in 1890 by the *Verein für Sozialpolitik*'s inquiry into the condition of agriculture in Eastern Germany) in the shift of farm labor from a condition of "status" to one of "contract." But the form in which this early interest developed into Weber's large-scale comparative treatment of society is surely, in ample measure, the consequence of the impact of Tönnies' theoretical constructs.

The communal ethic is central in Weber. Like Tönnies, Weber saw European history as a kind of falling away from the patriarchalism and brotherhood that had characterized medieval society. For Tönnies this falling away was expressed, as we have seen, by *Gesellschaft,* considered (as Tönnies explicitly considered it) as process. For Weber it is the consequence of the process of "rationalization." The two processes are, however, strikingly alike.

More to the point of the present discussion we see the effect of Tönnies' typology in Weber's treatment of the nature of social action and of social relationships. Weber's is the more subtle and, on the whole, sophisticated treatment, but its roots in Tönnies' distinction between the two types of association are clear.

We see this plainly in Weber's notable characterization of his four types of social action: orientation (1) to interpersonal ends, (2) to absolute value-ends, (3) to emotional or affectual states, and (4) to tradition and convention. Allow all we will to Weber's superior classification, its relation to Tönnies' analysis of the two types of will and his analysis of social norms and social values is inescapable. The same is true of Weber's analysis of types of social relationship. The very priority (in logical terms) that Weber gives to them in the larger institutional structures in which these types of social relationship are found—political, economic, religious, etc.—is testimony to the power exerted by Tönnies' treatment of the priority of types of will and relationship. Underlying the whole of Weber's treatment of social action, modes of orientation of social action, and "legitimacy" of social order is the image of the contrast between *Gemeinschaft* and *Gesellschaft*.

Let us turn, however, to Weber's specific use of the concept of "community" and its antithesis. We find this in his treatment of types of "solidary social relationship" where he makes the fundamental distinction between "communal" and "associative." These are types that Weber finds everywhere in human history, and they become for him exactly what *Gemeinschaft* and *Gesellschaft* are for Tönnies—ideal types. A relationship is communal, Weber tells us, when it is based on a subjective feeling of the parties that they belong to each other, that they are implicated in each other's total existence. Examples are the closely bound military unit, the labor union, the religious brotherhood, the ties of lovers, and the school or university; these in addition to such obvious types as family, parish, and neighborhood.

A relationship is associative for Weber when it rests on a "rationally motivated adjustment of interest or a similarly motivated agreement." It does not matter whether it is oriented to expediency or moral value; it is associative if it flows from rational calculation of interest or will rather than from emotional identification. The purest instances of associative relationships are to be found in the free market or open society. Here are to be found the associations that represent compromise of opposed but complementary interests. Here is the voluntary association that rests solely on self-interest or belief and contractual assent; to be seen in not only economic behavior but also religious, educational, and political.

These are the two basic types of relationship that Weber finds in human society. They are, for Weber, perspectives, ideal types, and much of Weber's treatment of them emphasizes the fact that both may be seen participating in the same social structure. "Every social relationship which goes beyond the pursuit of immediate common ends, which hence lasts for long periods, involves relatively permanent social relationships between the same persons, and these cannot be exclusively confined to the technically necessary activities." [31] Hence the tendency even in economic relationships based upon contract for the more communal type of atmosphere to begin to develop when the relationship endures for any length of time. "Conversely, a social relationship which is normally considered primarily communal may involve action on the part of some or even all of the participants, which is to an important degree oriented to considerations of expediency. There is, for instance, a wide variation in the extent to which the members of the family group feel a genuine community of interest or, on the other hand, exploit the relationship for their own ends." [32]

Weber goes beyond the simple distinction between communal and the associative to describe what he calls open and closed relationships:

"A social relationship, regardless of whether it is communal or associative in character, will be spoken of as "open" to outsiders if and insofar as participation in the mutually oriented social action relevant to its subjective meaning is, according to its system of order, not denied to anyone who wishes to participate and who is actually in a position to do so. A relationship will, on the other hand, be called "closed" against outsiders so far as, according to its subjective meaning and the binding rules of its order, participation of certain persons is excluded, limited, or subjected to conditions." [33]

Whether a relationship is open or closed has nothing to do, intrinsically, with whether it is communal or associative. There are associative relationships—business partnerships, select clubs, for example—that are just as closed as the most isolated tradition-bound kinship community. Closure, in short, may be for traditional, emotional, or purely calculative reasons. It is, however, the communal type of relationship that tends most frequently to manifest the social and moral qualities of the closed order. For, once a relationship becomes associative—that is, the product of interest or volition rather than tradition or kinship—it becomes difficult to enforce the criteria of closure.

The most notable demonstration of this in Weber is with respect to the city. Even by present standards, Weber's comparative study of urban structure and behavior remains a remarkable achievement, one that is as central to his study of capitalism as is his work on the Protestant ethic, though this fact is too often overlooked by Weber's critics. The major difference, Weber tells us, between cities of the ancient world and those of the European Middle Ages lies in the fact that the former were generally associations of *communities*—that is composed of tightly knit and legally indissoluble ethnic or kinship groups—whereas medieval cities were from the beginning associations of *individuals* (Christian individuals, to be sure, since Jews were denied the rights of citizens in consequence of their inability to participate in the Mass) in which allegiance was sworn to the city *as* individuals, *not* as members of kindreds or other groups. Every medieval town was, in the beginning, "a confessional association of individual believers, not a ritual association of kinship groups."

As Weber shrewdly notes, this fact carried with it two divergent and notable consequences. On the one hand, the fact of the individualism of its membership—that is, the legal disengagement of its individual members from other social groups—made for an increasing communality and autonomy of the medieval town itself. It was a community in the beginning in nearly as full a sense as the monastery or guild. But individualism of membership also meant that there would be from the beginning a structural strain toward *associational* character, one in which the rights of individuals would become ever more prominent, one that would make it increasingly easy for outsiders to become accepted as citizens of the towns and that would thus pose a challenge to the guilds and other closed groups within the town, thus aiding in the general development of capitalism and modern secular rationality.[34]

COMMUNITY AS METHODOLOGY

In Durkheim we find the idea of community used not merely substantively, as in Le Play, not merely typologically, as in Tönnies, but also methodologically. That is, in Durkheim's hands community becomes a framework of analysis within which such matters as morality, law, contract, religion, and even the nature of the human mind are given new dimensions of understanding.

Quite apart from Durkheim's direct influence upon sociology, his use of the idea of community was to inspire a considerable number of scholars in fields as distant from sociology as classical history, jurisprudence, and the study of Chinese culture. In Gustave Glotz's studies of ancient Athens we see the integration and disintegration of the Athenian community made the perspective of analysis of philosophy and art as well as of culture and polity. The same is true of Leon Duguit's philosophical works in jurisprudence, of J. Declareuil's interpretation of the history of Roman law, and of Marcel Granet's complex and subtle interpretations of Chinese culture. In all of these, and in many other works as well, community is transposed from mere collectivity, from a substantive type of human relationship, to a means of analysis of human thought behavior.

Durkheim shares with Freud a large part of the responsibility for turning contemporary social thought from the classic rationalist categories of volition, will, and individual consciousness to aspects which are, in a strict sense, non-volitional and non-rational. Freud's has been the more widely recognized influence. But there is every reason to regard

Durkheim's reaction to individualistic rationalism as more fundamental and encompassing than Freud's. Freud, after all, never doubted the primacy of the individual and intra-individual forces when he analyzed human behavior. Non-rational influences proceed, in Freud's interpretation, from an unconscious mind *within* the individual, even though it is related genetically to a racial past. The individual, in short, remains the solid reality in Freud's thought. In Durkheim, however, it is community that has prior reality, and it is from community that the essential elements of reason flow.

It is instructive to note that in Durkheim the tables of individualism are turned. Where the individualist perspective had reduced all that was traditional and corporate in society to the hard and unchanging atoms of individual mind and sentiment, Durkheim, in diametrically opposite fashion, makes the latter manifestations of the former. We have thus a kind of reverse reductionism, one that takes some of the deepest states of individuality—for example, religious faith, the categories of the mind, volition, the suicidal impulse—and explains them in terms of what lies outside the individual: in community and in moral tradition. Even such incontestably rational forms of relationship as contract and political decision are reduced by Durkheim to pre-rational and pre-individual states of communal and moral consensus. Crime, insanity, religion, morality, economic competition, and law are all approached from a methodology based on the priority of community.

What we noted earlier about the altered referent of "social" in European sociology applies with special force to Durkheim. The stringency of his criticism of utilitarian individualism is based in part upon what Durkheim regarded as the inadequacy of its view of the nature of society: an impersonal constellation of interests and agreements. This, for Durkheim, will never do. In his mind the real roots of the word *society* lie in *communitas,* not *societas.* "Society cannot make its influence felt unless it is in action, and it is not in action unless the individuals who compose it are assembled together and act in common. It is by common action that it takes consciousness of itself and realizes its position; it is before all else an active cooperation." [35]

From this communal envisagement of the nature of society proceeds the all-important concept of the collective conscience, which he defines appropriately in terms of "beliefs and sentiments held in common." Such a view of social organization manifestly shares little with the utilitarians of the nineteenth century. They, like the *philosophes* before them, took as their unconscious referent *societas* when they wrote of society. For them, Durkheim's image would have seemed intolerably corporate. Durkheim's thinking was deeply affected by the whole revival, in the nineteenth century, of the values and properties of community— community in the sense of groups formed by intimacy, emotional cohesion, depth, and continuity. For Durkheim, society is simply *community* written large.

It is important to note that Durkheim's initial interest in the metaphysical properties of society began with his effort to prove the irrelevance to modern life of the constraints and disciplines embodied in traditional, historical types of social organization. *The Division of Labor* was conceived, quite literally, to prove that the function of the division of labor in modern society is the integration of individuals through their pursuit of complementary and symbiotic specializations, thus making possible—for the first time in history—the termination of traditional mechanisms of social constraint. The function of the division of labor is social: that is, integration. With integration must come new relationships and new laws. The traditional types of relationship and law—based upon repression, mores, and communal sanctions—are gradually expelled. This was the motivation of the book. It was not, however, the conclusion.

In *The Division of Labor* Durkheim distinguishes between two types of social solidarity: mechanical and organic. The first is that which has existed throughout most of the history of human society. Based on moral and social homogeneity, it is reinforced by the discipline of the small community. Within such a framework, tradition dominates, individualism is totally lacking, and justice is overwhelmingly directed toward the subordination of the individual to the collective conscience. Property is communal, religion is indistinguishable from cult and ritual, and all questions of individual thought and conduct are determined by the will of the community. And the ties of kinship, localism, and the sacred give substance to the whole.

The second form of solidarity, which Durkheim calls *organic,* is based on the primacy of division of labor. With the rise of technology and the general emergence of individuality from the restraints of the past, it becomes possible—for the first time in human history—for social order to rest, not on mechanical uniformity and collective repression, but on the organic articulation of free individuals pursuing different functions but united by their complementary roles. Within the framework of organic solidarity there can be a general disengagement of man from the traditional restraints of kinship, class, localism, and the generalized social conscience. Justice will be restitutive rather than penal; law will lose its repressive character, and there will be a diminishing need for punishment. Heterogeneity and individualism will replace homogeneity and communalism, and division of labor will provide all that is necessary to unity and order.

Such was the initial conception of *The Division of Labor* that may be fairly easily inferred from its opening chapters, especially in the light of what Durkheim had written during the three or four years immediately preceding the publication of the book. There is little doubt that the theme of progressive, individualistic rationalism was considerably stronger in his mind at the beginning of the book than it was at the end. Given the essentially progressive nature of the framework of change in which Durkheim first sought to place the two types of society, his conclusions would have had an amusing similarity to those of Herbert Spencer—for Spencer's argument, reduced to its essentials, stressed the progressive ascendancy of ties based on restitutive sanctions and division of labor over those rooted in tradition and community.

But Durkheim went further. The distinctive contribution of *The Division of Labor* lies in the fact that, even in the process of arguing what he had conceived as the initial thesis of this work, he saw the inherent weaknesses of that argument when pushed to its logical conclusion and, seeing them, subtly but powerfully altered his thesis. Like Weber, Durkheim could see that, although the conceptual distinction between the two types of solidarity or association was a real one, the institutional stability of the second had to be deeply rooted in the continuation—in one form or another—of the first. The progressive rationalists of the time argued, rather, the replacement of the one by the other. What Durkheim, above even Weber, demonstrated was that such replacement would lead, in fact, to a sociological monstrosity.

The unraveling of the somewhat tangled threads of Durkheim's demonstration (and it is this that makes the study of *The Division of Labor* more fascinating than that of any other of his works) is not an easy one. Indeed, in a sense the book is a kind of palimpsest, and more than a little ingenuity is needed to discern the point at which the secondary argument begins to overshadow the initial thesis.

The secondary argument, the argument that close analysis reveals to be developing from about the mid-point of the book, is best expressed in the following passage: "The division of labor can be produced only in the midst of pre-existing society. There is a social life outside the whole division of labor, but which the latter presupposes. That is, indeed, what we have directly established in showing that there are societies whose cohesion is essentially due to a community of beliefs and sentiments, and it is from these societies that those whose unity is assured by the division of labor have emerged." [36]

The passage is a crucial one, but Durkheim is being a little less than candid. Although it is true that he has been concerned with the type of cohesion he has labeled *mechanical*—analyzing its modes of law, custom, and belief—it is hardly true that he has been stressing the continuing necessity in modern organic society of sinews of stability that are mechanical in character. The brief analysis of contract and of the indispensable roots of contract in noncontractual forms of authority and relationships may be said to be the watershed of Durkheim's argument.

It is important to emphasize this aspect of *The Division of Labor:* Durkheim's "reversal" of argument. It is crucial to an understanding of his life's work and is the only way in which his succeeding works can be made congruent with this one. It is a matter of record, of course, that Durkheim never went back, in later studies, to any utilization of the distinction between the two types of solidarity, nor to the division of labor as a form of cohesion, much less to any rationalization of conflict and anomie in society as mere "pathological forms of division of labor." The kinds of society, constraint, and solidarity dealt with in all his later works—either in theoretical or practical terms—have nothing whatsoever to do with the attributes that he had laid down for an organic and (presumably) irreversibly modern society in *The Division of Labor*. On the contrary, society—in all its guises, functions, and historical roles—becomes, for Durkheim, a compound of social and psychological elements that he had first relegated to folk or primitive society. Not only is normal society founded, he would ever after declare, on such traits as collective conscience, moral authority, community, and the sacred, but the only appropriate response to modern conditions is the strengthening of such traits. Thus, and only thus, will suicide, economic conflict, and the gnawing frustrations of anomic life be moderated.[37]

In *The Rules of Sociological Method,* which, chronologically, falls between *The Division of Labor* and *Suicide,* Durkheim transmuted the attributes of mechanical solidarity into the eternal characteristics of social facts in general. This was but a bold heightening of his earlier conclusion that, however one proceeds in the study of human behavior, facts of social exteriority, constraint, and tradition—all of them prime elements of mechanical solidarity—are the only facts that sociologists *qua* sociologists can properly be concerned with. The fundamental thesis of this small work is that social facts cannot be decomposed or reduced to individual, psychological, or biological data, much less to mere reflections of geographic or climatic substance.[38]

At the time *The Rules of Sociological Method* was published it must have appeared—in that ultra-individualistic age of social science— as hardly more than a vision of the absolute social mind, a scholastic exercise in reification. As one looks back on that age, it is clear that there were then as few sociologists capable of assimilating Durkheim's central argument into the individualist categories of their minds as there were, a decade or two later, physicists capable of assimilating Einstein's relativity theory into the classical categories of their lectures on mechanics. Today, Durkheim's *Rules,* read carefully and with allowance only for polemical emphases and vagaries of expression, seems to contain little that goes beyond what sociologists regularly assume about the nature of social reality in their empirical studies of institutionalized behavior. Nevertheless, such is the tenacity of descriptive stereotypes in the history of social thought that the criticisms which formed the first response to Durkheim's *Rules* have largely endured, despite the fact that the climate of analytical individualism within which they were made has long since been succeeded by one generally congenial to Durkheim's methodological values.

What was born in *The Division of Labor* and baptized, so to speak, in *The Rules of Sociological Method* received successive confirmations in *Suicide* and *The Elementary Forms of Religious Life*. For too long students of Durkheim have persisted in placing these works in separate intellectual categories, as though they marked discontinuous phases of his life's labors. The opposite is true: the methodology that is emphasized in *The Rules of Sociological Method* has deep roots in *The Division of Labor*. Equally to the point is the fact that the concrete empirical content of *Suicide* and the far-reaching scholarly substance of *The Elementary Forms of Religious Life* both flow clearly and rigorously from the insights and proposals that are stated abstractly in the *Rules*. It will not do, in short, to divide Durkheim's thought into mutant and disconnected phases labeled *evolutionary, metaphysical, empirical,* and *functional-institutional* and to assert that these reflect, in that order, his four major published works.

What all four works have in common—and this applies also to the books posthumously published as well as to the articles that appeared in *L'Année* and elsewhere—is a social metaphysic and a methodology rooted in the conviction that took shape in Durkheim's mind as he wrote

The Division of Labor: that all human behavior above the level of the strictly physiological must be regarded as either emanating from, or else sharply conditioned by, society: that is, by the totality of groups, norms, and institutions within which every individual human being consciously and unconsciously exists from the moment of his birth. Social instincts, prepotent complexes, natural sentiments—all of these may indeed exist in man (Durkheim never denied their existence), but viewed against the determinative effects of society on such matters as moral, religious, and social conduct, they are negligible in influence, supplying barely more than an organic base. They are, in any event, impossible to get at—in sociological terms—until all possible consequences of the social have been exhausted. This last point is the major truth so widely overlooked by the individualistic-utilitarian minds of the nineteenth century, as indeed it continues to be overlooked by many even now.

It is easy enough, no doubt, to demolish some of Durkheim's metaphysical constructs, and many critics have so engaged themselves. Considered abstractly, how long can such ideas as the *collective conscience, collective representations,* and *the absolute autonomy of society* stand against the onslaughts of critical empiricism, linguistic analysis, and other manifestations of contemporary philosophy's remorseless hunting down of all that is not conceptually atomic? Let it be conceded immediately: not very long.

But one cannot deal with Durkheim by confining himself to definitions of such terms as *collective representations, individual representations,* and *anomie* any more than he can by seeking to deduce the complexity and subtlety of Durkheim's work from, say, the concepts of structure or function. One must turn to the actual, empirical problems in which Durkheim was interested and which he sought to explain. This is the best way to see the kind of substantive conclusions that are reached on the basis of premises that may indeed be attacked in the abstract as metaphysically "meaningless."

Let us look, first, at his analysis of the nature and substance of morality. Durkheim never tired of insisting on the centrality of the moral. All social facts are, at one and the same time, moral facts. He wrote in the final pages of *The Division of Labor:* "Society is not . . . a stranger to the moral world or something which has only secondary repercussions upon it. . . . Let all social life disappear and moral life will disappear with it, since it would no longer have any objective." [39] He put the matter even more forcibly in *Moral Education:* "If there is one fact that history has irrefutably demonstrated, it is that the morality of each people is directly related to the social structure of the people practicing it. The connection is so intimate that, given the general character of the morality observed in a given society, . . . one can infer the nature of that society, the elements of its structure and the way it is organized. Tell me the marriage patterns, the morals dominating family life, and I will tell you the principal characteristics of its organization." [40]

Far from being social morality that is the abstraction, it is individual morality, he emphasizes, that is the abstraction, for where other than within the community can the moral life be seen? "Moral life, in all its forms, is never met with except in society. It never varies except in relation to social conditions. . . . The duties of the individual towards himself are, in reality, duties towards society." [41]

Moral Education provides the opportunity to see in detail how Durkheim utilized the perspective of community in the clarification of morality. (Fully half of this remarkable volume, published posthumously, is taken up with the ways in which moral codes become internalized in the mind of the child. This discussion can deal only with the central proposition of this work.) There are three essential elements of morality.

1. THE SPIRIT OF DISCIPLINE   All moral behavior "conforms to pre-established rules. To conduct one's self morally is a matter of abiding by a norm. . . . This domain of morality is the domain of duty; duty is prescribed behavior." What is the source of this prescriptive element? Not, certainly, the germ plasm. Those who answer "God" have at least the merit of looking outside the individual to an authority capable of command. But for Durkheim, God is but a mythicization of society; his answer, therefore, is "Society." It is society alone—through its kinship, religious, and economic codes, through its binding traditions and groups—that possesses the authority necessary to make the sense of *ought* (which can never be reduced, Durkheim repeatedly contends, to mere interest or convenience) one of the most directive and tenacious forces in human life. It is this unalterable relation of morality to "oughtness," to discipline incapable of reduction to mere inner drive in man, that leads Durkheim to the logical, if dramatic, declaration that "the erratic, the undisciplined, are morally incomplete." [42]

2. THE ENDS OF MORALITY   Discipline is not enough; for it to become effective, for its function to be made manifest and determining, there must also be ends of morality. These are invariably impersonal, for action oriented to exclusively personal goals—whatever its benefits—is the very opposite of moral action. Whence comes the impersonality that

communicates itself, through discipline, to the individual? From society, from the individual's attachment to society: "[Morality] consists in the individual's attachment to those social groups of which he is a member. Morality begins, accordingly, only insofar as we belong to a human group, whatever it may be. Since, in fact, man is complete only as he belongs to several societies, morality itself is complete only to the extent that we feel identified with those different groups in which we are involved—family, union, business, club, political party, country, humanity." [43] It is membership in the social group, then, that provides the indispensable context of mediation whereby ends become impersonal ends endowed with the authority that alone makes a reality of discipline.

3. AUTONOMY OR SELF-DETERMINATION This third element has nothing to do with Kantian autonomy and Durkheim devotes a good part of his argument to a demonstration of the inadequacies of Kant's individual-oriented categorical imperative. Personal autonomy—that is, self-responsibility—is indeed a crucial element of moral behavior, but this, Durkheim argues, is not less a part of society than discipline and group membership. Autonomy is simply the human being's rational awareness of reasons for what he does under the impulsions of discipline and attachment: "To act morally, it is not enough—it is no longer enough—to respect discipline and to be committed to a group. Beyond this, and whether out of deference to a rule or devotion to a collective idea, we must have knowledge, as clear and complete an awareness as possible of the reasons for our conduct. This consciousness confers on our behavior the autonomy that the public conscience from now on requires of every genuinely and completely moral being. Hence, we can say that the third element of morality is the understanding of it." [44] With the development of human society, there is a powerful tendency for man's awareness to become ever more acute and sensitive. The need for discipline and attachment remains as great as ever. (This, in answer to contemporary individualists who were proclaiming a new morality, one in which man forever was liberated from social disciplines and attachments and free to govern himself.) But, with his reason, man can know what he is doing and thus achieve a form of intellectual (but not social) autonomy unknown to primitive man.

A second and equally influential use of the perspective of community is the analysis of contract. This begins in *The Division of Labor* and is made the subject of exhaustive treatment in the later *Professional Ethics and Civic Morals*. In a number of respects the treatment of contract must rank among the more brilliant *tours de force* of modern social analysis. The point of departure is a refutation of Spencer's position, one in which contract is conceived as the simple, atomic act of two or more individuals achieving union through self-interest supplemented by reason. But it would be an error to limit Durkheim's treatment of contract to this. In proper focus, Durkheim's treatment is a profound attack on a vein of thought that began in the seventeenth century with Hobbes and his contemporaries and continued through the Enlightenment to become, in the nineteenth century, the essence of the utilitarian movement.[45] In this vein, contract is the residual model of all social relationships. Hobbes had endeavored to rationalize even the family tie as an implicit contract between child and parent. In the rationalist-utilitarian tradition of the eighteenth and nineteenth centuries, all that could not be rationalized—legitimatized—by contract, real or imaginary, was suspect. The only reality and, therefore, the proper object of scientific attention, is that which emanates from man himself, his instinct and his reason. Social union, however it may appear to simple perception, is in fact the product of some form of contract. In this view, in short, contract is the microcosm of society, the image of human relationships.

This is the image that Durkheim repudiates. Contract, he argues, taken as either historically or logically primordial, is untenable and meretricious. How, Durkheim asks, can men ever be expected to honor a contractual agreement if it rests only on the individual interest or fancy that supposedly brings it into being? "Where interest is the only ruling force, each individual finds himself in a state of war with every other since nothing comes to mollify the egos, and any truce would not be of long duration. There is nothing less constant than interest. Today, it unites me to you; tomorrow it will make me your enemy. Such a cause can only give rise to transient relations and passing associations." [46]

Contract of any type could not be sustained for a moment, Durkheim argues, unless it was based on conventions, traditions, codes in which the idea of an authority higher than contract was clearly resident. The idea of contract, its very possibility as a relationship among men, appears late in the development of human society. And it comes into existence only in the contexts of already sovereign mores which cannot, by any stretch of the imagination, be reduced to self-interest. These mores have their origin and continuing reality in community, not in states of individual consciousness.

Our third example of Durkheim's use of the perspective of community is his famous study of suicide. Here Durkheim's perspective is at its most boldly empirical. To have flung down the gauntlet before the rationalist idol of contract was daring enough. But to take suicide, that most intimate and plainly individual of all acts, and subject it, too, to the methodology of society—this, surely, must have been more than the utilitarians of that day could easily bear. What had been suggested in *The Division of Labor* about suicide—that is, its relation to periods of social disintegration—was now made the subject of investigation, and precisely in terms of the methodology he had laid down in *The Rules of Sociological Method*.

There are, of course, several motivations behind the work. There is, most obviously, the scientific. Suicide was plainly a problem of interest to many; it had already been studied, and much material of a demographic nature was accessible. This Durkheim acknowledges: "Suicide has been chosen as its subject, among the various subjects that we have had occasion to study in our teaching career, because few are more accurately to be defined and because it seemed to us particularly timely; its limits have even required study in a preliminary work." [47]

But there are also two other motivations behind the work, and these have been less noted. First, Durkheim maintains, the "possibility of sociology" as a distinct field of study will be made more evident by this discovery of laws affecting suicide that flow directly from the distinctive subject matter of sociology—that is, society and social facts. There is, in short, a practical, professional objective, and that this was never lost on Durkheim is plain in the repeated references to this point in *Suicide*.

"Sociological method, as we practice it, rests wholly on the basic principle that social facts must be studied as things: that is, as realities external to the individual. There is no principle for which we have received more criticism; but none is more fundamental." For a sociology to be possible, it must have an object distinctively its own. It must take cognizance of a reality that is not already in the domain of other sciences. If no reality exists outside individual consciousness, then sociology lacks any material of its own. For then the only possible subject of observation is the mental states of the individual; these, however, form the field of psychology. From the psychological point of view, the essence of marriage, for example, or of the family, or of religion consists of individual needs to which these institutions supposedly correspond: paternal affection, filial love, sexual desire, the so-called religious instinct. "On the pretext of giving the science a more solid foundation by establishing it upon the psychological constitution of the individual, it is thus robbed of the only object proper to it. It is not realized that there can be no sociology unless societies exist; and that societies cannot exist if there are only individuals." [48] Here, plainly stated, is the translation of metaphysics into practical methodology. Rarely has it been done more effectively.

Having justified the study of suicide on demographic and methodological grounds—in each instance, be it noted, stressing the autonomy of the social for what can alone be sociological consideration—Durkheim adds the final justification of his work: a moral one. Suicide, he says, falls in a category that includes economic conflict, crime, and divorce and marks the pathological state of contemporary European society. Remedies must therefore be proposed that might serve to moderate the incidence of suicide as well as that of other forms of social disintegration. It is in this practical, moral, light that Durkheim refers to "some suggestions concerning the causes of the general contemporary maladjustment being undergone by European societies and concerning remedies which may relieve it." Suicide, he emphasizes, as it is found today, "is precisely one of the forms through which the collective affection from which we suffer is transmitted; thus it will help us to understand this." [49]

The conclusions Durkheim reached in this remarkable volume can even today be regarded as a triumphant demonstration of the results he had forecast abstractly in *The Rules of Sociological Method*. His emphasis on society rather than on the individual is unremitting in the work, and it is fully sustained by the data and by his verification of hypotheses. His own summarizing words are graphic: "Wholly different are the results we obtained when we forgot the individual and sought the causes of the suicidal aptitude of each society in the nature of the societies themselves. The relation of suicide to certain states of social environment is as direct and constant as its relation to facts of a biological and physical character were seen to be uncertain and ambiguous." [50]

What are the specific modes by which society becomes the chief determinant of so individual an act as suicide? There are three in particular:

EGOISTIC SUICIDE This occurs when cohesion in the groups to which men belong declines to the point of no longer offering the support to ego that is normally given. "Suicide," Durkheim declares in one of his most celebrated propositions, "varies inversely with the degree of integration of the social groups of which the individual forms a part." When society is strongly integrated, it restrains individuals, considers them at its service, "and thus forbids them to dispose willfully of themselves." Among all those in modern populations whose associative ties are relatively weak—Protestants, urban dwellers, industrial workers, professional men—suicide rates are higher than those among aggregates of opposite character.[51]

ANOMIC SUICIDE Paralleling egoistic suicide is anomic suicide, caused by the sudden dislocation of normative systems, the breakdown of values by which one may have lived for a lifetime, or the conflict between ends desired and abilities to achieve them. It is not poverty that impels toward suicide. Durkheim refers to the "remarkable immunity of the poor countries": "[Poverty] protects against suicide because it is a restraint in itself. Wealth, on the other hand, by the power it bestows, deceives us into believing that we depend on ourselves only. Reducing the resistance we encounter from objects, it suggests the possibility of unlimited success against them. The less limited one feels, the more intolerable all limitations appear." [52] Anomie is, in short, a breakdown of *moral* community just as egoism is a breakdown of *social* community.

ALTRUISTIC SUICIDE The third form of suicide is no less social in its governing context than the other two types, but it manifests itself when involvement in a social relationship is so great that the individual is led to take his life because he believes some act of his has brought obloquy upon the social relationship. The essence of such suicide, as Durkheim notes, is not escape but self-punishment. Although this type of suicide is more likely to be found (but rarely even there) in primitive societies where tribal consensus can be overpowering, it is also to be seen occasionally in those areas of modern society—such as the officer corps of established military organizations—where tradition is dominant and penetrating.[53]

According to Durkheim: ". . . Each human society has a greater or lesser aptitude for suicide; the expression is based on the nature of things. Each social group really has a collective inclination for the act, quite its own, and is the source of all individual inclinations, rather than their result. It is made up of the currents of egoism, altruism, or anomie running through the society under consideration with tendencies to languorous melancholy, active renunciation, or exasperated weariness derivative from these currents. These tendencies of the whole social body, by affecting individuals, cause them to commit suicide. The private experiences usually thought to be the proximate causes of suicide have only the influence borrowed from the victim's moral predisposition, itself an echo of the moral state of society." [54]

This passage, abstracted from context and approached in strictly analytical terms, might easily be subjected to the same kind of assault that has been visited upon other passages and concepts in Durkheim's works. Can a human society have an "aptitude"—a group, a "collective inclination"—for suicide? Can a social body have "tendencies to languorous melancholy," and so on? The accumulated presuppositions of several centuries of Western individualism would say, emphatically, "No," and said so volubly in Durkheim's own day. Let us not pause, however, to wonder once again at the massive effects on Western thought of an analytical individualism that paradoxically has prevented more knowledge of man, actual man, than it has made possible, nor pause to seek to rescue Durkheim from familiar charges of reification. Argument is almost always futile and self-perpetuating. Let us instead emphasize this fact only: It was precisely on the basis of the view of society ably summarized in the passage just quoted that Durkheim evolved a methodology and worked by crucial verification to conclusions (very precise conclusions!) on the incidence of suicide in society that have, in only minor ways, been challenged in the seventy years that have elapsed since the publication of *Suicide*. *Suicide* remains one of the half-dozen great scientific studies in sociology; one need not even lean on the word *classic* to make this judgment.

Our fourth, and in the long run most fundamental, example of Durkheim's methodological use of community is his treatment of the nature of man. There may be little today, with two generations of social psychology intervening, to arrest attention in Durkheim's treatment of the social sources of the self. But in that day his approach was original enough to arouse incomprehension and epithet. So deeply rooted was the individualist perspective of self, mind, and personality, that Durkheim's critics (chief among them Tarde, whose own emphasis upon "imitation" as the crucial process rests upon conceptualized individuals that are preformed, so to speak, for social purposes) made charges of "group mind" and "social realism" central in their attacks. The individual, it was then widely charged (with echoes persisting to the present day), disappears utterly in Durkheim's sociology.

But if we look at what Durkheim actually wrote about individuality and the nature of personality-forming processes, there is little that can today seem exceptional. Society, Durkheim took care to write, "exists and lives only in and through individuals."

"If the idea of society were extinguished in individual minds, and the beliefs, traditions and aspirations of the group were no longer felt and shared by the individuals, society would die. We can say of it what we . . . said of the divinity: it is real only insofar as it has a place in human consciousnesses . . ." [55]

So much is true, but it does not follow that man is the self-contained and primary entity of utilitarian thought. On the contrary, man is double: biological and social.

"There are two beings in him: an individual being which has its foundations in the organism and the circle of whose activities is therefore strictly limited, and a social being which represents the highest reality in the intellectual and moral order that we can know by observation—I mean society. This duality of our nature has as its consequence in the practical order the irreducibility of a moral ideal to a utilitarian motive, and in the order of thought, the irreducibility of reason to individual experience. Insofar as he belongs to society, the individual transcends himself, both when he thinks and when he acts."

Elsewhere Durkheim writes: "Social man superimposes himself upon physical man. Social man necessarily presupposes a society which he expresses and serves. If this dissolves, if we no longer feel it in existence and action about and above us, whatever is social in us is deprived of all objective foundation. All that remains is an artificial combination of illusory images, a phantasmagoria vanishing at the least reflection; that is, nothing which can be a goal for our action. Yet this social man is the essence of civilized man; he is the masterpiece of existence." [56]

Durkheim's view of the individual is thus as radically social as his view of morality. Man is unknowable, at least to the social scientist, except as a manifestation, a node, of community. The discipline of mind and character is but the personalization of the discipline of the forming group. Normal personality is a reflection of normal integration with community. Abnormal personality is a reflection of the breakdown of this group integration.

Even into the recesses of individual mind does Durkheim carry his perspective of community. There is the authority of reason, but whence does this authority come? "It is the very authority of society, transferring itself to a certain manner of thought which is the indispensable condition of all common action. The necessity with which the categories are imposed upon us is not the effect of simple habits whose yoke we could easily throw off with a little effort; nor is it a physical or metaphysical necessity, since the categories change in different places and times; it is a special sort of moral necessity which is to the intellectual life what moral obligation is to will." [57]

Not only is the discipline of reason a reflection of communal discipline, but so also are the categories of reason—such categories as time, space, causality and force—reflections of community. Here, of course,

Durkheim is in highly debatable epistemological territory, and it would be folly to pretend that his views here have gained the kind of acceptance won by other aspects of his thought. But they nonetheless deserve mention. Empiricists had tried, with Hume, to explain these categories in terms of individual experience; apriorists had argued, with Kant, that the categories must be regarded as innate, as a part of the very frame of the mind. We find Durkheim challenging both views, arguing that each category is but a reflection of community. Thus, Durkheim contends, the idea of time arose with the social commemoration of religious feast days, with calendars, whose earliest significance was that of marking religious rites. Only the power of religious community and its rites could have imprinted the *general* idea of time on man's consciousness. Similarly with the other categories of mind. Conceptions of space among primitive peoples, Durkheim tells us, are always conceived after the manner in which their social units are juxtaposed: for example, concentrically or rectangularly. The idea of force is conceived in terms of the enlargement of the power of the tribal or other collective unit. And so on. Durkheim, it is plain, is not merely the sociologist of community; he is also the epistemologist and metaphysician.

That Durkheim's efforts to explain the "categories" of the mind have had little effect upon epistemology—where they have never been taken very seriously—is of less importance than that they have served admirably as perspectives in the sociology of knowledge and culture.

THE MOLECULAR COMMUNITY—SIMMEL

The final form in which the perspective of community is manifest in the sociological tradition lies in the micro-sociological sphere: the sphere of the small and intimate patterns of relationship which underlie the visible groups and associations of society. Here, of course, we turn to Simmel.

Simmel is the microscopist of society. He is endlessly fascinated by the small and the intimate. What has so often been called his formal sociology is more than simply an effort to classify forms of behavior. His treatments of such groups as the dyad and the triad and of such social bonds as friendship, obedience and loyalty should be seen as a search for the molecular elements of society: the smallest possible units into which institutions and associations could be analyzed.

He is interested in minute process as well as in structure. The interaction of dyads or triads in the form of co-operation, of trust, of secrecy, interested him as much as did the relationship itself. So did the negative elements of conflict and competition, elements which, he had no difficulty in showing, were as vital as the positive elements of love and co-operation in welding individuals and groups to one another. It is Simmel's microscopic eye, penetrating the over-layers of history and convention, that gives so timeless and universal a cast to his observations. Simmel knew that there is an important continuity of the fundamental elements of association from age to age; that no matter what the gross differences of institutions and cultural patterns of historical ages, such structures as dyads and triads possess continuing identity and indestructible influence upon the larger and more overt forms of society.

Everett Hughes has called Simmel the Freud of society, and the analogy is a useful one. Precisely as Freud devoted himself to the states and processes in the individual unconscious that lie beneath, and give orientation to, the conscious mind, Simmel devoted himself to the "unconscious" relationships of the social order: to dyads, triads, and other timeless, constitutive elements of the social bond. These, like the unconscious mind of the individual, have a profound effect upon the direction of change and the structure of the larger associations in society.

Simmel's reaction to analytical or utilitarian individualism is as sharp and encompassing as Durkheim's, though it is less obvious and is couched in terms which permit the occasional misconception of his work as individualist in character. That Simmel had a clear and unwavering view of individuality is incontestable. What he called the "capacious and far-reaching collision between society and the individual" haunted Simmel's ethical sensibilities as it preoccupied his sociological inquiries. A conceptual reality is granted by Simmel to individuality that is generally lacking in any of the sociologists we have thus far considered. But there is nevertheless a world of difference between Simmel's image of the individual and that to be found in the writings of the utilitarians. It is an image proceeding from a conception of society that has a striking resemblance to Durkheim's, as the following passage suggests: "Society lives a life of its own in a particular combination of abstractness and concreteness, and each individual contributes to it certain of his characteristics and strength; society grows through the contributions of the individuals who—beyond it—form or try to form their existence as individualities." [58]

Simmel was not insensitive to the larger forces of society or the historical tendencies that had brought them into being. Far from it. He may have been the microscopist, but he did not cease being the anatomist—and ecologist. His work, quite as much as Weber's or Tönnies', has for its background that great shift in the nature of society caused by the two revolutions. He was vividly aware of historical forces, and a large number of his illustrations and allusions are drawn from other historical ages. Thus, his essay on group affiliations is sprinkled with the same historical contrast between medieval and modern society that we have seen in the other sociologists. The contrast is the basis indeed of his perspective of individuality, one that is based upon historical release of man from the medieval community. "In the Middle Ages affiliation with a group absorbed the whole man. It served not only a momentary purpose, which was defined objectively. It was rather an association of all who had combined for the sake of that purpose while the association absorbed the whole life of each of them." [59] This does not mean that medieval man was stifled by membership. The "enrichment" of the individual as a social being "under the medieval type was considerable, for what the individual obtained from his affiliation with the larger group was in no way contained in the affiliation with his immediate groups. . . . The concentric pattern is a systematic and often also an historical stage, which is prior to that situation in which the groups with which persons affiliate are juxtaposed and 'intersect' in one and the same person." [60] Modern society differs profoundly from the medieval concentric pattern of group affiliations, and it is in this organizational difference that the distinctness of the modern individual lies, an *emergent* distinctness that is the historical background for modern philosophies of individualism. In modern society, unlike medieval, the individual may accumulate group affiliations almost endlessly. "The mere fact that he does so is sufficient, quite apart from the nature of the groups involved, to give him a stronger awareness of individuality in general, and at least to counteract the tendency of taking his initial group's affiliations for granted." [61] This, then, for Simmel—almost as it is for Durkheim—is the time perspective in which to place individualism.

Similarly, his notable essay, "Metropolis and Mental Life," is concerned fundamentally with the historical passage of Europe from cohesive and traditional forms of community to the anonymous urban-industrial complexes. Simmel's emphasis in this essay is on the lights of the city, but he makes us see the shadows left by receding community and tradition. The sophistication, anonymity, and reserve of metropolitan life are given a kind of counterpoint relation to the simplicity, directness, and warmth of the traditional community.

The same counterpoint is to be seen, more systematically stated, in his study of money.[62] Money is the symbol not only of the conversion of qualitative values to quantitative but also of the release of individuals from the communal contexts of pre-industrial Europe. Only Spengler's *Decline of the West* presents us with as detailed and imaginative a picture of money and credit as the alembic within which the Western mind became transposed from preoccupation with metaphysical and social essence to quantity and variations of quantity. Simmel shows us how the rise of money as an instrument and a measure of exchange in the economy of the Italian city-state and then in Europe as a whole, paralleled the rise of a world view in which the organic is succeeded by the merely quantitative and mechanical—in society as well as in philosophy and morality. In Simmel's hands, the social, moral, and intellectual history of Europe becomes indeed a succession of individual emergences from medieval community and tradition—to be seen in the rise of monarchs, in the rise of businessmen, bankers, artists, and intellectuals. The weakening of the medieval community and the thrusting forward of individuals could not have taken place until there was an impersonal means of value —matching an environment of impersonal law—by which individuals could become related to one another directly.

But Simmel was not content to leave the social transformation of Europe in these terms—the larger terms of transition from traditional community to impersonal society. He looked for the minute manifestations and the underlying elements that were involved in the change. Simmel's emphasis upon the primary forms of sociation was in part a search for a distinctive subject matter for sociology, one that would avoid duplicating what the other social sciences were doing, one that would remove sociology from the charge of being a mere "omnium-gatherum." But in larger part it reflects a desire to translate the forces involved in the larger transformation of European society into the specific social elements that were involved.

There is a splendid passage in his essay on religion that illustrates this. He writes: "Social life involves the mutual correlation of its elements, which occur in part in instantaneous actions and relations, which partly manifest themselves in tangible forms: in public functions and laws, orders and possessions, languages and means of communication. All such social mutual co-relations, however, are caused by distinct interests, ends and impulses. They form, as it were, the matter which realizes itself socially in the 'next to each other' and 'with each other,' the 'for each other' and 'against each other' of individuals." [63] It is the insistence that everything large in the way of social relationships and changes must be translated into the "next to each other," the "for each other," and so on, that marks Simmel's distinctive genius. No matter what he concerned himself with, political power, capitalism, religion, he was not content until he had brought the analysis down to the primary level of the elements which characterize the relationships and processes within which men live.

The special and distinctive character of Simmel's interest in the elements of community is best seen, not in his treatment of geometric forms such as dyads and triads, nor of the processes of co-operation and conflict—both types of interest admittedly relevant to the nature of community—but rather in his matchless analyses of friendship, loyalty, love, dependence, gratitude, confidence, and other primary elements of human relationship. Simmel's sensitivity to these and his trenchant ability to relate them to larger forces in society have no equal in modern thought except in the writings of certain novelists, dramatists, and other artists.

Friendship, dependence, confidence, loyalty: these are among the social atoms, as it were, of the traditional community. Interest in them is inevitably great in any society or age undergoing the kind of changes that were ascendant in the Europe of the late nineteenth century. Just as the breakdown of traditional class structures makes men aware for the first time of the complexities and nuances of status, so the rupture of community leaves men preoccupied by the nature of friendship, the allowable boundaries of intimacy, the canons of discretion, and the limits of loyalty. To traditionalists, in such an age of change, real friendships, confidences, and loyalties can appear as, at best, shards of community that once existed but now is dead, as pieces of jetsam afloat on the seas of economic and political egoism. There were many in Simmel's day for whom these figures of speech had meaning.

Simmel was far from being a traditionalist in these terms, but it is plain that the contrast between traditional community and modern society forms the essential background against which his microscopic analyses of primary ties take on their extraordinary vividness. What he called "the sociology of intimate relations" was rooted in no abstract geometry but in the currents of change that had been generated by the industrial and political revolutions.

There is no single work of Simmel's in which the full flavor of his distinctive analysis of community can be as well acquired as in his famous study of secrecy.[64] What Durkheim does with suicide, Simmel does, in a modified but related sense, with secrecy: that is, take it from the confines of the individual who "holds" the secret, as we say, and place it squarely among the relationships and processes of society. Suicide and secrecy: each is, in its own way, the ultimate of what belongs in the recesses of individual motivation, yet each is comprehensible only in its relation to society.

There is, first, the relation of secrecy to the process of human communication. It is an unbreakable relation, for all that we communicate to another, no matter how close and trustworthy the recipient may be, and no matter how "whole" the truth may be that we utter, it must still present a selection "from that psychological-real whole whose absolutely exact report (absolutely exact in terms of content and sequence) would drive everybody into the insane asylum." [65] We select and modulate, leaving whole areas of "reality" out.

Consciously or unconsciously, we lie. "Every lie, no matter how objective its topic, engenders by its very nature an error concerning the lying *subject*." [66] The lie consists in the fact that the liar hides his true idea from the other. A lie is the more bearable the farther in time or social space the liar is from us. "The farther removed individuals are from our most intimate personality, the more easily can we come to terms with their untruthfulness, both in a practical and in an intimate psychological sense—while if a few persons closest to us lie, life becomes unbearable." [67] But there is no society, no form of relationship, in which the lie in some degree is not permissible. It is even necessary, for as long as the outer society is graduated in terms of the degrees to which others are entitled to the "whole truth," so long will there be lies. "However often a lie may destroy a given relationship, as long as the relationship existed, the lie was an integral element of it. The ethically negative value of the lie must not blind us to its sociologically quite positive significance for the formation of certain concrete relations." The lie is "the positive and, as it were, aggressive technique, whose purpose is more often attained by mere secrecy and concealment." [68]

Simmel now moves from the socio-epistemological to the unqualifiedly social. "Before coming to the secret in the sense of a consciously desired concealment, one must note the different degrees to which various relationships leave the reciprocal knowledge of the total personalities of their members outside their province." There are interest groups which make no claim upon the whole individual, and these predominate in modern society. "The increasing objectification of our culture, whose phenomena consist more and more of impersonal elements and less and less absorb the subjective totality of the individual (most simply shown by the contrast between handicraft and factory work), also involves sociological structures." [39]

The whole social and moral area of *confidence* has been altered by this objectification of culture, for what one needs to be confident of in another human being has been, as it were, fragmented and localized—as in employer and employee, banker and borrower. So have the qualities of "acquaintance" and "discretion" been sharply changed. "Discretion is a special form of the typical contrast between the imperatives, 'what is not prohibited is allowed' and 'what is not allowed is prohibited.' Relations among men are thus distinguished according to the question of mutual knowledge—of either 'what is not concealed may be known' or 'what is not revealed must not be known.' "

There are also the roles of friendship and intimacy, each profoundly affected by modern social change. There are two crucial contexts in which, typically, intimacy resides: friendship and marriage. "To the extent that the ideal of friendship was received from antiquity and (peculiarly enough) was developed in a romantic spirit, it aims at an absolute psychological intimacy. . . . This entering of the whole undivided ego into the relationship may be more plausible in friendship than in love for the reason that friendship lacks the specific concentration upon one element which love derives from its sensuousness." [70] Admittedly, especially in modern society, it is sexual love that "opens the doors of the total personality more widely than does anything else. For not a few, in fact, love is the only form in which they can give their ego in its totality, just as to the artist the form of his art offers the only possibility for revealing the whole inner life." So much is true, yet, as Simmel emphasizes, "the preponderance of the erotic bond may suppress . . . the other contacts (practical-moral, intellectual) as well as the opening up of those reservoirs of the personality that lie outside the erotic sphere." Friendship lacks the fine intensity of love but also the frequent unevenness, and it "may be, therefore, more apt than love to connect a whole person with another person in its entirety; it may melt reserves more easily than love does—if not as stormily, yet on a larger scale and in a more enduring sequence. Yet such complete intimacy becomes probably more and more difficult as differentiation among men increases. Modern man, possibly, has too much to hide to sustain a friendship in the ancient sense." [71]

When we turn to marriage and intimacy, "the measures of self-revelation and self-restraint, with their complements of trespass and discretion, are more difficult to determine." The problem here in what Simmel specifically calls "the sociology of intimate relations" is "whether the maximum of common values can be attained under the condition that the personalities reciprocally relinquish their autonomies altogether, or under the condition of reserve." The problem is less intense in earlier ages because marriage "is not an erotic but, in principle, only a social and economic institution. The satisfaction of the desire for love is only accidentally connected with it." In such cultures there probably exists "neither the need for any intimate, reciprocal self-revelation, nor the possibility of it. On the other hand, there is probably an absence of certain reserves of delicacy and chastity which, in spite of their seemingly negative character, are yet the flower of a fully internalized and personal intimate relation." [72]

In our society, Simmel notes, where the marriage relationship is increasingly the only intimate relationship—friendship in the true sense diminishing under pressures of modernism—there is a strong temptation to make it carry more than it is structurally able to. "During the first stages of the relationship there is a great temptation, both in marriage and in marriage-like free love, to let oneself be completely absorbed by the other, to send the last reserves of the soul after those of the body, to lose oneself to the other without reservation. Yet, in most cases, this abandon probably threatens the future of the relationship seriously." [73] For, Simmel emphasizes, only those individuals can give themselves *wholly* who *cannot,* as it were, give all of themselves. These rare individuals have a reservoir of latent psychological possessions that never dries up. They replenish as they give. "But other individuals are different. With every flight of feeling, with every unconditional abandonment, with every revelation of their inner life, they make inroads (as it were) into their capital, because they lack the mainspring of ever renewed psychic affluence which can neither be exhaustively revealed nor be separated from the ego." [74]

Now, we come to secrecy as such, its clear relationship to dissimulation, confidence, discretion, and intimacy having been established. The secret, Simmel writes, is one of man's greatest achievements. In comparison with the childish stage of uninhibited display, "the secret produces an immense enlargement of life." The secret offers the possibility of a second world alongside the visible world, one in which as much truth, good, and right exist as in the manifest world, but one in which there may also be contained evil. The one world influences the other.

The secret is a morally neutral mechanism that rises above its contents. It may absorb the noblest of values and be maintained under the duress of punishments or tortures, or it may embody knowledge or motive of the most maleficent character. There is an inherent fascination in secrecy, for the secret gives one a position of exception. It is a means of identity enhancement, of achievement too, of intimacy. But there is also, Simmel notes, a fascination in *betrayal,* for "the secret contains a tension that is dissolved in the moment of its revelation. This moment constitutes the acme in the development of the secret; all of its charms are once more gathered in and brought to a climax—just as the moment of dissipation lets one enjoy with extreme intensity the value of the object. . . . The secret, too, is full of the consciousness that it *can* be betrayed; that one holds the power of surprises, turns of fate, joy, destruction—if only, perhaps, of self-destruction." [75]

Secrecy is closely related to individualization. "Social conditions of strong personal differentiation permit and require secrecy; and, conversely, the secret embodies and intensifies such differentiation. In a small and narrow circle, the formation and preservation of secrets is made difficult even on technical grounds: everybody is too close to everybody else and his circumstances, and frequency and intimacy of contact involve too many temptations of revelation. But further the secret is not even particularly needed, because this type of social formation usually levels its members. . . ." [76]

But with the enlargement of the community, all this changes radically. There is, Simmel notes, a certain paradox in modern society. "It seems as if, with growing cultural expediency, general affairs become ever more public, and individual affairs ever more secret." Politics, administration, and even business have thus "lost their secrecy and inaccessibility in the same measure in which the individual has gained the possibility of ever more complete withdrawal, and in the same measure in which modern life has developed, in the midst of metropolitan crowdedness, a technique for making and keeping private matters secret, such as earlier could be attained only by means of spatial isolation." [77] Simmel notes that the secret has one further social attribute: adornment. It is the nature and function of adornment to lead the eyes of the other to the adorned. "Although, in this sense, it is the antagonist of secrecy, not even the secret (it will be remembered) is without the function of personal emphasis."

Now Simmel comes directly to the secret society and its function. "The essence of the secret society is to give autonomy." [78] This means autonomy from invasions of privacy, from random and distasteful recognition, from impersonality and heterogeneity. The secret society has an aristocratic motive: it permits seclusion from those qualities that identify everyone and, therefore, no one. The secret society is a means of inclusiveness and exclusiveness. It is a means of clarifying and specifying confidence and trust, of pledged friendship and devotion. "Finally, the isolation of the secret society from the surrounding social syntheses removes a number of occasions for conflict." The collisions of interest and power and prestige to be found in all societies and ages, and especially in our own, are moderated by the very social isolation of the secret society.

What of its internal problems? There is a certain susceptibility to extreme centralization of authority in the secret society, for its very structure—secrecy—tends to promote special measures to guard it. The more secret the organization (as in a criminal conspiracy) the more heightened the centralization. The pressure for solidarity becomes nearly overwhelming. The more isolated or challenged the secret society comes to feel in the social order, the more its cohesion will take authoritarian form. However, by the same token, the more welcome this communal authority will be to the individual.

There is paradox for the individual in the process. All that gives him identifying feelings of recognition and individuality in the secret society tends to separate him from the environing society: the more of the one, the more of the other. Thus, Simmel points out, even as he is being "personalized" within the secret society, he is being "depersonalized" in the social order at large.

Equality is the essence of community, and the secret society is no exception. To each according to his needs, from each according to his ability. But secrecy can, when intensified, convert equality to leveling, which in turn acts to strengthen central power within the group.

From function to dysfunction might have been the subtitle given by Simmel to his study of secrecy. For its genius consists precisely in the demonstration that the very qualities that support the secret society also threaten it. Conceived as a means of bridging the gulf between the alienated individual and an impersonal society, of granting status, equality, sense of membership, and the various other values of community, the secret society, by virtue of pressure of the forces which lead to its creation, can become, not a means of socialization but of de-socialization, not a part of the social order but, under the hostile gaze of the masses and the central government, an enemy.

4 AUTHORITY

THE SPECTER OF POWER

"In our days," Tocqueville wrote, "men see that the constituted powers are crumbling down on every side; they see all ancient authority dying out, all ancient barriers tottering to their fall, and the judgment of the wisest is troubled at the sight; they attend only to the amazing revolution that is taking place before their eyes, and they imagine that mankind is about to fall into perpetual anarchy. If they looked to the final consequence of this revolution, their fears would perhaps assume a different shape. For myself, I confess that I put no trust in the spirit of freedom which appears to animate my contemporaries. I see well enough that the nations of this age are turbulent, but I do not clearly perceive that they are liberal; and I fear lest, at the close of those perturbations, which rock the base of thrones, the dominion of sovereigns may prove more powerful than it ever was." [1]

Precisely as the breakup of the old order made men aware of the loss of traditional community, it made them aware also of the loss of traditional authority: of the constraints, normative disciplines, and patriarchal bonds that had been for so long embedded in culture that they were scarcely recognized until the onset of the two revolutions dramatized them through threatened extinction. And just as the erosion of accustomed community led to sociological premonitions of mass society, so the decline of ancient authorities led to premonitions of disorganization, on the one hand, and, on the other, of new types of power, more encompassing and penetrating than any known before in history.

In traditional society authority is hardly recognized as having separate or even distinguishable identity. How could it be? Deeply embedded in social functions, an inalienable part of the inner order of family, neighborhood, parish, and guild, ritualized at every turn, authority is so closely woven into the fabric of tradition and morality as to be scarcely more noticeable than the air men breathe. Even in the hands of the king, authority in such a society tends to maintain this diffused and indirect character. Such is the tendency of monarchical power to become submerged in the whole ethos of patriarchalism that the power of the king seems to its subjects as but little different from that exercised by fathers over sons, priests over communicants, and masters over apprentices. The entire weight of morality—which is typically the morality of duty and allegiance—makes authority an undifferentiated aspect of the social order, the government hardly more than a symbolic superstructure.

But when men become separated, or feel themselves separated, from traditional institutions, there arises, along with the specter of the lost individual, the specter of lost authority. Fears and anxieties run over the intellectual landscape like masterless dogs. Inevitably in such circumstances, men's minds turn to the problem of authority. What, it is asked, shall be the source and nature of an authority sufficient to replace lost authority, to restrain the natural anarchy that even in civilized society thrusts itself now and then through the crevices of law and morality? And, paralleling this question: What shall be the means of checking the kind of power that always threatens to rise on the ruins of constituted authority?

Purely individual rights may not be enough. Such rights may even, as Burckhardt wrote, echoing sentiments that Burke had first uttered, intensify the growth of new and more awful forms of power. "The great harm was begun," wrote Burckhardt, "in the last century, mainly through Rousseau, with his doctrine of the goodness of human nature. Out of this, plebs and educated alike, distilled the doctrine of the golden age that was to come infallibly, provided people were left alone. The result, as every child knows, was the complete disintegration of the idea of authority in the hands of mortal men, whereupon, of course, we periodically fall victims to sheer power." [2]

Of all the faces of the French Revolution the one that was to torment post-Revolutionary conservatism most insistently was the face of power: power that seemed to the conservative mind to be born of the Revolution's vaunted system of individual liberty, rights, and equality. To the conservatives, beginning with Burke, all that had been taken away by the Revolutionists from the traditional authorities of guild, commune, church, and patriarchal family and vested precariously in individual and in popular will amounted in fact to a magnification of political power without precedent in European history. "In all senses, we worship and follow after Power," wrote Carlyle. This theme runs like a scarlet thread through nineteenth-century conservatism. The individual alone, alienated from historic community, would never prove sufficient, it was argued, despite his newly granted rights and equalities, to offset the kind of power that the revolutionary, democratic state represented.

From the point of view of the nineteenth-century sociology of power, four aspects of the Revolutionary and Napoleonic orders are notable. Each of them, as we shall see, furnishes potent stimulus and vivid theme to the works of all the major sociologists, from Tocqueville to Simmel.[3] Rarely in the sociology of ideas is the relation between social event and intellectual response as clear and direct as with respect to these four aspects of the Revolution.

1. The TOTALISM of Revolutionary power. It was not total at first, of course, but by the time of the Committee of Public Safety more than a few zealots were convinced that unless the power of the people over its enemies, internal and external, was made absolute and penetrating, the liberty of its citizens could not be secured. Hence Robespierre's ringing declaration that "the government of the Revolution is the despotism of freedom against tyranny." Given an underlying belief in the absolute morality of intent, it was an easy step to belief that the power to effect intent was also moral and must be total, must extend itself to every realm of man's life and being. Totalitarianism is not, of course, the word to describe Jacobin France, for between the aspiration of a Saint-Just and the political reality of his France there lay too many institutional barriers —persistences of traditional allegiance and authority. But it is only too clear that the *idea* of "democratic totalitarianism" was born in 1793.

2. The MASS BASE of Revolutionary power. Legitimacy of power does not lie, it was declared by the Revolutionists, in divine decree, in heredity, or in tradition. Legitimacy is given only by the mass of people who participate in it and who, by the very fact of participating, cannot therefore be said to be enslaved by it, no matter what its intensity. This thesis became steadily more important as the Revolution progressed until, in time, virtually everything came to be justified in the name of the people. It was the invocation of "the people" that made Revolutionary armies the first mass armies in Europe's history, and it was the same invocation that justified extension and penetration of governmental power beyond anything known since the age of Diocletian in ancient Rome. Not economic man, not religious man, not moral man, but *political* man, was the key figure of the Revolution. Hence the exaltation of

citizen. Mass participation in power, as we have seen, could appear inextricably related to the cherished perquisites of freedom, equality, and brotherhood.

3. The CENTRALIZATION of Revolutionary power. French centralization, as Tocqueville was to emphasize, had begun centuries earlier, in the latter part of the Middle Ages, but it had long been checked by institutions such as guild and commune that the Revolution was able to exterminate for once and all. Paris became the capital of French society in the Revolution to a degree never achieved by the Bourbons. Centralization of administration followed from the ideal of mass participation in power. How could the people as a whole be endowed with residual power unless all the intermediate authorities, all the ancient divisions of power, were disendowed, with their historic authorities passing to the people now, for the first time, represented by their government? By 1793 it was the conviction of many Revolutionary leaders, the Jacobins foremost, that in centralized government lay the best means of discovering and expressing the real will of the people. If five hundred persons could express the will of the people, why not fifty? If fifty, why not three? And from this it was but a short step to the fateful idea that in one man might lie possibility of fulfillment of popular will—the real will—that ordinary representative government could never equal.

4. The RATIONALIZATION of power. This, too was a process that, as Tocqueville and Weber were to emphasize, had been going on ever since the late Middle Ages. But the Revolution made it vivid, dramatized it, and rationalization became a consecrated principle of government. One sees it in the Revolution at all levels of importance. There was the rationalization of the currency, of the system of weights and measures, of the calendar. There was the rationalization of the educational system, replacing the historic autonomy of educational units by the one great public system, from elementary grades to university, that would reach every part of France and be directed from Paris. The historic irregularities of political communes and provinces were abolished, to be replaced by symmetrical departments and other units that would reflect administrative reason, not tradition. There was the rationalization of the army, including its system of command and its techniques of warfare. And there was, surmounting all of these, the whole rationalized system of bureaucracy.

These are the four aspects of the Revolution, the four faces of Revolutionary power, that were to impinge most sharply on nineteenth-century ideology and to penetrate most deeply philosophical reflection on the age-old problem of authority in society. In sociology, as we shall see, each of the four aspects becomes an insistent and directive theme.

AUTHORITY VERSUS POWER

The theoretical context of their assimilation in social thought is the important distinction between authority and power that began to be made before the Revolution had run its course. And, giving political shape and moral urgency to this distinction was the conflict between conservatism and radicalism. What Comte wrote on conservatives and radicals in this connection is highly illuminating:

"The two parties seem to have changed sides. The retrograde doctrine, notwithstanding its proud pretensions to order and unity, preaches the distribution of political centres, in the secret hope of preserving the old system yet a while longer among the most backward of the population, by keeping them aloof from the general centres of civilization; while the revolutionary policy, on the other hand, proud of having withstood, in France, the coalition of the old powers, discards its own maxims to recommend the subordination of the secondary to the principal centres. . . . In brief, the revolutionary school alone has understood that the increasing anarchy of the time, intellectual and moral, requires, to prevent a complete dislocation of society, a growing concentration of political action, properly so called." [4]

Later, in *The Positive Polity,* Comte would unfold a system of authority hardly distinguishable, in its medieval values, from the conservative philosophy. When he wrote these lines, however, he was still under the spell of a rationalism which, if it rejected the natural rights premises of the Revolution, was nonetheless influenced by the rationalizing and centralizing tendencies of the Revolution.

The essence of the difference between conservative and radical lay, as Comte suggests, between the contrasting philosophies of pluralism and centralization. Conservative philosophy, rooted in medieval values, made "distribution of political centers" its essence: that is, pluralism of authority resting first and foremost upon local community, family, guild, and the various other sources of custom and tradition. The conservatives saw in Revolutionary centralization and rationalization of authority a malign preview of what all European culture would one day become unless these forces were checked by reassertion of localism and decentralization, of tradition rather than of administrative decree. The radicals on the other hand could not help but see the Revolution as the work, or at least the beginning of the work, of liberation of man from oppressive authorities and his incorporation in a new system of power resting upon the people and given direction by rational thought.

It is in these terms—the terms established by the Revolution's impact upon traditional society—that the seminal distinction between authority and power is made. Whether for conservative or radical, the image of *social authority* is cast from materials drawn from the old regime; the image of *political power*—rational, centralized, and popular—from the legislative pattern of the Revolution. Social authority *versus* political power is precisely the way in which the issue was drawn, first by the conservatives and then all the way through the century to Durkheim's reflections on centralization and social groups and Weber's on rationalization and tradition. The vast and continuing interest in social constraint, social control, and normative authority that the history of sociology reveals, as well as its own special distinction between authority and power, has its roots in the same soil that produced its interest in community.

Burke began it with the contrast, which continues unabatedly all through his denunciations of the Revolution, between the old order resting on tradition and the new order manufactured out of unaided reason. Burke had only contempt for what he called the "geometric" system of the Revolutionaries in which a calculated, centralized program of administrative law was set up in place of what had been a seamless web of tradition and authority, beginning in the family, rising through the community and province until it reached the king, whose rule, Burke insists, was hardly more than symbolic. The essence of the system was the individual's loyalty to social group. "No man was ever attached by a sense of pride, partiality, or real affection to a description of square measurements . . . We begin our public affections in our families . . . We pass on to our neighborhoods, and our habitual provincial connections." [5]

In France, a few years later, we see the identical contrast in the works of Bonald, especially in his massive *Théorie du Pouvoir*. Here Bonald makes explicit the medieval-pluralist distinction between spheres of authority. The family has an authority, Bonald writes, that is properly absolute within its own domain; so has the church, the guild, and so, finally, does the state have a proper and constituted authority. But when the state's natural authority spreads out, to contravene the internal authorities of other associations in society, it becomes despotism, that is, *power*. It is in these terms that Bonald expresses his preference for monarchy over democracy. The former, by its nature, recognizes the authorities of the social and religious groups which comprise society. The latter, resting upon the revolutionary doctrine of the general will, does not and cannot. The former is essentially limited despite its historic claim of absolutism; the latter must become unlimited through the dissolving effect of its sovereignty upon all groups that interpose themselves between democratic mass and the individual.[6]

Hegel was equally concerned with the protection of authority from the inroads of centralized, rationalistic power. His preference for monarchy (though elective) was based in considerable part on his belief that political authority could be mediated, could be fused in the society more effectively than would be the case in a direct democracy. Hegel, too, is critical of the revolutionary theory of power in France, seeing in it not merely the isolation of the individual, but an intensification of political authority that would result from loss of intermediate institutions. "The constitution," he wrote in his *Philosophy of Right*, "is essentially a system of mediation. In despotisms where there are only rulers and people, the people is effective, if at all, only as a mass destructive of the organization of the state." [7]

Like Bonald, Hegel argues the necessity of institutions which will give the individual security and form a buffer between him and the government. Hence his advocacy of occupational corporations. "It is true," writes Hegel, "that these associations won too great a measure of self-subsistence in the Middle Ages, when they were states within states . . . but while that should not be allowed to happen, we may nonetheless affirm that the proper strength of the state lies in these associations. In them the executive meets with legitimate interests which it must respect, and since the administration cannot be other than helpful to such interests, though it must also supervise them, the individual finds protection in the exercise of his rights and so links his private interest with the maintenance of the whole . . . It is of the utmost importance that people should be organized because only so do they become mighty and powerful. Otherwise, they are nothing but a heap, an aggregate of atomic units. Only when the particular associations are organized members of the state are they possessed of legitimate power." [8] Hegel is as apprehensive of mass society as Burke or Bonald.

Hegel's theory of authority is premised on the evil of the kind of direct power that the Revolution and Napoleon had made manifest: power unmediated by social bodies. He thus emphasized the continuing importance of social classes, estates, local communities, as well as that of the occupational associations. In the articulation of all these groups lies the best basis of representation in the legislature.

Later in the century we find Le Play using the phrase "social authorities" explicitly for the purpose of describing what were for him the central and legitimate sources of the real authority of a society: patriarchal family, community, guild or business enterprise, and religion.[9] Tocqueville uses the words "secondary" and "intermediate" to describe these and other authorities that are, he tells us, at one and the same time buttresses to the security of the individual and barriers to the extension of political centralization.[10]

It would be false to think of this distinction between social authority and political power as one resting solely in conservative thought. The distinction began there, but it spread widely. Later, the anarchists were to make strong use of it. For them, the problem of power in modern society took on much of its intensity from the enormous enhancement that the Revolution had given the idea of the state. "Democracy is merely the state raised to the nth power," wrote Proudhon, echoing Bonald, whom he admired.[11] As we have already noted, Proudhon was profoundly interested in localism and in the multiplication of centers of authority in society as the means of restraining the mass-based centralization that he could see developing and which a mere change of economic system alone would not, he thought, significantly alter. The pluralism and decentralization which are such striking aspects of nineteenth-century anarchism—from Proudhon to Kropotkin—both stem from a vivid sense of the distinction between social authority, which is, by anarchist definition, multiple, associative, functional and autonomous, and the political power of the state, which is, no matter how "democratic" at root, bound to become centralized and bureaucratized unless offset by the authorities resident in localism and free association.

A significant vein of social liberalism also took up the distinction between authority and power. Here Lamennais, who began his life's work as an ultramontane Catholic conservative, is the key figure.[12] His early, militant defense of the Church against the state was predicated on a principle of authority that was, at bottom, pluralist. In the beginning he was united with Bonald and Chateaubriand, Balmes, and other Catholic conservatives, for he saw their vision of the Church's freedom in society as one containing by implication the freedom of other associations as well: family, co-operative, labor union, and locality. Only when Lamennais came to realize the disharmony between his purposes and those of certain Catholic conservatives did he break with them and with the

Church, bringing on his head, eventually, excommunication. But his essential work had been done, and with such others in the Church as Montalembert and Lacordaire to lead the way, modern social Catholicism, with its pluralist orientation, was a reality. Lamennais became, after his excommunication, a leading figure in the cause of co-operatives and labor unions in France. His ideological emphasis remained strongly decentralist. "Centralization," he wrote, "induces apoplexy at the center and anemia at the extremities." In an early issue of the newspaper *L'Avenir,* which he founded in 1830 while still in the service of the Church, decentralization and freedom of association are put among the foremost demands of the time.

Lamennais clearly precedes Tocqueville in these and related themes. And as the context for all of Lamennais's demands and pleas is his unremitting emphasis on the necessity of social authority as the basis of true freedom. "If one wants to get a just idea of our present condition, one must first understand that no government, no police, no order, would be possible if men were not united beforehand by ties which already constitute them in a state of society." And, more powerfully, and in direct antithesis to Rousseau's ideal of a polity in which each man would be "completely independent of his fellow men and completely dependent upon the state," Lamennais writes:

"From equality is born independence, and from independence isolation. As each man is circumscribed, so to speak, in his individual life, he no longer has more than his individual strength for defending himself if he is attacked; and no individual strength can offer sufficient guarantee of security against the abuses of that incomparably greater force which is called sovereignty and from which arises the necessity of a new liberty, the liberty of association." [13] These words were written nearly a decade before Tocqueville's *Democracy in America.*

But the most lasting effect of the distinction between social authority and political power was philosophical. For two centuries in social thought, philosophical emphasis had been on the state and on a doctrine of sovereignty that had become increasingly abstract. What Bodin began in 1576, with his momentous differentiation between the limited and conditional authorities of *society*—that is, of guild, monastery, corporation, and commune—and the absolute and unconditional authority of the *state,* to which alone he granted *sovereignty,* was continued with ever increasing power and subtlety: by Hobbes, by the whole school of natural law philosophers in the seventeenth century, and, eventually, by Rousseau. Hostility to traditional associations and their authorities ranged from Hobbes's likening of them to "worms in the entrails of natural man" to Rousseau's warning against all "partial associations" in the state. During the French Enlightenment distaste for traditional authority matched distaste for the traditional community. They were, after all, two sides of the same coin. For the Physiocrats, apostles of the natural order of economy, the good society could not even be brought into existence save by a political centralization that would extinguish these authorities, which, it was argued, clogged the arteries of commerce and finance.[14]

The result of two centuries of preoccupation with sovereignty had thus been to make political power appear as something either independent of or antithetical to moral tradition and social authority. True sovereignty, it had been argued from Hobbes to Rousseau, has its origin in, not tradition, not the historic social authorities, but in the nature of man and in contractual assent, either actual or implicit, and it gains its majesty and its rationality from its independence of all other types of authority.

It is on this point that we may best appreciate the significance of the sociological theories of authority that appear in the nineteenth century. We find, paralleling the rediscovery of community, the rediscovery of custom and tradition, of patriarchal and corporate authority, all of which, it is argued, are the fundamental (and continuing) sources of social and political order. In this view, the political state is converted into but one of the authorities in the larger society, conditioned, circumscribed, and limited by the others. It is in these terms that we may best see the significance of the sociologists with their rejection of the abstract or formal approach to the nature of sovereignty. And it is in these same terms that political pluralism as a systematic philosophy may be seen, along with syndicalist, guild-socialist, and other decentralist ideas. Historically, sociology's relation to them is close.[15]

THE DISCOVERY OF ELITES

A second consequence of the impact of the Revolution on the old regime was the beginning of modern intellectual interest in political elites. This interest flowed in the first instance from the problem posed for conservative minds by the seeming discontinuity of the French Revolution in the history of Europe. That is, given the conservative premise of the stability and essential harmony of the old order, how then could it have come to so sudden and drastic an end? Or even taking the view that that more dispassionate Tocqueville was to advance—that the centralization and rationalization of the Revolution were, along with its equalitarianism, the results of processes that had begun centuries earlier—how was the traumatic character of the Revolution to be explained?

For Burke, to whom the first of these two questions was the only real one, the answer lay clearly in the machinations of the *philosophes* in their struggle for power. Burke tells us that the philosophers of the Enlightenment were animated above all else by a passion for power and, with it, a hatred of the old order, which they desired to overthrow. Burke refers to the *philosophes* as "political men of letters." As a group, he notes dryly, they have rarely been averse to change and innovation. Having lost their roots, first in church and then in royal court, they were compelled to seek their own status in society. "What they lost in the old court protection, they endeavored to make up by joining in a sort of incorporation of their own; to which the two academies of France, and afterward the vast undertaking of the Encyclopedia, carried on by a society of these gentlemen, did not a little contribute." [16] They comprised, Burke tells us, a kind of cabal. Its first dedication was to "the destruction of the Christian religion. This object they pursued with a degree of zeal which hitherto had been discovered only in the propagators of some system of piety. They were possessed with a spirit of proselytism in the most fanatical degree; and from thence, by an easy progress, with the spirit of persecution according to their means." Burke puts little credence in the persecution which allegedly was visited upon the *philosophes*. The real persecution, he suggests, was *their* persecution of all who disagreed with them. "The resources of intrigue are called in to supply the defects of argument and wit. To this system of literary monopoly was joined an unremitting industry to blacken and discredit in every way, and by every means, all those who did not hold to their faction. To those who have observed the spirit of their conduct, it has long been clear that nothing was wanted but the power of carrying the intolerance of the tongue and of the pen into a persecution which would strike at property, liberty and life." [17]

Having dethroned religion, the intellectuals moved to a subversion of the social order around them. Here, too, "a spirit of cabal, intrigue, and proselytism pervaded all their thoughts, words and actions. And as controversial zeal soon turns its thoughts on force, they began to insinuate themselves into a correspondence with foreign princes; in hopes, through their authority, which at first they flattered, they might bring about the changes they had in view. To them it was indifferent whether these changes were to be accomplished by the thunderbolt of despotism, or by the earthquake of popular commotion . . . For the same purpose which they intrigued with princes, they cultivated, in a distinguished manner, the monied interest of France; and partly through the means furnished by those whose peculiar offices gave them the most extensive and certain means of communication, they carefully occupied all the avenues to opinion." [18]

Behind Burke's attack on political intellectuals lay, obviously, deep distrust of all influences which seemed to him to be antagonistic to social tradition, Christianity, and, above all perhaps, the landed class, with the gentleman as its symbol. That Burke was himself a political intellectual, with something of the same passion for party intrigue and for insinuating himself into circles of power and prestige, and with not a little of the same capacity for duplicity that he castigates in the intellectuals of the Enlightenment and Revolution, did not, of course, ever occur to him. It does not matter. From the historical point of view what does matter is the pattern of envisagement of the secular intellectual and his relation to power that Burke gave not only to conservative thought in nineteenth-century England and France but, later, to much sociology.

That distrust of the rootless intellectual and apprehension of his moth-like attraction to the circles of power should have become a fixed part of the conservative view—expressed in the writings of Coleridge, Carlyle, Maistre, and Taine—is a matter for no surprise. More interesting is the way in which it becomes translated into a "sociology of the intellectual" that was to persist from Comte to the present day.

Comte's words on the political intellectual are set in a larger context of condemnation of the politicization of thought that, he felt, was one of the worst manifestations of the "metaphysical" stage of thought. The most vital issues of polity have fallen, Comte tells us, "to the class which is essentially one under two names—the civilians and the metaphysicians, or, under their common title, the lawyers and men of letters, whose position in regard to statesmanship is naturally a subordinate one. We shall see hereafter that, from its origin to the time of the first French Revolution, the system of metaphysical polity was expressed and directed by the universities on the one hand and the great judiciary corporations on the other: the first constituting a sort of spiritual power and the other a temporal power. This state of things is still traceable in most countries of the continent; while in France, for above half a century, the arrangement has degenerated into such an abuse that the judges are superseded by the bar, and the doctors (as they used to be called) by mere men of letters; so that now, any man who can hold a pen may aspire to

the spiritual regulation of society, through the press or from the professional chair, unconditionally, and whatever may be his qualifications.
When the time comes for the constitution of an organic condition, the
reign of sophists and declaimers will have come to an end; but there will
be the impediment to surmount of their having been provisionally in possession of public confidence." [19]

Basically the same view of the political intellectuals lies in Tocqueville, particularly in *The Old Regime and the Revolution*. Like Burke
and Comte, Tocqueville calls our attention "to the remarkable, not to
say formidable, influence these men's writings (which at first sight might
seem to concern the history of our literature alone) had on the Revolution and, indeed, still have today." [20] Unlike Burke, Tocqueville can see
why the eighteenth-century political intellectual, as a social type, came
into existence: to combat the "ridiculous, ramshackle institutions, survivals of an earlier age, which no one had attempted to co-ordinate or to
adjust to modern conditions and which seemed destined to live on despite the fact that they had ceased to have any present value . . ."
Given these conditions, it was "natural enough that thinkers of the day
should come to loathe everything that savored of the past and should
desire to remold society on entirely new lines, traced by each thinker in
the sole light of reason." [21]

But in their distrust of past, their total inexperience with political
and social realities, and in their unwavering trust in what the light of
pure reason revealed to each of them, the political intellectuals became,
Tocqueville tells us, in almost Burkean words, unwitting instruments of a
new form of despotism: that emanating from subjection to "an imaginary ideal society in which all was simple, uniform, coherent, equitable,
and rational in the full sense of the terms." [22]

"Our men of letters," Tocqueville continues, "did not merely im-
part their revolutionary ideas to the French nation; they also shaped the
national temperament and outlook on life. In the long process of mold-
ing men's minds to their ideal pattern their task was all the easier since
the French had had no training in the field of politics, and they thus had
a clear field. The result was that our writers ended up by giving the
Frenchman the instincts, the turn of mind, the tastes, and even the eccen-
tricities characteristic of the literary man. And when the time came for
action, these literary propensities were imported into the political arena."
The French Revolution was conducted, Tocqueville observes, "in the
same spirit as that which gave rise to so many books expounding theories
in the abstract. Our revolutionaries had the same fondness for broad

generalizations, cut-and-dried legislative systems, and a pedantic symmetry; the same contempt for hard facts; the same taste for reshaping institutions on novel, ingenious, original lines; the same desire to reconstruct the entire constitution according to the rules of logic and a preconceived system instead of trying to rectify its faulty parts. The result was nothing short of disastrous; for what is a merit in a writer may well be a vice in the statesman and the very qualities which go to make great literature can lead to catastrophic revolutions." [23]

From the literary intellectuals came a new language of politics that was, henceforth, to alter profoundly the nature and dimension of politics. "Even the politicians' phraseology was borrowed largely from the books they read; it was cluttered up with abstract words, gaudy flowers of speech, sonorous clichés, and literary turns of phrase. Fostered by the political passions that it voiced, this style made its way into all classes, being adopted with remarkable facility even by the lowest." Tocqueville concludes his passage with dry malice: "All they needed, in fact, to become literary men in a small way was a better knowledge of spelling." [24]

The Roots of Power—Tocqueville

Tocqueville's *Democracy in America* is the first systematic and empirical study of the effects of political power on modern society. This work is much else also, but at bottom it is a study, and a remarkably dispassionate one, of the impact of democracy upon the traditions, values, and social structures descended from medieval society. In his second major work, *The Old Regime and the French Revolution,* Tocqueville explored the sources of modern political power, with its twin aspects of centralization and bureaucratization. Logically one might say that it precedes the earlier work. And no one reading *Democracy in America* will have any difficulty in seeing, between the lines, the thesis of the later work. Both studies have to be understood in the light of Tocqueville's obsession with the Revolution and its impact upon the social order.

Tocqueville's central thesis can be stated simply. All that alienates man in modern society from traditional authority—from class, guild, church, and so on—tends to drive him ever more forcefully into the haven of power, power conceived not as something remote and fearful but as close, sealing, intimate, and providential: the power, that is, of modern democracy with its roots in public opinion. This is Tocqueville's dominant theme. The decline of the aristocratic community and the release of men from old authorities were historically required, he repeatedly emphasizes, for modern power to make its appearance in the democratic-national state.

Unlike most of his contemporaries, Tocqueville saw democracy not primarily as a system of freedom but of power. Democracy with its emphasis upon equality, liberation from traditional authority, and its sense of the centralized, unified nation, is but the logical and inevitable outcome of forces that had begun centuries earlier in monarchical centralization which had, over several centuries, reduced medieval diversity and localism in favor of widening national aggregates based upon administrative power at the center. Whereas freedom is, for Tocqueville, *immunity* from power, democracy is, by its nature, a *form* of power, potentially greater in intensity and reach than any prior form of political government.

What are the sources of democratic power? Tocqueville finds these pre-eminently in the massive tendency of modern history toward equalization of status and the leveling of ranks. "In running over the pages of our history, we shall scarcely find a single great event of the last seven hundred years that has not promoted equality of condition." Equality has meant, however, the destruction of the estates, guilds, classes, and other associations which had, by virtue of the very inequality they conferred on the population, represented limits on the power of the king. "I perceive that we have destroyed those individual powers which were able, single-handed, to cope with tyranny; but it is the government alone that has inherited all the privileges of which families, guilds, and individuals have been deprived; to the power of a small number of persons, which, if it was sometimes oppressive, was often conservative, has succeeded the weakness of the whole community." [25]

The idea of the people, of the majority, the rock on which democratic power rests, could never have come into existence apart from the sterilization of hierarchical authority. In the Middle Ages men were conscious of themselves as churchmen, guildsmen, members of this or that family or province, but never as a nation, much less as a people, with independent, corporate existence. Conceptualization of the people as an entity is a gradual process in modern history; historically its basis is, first, the atomization of the medieval *social* identities of individuals and, second, the centralization and nationalization of political power, thus providing a legal atmosphere within which socially detached masses of individuals could live and have identity.

Between equality and centralization there is, therefore, a fateful affinity. Hence the necessity, in historical terms, of early powerful monarchs such as Louis XIV. By their attacks upon feudal enclaves of authority, they could not help but gradually widen the base of equality and enrich the taste for it. Similarly, all that loosened the bonds between the feudal associations and their members—such forces as war, trade, cities, the printing press—made the work of centralization correspondingly easier.

Having established the long-run tendency and roots of centralization, what are the causes of its variable intensity in modern times? Less or greater centralization in democracy is determined chiefly by whether or not a democracy comes into existence gradually, as in the United States, or as the consequence of sudden revolution. In the latter case, "As the classes that managed local affairs have been suddenly swept away by the storm, and as the confused mass that remains has yet neither the organization nor the habits which fit it to assume the administration of these affairs, the state alone seems capable of taking upon itself all the details of government, and centralization becomes, as it were, the unavoidable state of the country." Napoleonism, Tocqueville writes, was inevitable in France, for "after the abrupt disappearance of the nobility and the higher rank of the middle classes, these powers devolved on him, of course; it would have been almost as difficult for him to reject as to assume them." [26]

Tocqueville notes the affinity between the lower classes and centralized power. The central government is the only means whereby the people can wrest the management of local affairs from the aristocracy. The lower classes, or their representatives, thus tend to hold an ascendancy in the early phase of a revolution. But, Tocqueville emphasizes shrewdly, this balance changes. "Towards the close of such a revolution . . . it is usually the conquered aristocracy that endeavors to take over the management of all affairs to the state, because such an aristocracy dreads the tyranny of a people that has become its equal, and not infrequently its master. Thus, it is not always the same class of the community that strives to increase the prerogative of the government; but as long as the democratic revolution lasts, there is always one class in the nation, powerful in numbers or in wealth, which is induced, by peculiar passions or interests, to centralize the public administration, independently of that hatred of being governed by one's neighbor which is a general and permanent feeling among democratic nations." [27]

In England it is the lower classes that are striving to destroy local independence and to transfer administration to the center, and the upper classes endeavoring to retain administration in the local areas. But the time will come, Tocqueville predicts, when the very reverse will be the case.

A third factor in variability of intensity is the contrasting effect of mass illiteracy under an aristocracy and in a democracy. Ignorance of the masses does not necessarily lead to centralization in aristocracies "because in them instruction is nearly equally diffused between the monarch and the leading members of the community." Very different is the case in democracy where the intermediate powers have vanished. Mass ignorance here puts the people far more directly in the hands of the central government. "Hence, among a nation which is ignorant, as well as democratic, an amazing difference cannot fail speedily to arise between the intellectual capacity of the ruler and that of each of his subjects. This completes the easy concentration of all power in his hands: the administrative function of the state is perpetually extended because the state alone is competent to administer the affairs of the country." [28]

Fourth, warfare has a strongly centralizing effect on democratic administration. Success in war, Tocqueville notes, depends more on the means of easy transferal of all the resources of a nation to a single point than on the extent of those resources. "Hence, it is chiefly in war that nations desire, and frequently need, to increase the powers of the central government. All men of military genius are fond of centralization, which increases their strength; and all men of centralizing genius are fond of war . . . Thus, the democratic tendency that leads men unceasingly to multiply the privileges of the state and to circumscribe the rights of private persons is much more rapid and constant among those democratic nations that are exposed by their position to great and frequent war than among all others." [29]

But the foremost of the causes that centralize power in a democracy is the birth and character of the ruling individual. The people are never so happy about transferring powers to their leader as when they feel that he is one of them in origin and nature. "The attraction of administrative powers to the center will always be less easy and less rapid under the reign of kings who are still in some way connected with the old aristocratic order than under new princes, the children of their own achievements, whose birth, prejudices, propensities, and habits appear to bind them indissolubly to the cause of equality . . . In democratic communities the rule is that centralization must increase in proportion as the sovereign is less aristocratic.

"A revolution that overthrows an ancient regal family in order to place new men at the head of a democratic people may temporarily weaken the central power; but however anarchical such a revolution may appear at first, we need not hesitate to predict that its final and certain consequence will be to extend and to secure the prerogatives of that power.

"The foremost or indeed the sole condition required in order to succeed in centralizing the supreme power in a democratic community is to love equality, or to get men to believe you love it. Thus, the science of despotism, which was once so complex, is simplified, and reduced, as it were, to a single principle." [30]

Tocqueville's preoccupation with conflict between political power and traditional authority leads him to examine the effects of democratic power on social institutions. That it undermines, by its nature, localism and hierarchy we have seen. But there are other instances.

There is the authority of learning, of individual distinction, and of taste—weakened in each instance, he tells us, because the diffusion of power, or at least the myth of this diffusion, leads men to distrust all authority that does not seem to arise from public opinion, a power in democracy that Tocqueville declares to be more formidable than the Spanish Inquisition, which, after all, addressed itself only to the circulation of books. "The empire of the majority succeeds much better in the United States, since it actually removes any wish to publish them." [31]

There is the effect of popular power on the authority of the family. "Among aristocratic nations social institutions recognize, in truth, no one in the family but the father; children are received by society at his hands; society governs him, he governs them. Thus, the parent not only has a natural right but acquires a political right to command them; he is the author and the support of his family; but he is also its constituted ruler. In democracies, where the government picks out every individual singly from the mass to make him subservient to the general laws of the community, no such intermediate person is required; a father is there, in the eye of the law, only a member of the community, older and richer than his sons." [32]

Conflict between family and state is, then, conflict between the traditional authority of the father and the emerging power of other members of the family, the inevitable consequence of the individualization of family and the magnification of the role of each member as citizen.

"When men live more for the remembrance of what has been than for care of what is, and when they are more given to attend to what their ancestors thought than to think themselves, the father is the natural and necessary tie between the past and present, the link by which the ends of these two chains are connected. In aristocracies . . . the father is not only the civil head of the family, but the organ of its tradition, the expounder of its customs, the arbiter of its manners. He is listened to with deference, he is addressed with respect, and the love that is felt for him is always tempered with fear.

"When the condition of society becomes democratic and men adopt as their general principle that it is good and lawful to judge of all things for oneself, using former points of belief not as a rule of faith, but simply as a means of information, the power which the opinions of a father exercise over those of his sons diminishes as well as his legal power." [33]

With profession, class, and religion, the case is the same so far as authority is concerned. What is taken away by political power, and by public opinion adapting itself to political power, from the customary authority of each of these institutions is also taken away from their function in maintaining tradition or in serving as contexts of culture. Only the legal profession shows signs, Tocqueville believes, of maintaining traditional authority, and this is because of the inordinate number of lawyers who participate in politics and, by participating, are able to protect their professional identification along with the forms and rituals that so preeminently mark this medieval-born profession. In religion, Protestantism thrives by its very lack of organizational intensity and although Tocqueville seeks to demonstrate that there is greater natural affinity between Catholicism and democracy—because of the mass leveling within the Roman Church that papal centralization has effected—he notes that in liturgical and hierarchical terms American Catholicism is more "Protestant" than what is to be found in Europe.[34]

A final example of the impact of power on traditional authority is found in the military establishment. The spectacle of the Revolution's mass armies—continued in every equalitarian detail by Napoleon, who was himself a product of military democracy—left a deep impress on Tocqueville's thought, and he deserves to be called the first sociologist of militarism. He notes a deep internal conflict between *civil* democracy's preference for peace—based upon the desire to continue business affairs without the hindrance of war—and the preference of democratic armies for war. The reasons for the latter lie, he believes, in the nature of democratic military command. Whereas under aristocracy, officers are almost wholly drawn from the nobility, with nothing in war to affect a status that was ascribed by birth and hence independent of military careers, the case is very different in democracy. "In democratic armies the desire of advancement is almost universal: it is ardent, tenacious, perpetual; it is strengthened by all other desires and extinguished only with life itself. But it is easy to see that, of all armies in the world, those in which advancement must be slowest in time of peace are the armies of democratic countries. . . . All the ambitious spirits of a democratic army are consequently desirous of war, because war makes vacancies and warrants the violation of that law of seniority which is the sole privilege natural to democracy." [35]

There is the related fact, galling to status aspiration, that the military tends to be ignored, even despised, in times of peace. In an aristocracy this does not matter since the officers return in any event to noble status. It is very different in a democracy, where "military men fall to the lowest rank of the public servants; they are little esteemed and no longer understood. The reverse of what takes place in aristocratic ages then occurs; the men who enter the army are no longer of the highest, but of the lowest class." The successful, educated, and wealthy in a democracy shun military service, and the result is that "the army, taken collectively, eventually forms a small nation by itself, where the mind is less enlarged and habits are more rude than in the nation at large." [36]

Tocqueville finds noncommissioned officers in democratic armies more likely than others to be inclined toward war. After all, commissioned officers tend generally to have assured status in time of peace as well as in time of war. But the noncommissioned officer has none. "A desperate ambition cannot fail to be kindled in a man thus incessantly goaded on by his youth, his wants, his passions, the spirit of his age, his hopes, and his fears.

"Non-commissioned officers are therefore bent on war, on war always at any cost; but if war be denied them, then they desire revolutions, to suspend the authority of the established regulations and to enable them, aided by the general confusion and the political passions of the time, to get rid of their superior officers and to take their places. Nor is it impossible for them to bring about such a crisis, because their common origin and habits give them much influence over the soldiers, however different may be their passions and their desires." [37]

Democracies tend to be weak in early phases of a war but vastly stronger than aristocracies in the later phases. It is not easy in the beginning of war to separate democrats from customary civilian pursuits and attractions. But when the sheer duration of war leads inevitably to this separation, then people turn with all the more enthusiasm and even ferocity to prosecution of the war. "War, after it has destroyed all modes of speculation, becomes itself the great and sole speculation, to which all the ardent and ambitious desires that equality engenders are exclusively directed. . . . A long war produces upon a democratic army the same effects that a revolution produces upon a people; it breaks through regulations and allows extraordinary men to rise above the common level." [38] There is, moreover, a "secret connection" between military character and democratic character. The latter is passionately eager to acquire what it covets and to enjoy it. Democratic character tends to worship chance and to fear death less than difficulty. This is the spirit that men of a democracy bring to trade and commerce, and it is a spirit that lends itself easily to the contexts of war. "No kind of greatness is more pleasing to the imagination of a democratic people than military greatness, a greatness of vivid and sudden luster, obtained without toil, by nothing but the risk of life!" [39]

Tocqueville is also interested in the effect of democracy on administration, which he takes care to distinguish sharply from sovereignty. He emphasizes the significance of the transfer of administration, historically, from the voluntary and unpaid to salaried employees. This transfer, Tocqueville notes, has been going on since the Middle Ages, an aspect of the evolution of rationalized political power in Europe. But the process of bureaucratization has been vastly accelerated under democracies. It is possible indeed, Tocqueville suggests, to measure the progress of democracy in a country by the extent to which a salaried bureaucracy comes to replace the voluntary and unpaid. For, "if public officers are unpaid, a class of rich and independent public functionaries will be created who will constitute the basis of an aristocracy; and if the people still retain their right of election, the choice can be made only from a certain class of citizens.

"When a democratic republic requires salaried officials to serve without pay, it may safely be inferred that the state is advancing toward monarchy. And when a monarchy begins to remunerate such officers as had hitherto been unpaid, it is a sure sign that it is approaching a despotic or a republican form of government. The substitution of paid for unpaid functionaries is of itself, in my opinion, sufficient to constitute a real revolution." [40]

But there is a conflict between the development of bureaucracy—itself functionally related to democracy—and the preservation of popular participation in government, which is, after all, the moral cornerstone of democracy. Tocqueville did not describe this in the detail that Weber was to provide, but the insight is there nonetheless.

"All the governments of Europe have, in our time," he writes, "singularly improved the science of administration: they do more things, and they do everything with more order, more celerity, and at less expense; they seem to be constantly enriched by all the experience of which they have stripped private persons. From day to day, the princes of Europe hold their subordinate officers under stricter control and invent new methods for guiding them more closely and inspecting them with less trouble. Not content with managing everything by their agents, they undertake to manage the conduct of their agents in everything; so that the public administration not only depends upon one and the same power, but it is more and more confined to one spot and concentrated in the same hands. The government centralizes its agency while it increases its prerogative; hence a twofold increase of strength." [41]

There is a close, even reciprocal, relation between centralization and the form of *property* that predominates in democracies. The vast increase of fluid property associated with manufacturers has helped intensify the tendency toward more and more regimented, more and more centralized administration. "Manufacturing property . . . does not extend its rights in the same ratio as its importance. The manufacturing classes do not become less dependent while they become more numerous, but, on the contrary, it would seem as if despotism lurked within them and naturally grew with their growth." [42] As the nation becomes more engaged in manufactures, the lack of roads, canals, harbors, and other works of a semi-public nature, which are necessary to the further development of manufacturing, relentlessly leads to a widened scope of governmental administration.

Centralization has "everywhere increased in a thousand different ways. Wars, revolutions, conquests, have served to promote it; all men have labored to increase it." [43] Centralization of power feeds on popular revolt. Everywhere are to be seen people "escaping by violence from the sway of their laws, abolishing or limiting the authority of their rulers or their princes; the nations which are not in open revolution restless at least, and excited, all of them animated by the same spirit of revolt." But, paralleling this anarchy, is "the incessant increase of the prerogative of the supreme government, becoming more centralized, more adventurous, more absolute, more extensive, the people perpetually falling under the control of the public administration, led insensibly to surrender to it some further portion of their individual independence, till the very men who from time to time upset a throne and trample on a race of kings bend more and more obsequiously to the slightest dictate of a clerk.

Thus in our days two contrary revolutions appear to be going on, the one continually weakening the supreme power, the other as continually strengthening it; at no other period in our history has it appeared so weak or so strong." [44]

There is also the fateful affinity that Tocqueville could see between "Cartesian rationalism" and public opinion in democracy. In no country of the world, he declares, is less formal attention paid to philosophy than in the United States; Americans have no school of their own and they are indifferent to the schools of European thought. Yet for all this, there is a very real and potent "philosophical method" to be found among Americans. This is rationalism as Descartes defined it.

Even Americans who have never heard of Descartes follow his tenets eagerly, Tocqueville notes. They find his repudiation of all tradition (which, for Descartes, was the epistemological means of establishing the ground of pure truth from reason alone) a technique precisely adapted to a theory of government that seeks, in the name of freedom and equality, to repudiate traditional forms and dogmas. Such a method reinforces public opinion. It makes the common sense of each man (the common sense, Descartes had dryly noted, of which each man feels himself in equal and sufficient possession) an adequate guide to all difficulties and mysteries. Just as the union of equalitarianism and power has a sterilizing effect upon social distinctions, the union of Cartesian rationalism and public opinion has a sterilizing effect on intellectual distinctions. [45]

These, then—individualization, sterilization, and rationalization of traditional authority—are the processes that Tocqueville sees operating in the long run toward a magnification of political power in a democracy. Such power, he tells us, in one of the most celebrated chapters of *Democracy in America,* may in time come to seem not power but freedom. The democratic multitudes, separated from hierarchy, isolated from traditional communities, confined to the recesses of their individual minds and hearts, may come to regard the sole remaining power of the state, not as tyranny but as a form of higher and more benevolent community.

"Above this race of men stands an immense and tutelary power, which takes upon itself alone to secure their gratifications and to watch over their fate. That power is absolute, minute, regular, provident, and mild. It would be like the authority of a parent if, like that authority, its object was to prepare men for manhood; but it seeks, on the contrary, to keep them in perpetual childhood . . . After having thus successively taken each member of the community in its powerful grasp and fashioned him at will, the supreme power then extends its arm over the whole community. It covers the surface of society with a network of small complicated rules, minute and uniform, through which the more original minds and the most energetic characters cannot penetrate, to rise above the crowd . . . Such power does not destroy, but it prevents existence; it does not tyrannize, but it compresses, enervates, extinguishes, and stupefies a people, till each nation is reduced to nothing better than a flock of timid and industrious animals, of which the government is the shepherd.

"I have always thought that servitude of the regular, quiet, and gentle kind which I have just described might be combined more easily than is commonly believed with some of the outward forms of freedom, and that it might even establish itself under the wing of the sovereignty of the people." [46]

Such is Tocqueville's preview of totalitarianism: one born not of the patently evil in society but of forces and states which men everywhere were regarding as blessed by progress. What makes Tocqueville's analysis of modern totalitarianism superior to others is that he seeks to relate it to political values (rather, to corruption of values) that men prize, rather than those that are abhorred in a population. The grim vision that Weber later gives us of a Western society ground down into the robots produced by a humanitarian bureaucracy, one bereft of creative vitality, is not different from what we find in Tocqueville.

Yet it must not be thought that Tocqueville saw democracy only in the dark terms of necessary future transformation into plebiscitarian tyranny. That his vision became, before he died, a more and more governing one in his imagination is clear, but we should miss much of the sociological as well as the liberal essence of *Democracy in America* if we did not see the social checks and counter-forces to centralized power that Tocqueville found in the United States. There are many: the independence of the judiciary, the separation of religion and state, the autonomy and high status in which professions (particularly the legal profession) exist, the still intact authority of local community, the regional diversity, and the open frontier; all of these, Tocqueville emphasizes, stand as controls upon the type of political power that tends to emerge from politically dominant majorities and from the unrestrained sway of public opinion.

Even more important, he thought, is freedom of association.[47] Few things that he observed in America struck Tocqueville more forcibly and favorably than the profusion of associations that, in innumerable spheres, discharged social functions which in Europe were vested either in an aristocracy or in political bureaucracy. All societies require some degree of freedom of association, Tocqueville writes, but nowhere is the need for "intermediate associations" so great as in a democracy. For in a democracy it is only too easy to suppose that by virtue of sovereignty's locus in the people as a whole, the need for autonomous, non-political, functional associations is lessened. Associations serve the twin purposes, Tocqueville tells us, of providing a haven for the individual, thus freeing him of the desire to seek absorption in the mass, and of limiting the extent of governmental participation and centralization in society.

Tocqueville differentiates clearly between political associations and civil associations; the former are manifest largely in political parties, the latter in the great profusion of social, cultural, and economic associations that Tocqueville observed in the United States. From the point of view of the vitality of the social order and of protection of the individual, the latter are the more important. By their very existence they reflect a high degree of individual social action and membership. Logically, the prosperity of civil associations would appear to have little dependence upon political association. In fact, however, there is very close dependence.

"In all the countries where political associations are prohibited, civil associations are rare. It is hardly probable that this is the result of accident; the inference should rather be that there is a natural and perhaps a necessary connection between these two kinds of association . . . I do not say that there can be no civil associations in a country where political association is prohibited, for men can never live in a society without embarking on some common undertakings; but I maintain that in such a country civil associations will always be few in number, feebly planned, unskillfully managed, that they will never form any vast designs, or that they will fail in the execution of them." [48]

The more that government "stands in the place of associations, the more will individuals, losing the notion of combining together, require its assistance: these are causes and effects that unceasingly create each other." [49] Hence the vital importance of associations in the structure of authority in democratic society. In democracy, "the science of association is the mother of science; the progress of all the rest depends upon the progress it has made.

"Among the laws that rule human societies there is one which seems to be more precise and clear than all others. If men are to remain civilized or to become so, the art of associating together must grow and improve in the same ratio in which the equality of conditions is increased." [50]

THE USES OF POWER—MARX

In every important respect, Marx's view of the problem of power in society differs from Tocqueville's. There is no better way of accenting this contrast than by noting that whereas Tocqueville's philosophy is best seen as the *antithesis* of the four phases of revolutionary power described above—totalism, mass, centralization, and rationalization—Marx's philosophy is the lineal, conceptual *consequence* of these aspects. Marx shared utterly the Jacobin intellectual's hatred of traditional society, his distrust of pluralism and localism, and his repudiation of freedom of association. So did Marx share Jacobin faith in the people's will and in the long-run evanescence of power, so called, once the traditional status groups of society have been obliterated. The following passage is instructive:

"When, in the course of development, class distinctions have disappeared and all production has been concentrated in the hands of a vast association of the whole nation, the public power will lose its political character. Political power, properly so called, is merely the organized power of one class for oppressing another." [51]

This is, of course, pure Rousseau, pure Saint-Just. Despite its location in the *Communist Manifesto,* it is no mere call to action, no passing flight of tactical fancy. It reflects all that is central in the Marxian view, and this is as true of the early "philosophical" Marx as of the later "historical" Marx. From "On the Jewish Question" through the *Manifesto, The Class Struggles in France,* down to his final letters, there is a view of power in Marx precisely as antithetical to Tocqueville—and also, in large measure, to Tönnies, Weber, and Durkheim—as it is congruent with what we find in Rousseau's *Discourse on Political Economy* or in some of the decrees of the Committee on Public Safety. From such a view is bound to come philosophical indifference to the long-run consequences of the use of techniques of power in a revolution.

For, if men are convinced of the inevitable disappearance of power, once the proper economic and social conditions have been brought about why should not every possible technique of centralization and consolidation of power be employed during the revolution and the period immediately following it? And, if political power is indeed only the reflection of a dominant class in a class-torn society, then how can there be a problem of power in a society leveled of class (and all other social) distinctions?

Engels was but restating Marx's own view of the matter when he wrote of the state: "When at last it becomes the real representative of the whole of society it renders itself unnecessary. As soon as there is no longer any social class to be held in subjection . . . a state is no longer necessary. The first act by virtue of which the state really constitutes itself the representative of the whole of society—the taking possession of the means of production in the name of society—this is, at the same time, its last independent act as a state. State interference in social relations becomes, in one domain after another, superfluous, and then dies out of itself; the government of persons is replaced by the administration of things, and by the conduct of processes of production. The state is not 'abolished.' *It dies out.*" [52] The line between the Tocquevillian and the Marxian conceptions of the state could not be more sharply drawn than by Engels' passage. This is the view that even today underlies the nearly total indifference (scholarly as well as administrative) in Marxist nations and movements to the problems of bureaucracy, centralization, and political mechanization that, elsewhere, have proved to be the central preoccupations of liberal minds in the twentieth century.

The difference between Marx and Tocqueville may be reduced to this: for Tocqueville the greatest threats of political power must always occur in the most individualized—that is, atomized and leveled—societies; for Marx the greatest threats, indeed the *only* threats, occur in societies characterized by the reverse: where class and other modes of social differentiation are strongest. Tocqueville believed that there was more personal freedom under aristocracy than under democracy—where public opinion becomes, in his view, more despotic than the medieval Inquisition. For Marx, there was no real freedom under aristocracy. It is, for Marx, the special character of modern political development that the state, most notably in its democratic form, represents the beginning of a human emancipation that will only become complete after the socialist revolution. Then and only then will men know freedom. For Tocqueville political power is simultaneously a *cause* of alienation, through its invasions of the communities of membership which form society, and a *refuge* from alienation: that is, political power in a democracy becomes increasingly a fortress of escape from the ills and frustrations of civil society. For Marx political power *is* alienation; alienation in the special Marxian sense that pertains equally to property, class, and religion. Alienation and political power will both terminate when man knows, under socialism, full emancipation from all restraints. "Political emancipation is a reduction of man on the one hand to a member of civil society, an independent and egoistic individual, and on the other hand, to a citizen, to a moral person. Human emancipation will be complete only when the real individual man has absorbed into himself the abstract citizen; when as an individual man, in his everyday life, in his work, and in his relationships, he has become a species-being; and when he has recognized and organized his own powers (*forces propres*) as social powers so that he no longer separates this social power from himself as political power." [53]

The passage just quoted comes at the end of Marx's "On the Jewish Question," and there is no better place than in this essay, written five years before the *Manifesto,* to get at the essence of the Marxian view of the nature and role of political power in European history. The essay was written by Marx (as were so many of his briefer works) in refutation of the thesis of another philosopher: in this instance, Bruno Bauer's plea for the emancipation of the Jews and their elevation to political membership as Jews. For Marx such emancipation and elevation were chimerical. Bauer, he thought, failed to recognize the historical nature of the European state and its relation to religion. Marx's reply to Bauer's plea for Jewish political emancipation is given in a masterly review of the relation of the state to *all* forms of civil membership, religion included among economic, social, and cultural memberships. The purely polemical essence, which need not detain us here, is simply that there can be no *Jewish* membership in the state for the simple reason that there can be no *Christian* membership in the state. That is, the very idea of the state is predicated on the sterilization of religious identities for purposes of citizenship. If it is Jewishness (or Christianness either) that is declared fundamental, there can be no citizenship properly so called, for the idea of political citizenship has developed in terms of the emancipation of man from his pre-political identities.

It is the conflict between civil society and the state that strikes Marx's attention. Tocqueville too had seen this conflict, as we have observed, but in altogether different terms. For Marx it is not the state that is the decisive influence but rather civil society with its varied combinations of materialistic egoism and forms of alienation. The state offers man (and here we see again the strong substratum of Rousseau) a vision of community that stands in contrast to all that civil society represents. "Where the political state has attained to its full development, man leads, not only in thought, in consciousness, but in reality, in life, a double existence—celestial and terrestrial. He lives in the political community where he regards himself as a communal being and in civil society where he acts simply as a private individual, treats other men as means, degrades himself to the role of a mere means, and becomes the plaything of alien powers." [54] It is thus impossible, on moral grounds alone, for members of a religion as such to become members of the state, the political community. "The conflict in which the individual, as the professor of a particular religion, finds himself involved with his own quality of citizenship and with other men as members of the community, may be resolved into the secular schism between the political state and civil society." The difference between religious man and the citizen is exactly the same as that "between shopkeeper and citizen, between the day laborer and citizen, between the landed proprietor and the citizen, between the living individual and the citizen." [55]

It is, in short, the revolutionary tension between citizenship and membership in civil society that Marx, like Rousseau, is concerned with emphasizing. To be sure, political citizenship is not for Marx, as it was for Rousseau, the final answer, for it represents, as we have noted, in itself a mode of alienation. But as one reads this essay he cannot escape the thought that it is to some extent from the political ideal of citizenship —an identity man acquires through his legal and conceptual emancipation from other status identities—that Marx derives something (a model perhaps) of his apocalyptic vision of the final "human" emancipation in which he will be liberated from political as well as from all economic and religious and social identities. "Political emancipation certainly represents a great progress," Marx writes. "It is not indeed the final form of human emancipation, but it is the final form of emancipation within the framework of the prevailing order. It goes without saying that we are speaking here of real, practical emancipation." [56]

What Marx writes on the state and its role in European history is penetrating. European man, Marx tells us, has emancipated himself politically from religion "by expelling it from the sphere of public law to that of private law." Religion, from being a part of the fabric of the state, becomes, through such events as the Reformation and the rise of nationalism, a part of civil society only. "It has become the spirit of civil society, of the sphere of egoism and of the *bellum omnium contra omnes*. It is no longer the essence of community, but the essence of differentiation." [57]

Such a passage gives us the clue to Marx's view of civil society—an arena of economic, religious, and social tyrannies to which the individual is still subjected. Unlike Hegel, who found in civil society—family, class, and local community—the necessary complement of the state, Marx sees in civil society only fragmentation and alienation from which man must someday be extricated. He has Rousseau's repugnance for all that emphasizes man's separate, differentiated identity and all of Rousseau's love for that which emphasizes man in his communal, or what Marx calls "species," identity. It is in these terms indeed that Marx scorns the natural-law school's insistence upon *individual* rights—precisely as Rousseau had. Rousseau, in his *Social Contract,* had declared that once man entered into the true political community, he would surrender all of his individual rights and acquire new ones based upon his membership as a citizen. "None of the supposed rights of man," Marx writes, "go beyond the egoistic man, man as he is, as a member of civil society: that is, an individual separated from the community, withdrawn into himself, wholly preoccupied with his private interest and acting in accordance with his private caprice." [58] In *The Holy Family* Marx wrote again on this point: "It has been shown that the recognition of the rights of man by the modern State has only the same significance as the recognition of slavery by the State in antiquity. The basis of the State in antiquity was slavery; the basis of the modern State is civil society and the individual of civil society, that is, the independent individual, whose only link with other individuals is private interest and unconscious, natural necessity, the slave of wage labour, of the selfish needs of himself and others." [59]

Whenever the state, as a historical type, comes into being there must be conflict between it and the religious and economic elements of civil society. "Certainly, in periods when the political state as such comes violently to birth in civil society, and when men strive to liberate themselves through political emancipation, the state can, and must, proceed to abolish and destroy religion; but only in the same way as it proceeds to destroy private property, by declaring a maximum, by confiscation, or by progressive taxation, or in the same way as it proceeds to abolish life, by the guillotine. At those times when the state is most aware of itself, political life seeks to stifle its own prerequisites—civil society and its elements—and to establish itself as the genuine and harmonious species-life of man. But it can only achieve this end by setting itself in violent contradiction with its own conditions of existence, by declaring a permanent revolution." [60]

Given that passage, one does not have to search for extraneous, tactical influences to account for Marx's growing preoccupation with political power and the use of power to atomize remaining centers of privilege and hierarchy in society and to form a general association within which individuals, not groups and classes, would be the elements of polity. If it was from Hegel that Marx got his sense of the historical role of the state in Europe, it was from Rousseau (who had of course influenced Hegel) that he acquired his sense of the state as a structure resting on the unmediated loyalties and devotions of individuals, each freed of conflicting loyalties.

Like Rousseau, Marx could combine in a single passage elements of the rigorously analytical and the chiliastic. The individualizing functions of the historic state in its relation to feudal society served admirably for Marx, as for Rousseau, as the framework of speculation on the future. Rousseau's adjuration that within the general will and its exclusive association individuals shall become as completely as possible separated from competing relationships—thus forcing them to achieve their individualities—has reflections in the following passage from Marx on the subject of future society: "Religion, the family, the state, law, morality, science, art, etc., are only particular forms of production and come under its general law. The positive abolition of private property, as the appropriation of human life, is thus the positive abolition of all alienation, and thus the return of man from religion, the family, the state, etc., to his human, i.e. social life." [61] For Marx, as for Rousseau, there is always implicit a conception of man as containing naturally within himself sentiments and faculties which, over the course of social development, have become alienated from him and vested in external institutions which enslave him. Revolution is the only means by which the end of this alienation can be effected and man's faculties returned to him. Hence the vital political function of revolution in Marx's thought.

"The political aspect of a revolution consists in the movement of the politically uninfluential classes to end their exclusion from political life and power. Its standpoint is that of the state, an abstract whole, which only exists by virtue of its separation from real life, and which is unthinkable without the organized opposition between the universal idea and the individual existence of man. A revolution of a political kind also organizes, therefore, in accordance with this narrow and discordant outlook, a ruling group in society at the expense of society." [62]

Following this passage comes a key paragraph that extends analytical vision to messianic hope: hope of termination, for the first time in history, of the omnipresence of political power. "Revolution in general —the overthrow of the existing ruling power and the dissolution of existing social relationships—is a political act. Without revolution socialism cannot develop. It requires this political act as it needs the overthrow and the dissolution. But as soon as its organizing activity begins, as soon as its own purpose and spirit come to the fore, socialism sheds this political covering." [63] The last sentence is the crux, of course. This passage was written five years before the *Manifesto* appeared, and it is in many ways the single most important sentence Marx ever wrote so far as the future politics of socialism was concerned. It is the seed of the myth that permitted generations of Marxist intellectuals to combine without difficulty in their minds programs for the ruthless capture and absolute centralization of political power with fanatical confidence that, once the spirit and purpose of socialism had become morally sovereign, political power in the existential sense would disappear. Not without cause did Lenin style the Bolsheviks as "the Jacobins of contemporary Social-Democracy."

In the same way that organized power of the French Revolution served as a model for Marxian acceptance of the necessary totalism of revolutionary power, of atomization of traditional authorities and of rationalization and generalization of revolutionary political power, it served also as a model of the centralization that Marx and Engels never doubted would be crucial to socialist objectives in the first stages of a revolution. Marx expressed his admiration for the centralization of the French Revolution that had, like a "gigantic broom," swept away all the localism, pluralism, and communalism of traditional French society. "The centralized state power," he writes in opening words reminiscent of Tocqueville, "with its ubiquitous organs of standing army, police, bureaucracy, clergy, and judicature—organs wrought after the plan of a systematic and hierarchic division of labor—originates from the days of the absolute monarchy, serving nascent middle-class society as a mighty weapon in its struggles against feudalism. Still its development remained clogged by all manner of medieval rubbish, seignorial rights, local privileges, municipal and gild monopolies and provincial constitutions. The gigantic broom of the French Revolution of the eighteenth century swept away all these relics of bygone times, thus clearing simultaneously the social soil of its last hindrances to the superstructure of the modern state edifice raised under the First Empire . . ." [64]

For Napoleon too Marx had an appreciation not unlike Tocqueville's. Napoleon, Marx tells us, clearly understood the nature of the modern state, and he represented the last struggle of the revolutionary terrorism against civil society and its policy that had been begun by the Revolution. Napoleon, however, "practiced terrorism by substituting permanent war for permanent revolution." Marx's tactical understanding of the steps taken by Napoleon to nationalize, monopolize, and central-ize economic and intellectual life in France is clear. And there is little doubt that the model of both Jacobin and Napoleonic centralization was in his mind when, in the *Communist Manifesto,* he and Engels came to the steps that would be a necessary part of the Revolution in "the most advanced countries." These included centralization of credit and bank-ing, of placing the means of communication and transport in the hands of the state; extension of factories and other productive facilities owned by the state; establishment of industrial armies, and so forth.[65]

Marx was capable of writing highly sophisticated appreciations of the role of bureaucracy in the development of European government. "This executive power with its monstrous bureaucratic and military or-ganization, with its artificial state machinery embracing wide strata, with a host of officials numbering half a million, besides an army of another half million, this appalling parasitic growth, which enmeshes the body of French society like a net and closes all its pores, sprang up in the days of absolute monarchy, with the decay of the feudal system, which it helped to hasten. The seignorial privileges of the landowners and towns became transformed into so many attributes of the state power, the feudal digni-taries into paid officials and the motley pattern of conflicting medieval plenary powers into the regulated plan of a state authority, whose work is divided and centralized as in a factory. The first French Revolution, with its task of breaking all local, territorial, urban and provincial inde-pendent powers in order to create the bourgeois unity of the nation, was bound to develop what the absolute monarchy had begun—centraliza-tion, but at the same time the extent, the attributes and the agents of the governmental authority. Napoleon perfected this state machinery." [66] Tocqueville could not have improved on those words. They were written in 1852, seventeen years after the publication of *Democracy in America,* three years before publication of Tocqueville's study of the old regime. But there the matter stopped.

That socialism might have its own problems of bureaucracy in the light of the centralized assumption of economic powers that the *Commu-nist Manifesto* prescribes for the revolution seems to have given Marx's mind little trouble. In the same way that political power loses its politi-cal character once the capitalist class has been overthrown, so pre-sumably does governmental administration lose its bureaucratic nature. Lenin must have felt in keeping with Marxist understanding of these matters when he wrote of socialist administration: "The bookkeeping and control necessary for this have been simplified by capitalism to the utmost, till they have become the extraordinarily simple operations of watching, recording, and issuing receipts, within the reach of anybody who can read and write and know the first four arithmetical rules . . . When most of the functions of the state are reduced to this bookkeeping and control by the workers themselves, it ceases to be a "political" state. The public functions are converted from political into simple administrative functions . . . The whole of society will have become one office and one factory with equal work and pay." [67]

Although Marx and Engels were indifferent to any problem of *political* power that might emerge within classless society, they had, like Bentham before them, a rather well-developed conception of the factory as the embodiment of social authority within industrialism. In "On Authority," an essay written in 1874, Engels expressed his disdain for the anarchist expectation of the cessation of all authority once capitalism was overthrown. Far from any nirvana of surcease from all authority, there will be, Engels tells us, there *must* be, under socialism, the kind of continuing authority that is bound up with the disciplines of technology and the large-scale factory. Engels' words on the future work under socialism are emphatic.

"All these workers, men, women, and children, are obliged to begin and finish their work at the hours fixed by the authority of the steam, which care nothing for individual autonomy. . . . [T]he will of the single individual will always have to subordinate itself, which means that questions are settled in an authoritarian way. The automatic machinery of a big factory is much more despotic than the small capitalists who employ workers ever have been. At least with regard to the hours of work one may write upon the portals of these factories: *Lasciate ogni autonomia, voi che entrate.* If man, by dint of his knowledge and inventive genius, has subdued the forces of nature, the latter avenge themselves upon him by subjecting him, in so far as he employs them, to a veritable despotism, independent of all social organization. Wanting to abolish authority in large-scale industry is tantamount to wanting to abolish industry itself, to destroy the power loom in order to return to the spinning wheel." [68]

There was, it is plain enough, little of the utopian or romantic in Engels, and even if his words did not perfectly and wholly embody Marx's views on the subject, they certainly entered into the mainstream of the Marxist tradition that was to reach its culmination in Russia in 1919. And there is every reason to suppose that his words did in fact substantially express Marx's views, for Marx never repudiated them, and in any event they correspond to the view that he tirelessly proclaimed from earliest years, to wit: it is *history* that produces, within the womb of each stage of development, the true outlines and the true substance of the next stage. For Marx the glory of capitalism was the industrial and technological system that had formed within it. Capitalism as a set of social relations would be extinguished, along with political power, but not large-scale industry and technology and the disciplines they represented.

THE RATIONALIZATION OF AUTHORITY—WEBER

Contrast between traditional and modern society forms, for Weber as for Tocqueville and Marx, the essential background of his theory of power. In moral terms, there is the same gulf between Weber and Marx that lies between Tocqueville and Marx. There is, if possible, even more pessimism about the future of Western political power in Weber than in Tocqueville. All of the essential elements of Weber's analysis of the history of political power have their prototype in Tocqueville's treatment of the affinity between social equalitarianism and centralization of political power. The principle of rationalization serves Weber's purposes in much the same way that Tocqueville's were served by the principle of equality. In each instance a single, dominating aspect of modernism is endowed with dynamic, even causal, historical significance. What for Tocqueville is epitomized by "aristocratic" is epitomized for Weber by "traditional."

Weber, however, gives the central elements of his theory of power a degree of universality, a generality of sociological application, that is lacking in Tocqueville. There is little of the deliberately taxonomic in Tocqueville's treatment of authority, no effort to extract from the concrete materials of Western European or American society calculated perspectives of analysis to be used toward the clarification of the ancient world or non-Western societies. That Tocqueville could on occasion use the concrete as the basis of reflections having abstract and universal application is clear enough. But this is very different from Weber's determinedly scientific effort to formulate concepts that could be used, irrespective of time and place, in the study of society. Weber's success in his effort is amply attested by the almost universal incorporation of his basic categories in contemporary studies. It is hardly an exaggeration to say that the bulk of inquiries today into large-scale, formal organization and into the transitions of the new nations of the non-Western world from traditional to modern types of government take their departure from the categories that Weber used to account for the history of authority and power in the West. And Weber's analysis of bureaucracy, including its role in non-governmental spheres of society and culture, is not merely the point of departure of present inquiries; it is, with the rarest and most minute exceptions, still the sum of them. No one has yet added to Weber's theory (vision is the more accurate word) of bureaucracy any theoretical element that is not at least implicit in his own statements on the subject.

Let us begin with the three types of "domination" that Weber finds, in one degree or another, in all societies: the traditional, the rational, and the charismatic. The first two are, for analytical purposes, the more important in the sociology of authority. The third, the charismatic, exists, on Weber's own account, in pure form only for brief moments in history; its fate is to be converted almost immediately into the traditional or the rational. On this we shall be brief, for I believe the more relevant place for extended examination of the charismatic is in the chapter on the religio-sacred.

TRADITIONAL   "A system of imperative co-ordination will be called 'traditional' if legitimacy is claimed for it and believed in on the basis of the sanctity of the order and the attendant powers of control as they have been handed down from the past, 'have always existed.' The person or persons exercising authority are designated according to traditionally transmitted rules. The object of obedience is the personal authority of the individual which he enjoys by virtue of his traditional status. The organized group exercising authority is, in the simplest case, primarily based on relations of personal loyalty, cultivated through a common process of education." [69] Traditional authority thus draws its legitimacy not from reason or abstract rule but from its roots in the belief that it is ancient, that it has inherent and unassailable wisdom transcending any one man's reason. Its social essence is the direct personal relation between those affected: teacher to student, servant to master, disciple to religious leader, and so on. No clear differentiation in such a system is made between "political" and "moral" authority. The king's authority is primarily personal, not territorial, and is mediated through ranks of other rulers—dukes, earls, and so on—all of whom have a relation to vassals below them comparable to the king's relation to them. The "apparatus" appropriate to such a system consists either of personal retainers—household officials, relatives, favorites—or personally loyal vassals and tributary lords. The essential model for traditional authority for Weber is, as it was for all other sociologists, the Middle Ages.

RATIONAL AUTHORITY differs sharply in kind. It is characterized by bureaucracy, by rationalization of the personal relationships which are the substance of traditional society. Legal domination exists in a society when "a system of rules that is applied judicially and administratively in accordance with ascertainable principles is valid for all members of the corporate group." [70] Although this mode of authority is not equalitarian —it has its own strata of function and responsibility—it cannot help but place an emphasis on equality that is lacking in the traditional order. All are equal under the rules governing them specifically. The emphasis is on the rules rather than on persons or on mores. The organization is supreme and, by its nature, strives toward increasing rationalization of itself through reduction of the influence played by kinship, friendship, or the various other factors, including money, that so strongly influence the traditional system. Function, authority, hierarchy, and obedience all exist here, as they do in the traditional order, but they are conceived to flow strictly from the application of organizational reason.

CHARISMATIC AUTHORITY is that wielded by an individual who is able to show through revelation, magical power, or simply through boundless personal attraction, that he possesses *charisma,* a unique force of command that overrides in popular estimation all that is bequeathed by either tradition or law. Charismatic leadership, whether found in religion or politics, almost always involves at some key point in its arrival a dramatic stroke, whether of state or church. Jesus, Buddha, Mohammed, Caesar, Cromwell, Napoleon (whose own *coup d'état,* as I have noted, was the prime source of the nineteenth century's fascination with this type of authority), all represent not merely the eruption of individual genius (in the Latin sense) but of a dramatic conflict with either sacred tradition or rational administration. Revolution, whether religious or political, is the very essence of the exercise of charismatic leadership, for its very impact on the people must have a profoundly dislocating effect upon the traditions or rules by which men normally live. In its pure form, charismatic authority is not, however, indeed cannot be by its very nature, stable and lasting. "It is the fate of charisma," wrote Weber, "whenever it comes into the permanent institutions of a community, to give way to powers of tradition and of rational socialization. This waning of charisma generally indicates the diminishing importance of individual action. And of all those powers that lessen the importance of individual action, the most irresistible is *rational discipline.*" [71]

Charismatic authority is thus not a type of authority as much as, in its strict and pure form, a mode of change induced by the impact of some great individual. What happens then is that his "message" becomes traditionalized or rationalized—or both. Weber refers to the "routinization" of charisma: the inevitable aftermath of the disappearance of the great man or the great moment of inspiration. But the routinization of charisma shortly falls, as Weber himself makes clear and emphatic, into either of the two real types of authority: the traditional and the rational.[72]

Quite apart from the clear relation of Weber's concepts of the traditional and rational to currents of thought that arose in the aftermath of the French Revolution, there is a more specific relation between his concepts and Tönnies' *Gemeinschaft* and *Gesellschaft*. The influence Tönnies exerted on Weber's definition of community and its relation to association is paralleled by the influence of Tönnies' envisagement of the political state. Tönnies saw the modern state as a prime manifestation of *Gesellschaft*, its regularized legal codes and procedures fully as expressive of *Gesellschaft* as the economic elements that tend more often to be emphasized. We need consider only the following passage from Tönnies' book:

"The state frees itself more and more from the traditions and customs of the past and the belief in their importance. Thus, the forms of law change from a product of the folkways and mores and the law of custom into a purely legalistic law, a product of policy. The state and its departments and the individuals are the only remaining agents, instead of numerous and manifold fellowships, communities, and commonwealths which grow up organically. The characters of the people, which were influenced and determined by these previously existing institutions, undergo new changes in adaptation to new and arbitrary legal constructions. These earlier institutions lose the firm hold which folkways, mores, and the conviction of their infallibility gave to them." [73]

Here, almost certainly, is the immediate source of Weber's notable principle of rationalization, the principle that lifts his concepts of the traditional and rational from the merely classificatory to their position of elements in a philosophy of history fully as grand as Tocqueville's, Marx's, or Tönnies'. Just as Tocqueville saw the shape of modern power in terms of the formative influence of equality, as Marx saw it in terms of dialectical struggle, and Tönnies in the transition from *Gemeinschaft* to *Gesellschaft*, Weber epitomized it by a process of rationalization that began in the high Middle Ages and has continued down to the present day with its conclusion no more in sight than that of equalitarianism, the dialectic, or *Gesellschaft*.

Democracy and capitalism—the sovereign realities of the modern world for Tocqueville and Marx, respectively—are, in Weber's historical view, but special manifestations of the more fundamental force of rationalization. The rationalization of government—involving centralization, generalization, as well as abstraction of power—brought Europe from feudalism through the absolute monarchies to the contemporary nation-state in its democratic form. If it is prevented from evolving further to a more complete, even totalitarian, mode of bureaucratic rationalization, it will be only because of the continued force of moral and esthetic values which men will somehow continue to see as limits on pure rationality.

Similarly, the rationalization of economy—through improved cost accounting, rational modes of work, gradual separation of property from political power (*dominium*), and other means—brought what we call modern capitalism into existence. For Marx, capitalism was characterized primarily by the privateness of ownership of property and the separation of population into the two groups of owners and workers. For Weber, these elements are more nearly accident than essence. Moreover, and here is where Weber differed profoundly and lastingly with the Marxists, socialism, far from being the opposite of capitalism, would be only an intensification and widening of the essential properties of capitalism. Under socialism, rationalization, bureaucracy, and mechanization would become even more dominant in human lives than they are under capitalism.

Of all conceptual elements in Weber's theory of authority, the one for which he is most famous is bureaucracy. Bureaucracy falls, as we have seen, within Weber's category of rational domination; it is the mode of hierarchy that supplants patrimonial, charismatic, and/or traditional authority when economy or government (or religion, education, the military, or any other institution in society) becomes structured in the following specific ways:

Foremost is "the principle of fixed and official jurisdictional areas, which are generally ordered by rules, that is, by laws or administrative regulations." [74] Ordinary activities become distributed as official duties, and the authority to give commands is distributed in a stable and foreseeable way, thus replacing the random and sporadic character of kinship or patrimonial authority. Provision is made "for the regular and continuous fulfillment of these duties and for the execution of the corresponding rights." In public government such a system is always identified as bureaucracy, but the same basic system exists in modern business and is known as management.

From the basic principle of fixed and official jurisdiction flow such

vital practices and criteria as the regularization of channels of communication, authority, and appeal; the functional priority of the office to the
person occupying it; the emphasis upon written and recorded orders, in
place of random, merely personal, commands or wishes; the sharp separation of official from personal identity in the management of affairs and
the superintending of finances; the identification of, and provision for the
training of "expertness" in a given office or function; the rigorous priority of official to merely personal business in the governing of an enterprise; and, finally, the conversion of as many activities and functions as
possible to clear and specifiable rules; rules that, by their nature, have
both preceptive and authoritarian significance.[75]

Such is the essence of Weber's definition of bureaucracy. But to
leave the matter here would be to leave it in the realm of the merely
descriptive and taxonomic. What gives distinction to Weber's theory of
bureaucracy is the manner in which he relates it to the main currents of
European political, economic, and social history. *Bureaucratization* becomes for Weber a powerful manifestation of the historical principle of
rationalization. The growth of bureaucracy in government, business, religion, and education is an aspect of the rationalization of culture that has
also transformed, in Weber's view, the nature of art, drama, music, and
philosophy. Bureaucracy is, in short, a historical process through which
we may account for much of what distinguishes the modern from the
medieval world (and also, of course, for analogous differentiations in the
ancient and Asiatic worlds; bureaucracy in Weber is a means of illuminating Chinese, Indian, and ancient Roman society as well as European).

It is Weber's identification of bureaucracy as the essential and far-
flung ambience of modern Western man that lifts his sociology of authority from the empirically commonplace. Within it, as within his larger and
containing vision of rationalization, lie possibilities of both freedom and
despotism. Apart from a bureaucratization of society, with its implicit
emphasis upon the universal qualities of men and its theoretical exclusion of all personal or parochial attributes, a great deal of the history of
modern freedom and democracy would not have been possible. As
Tocqueville presented democracy as a phase of the history of collectivi-
zation and centralization of power, Weber presents it as a manifestation of
bureaucratization. Tocqueville's statement, that the progress of democracy in a country may be measured by the rate of its utilization of paid
officers, finds ready echo in Weber. Equally true, however, is the ease
with which the rules and the office and the files may come to exert a

broader and more penetrating despotism upon the spirit of man than anything within the capacity of a personal monarch or an aristocracy. We shall reserve for our final chapter consideration of Weber's melancholy reflections along this line, for it is a part of a temper of alienation that includes other subjects as well.

Weber is, above all others, the sociologist of "the organizational revolution." This is the revolution that Marx failed to sense, as he had to fail, given his single-minded emphasis upon the dominance of private property. What Weber demonstrates is that foremost among the tendencies of modern history is the gradual replacement of proprietary by organizational incentives. Long before Berle and Means wrote their notable study in the 1930s of the modern corporation and the "splitting of the atom of property" into passive possession and active administration, Weber had made this point the basis of his theory of modern organization. To administration, Weber noted, have been transferred many of the privileges, powers, and obligations that formerly were inseparable from property. In medieval society the concepts of "ownership" and "sovereignty" were but dimly known as independent essences, for it was a mark of traditional society that they were linked. It is testimony to the creative character of rationalization, Weber emphasizes, that, in the centuries following the Middle Ages, power and property became increasingly separated in practice and sharply distinguished in theory. But, with the coming of the twentieth century, rationalization has brought the process to a new level. Once again the two elements are dissolved into one, but this time the "one" is not property, not even power in the ordinary sense, but administration—more specifically, the administration that lies in the processes of bureaucratization, of organization taken as its own end. Thus the hospital reaches the point of serving, not human illness primarily, but the hospital; the university, the church, and the labor union, all become dominated, through processes of rationalization, by their intrinsic organizational goals; all of this, for Weber, is the natural and inevitable conclusion of a process that began when for the directness of domination based upon ownership there began to be substituted the more rational processes of management and administration.

With management—that is, "domination" in the old sense—made increasingly the responsibility of rational administration, the realm of "political" action is correspondingly changed, putting a premium, as Weber foresaw, on qualities in elected officials that would have less and less to do with organization as such and more and more with qualities that Weber summarized by the word demagogue. "Since the time of the constitutional state, and definitely since democracy has been established, the 'demagogue' has been the typical political leader of the Occident. . . . Modern demagoguery also makes use of oratory, even to a tremendous extent, if one considers the election speeches a modern candidate has to deliver. But the use of the printed word is more enduring. The political publicist, and above all the journalist, is nowadays the most important representative of the demagogic species." [76]

Hence the conflict between democracy and bureaucracy that Weber could see growing in modern nations. Like Tocqueville, he perceived the functional relation between democracy and bureaucracy, the one developing with the other, each feeding on the common enemy, inherited privilege. And, like Tocqueville, Weber could see also that, however related the two forces might be in functional terms, the time must come when the moral objective of democracy—rule by the people— could no longer be maintained, given the increasing centrality of the instrument of that rule: the bureaucracy. The robot would turn upon its master. This was the mode of dehumanization that became, for Weber, the increasing preoccupation of his apprehension.

In various ways it became the subject of other men's apprehensions as well: nowhere more penetratingly and presciently than in Robert Michels' *Political Parties: A Sociological Study of Oligarchical Tendencies of Modern Democracy*.[77] This remarkable book is much more than a critique of bureaucracy. It is a searching examination of all aspects of political modernism—popular sovereignty, the party system, administrative centralization, and of the politicization of moral and cultural values under the pressures of the masses. But we shall confine attention here to its treatment of bureaucracy, which is in the direct line of Max Weber's perspective.

"Bureaucracy," Michels writes, "is the sworn enemy of individual liberty, and of all bold initiative in matters of internal policy. The dependence upon superior authorities characteristic of the average employee suppresses individuality and gives to the society in which employees predominate a narrow petty-bourgeois and philistine stamp. The bureaucratic spirit corrupts character and engenders moral poverty. In every bureaucracy we may observe place-hunting, a mania for promotion, and obsequiousness towards those on whom promotion depends; there is arrogance towards inferiors and servility towards superiors. . . . We may even say that the more conspicuously a bureaucracy is distinguished by its zeal, by its sense of duty, and by its devotion, the more also will it show itself to be petty, narrow, rigid, and illiberal." [78]

Michels' words are set in the context of consideration of governmental—and particularly Prussian—bureaucracy, but the essence of his book lies in the characterization of mass democratic and socialist movements in precisely these terms. Where Weber had contented himself, for the most part, with the bureaucratization of official and governmental agencies, Michels carries the analysis forward to those working-class movements—Marxist among them—which were supposedly challenging the structure of bureaucratic government and bureaucratic capitalism. What we find, Michels concludes, is little else than a reordering of socialist organization and thought in the enemy's terms.

"The Marxist economic doctrine and the Marxist philosophy of history cannot fail to exercise a great attraction upon thinkers. But the defects of Marxism are patent directly we enter the practical domains of administration and public law, without even speaking of errors in the psychological field and even in more elementary spheres." Socialist theory has either collapsed in a cloudland of impossible individualism or else "it has made proposals which (doubtless in opposition to the excellent intentions of their authors) could not fail to enslave the individual to the mass." [79] For over half a century, Michels observes, the socialists have been working toward a model organization. "Now when three million workers have been organized—a greater number than was supposed necessary to secure complete victory over the enemy—the party is endowed with a bureaucracy which, in respect of its consciousness of its duties, its zeal, and its submission to the hierarchy, rivals that of the state itself; the treasuries are full; a complex ramification of financial and moral interests extends all over the country. . . . Thus from a means, organization becomes an end." [80]

It is in the light of what Michels regards as the inevitability of bureaucratization of political action—once it is successful and attracts large numbers—that he refers to "the iron law of oligarchy":

"Organization implies the tendency to oligarchy. In every organization, whether it be a political party, a professional union, or any other association of the kind, the aristocratic tendency manifests this very clearly. The mechanism of the organization, while conferring a solidity of structure, induces serious changes in the organized mass, completely inverting the respective position of the leaders and the led. . . . With the advance of organization, democracy tends to decline. Democratic evolution has a parabolic course. At the present time, at any rate as far as party life is concerned, democracy is in the descending phase. It may be enunciated as a general rule that the increase in the power of the

leaders is directly proportional with the extension of the organization." [81]
Such for Michels is the iron law of bureaucracy.

It was not to socialist democracy alone that Michels directed his
mordant analysis, but to democracy in general. The paragraph with
which he somberly concludes his book is in the straight tradition of
Tocqueville and Weber.

"The democratic currents of history resemble successive waves.
They break ever on the same shoal. They are ever renewed. This enduring spectacle is simultaneously encouraging and depressing. When democracies have gained a certain state of development, they undergo a
gradual transformation, adopting the aristocratic spirit, and in many cases
also the aristocratic forms, against which at the outset they struggled so
fiercely. Now new accusers arise to denounce the traitors; after an era of
glorious combats and of inglorious power, they end by fusing with the
old dominant class; whereupon once more they are in their turn attacked
by fresh opponents who appeal to the name of democracy. It is probable
that this cruel game will continue without end." [82]

THE FUNCTION OF AUTHORITY—DURKHEIM

Authority runs like a *leitmotif* through all of Durkheim's works.
Second only to community, it is the dominant theme of his sociology and
philosophy. In the beginning, indeed, he took law as the only real measure of social solidarity.[83] That he was led to abandon this stringent emphasis did not, however, in any way lessen his insistence on the proposition that true society and true morality exist only when authority over
individual mind and behavior is clearly present.

The centrality of authority in Durkheim's thought may be inferred
from some words he wrote on the relation between discipline and personality. "Ordinarily," he writes, "discipline appears useful only because
it entails behavior that has useful outcomes. Discipline is only a means
of specifying and imposing the required behavior. But . . . we must say
that discipline derives its *raison d'être* from itself; it is good that man is
disciplined, independent of the acts to which he thus finds himself constrained." [84]

Why is discipline good? The answer forms the explicit substance of
Moral Education, though it could be deduced easily from each of the
other works. Discipline is authority in operation, and authority is inseparable, even indistinguishable, from the texture of society. Society, he has

already told us in *The Division of Labor* and in the *Rules,* is manifest only in the diverse forms of constraint which rescue, as it were, the individual from the void. Authority and discipline form the very warp of personality; without authority man can have no sense of duty, no real freedom even. Only when traditions, codes, and roles have the effect of coercing, directing, or restraining man's impulses can it be said that society is genuinely in existence.

He is critical of Bentham and other utilitarians for their false view of the role of authority. "For Bentham, morality, like law, involved a kind of pathology. Most of the classical economists were of the same view. And doubtless the viewpoint has led the major socialist theoreticians to deem a society without systematic regulation both possible and desirable. The notion of an authority dominating life and administering law seemed to them to be an archaic idea, a prejudice that could not persist. It is life itself that makes its own laws. There could be nothing above or beyond it." [85]

In his *Professional Ethics,* Durkheim continues the theme. "There is no form of social activity which can do without the appropriate moral discipline . . . The interests of the individual are not those of the group he belongs to and, indeed, there is often a real antagonism between the one and the other." [86] Such interests are only dimly perceived by him: he may fail to perceive them at all. There must, therefore, be some system which brings them to mind, "which obliges him to respect them, and this system can be no other than a moral discipline. For all discipline of this kind is a code of rules that lays down for the individual what he should do so as not to damage collective interests and so as not to disorganize the society of which he forms a part." [87]

Authority, in its relation to man, not only buttresses moral life; it *is* moral life. Authority "performs an important function in forming character and personality in general. In fact, the most essential element of character is this capacity for restraint or—as they say—of inhibition, which allows us to contain our passions, our desires, our habits, and subject them to law." [88] This last suggests that Durkheim was not unaware of Freudians and others of his day who found in the rigor of moral authorities the immediate source of psychological disabilities. The contrast between Durkheim and Freudianism on the matter of discipline is of considerable interest.

Durkheim's views on authority bring him, of course, to the problem of freedom, and he does not hesitate to stress the absolute priority of authority in the establishment of any scene in which freedom is imaginable. "In sum, the theories that celebrate the beneficence of unrestricted liberties are apologies for a diseased state. One may even say that, contrary to appearances, the words 'liberty' and 'lawlessness' clash in their coupling, since liberty is the fruit of regulation. Through the practice of moral rules we develop the capacity to govern and regulate ourselves, which is the whole reality of liberty." [89]

In several places, starting with *The Division of Labor* and continuing through his last major work, Durkheim made plain that he considered the modern age one in which breakdown of authority was conspicuous. The necessity of moral authority, he writes, is a truth especially to be remembered at the present time: "For we are living precisely in one of those critical, revolutionary periods when authority is usually weakened through the loss of traditional discipline—a time that may easily give rise to a spirit of anarchy. This is the source of the anarchic aspirations that . . . are emerging today, not only in the particular sects bearing the name, but in the very different doctrines that, although opposed on other points, join in a common aversion to anything smacking of regulation." [90]

It is his theoretical concern with authority, in all its breadth and depth, that has so frequently invited charges of "collectivism," "authoritarianism," and "nationalism." Such charges are, however, incorrect. In the first place, such terms as these have political connotations, and their inevitable effect is to identify Durkheim with the unitary nationalist collectivism that was coming to flower in Europe. Such identification is false. In clear fact, Durkheim's political thought comes close to the opposite extreme. His analysis of the state and its relationship to social order, as we shall see in this section, is much nearer that of the syndicalists of his time than to either the integral nationalism of French conservatives or the more idealized variety that we find in England in the works of such men as T. H. Green and Bernard Bosanquet.

In terms of practical politics, Durkheim was a *Dreyfusard,* a term covering beliefs that went well beyond the innocence of Alfred Dreyfus to include such principles as legal equality, civil rights, the rule of law, and political liberty. The term also included anti-clericalism, and because of the emotional intensity with which all matters pertaining to the Church in political affairs were then charged, this could sometimes result in a degree of apparent anti-religious sentiment sufficient to alienate a few like Péguy. Durkheim never abandoned *Dreyfusard* principles and, given his known agnosticism, it was only too easy for supporters of the Church to distort his anti-clericalist, agnostic views into tacit support of political domination of all religious, intellectual, and moral matters.

But however easy such distortion may have been, it is not made the more acceptable. Far from being a monist, a nationalist, or a collectivist, Durkheim must be placed, like Tocqueville, among the pluralists. Durkheim's ideas were very close to those advanced in his day by such men as Duguit and Saleilles in France and by Maitland and Figgis in England. Durkheim's emphasis upon society, order, and authority is clear enough. But to make this synonomous with unitary nationalism or centralized economic collectivism, as many critics have, misses the essence of a theory of man's relation to society that culminates in *pluralism* of authority and rigorous insistence upon what he called the *corps intermédiaires*. These latter, associations lying intermediate to man and the state and forming the multiple substance of society, are the real units of Durkheim's theory of authority, just as abstract individuals are the units of utilitarian theory. Criticism of individualism does not mean, in Durkheim's thought, repudiation of freedom and acceptance of collectivism. Such criticism is, on the contrary, one of the very salients of any genuine critique of the traditional theory of monistic sovereignty.

Authority is the bedrock of society. But for Durkheim authority is plural, manifest in the diverse spheres of kinship, local community, profession, church, school, guild, and labor union as well as in political government. From the premise of the necessity of continuing authority over the individual in each of society's associations, and hence a limitation on legal and social individualism, Durkheim reaches a critique of the state every bit as pointed as that of the individualists and a good deal more securely grounded in history.

When Durkheim began his work he made juridical rules the only reliable manifestations of consensus in society. In *The Division of Labor* he had chosen law as the only clear and reliable means of identifying social solidarity. There he wrote: "It will be distinctly seen how we have studied social solidarity *through the system of juridical rules;* how, in the search for causes, we have put aside all that too readily lends itself to personal judgments and subjective appreciation, so as to reach certain rather profound facts of the social structure, capable of being objects of judgment and, consequently, of science." [91]

This is one of the most quoted remarks in all of Durkheim's work, and while it may be taken properly enough as important in *The Division of Labor,* it is too seldom realized that its significance is confined to that work alone. In that work, in principle anyhow, he makes repressive law the identifying attribute, the hallmark, of mechanical solidarity, just as he makes restitutive law the essence of organic solidarity. But he did not really restrict himself even there to juridical data alone. We find him admitting that the legalist approach fails to "take into account certain elements of the collective conscience which, because of their smaller power or their indeterminateness, remain foreign to repressive law while contributing to the assurance of social harmony. These are the ones protected by punishments which are merely diffuse." [92]

Fortunate for us is the fact that Durkheim, the scholar and scientist, did not let himself be cribbed and confined by Durkheim the methodologist—for if he had not let himself go beyond "juridical rules," we would today be without, not merely *Suicide, Elementary Forms of Religious Life, Moral Education,* but even large sections of *The Division of Labor* itself.

The main point here is that Durkheim's approach to the study of authority cannot be limited by the processes of either law or the state, and it is in the sharp distinction he makes between society and the state —the same distinction made by all pluralists—that we are able to see how an emphasis on authority is compatible with a political position that is incontestably liberal, by the standards of that day and now. Only when the individual is securely rooted in a system of social and moral authority is political freedom possible.

"Imagine," he writes, "a being liberated from all external restraint, a despot still more absolute than those of which history tells us, a despot that no external power can restrain or influence. By definition, the desires of such a being are irresistible. Shall we say, then, that he is all-powerful? Certainly not, since he himself cannot resist his desires. They are masters of him, as of everything else. He submits to them; he does not dominate them." [93] Authority, for Durkheim, is rooted in moral values which ultimately make for legitimacy or it is not authority, only the shell. And freedom is simply inconceivable save within the context of the rules and norms which define it.

Although the roots of Durkheim's pluralism lie in *The Division of Labor,* his first serious concern with the problem of the individual's triangular relation to social authority and the power of the state is to be found in the final pages of *Suicide.* Here we find him reflecting on the measures necessary to a restoration of the kind of authority sufficient to check the moral disorganization of which suicide is a conspicuous manifestation. First to be considered is a possible revival of the extreme penalties which were formerly visited on suicides and their families. But these must be rejected today, for they "would not be tolerated by the public conscience." The reason is that suicide "emanates from sentiments respected by public opinion"—even if the act itself is not—and, given these sentiments, the public would not bring itself to harsh measures. "Our excessive tolerance of suicide is due to the fact that, since the state of mind from which it springs is a general one, we cannot condemn it without condemning ourselves; we are too saturated with it not to excuse it in part." [94]

The family is no solution. It might have been once, but the modern family, the conjugal family, is not only too small to absorb the ills of the human spirit, it has been separated by the forces of modern history from centrality in the economic and political processes that govern man's life and attract his allegiances. The family, far from being a haven for man's fears and inadequacies, is itself in need of the kind of reinforcement that can come only from a role in a larger and more relevant form of association, something comparable functionally to the ancient but now defunct kindred or extended family. The problem of suicide and the present condition of the conjugal family are both, Durkheim concludes, instances of the modern decline of authority. His treatment of the family—in terms of loss of functional significance—must certainly be regarded as among the first, if not the first, in what has proved to be a long line. Others had distinguished the nuclear from the extended family, but Durkheim gave it relevance to the problems of contemporary authority and disorganization.

Education is irrelevant to the problem. Education "is only the image and reflection of society. It imitates and reproduces the latter in abbreviated form; it does not create it. The evil is moral and deepseated, and to expect education, which, after all, has but a part of each of its students, and for but a short time, to overcome deficiencies in the whole social order is absurd." [95]

The only remedy "is to restore enough consistency to social groups for them to obtain a firmer grip on the individual, and for him to feel himself bound to them. He must feel himself more solidary with a collective existence which precedes him in time, which survives him, and which encompasses him at all points. If this occurs, he will no longer find the only aim of his conduct in himself and, understanding that he is the instrument of a purpose greater than himself, he will see that he is not without significance. Life will resume meaning in his eyes, because it will recover its natural aim and orientation. But what groups are best calculated constantly to reimpress on man this salutary sentiment of solidarity?" [96]

Not political society, which is "too far removed from the individual" to affect him uninterruptedly and with sufficient force. The state, in any event, is one of the principal *causes* of the social atomization and moral emptiness of which suicide is an outcome.[97] Hardly more efficacious would be religious society. Once, yes, but not today, when so many currents of secular thought have made it impossible for most persons to return to the degree of dogmatic certitude required of a religion if it is to possess the authority sufficient to restrain individuals from suicidal impulses. Roman Catholicism's statistically demonstrable effectiveness is based on a degree of organizational and intellectual rigidity that would be intolerable, Durkheim thinks, for most persons today. New religions will indeed come into being, but they are likely to be even more liberal in doctrinal matters than the most liberal Protestant sects of the present, and these, as the demographic data show, have virtually no restraining influence.

We are preserved from egoistic suicide, Durkheim concludes, only *"insofar as we are socialized; but religions can socialize us only insofar as they refuse us the right of free examination.* They no longer have, and probably never will have again, enough authority to wring such a sacrifice from us. . . . Besides, if those who see our only cure in a religious restoration were self-consistent, they would demand the re-establishment of the most archaic religions. For against suicide Judaism preserves better than Catholicism, and Catholicism better than Protestantism." [98] And, as one is justified in concluding from Durkheim's systematic later study of religion, it is *primitive* religion, with its total subordination of the individual to the cult, that would be most efficacious of all. In primitive society, where everything is surcharged by the sacred, where all values are set in unremitting contexts of community, suicide, except in its rare "altruistic" form, is unknown. But modern European society can hardly be supposed capable of returning to this type of religion.

In the revival of an adapted form of the guild—that is, in an occupational association specifically adapted to the character of modern industry—Durkheim finds the mode of authority and type of membership most likely to supply the social substance now lacking in individual lives. Modern man is encompassed by economic life to a degree unknown in all earlier ages. But, at present, "European societies have the alternative either of leaving occupational life unregulated or of regulating it through the state's mediation, since no other organ exists which can play this role of moderator." [99] Hence, new forms of social organization must be devised to escape the contradiction involved presently in a horde of individuals whose lives are regulated but not really ruled by the distant, remote, and impersonal state.

"The only way to resolve this antinomy is to set up a cluster of collective forces outside the state, though subject to its action, whose regulative influence can be exerted with greater variety. Not only will our reconstituted corporations satisfy this condition, but it is hard to see what other groups could do so. For they are close enough to the facts, directly and constantly enough in contact with them, to detect all their nuances, and they should be sufficiently autonomous to be able to respect their diversity. To them, therefore, falls the duty of presiding over companies of insurance, benevolent aid and pensions, the need of which is felt by so many good minds but which we rightly hesitate to place in the hands of the state, already so powerful and awkward." [100] Such corporations would be, in the very relevance of their goals to economic and social need, repositories of moral authority sufficient to restrain the egoistic (and hence suicidogenic) impulses of human beings now scattered like so many grains of dust.

Both anomic and egoistic types of suicide would be checked, for the corporation would become, even as was the medieval guild, the center of legitimate moral authority. "Whenever excited appetites tended to exceed all limits, the corporation would have to decide the share that should equitably revert to each of the cooperative parts. Standing above its own members, it would have all necessary authority to demand indispensable sacrifices and concessions and impose order upon them. By forcing the strongest to use their strength with moderation, by preventing the weakest from endlessly multiplying their protests, by recalling both to the sense of their reciprocal duties and the general interest, and by regulating production in certain cases so that it does not degenerate into a morbid fever, it would moderate one set of passions by another, and permit their appeasement by assigning them limits. Thus, a new sort of moral discipline would be established, without which all the scientific discoveries and economic progress in the world would produce only malcontents." [101]

It is important that these new structures of authority be granted a measure of legal as well as strictly moral and social authority, for moral authority only follows legal recognition. Our historical development, Durkheim writes in a passage of Tocquevillian intensity, has swept away all older forms of intermediate social organization. "One after another, they have disappeared either through the slow erosion of time or through great disturbances, but without being replaced." [102] Originally kinship, through clan and family, possessed the requisite authority, but it soon ceased to be a political division and became only the center of private life. Territorial unities—hundreds, villages, communes—guilds, monasteries, and other forms of association followed, but they too have suffered dislocation and atomization.

"The great change brought about by the French Revolution was precisely to carry this leveling to a point hitherto unknown. Not that it improvised this change; the latter had long since been prepared by the progressive centralization to which the old regime had advanced . . . Since then, the development of means of communication, by massing the populations, has almost eliminated the last traces of the old dispensation. And since what remained of occupational organizations was violently destroyed at the same time, all secondary organizations of social life were done away with." [103]

Only the state has survived the tempest of modern history. Here we come to the true heart of Durkheim's political sociology. The modern state's action has involved profound paradox. Even as it has absorbed functions previously embodied in other groups, thus swelling further an already swollen bureaucracy, it has tended, by this very action, to level social ranks, to atomize social groups, leaving populations in the form of a sand heap. "It has often been said that the state is as intrusive as it is impotent. It makes a sickly attempt to extend itself over all sorts of things which do not belong to it, or which it grasps only by doing them violence . . . Individuals are made aware of society and of their dependence upon it only through the state. But since this is far from them, it can exert only a distant, discontinuous influence over them; which is why this feeling has neither the necessary constancy nor strength . . . Man cannot become attached to higher aims and submit to a rule if he sees nothing above him to which he belongs. To free him from all social pressure is to abandon him to himself and demoralize him. These are really the two characteristics of our moral situation. While the state becomes inflated and hypertrophied in order to obtain a firm enough grip upon individuals, but without succeeding, the latter, without mutual relationships, tumble over one another like so many liquid molecules, encountering no central energy to retain, fix and organize them." [104]

It is in these terms, and they are, at bottom, Tocquevillian terms, that Durkheim sets the juridical context for the establishment of his occupational associations. These will be the essential units of society—recognized equally by the state and by the families of their members—and, being units of society, they must have grants of *legal* authority that will render their moral authority sufficient to the necessities of integration and morality.

I have dealt with this aspect of Durkheim's thought at some length for reasons that go beyond the ephemeral importance of occupational associations. These are now well behind us in terms of historical likelihood. But too often they have been treated by students of Durkheim as random fragments of his thought. The reverse is true. In their first proposal, in the concluding pages of *Suicide,* published in 1896, lies the origin and essence of a *theoretical* approach to the problem of authority and power that was to influence a considerable number of historians, jurists, and ethnologists, all of whom found in Durkheim's dichotomy between social authority and political power a perspective of extraordinary utility in their studies of other cultures and historical periods.

Let us look more carefully at this theoretical approach to the relation between authority and power. What, for Durkheim, is political society? First, in its normal state, it is pluralistic. Durkheim quotes Montesquieu to the effect that political society involves "intermediary," subordinate, and dependent powers." Without these secondary authorities, the state, except in pathological form, is impossible. "Far from being in opposition to the social group endowed with sovereign powers and called more specifically the state, the state presupposes their existence; it exists only where they exist. No secondary groups, no political authority—at least no authority that this term can apply to without being inappropriate." [105]

But this is only a part of the picture. For, dependent though the normal state is on the body of secondary authorities which undergird it, there is nevertheless to be seen a *conflict,* sometimes actual, always potential, between the state and these authorities. The individual represents the third point of a triangular relation of forces. His freedom from the state's power is measured by his absorption in one or more of the secondary authorities—family, church, guild, and so on. Conversely, the individual's protection from the often overwhelming authorities of these groups is granted, history shows, and protected by the state, through the means of *private rights.* Private rights are created by the state.

This triangular relationship is universal in the history of human societies. In the beginning it is only latent. Both state and individual are but dimly conceived realities. It is the social group—clan, tribe, association—that is sovereign. "In the early stage, the individual personality is lost in the depths of the social mass and then later, by its own effort, breaks away. From being limited and of small regard, the scope of the individual life expands and becomes the exalted object of moral respect. The individual comes to acquire ever wider rights over his own person and over the possessions to which he has title. . . ." [106]

It is interesting to compare this branch of analysis with its root in *The Division of Labor*. There, in one of the most brilliant paragraphs on power and its relation to individualism ever written, Durkheim reveals an aspect of his mind that is (*mirabile dictu*) as Rousseauian as it is Tocquevillian. "Rather than dating the effacement of the individual from the institution of a despotic authority, we must, on the contrary, see in this institution the first step made toward individualism. Chiefs are, in fact, the first personalities who emerge from the social mass. Their exceptional situation, putting them beyond the level of others, gives them a distinct physiognomy and accordingly confers individuality upon them. In dominating society, they are no longer forced to follow all its movements. Of course, it is from the group that they derive their power, but once power is organized, it becomes autonomous and makes them capable of personal activity. A source of initiative is thus opened which had not existed before then. There is, hereafter, someone who can produce new things and even, in certain measure, deny collective usages. Equilibrium has been broken." [107]

The individual does not break away by his own efforts alone. War and commerce help create the state, and between state and individual a powerful affinity develops. What the history of both Athens and Rome reveals is the steady emergence of the individual from tribal society through the help of the also emerging central state. It is indeed the state, historically, that first creates the idea of individuality, first in legal, then, gradually, in economic and moral terms. The famous Cleisthenean reforms in ancient Attica demonstrate this. The individual, released from traditional society, is as necessary to the state, in its own development of jurisdiction and authority, as the state is to the individual in the achievement of, first, legal, then social and moral identity.

Apart from society (distinguished sharply, be it remembered, from the state), man would not, of course, have the nature that removes him from the animals. Society has carried man's individual psychic faculties "to a degree of energy and productive capacity immeasurably greater than any they could achieve if they remained isolated one from the other . . . richer by far and more varied than one played out in the single individual alone." But there is another side, a repressive side. "Whilst society thus feeds and enriches the individual nature, it tends, on the other hand, to subject that nature to itself and for the same reason." [108] It is of the nature of every form of association to become despotic if there are not external forces that restrain it through their competing claims upon individual allegiance. Until the tight communities of the ancient world were partially loosened, their members made in some degree independent particles, freedom, as we know it, was not possible.

"A man is far more free in the midst of a throng than in a small coterie. Hence, it follows that individual diversities can then more easily have play, that collective tyranny declines, and that individualism establishes itself in fact, and that, with time, the fact becomes a right." [109] The only way by which the secondary authorities, old or new, can be restrained from enveloping their individual members, depriving them of the diversity that individualization makes possible, is for there to be a greater, a larger, form of association that creates the legal possibility of *individual* identity, one distinguishable from the social groups to which human beings first belong.

What is taken from the social groups goes, in part, to the state, becoming lodged in its new system of law, but, in part also, to individual citizens in the form of prescribed rights It is in this sense that Durkheim refers to the main function of the state as being "to liberate individual personalities. It is solely because, in holding its constituent societies in check, it prevents them from exerting the repressive influences over the individual that they would otherwise exert." [110]

But Durkheim has not forgotten the quite opposite consequences of the state, those that he first emphasized in *Suicide*, consequences revealed in hypertrophy of state and atrophy of social groups. For it is easy for the state itself to become the leveler, the represser, the despot. And, unlike the smaller authorities, it cannot, by virtue of its vastness, ever give the individual the sense of community that the older forms of association can. Not, that is, without despotic consequences.

"The inference to be drawn from this is simply that, if the collective force, the state, is to be the liberator of the individual, it has itself need of some counter-balance; it must be restrained by other collective forces, that is, by those secondary groups we shall discuss later on . . . It is not a good thing for the groups to stand alone, nevertheless they have to exist. *And it is out of this conflict of social forces that individual liberties are born.* Here again, we see the significance of these groups; their usefulness is not merely to regulate and govern the interests they are meant to serve. They have a wider purpose; they form one of the conditions essential to the emancipation of the individual." [111]

THE FORMS OF AUTHORITY—SIMMEL

Despite important differences between Simmel and Durkheim, there is striking resemblance between their conceptions of the function of authority in the social order and in the genesis and maintenance of personality. There is a distinctness and even a priority of the individual in Simmel that is lacking in Durkheim. Yet the following passage might easily have been written by Durkheim instead of Simmel:

"Occasionally the consciousness of being under coercion, of being subject to a superordinate authority, is revolting or oppressive—whether the authority be an ideal or a social law, an arbitrarily-decreeing personality or the executor of higher norms. But for the majority of men, coercion is probably an irreplaceable support and cohesion of the inner and outer life. In the inevitably symbolic language of all psychology: our soul seems to live in two layers, one of which is deeper, hard or impossible to move, carrying the real sense of substance of life, while the other is composed of momentary impulses and isolated irritabilities. This second layer would be victorious over the first and even more often than it actually is; and, because of the onslaught and quick alternation of its elements, the second layer would give the first no opportunity to come to the surface if the feeling of a coercion interfering from somewhere did not dam its torrent, break its vacillations and caprices, and, thus, again and again give room and supremacy to the persistent undercurrent." [112]

It is in these terms that Simmel makes out a sociological case for the advantages possessed by institutions such as hereditary monarchy and sacramental marriage. The latter will illustrate. Nobody, Simmel says, will deny that the coercion of law and custom holds many marriages together which, from a strictly psychological standpoint, ought to break up. Here persons are subordinating themselves to a law that does not fit their case. Unhappiness is the consequence.

"But in other instances this same coercion—however hard, momentarily and subjectively, it may be felt to be—is an irreplaceable value, because it keeps together those who, from the moral standpoint, ought to stay together but, for some momentary ill-temper, irritation or vacillation of feeling, would separate if they only could, and thus would impoverish or destroy their lives irreparably." [113]

The function of authority is, for Simmel, therefore substantially what it is for Durkheim. Irrespective of what the *content* of moral law may be—good or bad, rational or irrational—the "mere coercion of the law to stay together develops individual values of an eudaemonistic and ethical nature (not to mention values of social expediency) which . . . could never be realized in the absence of all coercion." [114]

The function of authority is integrative, the indispensable cement of association, the constituent tie of human loyalties. Loyalties and obligations to the group would waver, would be constantly threatened with atrophy, were it not for the hard, unyielding structure of authority that serves not only the mission of the group and its values but also the vital tie between individual and group.

Let us return to the secret society, looking at it this time not from the point of view of its communal, but rather its authoritarian character. Simmel writes: "Corresponding to the outstanding degree of cohesion within the secret society is the thoroughness of its centralization. The secret society offers examples of unconditional and blind obedience to leaders who—although naturally they may also be found elsewhere—are yet particularly remarkable in view of the frequent anarchic character of the secret society that negates all other law. The more criminal its purposes, the more unlimited, usually, is the power of the leaders and the cruelty of its exercise . . . Secret societies which, for whatever reasons, fail to develop a tightly solidifying authority are, therefore, typically exposed to very grave dangers.[115]

Just as there is a close and reciprocal relation between the communality of a secret society and its members' sense of the impersonal, meaningless exteriority of the surrounding social order, so is there an equally close and reciprocal relation between the system of authority that the secret society embodies and the larger system of legal authority or power that surrounds the secret society.

There is inevitable conflict between the two systems; a conflict, Simmel emphasizes, arising not entirely from the structure of secrecy within the one but from the fact that it is partial and therefore, potentially, distractive and divisive. "Where the overall aim of the general society is strong (particularly political) centralization, it is antagonistic to all special associations, quite irrespective of their contents and purposes. Simply by being units, these groups compete with the principle of centralization which alone wishes to have the prerogative of fusing individuals into a unitary form. The preoccupation of the central power with 'special association' runs through all political history." To this Tocquevillian insight Simmel adds one distinctively his own: "The secret society is so much considered an enemy of the central power that, even conversely, every group that is politically rejected is called a secret society." [116]

The effect of conflict, of persecution, can be as vitalizing to the secret society's sense of internal freedom as it can to its sense of cohesion. Secret societies often combine an iron authoritarianism with intoxicating feelings of freedom on the part of their members. All that makes the members wish to withdraw from the felt oppressions and frustrations of the larger society causes them to wish to intensify the feeling of oneness within the secret society. Such intensification commonly leads also to centralization and rigor of authority within. Gradually the monolithic character of the small society comes to seem a very sign of the members' release from the tyrannies and corruptions of the outer society. In the totalism of its power, the secret society feels, not despotism, but a new form of freedom, one in which all may participate, one freighted with redemptive mission. The whole history of religious sects and revolutionary movements is illustrative of this.

Although it is the inner recesses of authority that chiefly interest Simmel, he is not blind to the relation of these to the larger institutions and the more generalized norms of society. A case in point is his elaboration of the "authority" manifest in certain cultural and social acts of individuals. In some persons this "authority," this instantaneous capacity for evoking response, may seem to arise directly from the special nature of the personality involved. "But the same result, authority, may be attained in the opposite direction. A super-individual power—state, church, school, family or military organization—clothes a person with a reputation, a dignity, a power of ultimate decision, which would never flow from his individuality." [117]

Simmel's treatment of authority is shot through with historical allusion, further indicating his awareness of the relation between the microsociological and the larger currents of society. He may not reveal the depth, diversity, and richness of historical knowledge of a Weber, but, if we compare him with Durkheim, there is far more evidence of historical (in contrast to ethnological) interest in the nature of authority. One finds almost perfect correspondence of analytical view between Simmel and Tocqueville on the history of political centralization, its effect on intermediate associations, and on the rise of the political mass in modern society. The difference is that these matters are of less obvious moral significance to Simmel than to Tocqueville; less rooted in ideological circumstance.

Simmel's characterization of the political mass is illustrative. In "The Individual's Superiority over the Mass," he gives us all the essential qualities of the modern mass state, which he refers to as a "sociological tragedy" through its reduction of individuality to a lower and primitively more sensuous level, its blurring of what is distinct in the person, and its formation of an undiversified whole resting on the least common denominator. The mass, he writes, is "a new phenomenon made up, not of the total individualities of its members, but only of those fragments of each of them in which he coincides with all others. These fragments, therefore, can be nothing but the lowest and most primitive." [118] But where Tocqueville largely confined his treatment of the mass to American democracy, Simmel puts it in more general and formal social type. And where, in Tocqueville, moral judgments are constantly explicit, Simmel prefers the subtler, more dispassionate, and objective approach. The essential point is that Simmel, working from the same historical vantage point as Tocqueville, chose to place the political mass in more universal and categorical mold.

Or consider Simmel's treatment of what he calls *tertius gaudens,* that is, the power wielded by a third person or party merely by virtue of being third. Within the space of three paragraphs he draws illustrations from European history as varied as the following: the relation of the Center party to the Liberals and the Social Democrats in his own day; the role played by England at the beginning of the modern political age with respect to Continental powers; the position of the Pope *vis à vis* conflicting elements within the late medieval church; the judicial role of William the Conqueror between Anglo-Saxons and his own Normans.

Closely related is his elaboration in sociological terms of *divide et impera.* Here a familiar and oft-noted tactic in politics is converted into an abstract form, one observable in contexts ranging from family to state or empire: in this a third party gains power by adroit promotion of division between two other parties. Simmel's examples include the relation of the Roman emperors to religious and economic associations; the position of Anglo-Norman kings with respect to the manors of feudal lords; and the factionalism promoted among Australian aborigines by colonial rulers, and the efforts of rulers of medieval Venice to divide the citizenry. Simmel may be primarily concerned with the forms that can be abstracted from the circumstances of history, but no one can accuse him of rootless abstraction.

When we turn to Simmel's major work on the nature of authority, *Superordination and Subordination,* we find the same contextual relation between his formal types of authority and the concrete historical development of modern Europe that we observed in Weber. Just as Weber's categories of "traditional" and "rational" turn out to be conceptualizations of phases through which Europe had passed, and was passing, in its transition to modernism, so do Simmel's three essential types. Behind what Simmel calls "individual centralization," "subordination under a plurality," and "subordination to a principle" lie, quite as clearly as in Weber, the historical models presented by the successive phases of modern European polity in its movement from monarchy to republic to domination by impersonal organizations and norms. Nearly all of his illustrations of the three types are drawn from European history. To observe this is in no way to diminish the scientific applicability of the three types to the comparative study of authority and power. It is merely to emphasize once again the deep roots that the central concepts of modern sociology have in a special set of historical circumstances.

Superordination and Subordination begins with an analysis of the nature of domination and its relation to the minute elements of human association. Authority, Simmel tells us, is by its nature *interactive*. Domination, far from being one-sided, as it might at first sight appear to be, is in fact determined by expectation of the nature of the *obedience* it will receive. In the most extreme cases of personal subordination, Simmel tells us, there is still a considerable measure of personal freedom. So-called absolute coercion is always relative; its condition is our desire to escape from the threatened punishment or from other consequences of our disobedience. Only in cases of direct physical violation can it be said that the subordinate's freedom has been wholly destroyed in a super-subordination relationship. Obedience, in short, shapes domination quite as much as domination shapes obedience. No one, Simmel observes, "wishes that his influence completely determine the other individual. He rather wants this influence, this determination of the other, to act back upon *him*. Even the abstract will-to-dominate, therefore, is a case of interaction. This will draws its satisfaction from the fact that the acting or suffering of the other, his positive or negative condition, offers itself to the dominator as the product of *his* will." [119]

In the most extreme case of domination—master and slave—there is still, Simmel insists, a residual degree of sociation that robs domination of the unilateral character commonly ascribed to it. But when, through processes of "objectification"—that is, the reduction of persons to objects—individuals become known chiefly as classes of *things* (as in the modern working class where individual workers are unknown to those hiring them and where an impersonal commodity, "labor," is sold), then there is "as little ground for speaking of sociation as there is in the case of the carpenter and his bench." [120] Authority of persons, in contrast to domination of things, "presupposes in a much higher degree than is usually recognized a freedom on the part of the person subjected to authority. Even where authority seems to 'crush' him, it is based not *only* on coercion or compulsion to yield to it."

The unique character of authority is significant for social life in the most varied ways. One of the most significant is the relation of authority to the gradually acquired sense of objectivity in human perception and judgment. A person of superior authority acquires "an overwhelming weight of his opinions, a faith, or a confidence which have the character of objectivity." . . . By acting "authoritatively," the quantity of his significance is transformed into a new quality; it assumes for his environment the physical state—metaphorically speaking—of objectivity.[121] Here too, plainly, Simmel and Durkheim are very close.

Reciprocity is the essence of personal authority, but something else comes into the picture with the large assemblage: a diminution of reciprocity and an intensification of sheer domination. "It is the absence of this reciprocity which accounts for the observation that the tyranny of a group over its own members is worse than that of a prince over his subjects." Simmel's development of this point is different from Tocqueville's but the result is approximately the same: the inexorable expansion of the tolerable limits of power over oneself when this power is conceived as arising from relationships of which one is a part. "The group—and by no means the political group alone—conceives of its members, not as confronting it, but as being included by it as its own links. This often results in a peculiar inconsiderateness toward the members, which is very different from a ruler's personal cruelty. Wherever there is, formally, confrontation (even if, continually, it comes *close* to submission), there is interaction; and, in principle, interaction always contains some limitation of *each* party to the process (although there may be individual exceptions to this rule). Where superordination shows an extreme inconsiderateness, as in the case of the group that simply *disposes* of its members, there no longer is any confrontation with its form of interaction, which involves spontaneity, and hence limitation, of both superordinate and subordinate elements." [122] What Tocqueville saw in public opinion, using large-scale political democracy as his framework, Simmel sees at every level of association, in the sociologically precise terms of subordination of individual role and identity to membership in the group.

We may turn now to Simmel's three fundamental types of superordination and subordination: (1) that wielded by an individual, as monarch, the father in a patriarchal family, manorial lord, or business proprietor; (2) that wielded by a group or association over its members, as in modern republics and democracies; and (3) that wielded by an objective principle in which office or impersonal organization or technology, rather than the personalities of human beings, is dominant. All three, as noted above, may be seen as conceptual distillations of European historical experience.

INDIVIDUAL CENTRALIZATION OF AUTHORITY What Simmel calls superordination by a single individual is reflective, he tells us, of the earlier history of Europe: in commonwealth, family, and church.

It is the rule of the single person that underlies the first unification of the group. The historic success of Judaism and Christianity in bringing individuals out of diverse tribal and kinship loyalties was the consequence of centralization: in these cases, centralization of deity. The rise of the modern state would not have been possible save in terms of the focal point represented by the one—the monarch. Only rule by one makes the *ruled* conscious of itself as a society with its own interests. This may result in conflict, in dissociation, but Simmel shows how such conflict may be the further basis of unity. He notes, as had Tocqueville, the interactive relation between centralization and leveling. There are, however, different types of leveling. "The leveling most welcome to despotism . . . is that of differences in rank, not in character. A society homogeneous in character and tendency, but organized in several rank orders, resists despotism strongly, while a society in which numerous kinds of characters exist side by side with organically inarticulate equality, resists it only slightly." [123] He observes the fondness of despots for persons of middle range of ability. Despots, he writes in a Tocquevillian epigram, "only love servants of average talent."

How does one rationalize normatively the disproportion involved in one-man rule? "The point is that the structure of a society in which only one person rules while the great mass lets itself be ruled makes normative sense only by virtue of a specific circumstance: that the mass, the ruled element, injects only *parts* of all personalities which compose it into the mutual relationship, whereas the ruler contributes *all* of *his* personality. The ruler and the individual subject do not enter the relationships with the same quantity of their personalities." [124] Here, under the rubric of authority, Simmel comes back to the theme that we found in his analysis of the group: the unequal "giving" by the individual, from group to group, of himself. Groups are characteristically "different according to the proportion between the members' total personalities and those parts of their personalities with which they fuse in the 'mass.' The measure of their governability depends on this difference in quanta." [125]

But leveling is not the only correlate of domination by a single individual. There is a second; one "in which the group takes on the form of a pyramid. The subordinates face the ruler in gradations of power. Layers whose volume becomes ever smaller and whose significance becomes ever greater lead from the lowest mass to the top of the pyramid." [126] The pyramid may originate in either of two ways: first, in the full autocratic power of the ruler who lets the content of his authority "glide downward" while holding its form and title to himself. Generally, over a period of time, the power of the highest echelons then tends to wither, resulting in ever increasing autonomy of the lower elements of the pyramid. Second, in the conversion of authorities previously autonomous into ordered phases of the power pyramid. Here the process begins at the bottom, autonomy is traded, as it were, for the security of membership in the pyramid. Both of these types originate clearly in the political history of Europe, and Simmel is as sensitive to this as Weber. But here, as elsewhere, it is their applicability to non-political structures—to church, school, class, and clan—that also interests him. There can be a mixture of the two types of gradation, and, as Simmel notes, the history of Western feudalism illustrates this mixture.

There is, Simmel concludes with Durkheim, an indestructibility and eternality of one-man rule. The image of the one remains long after revolution and change have swept away monarchs and emperors. "It is the peculiar strength of domination by one person to survive its own death, as it were—by transferring its own color to structures whose very significance is the negation of such domination." [127] Even revolutionary democracy, he notes, is conceived as "nothing but royalty turned upside down, and equipped with the same qualities. Rousseau's 'volonté générale' to which, he teaches, everybody must submit without resistance, has entirely the character of the absolute monarch." [128]

Simmel notes the recurrent phenomenon in history of the group subjecting itself by preference to the *outsider:* the person whose lack of inner knowledge of the group is magnificently compensated for by objectivity on, and immunity to, the group's inner hostilities and suspicions. In medieval society, Simmel remarks, it was unthinkable that anyone— noble, guildsman, churchman, or family member—be governed, judged, by one not of his own social kind. Modern life is more variegated, however. It has introduced a new attitude toward this. "In general . . . we can say that the lower a group is as a whole and the more, therefore, every member of it is accustomed to subordination, the less will the group allow one of its members to rule it. And, inversely, the higher a group is as a whole, the more likely it is that it subordinates itself only to one of its peers. In the first case, domination by the member, the like person, is difficult because everybody is low; in the second case, it is easier because everybody stands high." [129]

SUBORDINATION UNDER A PLURALITY   As the image of the monarch underlies the ideal type of the first, it is the image of the republic that underlies this second general type. Three points made by Simmel are deserving of emphasis.

In the first place, the *objectivity* of plural rule—that is, its incorporation of dominance within the laws and processes of the entire group rather than within the one symbolic figure—is matched by its tendency toward greater *impersonality*. This can have good consequences. The ancient slaves of Sparta, the feudal peasants of Prussia, and the modern inhabitants of India all showed understandable preference for governance by the state—state slavery, state domain, English state—over governance by private interests. But, by the same token, cruelties committed by republics to those outside often exceed those committed by individual rulers. The lot of subject peoples was harsher under the Roman republic than under the emperors and there are few examples of harsher treatment of groups—Irish, Dissenters, Scotch, Papists—than those revealed by the modern history of England, which on the other hand has the most resplendent record of all nations in its justice to *individuals*.[130] And repeatedly in European history we are struck, Simmel observes, by the greater proneness of the monarch to render popular aid than anything to be found in the collective will of the feudal nobility or the later republic. And, Simmel observes, while the modern state can legally condemn an individual to death, it cannot pardon him; pardon remains the prerogative of the individual monarch or president or governor.

The second point that Simmel makes is the historical tendency toward *increasing corporateness* of plural will or governance. Although personal rule is required to bring the identity of the group into being in the first instance, it is the gradual transference of the center of gravity from person to collectivity that gives the latter durability. Thus, "the growth of democratic consciousness in France has been derived (among other things) from the fact that, since the fall of Napoleon I, changing governmental powers followed one another in rapid succession. Each one of them was incompetent, uncertain, and trying to gain the favor of the masses—whereby every citizen was bound to become deeply aware of his own social significance. Although he was subject to every one of these governments, he nevertheless felt himself to be strong, because he formed the lasting element in all the change and contrast among the successive regimes." [131]

Simmel is also concerned with the process of what he calls the outvoting of minorities by majorities, by which he means the modern (in contrast to the medieval) practice of minority views becoming overruled, even dissolved, by the majority. To some students of Simmel this section has had the appearance of archaic oddity. What his often rarefied terminology covers, however, is the significant problem of the maintenance of cultural, ethnic, and geographic pluralism in a society which, having become increasingly politicized, reduces more and more matters of survival to the political processes of the vote. Groups, which in the ages of the past could maintain identity even in the face of armed hostility, find it increasingly difficult to do so when all issues and tensions are assimilated by the political process and, hence, at the mercy of majority vote. It is significant, he remarks, that only rarely has majority outvoting been defended on the simple ground of the superior right of the majority. More often, distinguishable will of the whole association is presumed to lie latent and majority supremacy is rationalized as the majority's revelation by vote of what the total or real will actually is. This, of course, is what Rousseau declared the legitimate function of voting to be in its relation to the General Will.

SUBORDINATION TO A PRINCIPLE Here Simmel is concerned with objective circumstance. He describes it as the "fundamental transition of the relationship of obedience from personalism to objectivism, a transition which cannot be derived from anticipation of utilitarian consequence." [132] He compares subordination to *objects*—for example, land or machines—with personal subordination, finding the former generally a "humiliatingly harsh and unconditional kind of subordination. For, inasmuch as a man is subordinate by virtue of belonging to a thing, he himself psychologically sinks to the category of mere thing." [133]

It is easy to see the relation of this type of domination to the whole pattern of modernism, with its triumph of process, organization, and sheer physical matter over the individual. Modern society leads, Simmel argues, to a multiplication of situations in which individuals find themselves under this "objective" type of power. The status of the modern worker is a case in point. As long as the relationship of wage labor was conceived of as "rental contract" something was retained of the worker's subordination to a *person*—to the entrepreneur." "But once the work contract is considered, not as the renting of a person, but as the purchase of a piece of merchandise, that is, labor, then this element of personal subordination is eliminated . . . The worker is no longer subject as a person but only as the servant of an objective, economic procedure." [134] Objective power, metropolis, alienation: the three comprise, for Simmel, an unholy trinity.

But there is a second connotation of objectivism: one that may ultimately amount to the same kind of impersonal power but that nonetheless requires differentiation. Objectivism can also mean a transfer of power from person or group to social *norm*. Thus, objectification of power is revealed by such conceptions as the supremacy of the law, of the office, of the command, of abstract moral commandment. In the beginning the adjuration against killing had force only because of the identity of the person who commanded against it—chief, king, or god. But in time, "thou shalt not kill" came to assume an impersonal, objective force. Simmel's discussion of objectivism, while very close to Durkheim's treatment of the authority of the collective conscience, differs in one important respect: for Durkheim, the collective precedes, historically, and always gives force to the personal; for Simmel, however, the personal precedes the collective and supplies the lasting element of the authority that inheres even in objective circumstance.

There remains the relation between domination and freedom. Like Tocqueville, Simmel sees freedom not only as the gain by an individual or group of liberation from power, but, equally, as the utilization of freedom for domination of others. "If liberation from subordination is examined more closely . . . it almost always reveals itself as, at the same time, a gain in domination—either in regard to those previously superordinate, or in regard to a newly formed stratum that is destined to definitive subordination." [135] He uses Puritanism in England as a case in point and also the role of the Third Estate in France during and after the Revolution. On the latter Simmel's words are perceptive and profound: "By means of its economic power, the Third Estate made the other, previously higher estates dependent upon itself; but, this effect and the whole emancipation of the Third Estate derived its rich content and its important consequences only because there existed (or, rather, there was formed in the same process) a Fourth Estate which the Third could exploit and above which it could rise." [136] A final example Simmel adduces is that of the history of the church in Western Europe. Freedom of the church, he writes, "usually does not consist in the liberation from superordinate secular powers alone but, through this liberation, in dominion over these powers. The church's liberty of teaching, for instance, means that the state obtains citizens who are inculcated by the church and stand under its suggestion; whereby the state comes often enough under the domination of the church." [137]

The freedom granted a group, Simmel observes, can have two aspects, depending on the spirit in which it is granted and the status of the group receiving it. On the one hand it can represent "esteem, a right, a power." But on the other hand it can reflect "exclusion and a contemptuous indifference on the part of the higher power." He cites the history of the Jews, in their relation to the society around them, as striking instances of each—either in single or mixed form.[138]

Between freedom and equality there is an eternally ambiguous relation. "To the extent that general freedom prevails, there also prevails general equality. For general freedom only entails the negative fact that there is no domination." But equality, although appearing as the early consequence of freedom, proves to be only a kind of transitional state. Simmel is virtually quoting Tocqueville when he writes: "Typically speaking, nobody is satisfied with the position he occupies in regard to his fellow creatures; everybody wishes to attain one which is, in some sense, more favorable." Thus the first affinity of freedom is broken quickly, for the impulse that generates, in the name of freedom, the first striving to become *equal* to the power that dominates continues to generate the desire to *exceed* that power and others like it.[139]

5 STATUS

THE EMERGENCE OF CLASS

"The owl of Minerva," Hegel wrote, "flies at twilight." In no area of sociology is the appositeness of this maxim more striking than with respect to the study of social class. Only after the historic and essential bases of social class in European society had become tenuous and uncertain, had become threatened by forces such as political centralization, citizenship, and mass education—forces which would, in the long run, make class the weakest of all the traditional social unities under the modern regime—did the study of social stratification burst forth in full brilliance. Central to sociology's interest in stratification is its sharp distinction, from Tocqueville on, between social class and social status.

Interest in social hierarchy is not, to be sure, peculiar to the nineteenth century. The far-reaching idea of "the great chain of being" that had, from Plato down to the modern Enlightenment, fascinated European philosophers, suffusing metaphysics, biology, and cosmography, could not but have included the notion of a *social* chain of being: one that stretched from the lowly peasant through intermediate ranks and stations to monarch or emperor. References to "ranks," "orders," and "degrees" are strung out continuously in social and moral thought from the late Middle Ages on. A great deal of the social philosophy of Thomas Aquinas concerns the hierarchy of the organic community. Aside from a few religiously inspired equalitarian groups spawned for the most part by the Reformation—the chiliastic, millennial, and apocalyptic—it is hard to find moral philosophers prior to the mid-seventeenth century who would not have concurred with Shakespeare's words: "Take but degree away, untune that string, and hark! what discord follows; each thing meets in mere oppugnancy." Elizabethan dramatists and philosophical

174

essayists were literally obsessed by rank, estate, and station and their absolute necessity in the social order.[1]

When we come to Hobbes, however, in the middle of the seventeenth century, we find a suspicion of both aristocracy and the middle class; a suspicion founded on Hobbes's distrust of all intermediate social bodies in the monolithic structure of his Leviathan.[2] In natural-law theory as a whole in the century there is, with the one remarkable exception of Althusius, an exclusion of social class and rank from systematic consideration. The hostility that natural-law theorists manifested for the most part toward guilds and other corporations was extended, in theory at least, to aristocracy. Unlike such essential concepts as those of individual, state, and contract, the concept of social class had little if any theoretical role. Althusius, as I have suggested, is a major exception. His vision of society had as much room in it for the ordered gradations of social hierarchy as for community and corporation. But he stands alone.

With the onset of the Enlightenment, we see a sharp rise in criticism of traditional hierarchy—proceeding from the *philosophes'* general distaste for everything feudal in origin—and also in analytical interest in stratification. Rousseau's *Discourse on the Origin of Inequality,* for all its polemical overtones, contains a remarkable account of social stratification set within a developmental perspective and pivoted upon private property. Some of the Scottish moral philosophers—Hume, Ferguson, Adam Smith, and especially John Millars—gave searching attention to stratification. The latter's *Observations Concerning the Distinction of Ranks in Society* is a masterpiece of historico-ethnographic description and analysis.

But all of this is nothing compared to the intensity and comprehensiveness of treatments of stratification to be observed after the forces of revolutionary democracy and industrialism had gotten well under way in the nineteenth century. Conservatives, liberals, and radicals alike made the concept of social class fundamental to their writings. Such indeed was the fascination that the word "class" came to exert on the minds of intellectuals that John Stuart Mill was led to write in 1834: "They revolve in their eternal circle of landlords, capitalists and laborers, until they seem to think of the distinction of society into those three classes as if it were one of God's ordinances, not man's, and as little under human control as the division of day or night. Scarcely any one of them seems to have said to himself as a subject of inquiry, what changes the relations of those classes to one another are likely to undergo in the progress of society."[3] Mill's words applied to the economists, certainly, but not to the sociologists. As I shall emphasize in this chapter, it was of the very essence of sociology to be concerned with the future of class under the operation of historical forces. Indeed, in this concern lay the basis of the central conflict among sociologists in the century, with Tocqueville at one point on the continuum and Marx at the other.

The concept of social class, in distinction from the earlier concepts of hierarchy, is late eighteenth century. As Asa Briggs has written: "The concept of social 'class' with all its attendant terminology was a product of the large-scale economic and social changes of the late eighteenth and early nineteenth centuries. . . . There was no dearth of social conflicts in pre-industrial society, but they were not conceived of at the time in straight class terms. The change in nomenclature in the late eighteenth and early nineteenth centuries reflected a basic change not only in men's ways of viewing society but in society itself." [4]

Why did social class seem so paramount a reality to many minds when, as we have seen, processes of individualization, leveling, and fragmentation were endemic in the transition to the modern regime? Putting the question differently, why did the age-old conception of the *continuity* of hierarchy in society, the notion of a chain of being, now become supplanted by presentiments of discontinuity, even of conflict, among classes? The answer lies, in considerable part, in what Ostrogorski has called the "new species of subordination" that arose in the industrial world. "When manufacturing took the place of domestic labour, direct intercourse between the owners of factories and the shifting masses of workmen became impossible; henceforth their only points of contact were work and wages, governed by the stern law of supply and demand; they became anonymous abstractions one to the other; they came together and parted without seeing each other. . . . They now belonged to different strata of society . . . marked by distinctions which varied according to the income of their members, and each distinction constituted a new line of demarcation and separation." [5] Whether these new strata were simply levels—tenuous and evanescent in the long run—or the hard social classes Marx thought them to be is not here the point. What is important is the sudden appearance of the terminology of class, a terminology that was to remain vital in social science for a full century.

It is even possible, as Raymond Williams has shown, to date the successive appearances of the new terms of class. "It is only at the end of the eighteenth century that the modern structure of *class,* in its social sense, begins to be built up. First comes *lower classes* to join *lower orders,* which appears earlier in the eighteenth century. Then, in the 1790s we get *higher classes; middle classes* and *middling classes* follow at once; *working classes* in about 1815; *upper classes* in the 1820s. *Class prejudice, class legislation, class consciousness, class conflict* and *class war* follow. . . ." [6]

THE MODEL OF CLASS

Something must be said of the significant role held by the English landed class in the minds of those who, from the late eighteenth century on, were concerned with the probable shape of stratification in the new society that was forming around industry. Nothing quite like the English landed class existed on the Continent, a fact emphasized by the references to it that we find in French and German writings throughout the nineteenth century. That this class was, in one way or another, a model for all those in England whose intellectual roots lay in Burke's admiration for it is hardly strange. It also excited the respect of Hegel, Tocqueville, and Taine. I am more interested, however, in its conceptual function in providing the *pattern,* so to speak, of what writers were to take as the substance of true class, in whatever context. I believe it was the English landed class above any other that became the analytical model for what, it was widely assumed, would be fulfilled, *mutatis mutandis,* in the new economy of capitalism. The English landed class was, I think we are justified in saying, the *known* from which many students of stratification —including Marx—mapped their way into the new unknown of industrial society. A good many radicals and conservatives alike foresaw the industrial bourgeoisie as the successor of the landed class, like it in structure, status, and power, differing only in economic context.

The relevance of the English landed class to both radical and conservative theories lies in its detachment from any formal system of political law and from any apparent external force. In France and on the Continent in general social classes of the older order had been more nearly in the nature of estates, bounded, reinforced, and maintained by laws of the realm. Not so in England. Despite the powerful role that this class played in political affairs, it was not a creature of law and nothing in the English constitution pertained to it.

There was, first, its economic unity founded largely upon landed property. It would be wrong to say that no other forms of property were recognized, but it is fair to note that men who made their fortunes in commerce and business did not usually gain recognition from this class until they had acquired land and based their existence upon it. From generation to generation landed property tended to remain in the same family hands.

Equally notable was the political unity of the class. Economic ownership and political power coalesced almost perfectly. This was to be seen not merely in the overwhelming number of Parliamentary seats that went to members of the landed class and in the astonishing degree of consensus that reigned among them, but in the monopoly they held of administrative functions in local and county government. "The great unpaid," as they were to be called by a later historian, is an apt term. Without formal compensation of any kind, without indeed any position in the law of the land, they performed throughout England the essential tasks of administration, including much of the dispensing of justice. It was the generally high sense of responsibility with which this class operated at local levels—coupled with the absence of the kind of aggressive and independent legal profession that France had produced—that for long restrained a true bureaucracy in England and made of this class a model for all conservatives.

There was little if any element of caste. No legal boundaries existed to mark classes and no restrictions of a legal sort prevented others from participating. We know that occasionally men did rise from below to attain influential places in government and society. But they were rare for, although the landed class was not closed, openings were few and could close with extraordinary speed. Overwhelmingly, national politics, local administration, justice, and service in the commissioned areas of the armed forces were the functions of this one, socially homogeneous class.

So too was there a high degree of convergence of the various attributes of social status. Except for the handful of intellectuals largely concentrated in London, the only people of education were members of this class, and both the public schools and the two great universities were shaped in purpose and result by landed class needs. The norms of what constituted an educated man were universally understood. Language, including accent, could identify a man in a moment as belonging to this class. All were of the Established Church, most of the higher clergy were themselves products of the landed group, and even when they weren't, their loyalties to it were strong.

Over the whole structure towered the governing conception of the gentleman. Hard to define in abstract terms, perhaps, the reality of the gentleman was nevertheless as unmistakable and as universal as that of

the land itself. In dress, opinion, taste, and conviction the landed gentleman set the life style of all that was invested with prestige and power. It
was the pervasive image of the gentleman that had so much to do with
maintaining the solidarity of this class, with shoring up its political and
economic strength, and with making its behavior and desires so universal
in England of that day. All of this we know from the countless letters
and diaries of the age.

We should note that this class was functional in sociological respects. Between the social attributes of prestige and the realities of economic and political power there was an almost perfect convergence, leading to a degree of solidarity and self-awareness that could hardly have
been exceeded. Criteria of class were clear, easily identifiable, and substantially the same everywhere in England. Knowledge of a family's
standing with respect to any one of the criteria was sufficient to place
that family fairly accurately with respect to other criteria. Finally, there
was stability of this convergence of attributes from one generation to
another. In sum, if it was the social norm of the gentleman that surmounted the structure, it was the near monopoly of political power and
its deep roots in property that provided the foundations.

The rugged strength of this landed class may be inferred from the
extent to which its purely cultural properties—intellectual interests, education, mode of speech, life style in general—remained evocative in England after its real economic and political roots had been cut by economic
change and political reform. Nowhere else in Europe, much less in the
United States, has the cultural reality of an upper class remained so
vivid, so continuously influential in all spheres of government and society, as in England. Despite profound changes in political structure and in
the character of wealth, despite the broadening of the educational base,
an upper-class culture remains even today significant beyond anything
known elsewhere in Western society. And no matter what the diversity of
economic channels through which this culture flows today—industrial,
governmental, and other—its historical source is the landed class I have
just described.

The Challenge to Class

From our point of view, however, the essential significance of this
class in the nineteenth century was conceptual. It became, as I have suggested, a kind of ideal type, a theoretical model, of what substantive

social class is and what its political and economic power in society might be. This class was, of course, pre-capitalist, quasi-feudal in character. It had a great deal more to do with the stability of the new economic and political orders than spokesmen of either of the latter were willing to admit. They, chiefly the economists—classical and socialist alike—contented themselves with describing the new classes that capitalism was supposedly ushering in: industrial owners and workers. Given the abstract mode of economic analysis and the assumption of an autonomous, self-operating economic order, the reinforcing and often vital influence of the landed class was rarely perceived. Nor were the intricate interweavings of landed and industrial wealth in both old and new families. Economists, for the most part, were prisoners of categories bequeathed by Smith and Ricardo.

But to the sociologically minded the outlines of the old, landed class were distinct and brilliant. And a large number of minds sought in the new economic strata of capitalism the same convergence of political, economic, and cultural elements that were so plain in pre-capitalist classes of aristocracy and peasantry. Why, it was asked, should not the future of capitalism reveal the development of an upper and a lower class within its own economic structure that would be as politically and socially distinct, as culturally pervasive, as anything to be found in the pre-capitalist order? It was in reply to this question that the two major types of evaluation of European stratification were predicated.

The major controversy in the study of stratification, at least among the sociologists, was not that of social class versus equalitarianism. It was the subtler and theoretically more fundamental one of *social class* versus *social status:* of a view of the new society resting upon the assumed existence of solid, substantive social class opposed to a view resting upon the assumption of the erosion of class and its replacement by fluctuant, mobile, status groups and by status-seeking individuals.

We may put the question in this fashion: Was the new society that was being ushered in, a society founded upon citizen, entrepreneur, and technologist, a society based on the imperious, if uncertain and often misled, will of the masses, dominated by new structures of administrative power and flooded by new forms of wealth, driven by novel and incessant pressures for educational, religious, and social equality; was this society to be, as had been all previous forms of society, organized primarily in terms of class layers, each holding the same union of economic, intellectual, educational, and political properties that had characterized social ranks in the old order? Or, in sharp contrast, could the acids of

modernity be seen working in as destructive a fashion upon the bases of
social class—in any viable sense of that word—as they were upon village
community, extended family, and the whole network of moral-cultural
relations that had also been born in the pre-capitalist, pre-democratic,
pre-rationalist age?

Answers to these questions form a major aspect of sociology in the
century and they are, of course, closely related to treatments of other
elements of the social and political order. That is, how one approached
the problems of community and authority foretold much of how he
would approach the problem of stratification. Bias was as vivid here as it
was in all other major issues in the century. On the one hand were those
who argued that social, political, and economic inequalities in the new,
emerging society could be as accurately described in terms of social class
as the inequalities that had been contained in the old order. In the bourgeoisie, exponents of this view—radicals for the most part—could see,
or foresee, the same kind of formidable unity of power, wealth, and
status in the industrial world that had characterized the landed aristocracy for hundreds of years in Europe and was even yet a force to be
reckoned with. Marx became, as we know, the pre-eminent representative of this body of interpretation, and the impress of his ideas is with us
still.

On the other hand, and in sharp contrast, were those who, from the
very beginning, saw no more likelihood of substantive social class forming within the new order than they did genuine community, of which
class, in their eyes, was a notable type. The fragmentation of the old
order, resulting in the release of long-pent-up elements of wealth and
power and status, would lead, it was argued, to a scrambling of social
categories, to an individualization of stratification that would result in
the ascendancy not of class but of social status—which is at once more
mobile, individually autonomous, and diversified than class. Tocqueville
is the major representative of this view.

I do not wish to overdraw the contrast. It is not black and white.
None of the sociologists was oblivious to class in one degree or another.
Even Tocqueville could refer to the "class" of manufacturers and to an
economic power wielded by manufacturers that seemed to him fraught
with danger to democracy. But, as we shall see, Tocqueville uses the
term class in so denatured a sense that it is left merely as a kind of level,
at best an interest group; not a social stratum characterized by the kind
of solidification of political, economic, and social elements that had
characterized the structure of the landed aristocracy.

The difference between political conservatives and radicals on the nature and reality of social class is a kind of anagram of the existential and the utopian. Conservatives, beginning with Burke, said, in effect, that while social class should be one of the supports of a truly stable and free society, it was all too likely that the combined effect of political centralization, social atomization, new types of wealth, and the transfer of the center of political gravity from rural to urban areas would in fact destroy the substance of social class, reduce it to mass rubble. No single element is more central to the social philosophies of Burke, Coleridge, and Carlyle in England, to Bonald, Maistre, and Balzac in France, and to Haller and Hegel in Germany than that of social hierarchy. And, equally, nothing is more common to these writers than the assumption that economic and political modernism was rapidly destroying the contexts of hierarchy. Auguste Comte was powerfully affected by conservative veneration for hierarchy, and we find in his early writings sharp criticism of the egalitarian doctrines of Enlightenment and Revolution and, in his *Positive Polity,* rigorous prescription for the organization of the Positivist utopia in terms of distinct social classes.

Radical thinkers, on the other hand, took the position that while the extermination of social hierarchy had the highest priority in social action and while equality was, even over freedom, the sovereign value in their axiology, the harsh facts were that capitalist society would be as class-structured, as class-dominated, and class-oriented as was any preceding stage of man's social development. And political democracy would not, could not, affect this. From William Cobbett in England, through Proudhon in France, to Marx in Germany, radical doctrine made the reality of social class in capitalism fundamental to its thinking.

These two ideological positions are, so to speak, magnetic poles in the study of stratification in the nineteenth century. Among the sociologists, Tocqueville is as perfectly expressive of the one as Marx is of the other, and what eventually emerges—chiefly in Weber—as the dominant sociological view of stratification is best seen as a resultant of the two forces represented by Tocqueville and Marx. If for a long time the Marxian view exerted the greater influence, it was never absolute (except among Marxists), and more recently it is clear that Tocqueville's perspective has become ascendant.

THE TRIUMPH OF STATUS—TOCQUEVILLE

Tocqueville is the first and, throughout the nineteenth century, the major exponent of the view that the modern regime is characterized not by the solidification but by the fragmentation of social class, with the key elements dispersed: power to the masses and to centralized bureaucracy, wealth to an ever-enlarging middle class, and status to the varied and shifting sectors of society which, in the absence of true class, become the theaters of the unending and agonizing competition among individuals for the attainment of the marks of status.

The clue to the modern order lies for Tocqueville in the relentless leveling of classes that has characterized the history of the West since the end of the Middle Ages. "In running over the pages of our history, we shall scarcely find a single great event of the last seven hundred years that has not promoted equality of condition." [7] Given this formidable background of history, is it likely, he asks, that capitalism or any other feature of modern society will arrest a tendency now so deeply embedded in historical reality?

"The gradual development of the principle of equality is a providential fact. It has all the chief characteristics of such a fact: it is universal, it is durable, it constantly eludes all human interference, and all events as well as all men contribute to its progress. Would it be wise to imagine that a social movement, the causes of which lie so far back, can be checked by the efforts of one generation? Can it be believed that the democracy which has overthrown the feudal system and vanquished kings will retreat before tradesmen and capitalists? Will it stop now that it has grown so strong and its adversaries so weak?" [8]

Tocqueville's answer to these questions forms the theme of his sociology of stratification. The dissolution of social class that began in the late Middle Ages under the twin impacts of political centralization and social individualism can only complete itself in the modern order. The dispersion of power among the democratic mass, the ever more prominent place occupied by political bureaucracy, the virtual enshrinement of the norm of equality, the incessant competition for wealth in the fluid forms that capitalism has brought, and the profound urge to status achievement in a society where each man regards himself as the equal of all—these and other forces make true social class impossible. There are, of course, economic strata, even extremes of wealth. But these do not promote a sense belonging to a class.

"I am aware that among a great democratic people there will always be some members of the community in great poverty and others in great opulence; but the poor, instead of forming the great majority of the nation, as is always the case in aristocratic communities, are comparatively few in number, and the laws do not bind them together by ties of irremediable and hereditary penury. . . . As there is no longer a race of poor men, so there is no longer a race of rich men; the latter spring up daily from the multitude and relapse into it again. Hence, they do not form a distinct class which may be easily marked out and plundered; and, moreover, as they are connected with the mass of their fellow citizens by a thousand secret ties, the people cannot assail them without inflicting an injury upon themselves.

"Between these two extremes of democratic communities stands an innumerable multitude of men almost alike, who, without being exactly either rich or poor, possess sufficient property to desire the maintenance of order, yet not enough to excite envy." [9]

It is in these terms exactly that Tocqueville's view of class, class consciousness, and class conflict may be seen as the obverse of Marx's. The tensions of democratic-commercial society, far from promoting revolution, constantly diminish the possibility of revolution. "Such men," Tocqueville writes of the great democratic middle, "are the natural enemies of violent commotions; their lack of agitation keeps all beneath them and above them still and secures the balance of the fabric of society. Not, indeed, that even these men are contented with what they have got or that they feel a natural abhorrence for a revolution in which they might share the spoil without sharing the calamity; on the contrary, they desire, with unexampled ardor, to get rich, but the difficulty is to know from whom riches can be taken. The same state of society that constantly prompts desires, restrains these desires within necessary limits; it gives men more liberty of changing, and less interest in change." [10]

Such class lines as do persist are waning evidences of the mild influence that the landed class once held in such places as New York and the stronger influences that the planters held in the South before the American Revolution. "In most of the states situated to the southwest of the Hudson some great English proprietors had settled who had imported with them aristocratic principles and the English law of inheritance . . . They constituted a superior class having ideas and tastes of its own and forming the center of political action. This kind of aristocracy sympathized with the body of the people, whose passions and interests it easily embraced; but it was too weak and too shortlived to excite either love or hatred. This was the class which headed the insurrection in the South and furnished the best leaders of the American Revolution." [11]

But the gathering tides of democracy after the American Revolution sterilized the role of the quasi-aristocracy, and there are left, Tocqueville emphasizes, only the shifting categories of rich and poor, categories not likely to produce classes in the true sense; and so far as political power is concerned, it is more likely, in a democracy, Tocqueville argues, to lie with the masses of the poor than with the rich. "Among civilized nations, only those who have nothing to lose ever revolt," and while "the natural anxiety of the rich may produce a secret dissatisfaction," their sheer devotion to wealth and property will ensure almost any degree of political compliance.[12]

The character of wealth in a democracy tends to make true class impossible. It is typically commercial, trading, and manufacturing wealth, not landed. Democracy not only "swells the number of workingmen, but leads men to prefer one kind of labor to another; and while it diverts them from agriculture, it encourages their taste for commerce and manufactures." [13] Commerce does not stimulate the democratic passion for well-being; the reverse is true. "All the causes that make the love of worldly welfare predominate in the heart of man are favorable to the growth of commerce and manufactures. Equality of conditions is one of those causes; it encourages trade, not directly, by giving men a taste for business, but indirectly, by strengthening and expanding in their minds a taste for well-being." [14]

It is, in short, a political interpretation of capitalism that Tocqueville gives us and, characteristically, he places the interpretation in the context of democracy's difference from aristocracy. Under aristocracy, the rich are at the same time the governing power; they do not have time for the responsibilities of trade and commerce, and where an aristocrat does attempt, now and then, to enter trade, the counteractive opinion of his peers is sudden and compelling.

In democratic countries, on the other hand, "where money does not lead those who possess it to political power, but often removes them from it, the rich do not know how to spend their leisure. They are driven into active life by the disquietude and the greatness of their desires, by the extent of their resources, and by the taste for what is extraordinary, which is always felt by those who rise, by whatever means, above the crowd. Trade is the only road open to them." [15]

In one respect only does Tocqueville see the outlines—though only the outlines—of a class, a new mode of aristocracy forming within capitalism. This is the manufacturing class. Tocqueville did not regard the system of division of labor in the optimistic light of his liberal contemporaries. It is one of the marks of his alienated view of modern society that he sees, not improvement, but degradation in the specialization of the worker. Such degradation he thought a permanent aspect of the system and one that would only heighten the superiority and influence of the manufacturing class in democracy. The latter becomes more powerful and, as a *category,* more intrenched, as the working class becomes more degraded. "Men grow more alike in the one, more different in the other; and inequality increases in the less numerous class in the same ratio in which it decreases in the community. Hence it would appear, on searching to the bottom, that aristocracy would naturally spring out of the bosom of democracy." [16]

So it might seem. But what Tocqueville sees as the perpetual mobility of commercial democracy makes such an aristocracy impossible, in fact. There is too much circulation of the members of the classes—especially of the rich class, which is constantly losing its members, to be replaced by others. Thus, and here is the essence of Tocqueville's view of class in capitalism, the very converse of Marx's: "though there are rich men, the class of rich men does not exist; for these rich individuals have no feeling or purposes, no traditions or hopes, in common; there are individuals, therefore, but no definite class.

"Not only are the rich not compactly united among themselves, but there is no real bond between them and the poor. Their relative position is not a permanent one; they are constantly drawn together or separated by their interests. . . . The one contracts no obligation to protect nor the other to defend, and they are not permanently connected either by habit or by duty. . . . An aristocracy thus constituted can have no great hold upon those whom it employs, and even if it succeeds in retaining them at one moment, they escape the next; it knows not how to will, and it cannot act." [17]

The differences here between Marx and Tocqueville are engaging. It is precisely *because* of the lack of reciprocal obligation between the manufacturers and workers, *because* of the dissolution of uniting bonds of protection and defense, that Marx sees the two classes becoming ever more distinct, each ever more inclusive of habits, ideas, and beliefs. But for Tocqueville true class can exist *only* in the presence of reciprocality, co-operation, and mutual dependence, and where these are gone, there can remain only levels, abstract strata, not true classes.

It is love of money and of the well-being associated with money that

Tocqueville finds the single most important factor in establishing the status system of democracies. This is indeed the major difference between democracy and aristocracy. In the latter, men enjoy physical comforts without really caring for them. "The heart of man is not so much caught by the undisturbed possession of anything valuable as by the desire, as yet imperfectly satisfied, of possessing it and by the incessant dread of losing it." [18]

"When . . . the distinctions of ranks are obliterated and privileges are destroyed, when hereditary property is subdivided and education and freedom are widely diffused, the desire of securing the comforts of the world haunts the imagination of the poor, and the dread of losing them that of the rich. Many scanty fortunes spring up; those who possess them have a sufficient share of physical gratifications to conceive a taste for these pleasures, not enough to satisfy it. They never procure them without exertion, and they never indulge in them without apprehension. They are therefore always straining to pursue or to retain gratifications so delightful, so imperfect, so fugitive." [19]

Not even Marx could exceed the emphasis Tocqueville places upon the role of money in democratic society and its determinative influence in matters of status. "Men living in democratic times have many passions, but most of their passions either end in the love of riches or proceed from it. The cause of this is not that their souls are narrower, but that the impotence of money is really greater at such times. When all the members of a community are independent of or indifferent to each other, the co-operation of each of them can be obtained only by paying for it: this infinitely multiplies the purposes to which wealth may be applied and increases its value. When the reverence that belonged to what is old has vanished, birth, condition, and profession no longer distinguish men, or scarcely distinguish them; hardly anything but money remains to create strongly marked differences between them and to raise some of them above the common level. The distinction originating in wealth is increased by the disappearance or diminution of all other distinctions. Among aristocratic nations, money reaches only to a few points on the vast circle of man's desire; in democracies, it seems to lead to all." [20]

Hence the incessant preoccupation with individual achievement, with social superiority and inferiority, with prestige, in democracy. The fateful combination of recession of social class and dissemination of political and moral equality leads to gnawing concern with status. Equality is, by its nature, a mercurial and elusive goal. It is possible to imagine a degree of freedom, Tocqueville writes, that would satisfy all men, but men will never establish any equality with which they can be contented. No matter how completely they equalize political, legal, and even economic conditions, the remaining differences and inequalities among them —intellectual, cultural, social—will only be magnified. "When inequality of conditions is the common law of society, the most marked inequalities do not strike the eye; when everything is nearly on the same level, the slightest are marked enough to hurt it. Hence the desire for equality always becomes more insatiable in proportion as equality is more complete." [21] Men become the more anxious about their own status and more apprehensive of that of others in proportion as the fixed lines of class dissolve and the ethos of democratic equality spreads. The role of money heightens this.

"Since in such communities nothing is stable, each man is haunted by a fear of sinking to a lower social level and by a restless urge to better his condition. And since money has not only become the sole criterion of a man's social status but has also acquired an extreme mobility—that is to say it changes hands incessantly, raising or lowering the prestige of individuals and families—everybody is feverishly intent on making money or, if already rich, on keeping his wealth intact." [22]

Quite apart from status anxiety, there is a built-in indecisiveness about one's status in the minds of those who live in times when aristocracy is fading. "When it is birth alone, independent of wealth, that classes men in society, everyone knows exactly what his own position is in the social scale; he does not seek to rise, he does not fear to sink. In a community thus organized, men of different castes communicate very little with one another; but if accident brings them together, they are ready to converse without hoping or fearing to lose their own position. Their intercourse is not on a footing of equality, but it is not constrained." [23]

But where a moneyed aristocracy succeeds to an aristocracy of birth, the reverse occurs. "As the social importance of men is no longer ostensibly and permanently fixed by blood and is infinitely varied by wealth, ranks still exist, but it is not easy to distinguish at a glance those who respectively belong to them. Secret hostilities then arise in the community; one set of men endeavor by innumerable artifices to penetrate, or to appear to penetrate, among those who are above them; another set are constantly in arms against these usurpers of their rights; or, rather, the same individual does both at once, and while he seeks to raise himself into a higher circle, he is always on the defensive against the intrusion of those below him." [24] Particularly in England, Tocqueville notes, are these phenomena of status invasion and status rejection notable.

In the United States, where a genuine aristocracy of birth was never more than faint and where money has become the controlling medium of everyone's social status, social intercourse is easier and freer of hostilities. The reserve that characterizes the Englishman's wary protection of status is lost to the American for whom failure to respond quickly and enthusiastically to any overture is cause for suspicion of snobbery. The American is slow to take insult in the easy idiom of democratic equality. "Despising no one on account of his station, he does not imagine that anyone can despise him for that cause, and until he has clearly perceived an insult, he does not suppose that an affront was intended." [25] Distinctions of rank in civil society being negligible and in political society nonexistent, the American does not feel compelled to either pay or require special attention from others.

It is different, however, when the American goes to Europe. There, for the first time, status, beginning with his own, becomes a perplexing problem. He becomes sensitive and captious, Tocqueville observes. Traces of rank persist, the privileges of birth and wealth cannot be overlooked, but they are not easily defined. "He is, therefore, profoundly ignorant of the place that he ought to occupy in this half-ruined scale of classes, which are sufficiently distinct to hate and despise each other, yet sufficiently alike for him to be always confounding them. He is afraid of ranking himself too high; still more is he afraid of being ranked too low. This twofold peril keeps his mind constantly on the stretch and embarrasses all he says and does." [26]

For such a man, society is not a recreation but a serious toil, Tocqueville writes. "He is like a man surrounded by traps. . . . He weighs your least actions, interrogates your looks, and scrutinizes all you say lest there should be some hidden allusion to affront him. I doubt whether there was ever a provincial man of quality so punctilious in breeding as he is: he endeavors to attend to the slightest rules of etiquette and does not allow one of them to be waived towards himself; he is full of scruples and at the same time of pretensions; he wishes to do enough, but fears to do too much, and as he does not very well know the limits of the one or of the other, he keeps up a haughty and embarrassed reserve." [27]

Americans, Tocqueville notes, are forever talking, when abroad, of the absolute equality that prevails in the United States. All praise it openly, yet it is as though each of them privately aspires to show that, for his part, he is an exception to the general equality of birth that he boasts of. Hardly an American exists "who does not claim some remote kindred with the first founders of the colonies; and as for the scions of the noble families of England, America seems to be covered with them." When an American of wealth reaches Europe, his first care is to surround himself with luxuries; "he is so afraid of being taken for the plain citizen of a democracy that he adopts a hundred distorted ways of bringing some new instance of his wealth before you every day. His house will be in the most fashionable part of the town; he will always be surrounded by a host of servants . . ." [28]

Reading the foregoing words, one cannot conquer the feeling that their chief relevance, as well as charm of insight, is to the status system in the United States itself—though not perhaps until a generation or two after Tocqueville's visit. Like so much in Tocqueville, his words have a value to the empirical realities of an American society that became manifest only in the 1880s. Tocqueville consistently underplays the role of the quasi-aristocracy in the United States formed by the great families of wealth and breeding that could trace their ancestry and holdings back to early colonial days. His words on the American in the presence of European aristocracy have in fact as much point when directed to the *new* American rich in the presence of these older strains of American wealth found in New York, Boston, and Charleston. His notebooks show that he was well aware of this.

Tocqueville was profoundly impressed by the master-servant relation in modern democratic-commercial society. His chapter on this subject is a kind of paradigm of the impact of democracy on the status structure of traditional society and is among the most important in the book.[29]

Under an aristocracy, Tocqueville notes, such as that in England, servants form a distinct class. Gradations of status within this class are as deeply textured as within the master class. Generations of servants may succeed one another without any change of position. Masters and servants form two communities and "are superposed one above the other, always distinct, but regulated by analogous principles. This aristocratic constitution does not exert a less powerful influence on the motions and manners of servants than on those of masters; and although the effects are different, the same cause may be traced." In such a servant class, notions of honor, service, virtue, and fame can take root, *mutatis mutandis,* even as they do among the masters. There is indeed a sort of "servile honor," and it is still possible in England to find men of noble and vigorous minds in the service of the great. Once, of course, this was

common, and there were many "who did not feel the servitude they bore
and who submitted to the will of their masters without any fear of their
displeasure." [30]

But, lower down, are the menials, those for whom the term *lackey*
was invented by the French in the old regime. "This word *lackey* served
as the strongest expression, when all others were exhausted, to designate
human meanness." [31] Permanent inequality of conditions inevitably creates a class whose very essence is willing and constant obedience; whose
own norms of achievement are bounded by unflagging obedience and
even anticipation of command. "In aristocracies the master often exercises, even without being aware of it, an amazing sway over the opinions,
the habits, and the manners of those who obey him, and his influence
extends even further than his authority.

"In aristocratic communities not only are there hereditary families
of servants as well as of masters, but the same families of servants adhere for several generations to the same families of masters (like two
parallel lines, which neither meet nor separate); and this considerably
modifies the mutual relations of these two classes of persons. Thus, although in aristocratic society the master and servant have no natural
resemblance, although, on the contrary, they are placed at an immense
distance on the scale of human beings by their fortune, education and
opinions, yet time ultimately binds them together. They are connected by
a long series of common reminiscences, and however different they may
be, they grow alike; while in democracies, where they are naturally almost alike, they always remain strangers to one another." [32] In the same
way that masters, in an aristocracy, come to regard their servants as
secondary and inferior extensions of themselves, servants regard themselves in the same light, and feel their own moods, fancies, pride, and
despair fluctuate with those of their masters.

But consider now the effects of the democratic revolution on this
relationship. "The laws and, partially public opinion, already declare
that no natural or permanent inferiority exists between the servant and
the master. But this new belief has not yet reached the innermost convic-
tions of the latter, or rather his heart rejects it; in the secret persuasion of
his mind the master thinks that he belongs to a peculiar and superior
race; he dares not say so, but he shudders at allowing himself to be
dragged to the same level. His authority over his servants becomes timid
and at the same time harsh; he has already ceased to entertain for them
the feelings of patronizing kindness which long uncontested power always produces, and he is surprised that, being changed himself, his serv-

ant changes also. He wants his attendants to form regular and permanent habits, in a condition of domestic service that is only temporary; he requires that they should appear contented with a pride of a servile condition which they will one day shake off, that they should sacrifice themselves to a man who can neither protect nor ruin them, and, in short, that they should contract an indissoluble engagement to a being like themselves and one who will last no longer than they will." [33]

And the servants? What Tocqueville calls a "confused and imperfect phantom of inequality" haunts their minds. They rebel in their hearts against a subordination that they have nominally chosen. "They consent to serve and they blush to obey; they like the advantages of service, but not the master; or, rather, they are not sure that they ought not themselves to be masters, and they are inclined to consider him who orders them as an unjust usurper of their own rights." [34]

"Then it is that the dwelling of every citizen offers a spectacle somewhat analogous to the gloomy aspect of political society. A secret and internal warfare is going on there between powers ever rivals and suspicious of one another . . . The lines that divide authority from oppression, liberty from license, and right from might are to their eyes so jumbled together and confused that no one knows exactly what he is or what he may be or what he ought to be. Such a condition is not democracy, but revolution." [35] Such a condition, in Tocqueville's mind, characterized France after the Revolution.

American society Tocqueville finds somewhere in between the two extremes of master-servant relations. The Americans, he writes, not only are unacquainted with the kind of man who forms the fixed servant class of aristocratic nations, they cannot believe that he ever existed. There is, to be sure, a class of menials and a class of masters, but like all other classes in democracy, "these classes are not always composed of the same individuals, still less of the same families; and those in command are not more secure of perpetuity than those who obey." [36]

In a fully developed democracy like the United States, servants are not only equal among themselves, "but it may be said that they are, in some sort, the equals of their masters." Within the terms of the covenant of domestic service, one is superior, the other inferior, but "beyond it they are two citizens of the commonwealth, two men." The American master-servant relation is comparable to the officer-soldier relation in democratic armies. Within the contract, subordination; out of it, equality.

The money contract of service will produce able and willing service within democracy's households, but there is not, cannot be, the kind of mutual devotion, the "warm and deep-seated affections which are sometimes kindled in the domestic service of aristocracy," nor will there be comparable instances of self-sacrifice. "In aristocracies masters and servants live apart, and frequently their only intercourse is through a third person; yet they commonly stand firmly by one another. In democratic countries, the master and the servant are close together; they are in daily personal contact, but their minds do not intermingle; they have common occupations, hardly ever common interests." [37]

Most of the servants Tocqueville found in the Northern states were Negro freedmen or children of freedmen. These, he writes, "occupy an uncertain position in the public estimation; by the laws they are brought up to the level of their masters; by the manners of the country they are firmly kept below it. They do not themselves clearly know their proper place and are almost always either insolent or craven." [38]

Tocqueville was deeply struck—and appalled—by the position of the Negro in the United States. He was horrified by the paradox of educated and morally cultivated Southern whites able to inflict awful punishments and deprivations upon their Negro slaves without remorse. It was proof, in Tocqueville's mind, of the dependence of modern Western humanitarianism upon equality rather than upon level of education or civilization. No nation, he thought, approached the United States in the humaneness of its penal institutions and the relative gentleness of its criminal laws. But all of this was within the context of white society alone, where equalitarian sentiment dominated. Very different was the state of the Negro under slavery; Southern white masters might be educated and be humane among themselves, "yet the slaves still endure frightful misery there and are constantly exposed to very cruel punishments." The same man "who is full of humanity toward his fellow creatures when they are at the same time his equals becomes insensible to their afflictions as soon as that equality ceases. His mildness should therefore be attributed to the equality of conditions rather than to civilization and education." [39]

From this, however, it does not follow in Tocqueville's mind that the only requisite for establishment of an equalitarian temper between white and Negro is legal emancipation. Abolitionists often wrote as though simple emancipation would solve everything, but Tocqueville could see in a liberation that was *only* legal the seed of bitterness and hostility that could eventually erupt into revolution. The one possibility indeed that he could see of revolution in the United States was that engendered by the Negro *after* he had been formally freed by law.[40] The following words are prescient:

"I am obliged to confess that I do not regard the abolition of slavery as a means of warding off the struggle of the two races in the Southern states. The Negroes may long remain slaves without complaining; but if they are once raised to the level of freemen, they will soon revolt at being deprived of almost all their civil rights; and as they cannot become the equals of the whites, they will speedily show themselves as enemies." [41]

There are but two modes of action really feasible with respect to Negro slaves, Tocqueville thinks; either emancipate them and immediately intermingle with them or, remaining isolated from them, keep them in slavery. "All intermediate measures seem to me likely to terminate, and that shortly, in the most horrible of civil wars and perhaps in the extirpation of one or the other of the two races." [42]

Tocqueville saw that the essence of the Negro-white relationship was social, not racial, not economic, not political. He was perhaps the first to be aware of the paradox that political democracy, far from facilitating the intermingling of the two races that would be ultimately required for their peaceful equality, was in fact a mighty barrier. For democracy rests upon public opinion and it is the heavy weight of public opinion in a democracy that, above all else, tends to defeat assimilation.

"An isolated individual may surmount the prejudices of religion, of his country, or of his race; and if this individual is a king, he may effect surprising changes in society; but a whole people cannot rise, as it were, above itself. A despot who should subject the Americans and their former slaves to the same yoke might perhaps succeed in commingling their races; but as long as the American democracy remains at the head of affairs, no one will undertake so difficult a task; and it may be foreseen that the freer the white population of the United States becomes, the more isolated will it remain." [43]

All that Tocqueville saw in the North, where Negroes were legally free and, often, politically and even economically accepted, confirmed him in his conviction that the status factor was dominant and, he feared, unalterable. The Northern whites, he writes, "avoid the Negroes with increasing care in proportion as the legal barriers of separation are removed. . . ." [44] How, then, can anything different and better be predicted for the South, where the Negroes exist in large numbers? It is clearly to the abolitionists of the time that Tocqueville is speaking when he writes: "If I were called upon to predict the future, I should say that the abolition of slavery in the South will, in the common course of things, increase the repugnance of the white population for the blacks." [45]

The merit of Tocqueville's analysis of the Negro problem in the United States rests upon his conversion of the problem from the perspective of race or of simple minority group to the perspective of status and status relationships. He correctly places the problem in the turbulent arena of American democracy's quest for status and status identity. Had there been a social scene in which the dominant white majority was not itself preoccupied by status, by mobility, and by status anxiety, the problem for the Negro would have been a simpler one. But this, as Tocqueville emphasizes, is not the case in American democracy—or in democracy anywhere. The tragic consequence is that the Negro can only appear as threat to a white status already made fragile and uncertain by currents of history that have nothing to do with the Negro.

In final complication of the Negro's plight, there is his *visibility*. The history of equalitarian democracy has been, Tocqueville emphasizes, a history of the erosion of those attributes, those "stigmata," by which visible, inferior groups in the population were rendered somehow less visible. Consider, he says, how long was required for the assimilation into the general population of the peasant, whose only *original* visibility was legal. "Yet these divisions existed for ages; they still exist in many places; and everywhere they have left imaginary vestiges, which time alone can efface." [46]

"If it be so difficult to root out an inequality that originates solely in the law, how are those distinctions to be destroyed which seem to be based upon the immutable laws of Nature herself? When I remember the extreme difficulty with which aristocratic bodies, of whatever nature they may be, are commingled with the mass of the people, and the exceeding care which they take to preserve for ages the ideal boundaries of their caste inviolate, I despair of seeing an aristocracy disappear which is founded upon visible and indelible signs." [47]

And, in a final burst of pessimism, Tocqueville writes:

"Whoever has inhabited the United States must have perceived that in those parts of the Union in which the Negroes are no longer slaves they have in no wise drawn nearer to the whites. On the contrary, the prejudice of race appears to be stronger in the states that have abolished slavery than in those where it still exists; and nowhere is it so intolerant as in those states where servitude has never been known." [48]

A Note on Le Play, Taine, and Durkheim

Such was the appeal in France of Tocqueville's envisagement of stratification in modern democratic society that it formed a lasting theoretical model. I know of no other explanation of the extraordinary lack of attention to social class that French sociological literature reveals. The Tocquevillian vision of modern society—atomized, centralized, bureaucratized and classless—remained the dominant one until after World War I, when, for the first time, Marxism became influential among intellectuals. In Le Play, Taine, and Durkheim, Tocqueville's perspective of stratification is a governing one.

Le Play was vividly aware, as we have seen, of stratification of occupation and type of economic contract between employer and employee. But his discussion of this falls only within his analysis of family and community. He was also well aware of the role of social class in the historical past of Europe and in existing non-European countries. And, as a conservative, his ideal of the good society was built on the desirability of social classes bound by ties of respect and responsibility. Le Play is an excellent illustration of what, at the beginning of the chapter, I called the anagram of fact and ideal that characterizes ideologies of stratification in modern thought. Prizing social class as an ideal, along with family and community and church, his observation told him there was no real social class to be found in the world created by the Revolution.

What Le Play, like Tocqueville, sees is the triumph of status mobility. So ingrained is inequality in the human condition, thought Le Play, that the extermination of the classes by political centralization and economic individualism can only magnify the passion for status. And nowhere, he thought, was this more evident than in the France of his own day.

"I have even established the fact that my fellow citizens, more than any other European people, are disposed to adopt habits of *inequality,* and those even which are far from being tolerated by experience and reason. In the number of these which have occasioned most astonishment among our rivals are: the general practice of assuming titles of nobility, and the ridiculous fondness shown by the newly enriched for titles thus usurped; the extreme covetousness incessantly exhibited in acquiring orders of chivalry, whether French, or of other countries; repugnance for those free corporations, which, among our rivals, unite all minds devoted to the culture of the liberal arts; the high estimate accorded to academies vested with special privileges; that inveterate propensity to establish categories designating places for the various classes of society, on occasions of public reunions and even in the sacred temples; the infinite variety in civil formalities, including the new epistolary style; the abuses of the influence and privileges conferred upon public functionaries; finally, that insatiable desire for privilege which incessantly leads, in spite of the pompous declarations of our legislators, to venal charges against ministerial officers and innumerable varieties of commercial and professional monopolies." [49]

It is, Le Play argues, the irrational political and intellectual opposition to true hierarchy, the hierarchy that all prosperous societies know to be essential to order and freedom, that leads to eruptions of status competition and exploitation which are frequently worse than anything to be found in frankly aristocratic societies. "Everyone knows that those who begin to rise treat their equals of the previous day with a severity always rare among persons who from their birth have occupied elevated position. This view of *parvenus* is severely felt by those who still remain in the lower ranks, and it contributes more than is generally believed to reconcile the poor to those who have enjoyed wealth from their birth." [50]

There is much insight in the following passage: "When the social hierarchy is established by tradition upon virtue, talent, property, and regard for services rendered, the ruling classes will have an interest in making good their claims to the pre-eminence bestowed upon them. They will exert themselves to preserve the affection and favor the wishes of their constituents. On the contrary, where they are incessantly subjected to hatred and envy, the chiefs of society are disposed to put down all those who in future might come in competition with them. The extravagance which at the present time desolates our society seems, in many families, to be a means of demonstrating that inequality which really exists between the various conditions. Chafed to find the poor refuse them certain traditional signs of deference, the rich indulge themselves in extravagant expenditures in order to establish their superiority. The false notion of equality creates most directly upon the lower classes to produce social antagonism. It gives rise to feelings of ambition which cannot be satisfied except in persons possessed of uncommon qualities." [51]

Taine, whose successive volumes on the old regime, the Revolution, and the modern regime represent (albeit distortedly and inadequately) the design that Tocqueville had cherished for his own life's work, presents an almost identical view of the relation between social class, political power, and social status that we find in Tocqueville.

The following passage manifests a degree of nostalgic romanticism, not to say reaction, that the more dispassionate Tocqueville would not have displayed, but it is nevertheless Tocquevillian in substance. Taine is writing of French society in the age of the second Napoleon.

"To make one's way, to get ahead, and succeed in the world is now the dominant thought in the minds of men. Before 1789, this thought had not acquired sovereign control in their minds; it found that there were rival ideas to contend with, and it had only half developed itself; its roots had not sunk down deep enough to monopolize the activity of the imagination, to absorb the will and possess the mind entirely; and the reason is that it lacked both air and aliment." [52]

In the old order men were not haunted by fears of loss of status nor intoxicated by efforts to gain it. Then the class structure of society was like a "great social staircase."

"The great social staircase led to several stories; each man could ascend every step of his own flight, but he could not mount above it; the landing reached, he found closed doors and nearly insurmountable barriers. . . . Through this visible separation of stories, people had acquired the habit of remaining in the condition in which they were placed; they were not irritated by being obliged to stay in it. . . . Life, thus restricted and circumscribed, was more cheerful then than at the present day; souls, less disturbed and less strained, less exhausted and less burdened with cares, were healthier. The Frenchman, exempt from modern preoccupations, followed amiable and social instincts, inclined to take things easily, and of a playful disposition owing to his natural talent for amusing himself by amusing others, in mutual enjoyment of each other's company and without calculation. . . ." [53]

Taine tells us that under this system those of great individual talent who, seeing they could not employ their talents at home because the social staircase was closed to them by birth, were moved to go abroad; hence the vast number of Frenchmen who explored the New World and who there took positions of responsibility or daring or power.

"But the Revolution came on and the ambitions which, under the ancient regime, found a field abroad or cooled down at home, arose on natal soil and suddenly expanded beyond all calculation. After 1789 France resembles a hive in a state of excitement; in a few hours, in the brief interval of an August morning, each insect puts forth two huge wings, soars aloft and all whirl together pell-mell; many fall to the ground half cut to pieces and begin to crawl upward as before; others, with more strength or with better luck, ascend and glitter in the highways of the atmosphere. . . ." [54]

"At the same time, and in a counter-sense, a revolution is going on in minds and the moral effect of the spectacle becomes grander and more lasting than the spectacle itself; souls have been stirred to their very depths; torpid passions and slumbering pretensions are aroused. . . . This new sentiment must be taken into account: for, whether reasonable or not, it is going to last, to maintain its energy, stimulate men with extraordinary force and become one of the great mainsprings of will and action. Henceforth government and administration are to become difficult matters; the forms and plans of the old social architecture are no longer applicable . . ." [55]

When we come to Durkheim, we are struck by the almost total absence of attention to social class as a significant feature in the study of any society—past or present, Western or non-Western. He wrote, as we know, a good deal on professional groups; he was vividly aware of industrial strife in his own age; there are frequent references to historical ages other than his own—ancient-classical, medieval included—but even in these the subject of social class does not enter into his thought, as does, for example, family, tribe, city, and guild. Only in the final pages of *The Division of Labor* do we encounter a discussion of class, and this is to show (appropriately to the argument of that volume and also to the whole tenor of French sociological thought) that it is the nature of modern social development to sterilize social classes and to remove social inequalities.[56] The discussion of "hierarchy" that we find in his *Elementary Forms of Religious Life,* designed to show the origin of man's capacity for logical classification, bears no relation to stratification in the sense used in this chapter. Some of Durkheim's students—notably Gustave Glotz, in his treatment of the ancient Athenian community, Celeste Bouglé, in his *Essai sur le régime des castes,* and, above all, Maurice Halbwachs, in his remarkable and too little appreciated *The Psychology of Social Classes*—took up the study of stratification, but there is little except method that they could have drawn directly from Durkheim himself.

THE CRYSTALLIZATION OF CLASS—MARX

In Germany the situation is strikingly different. It would be hard to find any social concept possessed of more pivotal importance after 1849 than the concept of class. Even when, as with Tönnies and Weber, we find major modifications of the class perspective, class and the whole terminology of stratification retain a degree of importance lacking in French thought. Marx is, of course, the prime source of all this.

In Marx we find no picture of social class pulverized by the forces of modernism, of power passing from social hierarchy to political masses, of frenzied competition for status. What Marx gives us is a view of modern society resting upon the solid reality of class, a reality in which power, wealth, and status are as class-based as they were under feudalism. He might have been directing the following words at Tocqueville: "The modern bourgeois society that has sprouted from the ruins of feudal society has not done away with class antagonisms. It has but established new classes, new conditions of oppression, new forms of struggle in place of old ones. Our epoch, the epoch of the bourgeoisie, possesses, however, this distinctive feature: it has simplified the class antagonisms. Society as a whole is more and more splitting up into two great hostile camps, into two great classes directly facing each other: bourgeoisie and proletariat." [57]

Some students of Marx's thought have suggested that beneath his vision of the two great classes in capitalism—bourgeoisie and proletariat —lies the model of ancient master and slave classes. But I do not think we need go back so far in history. We need look only to the classes of landed gentry and peasant that were still solid structures in Marx's time to find his model. As I have suggested, English landed society alone was sufficient in this respect. Did it not prove that there could be united in a single social class the attributes of political power, wealth, social status, and all the controlling forces for a society reflected in culture, life style, education, and religion? Was it not obvious that what had existed for centuries in the *landed* aristocracy was now forming in an *industrial* aristocracy, the bourgeoisie, to survive until the gathering forces of revolution would destroy this class, just as revolutions had destroyed all preceding forms of class in history? Only this time there would be left not still another sovereign class but, for the first time in history, the structure of a society without any classes at all.

Marx's fascination with the bourgeoisie is at the heart of his theory.

No spokesman for Manchester could have given us more laudatory words on this class than Marx wrote in the early pages of the *Manifesto:* "The bourgeoisie, during its rule of scarce one hundred years, has created more massive and colossal productive forces than have all preceding generations together." [58] The development of scientific technology, the command of nature's resources, the erasure of local and national boundaries, the rise of cities, the spread of communications, the creation of a world market, and the rise of common people into political areas previously governed by nobility alone—all of this, Marx tells us, is the work of a single social class: the bourgeoisie.

In Marx's praise there is of course special and revolutionary intent. All that he gives in revolutionary importance to the bourgeoisie in the making of modern Europe he transfers to the proletariat for the making of future Europe: the socialist, classless society which must, Marx argued, evolve as inexorably as each preceding stage of society had evolved. What the bourgeoisie has done in our era to dislocate the landed aristocracy, the proletariat must do eventually, through operation of identical dialectical-historical forces, to the bourgeoisie. For the present, however, the health of the bourgeoisie is absolutely essential to the embryonic development of the proletariat. On this point Marxian "science" rested squarely.

"The development of the industrial proletariat is, in general, conditioned by the development of the industrial bourgeoisie. Only under its rule does the proletariat gain that extensive national existence which can raise its revolution to a national one and does itself create the modern means of production, which become just so many means of its revolutionary emancipation. Only its rule tears up the material roots of feudal society and levels the ground on which alone a proletarian revolution is possible." [59] Elsewhere, as in the *Communist Manifesto* and *The German Ideology,* Marx would emphasize the international aspect of the development of the proletariat. "Empirically, communism is possible only as the act of the dominant peoples 'all at once,' or simultaneously, which presupposes the universal development of productive forces and the world intercourse bound up with them. . . . The proletariat can thus exist only *world historically,* just as communism, its movement, can only have a 'world-historical' existence." [60] But the bourgeoisie is absolutely fundamental to the development of the proletariat. The bourgeoisie is for Marx what democracy is for Tocqueville: the cause and the shape of all that is central in the modern regime.

In stark contrast to Tocqueville, Marx sees ever more extreme *in-*

equality as the dominant social characteristic of the time. Tocqueville had stressed the bland and uniformitarian aspects of modernism: aspects that would eventually sterilize all significant social and political differences. Marx, however, saw social and political differences among men increasing and, given the structural contradictions of capitalism, made ever more revolutionary in implication. Where Tocqueville saw at best economic *levels* in industrial society, Marx saw classes and, between them, inevitable and relentless struggle.

Class struggle is for Marx a principle, *the* principle, of history: comparable in scope and force to Comte's law of three stages, to Tocqueville's political centralization, to Weber's rationalization. Class struggle is the most fundamental social manifestation of the dialectic in history; it is the "efficient cause" of the movement of society from one stage to another. The modern emergence of the bourgeoisie is the consequence of "a series of revolutions in the modes of production and exchange." The bourgeoisie has, from dialectical necessity, become a revolutionary force, the most revolutionary indeed in all history. Wherever it has got the upper hand, Marx tells us in one of his most celebrated statements, it has put an end to all forms of relationship—kinship, religious, professional, personal—founded on assertedly moral or personal values.[61] Only "cash-payment" is left.

Let us look more closely at the Marxian conception of the nature of class. Despite the fact that social class is the very basis of Marxian sociology, and despite the abundance of general references to social class— most notably to the bourgeoisie and the proletariat—a clear, analytical conception of social class is not easy to derive from a reading of Marx. The one place in his works where it would appear that a genuine sociological analysis is under way—at the very end of the third volume of *Capital*—the discussion comes to a quick and uncertain ending. We shall return to this momentarily. It is first necessary to deal with the larger picture of social class that Marx gives us. We begin with the centrality of work.

For Marx, what man does economically is the single most important and determining thing about his life. The type of work he performs, his position in the larger system of production in society, and the differential rewards he receives for his work—these are the essential elements on which a sociology of class must be built. Given the crucial role of work in man's life, it follows that the position man holds in society's stratification of work and rewards is bound to affect not only the degree of power he possesses but also his social status and even his personality.

"The general conclusion at which I arrived and which, once reached, continued to serve as the leading thread in my studies may be briefly summed up as follows: In the social production which men carry on they enter into definite relations that are indispensable and independent of their will; these relations of production correspond to a definite stage of development of their material powers of production. The sum total of these relations of production constitutes the economic structure of society—the real foundation, on which rise legal and political superstructures and to which correspond definite forms of social consciousness. The mode of production in material life determines the general character of the social, political, and spiritual processes of life." [62]

This principle is as relevant to the societies of the ancient world as it is to those of the present. It was the system of production that divided ancient economies into master and slave, feudal society into noble and serf, and modern capitalism into capitalist and worker. Social movement in history is always caused by revolution in which the struggle between classes is the central element. This struggle is invariably the consequence of a contradiction that develops between "material forces of production" (technology) and "existing relations of production" (the social classes).

"From forms of development of the forces of production these relations turn into their fetters. Then comes the period of social revolution. With the change of the economic foundation the entire immense superstructure is more or less rapidly transformed. . . . In broad outlines we can designate the Asiatic, the ancient, the feudal, and the modern bourgeois methods of production as so many epochs in the progress of the economic formation of society. The bourgeois relations of production are the last antagonistic form of the social process of production—antagonistic not in the sense of individual antagonism, but of one arising from conditions surrounding the life of individuals in society; at the same time the productive forces developing in the womb of bourgeois society create the material conditions for the solution of that antagonism." [63]

The relation between social class and the rest of society is therefore direct and unalterable. So is the relation between social class and ideas, which form, in their totality, an *ideology*—that is, a set of mental representations—of class position. "The ideas of the ruling class are, in every age, the ruling ideas: *i.e.*, the class which is the dominant material force in society is at the same time its dominant intellectual force. The class which has the means of material production at its disposal has control at the same time over the means of mental production, so that in consequence the ideas of those who lack the means of mental production are in general subject to it. The dominant ideas are nothing more than the ideal expression of the dominant material relationships, the dominant material relationships grasped as ideas, and thus of the relationships which make one class the ruling one; they are consequently the ideas of its dominance." [64]

What has been true in the historical past is equally true of the bourgeois-dominated present. Literature, art, music, along with prevailing ideas of the good society, morality, and even metaphysics, are all, in their dominant forms, *bourgeois* representations. Only through revolution or, for the immediate future, through disciplined awareness of the necessity of revolution and of identification with the interests of the working class, is it possible for one to escape the total cultural domination of the bourgeoisie. Hence the Marxian emphasis on the necessity of *developing* a proletarian class interest and, with it, a proletarian mind, culture, and world view.

The end of bourgeois culture and ideology is, of course, foredestined by the laws of historical development and of internal capitalist contradiction. Just as each dominant class in past ages has sown the seeds of its own destruction, so has the bourgeoisie. "Modern bourgeois society . . . is like the sorcerer who is no longer able to control the powers of the nether world whom he has called up by his spells. . . . The weapons with which the bourgeoisie felled feudalism to the ground are now turned against the bourgeoisie itself. But not only has the bourgeoisie forged the weapons that bring death to itself; it has also called into existence the men who are to wield those weapons, the proletarians." [65]

"In proportion as the bourgeoisie, *i.e.,* capital, is developed, in the same proportion as the proletariat, the modern working class, developed —a class of laborers, who live only so long as they find work, and who find work only so long as their labor increases capital. These laborers, who must sell themselves piecemeal, are a commodity, like every other article of commerce, and are consequently exposed to all the vicissitudes of competition, to all the fluctuations of the market." [66]

Out of the workingman's awareness of the class position which is forced upon him will come, must come, *collective* proletarian awareness. But for this to be accomplished, conflict with the bourgeoisie is an iron necessity. Despite the importance of work and productive role in the formation of class, it is the *conflict* of classes that exercises the major influence in Marx's mind in fixing the class structure of loyalties and consciousness and in preventing the fragmentation of class ties that would, apart from conflict, reduce class to a tenuous "level." We must stress this point. Too many contemporary students of class assume, with a naïveté that Marx would scarcely relish, that while class *conflict* is a negligible feature of contemporary social democracy, *the lines and loyalties of class* remain strong nevertheless. Marx was much more sophisticated.

"The separate individuals form a class *insofar as they have to carry on a common battle against another class;* otherwise they are on hostile terms with each other as competitors. On the other hand, the class, in its turn, achieves an independent existence over against the individuals, so that the latter find their conditions of existence pre-destined, and hence have their position in life and their personal development assigned to 'hem by their class, become subsumed under it. This is the same phenomenon as the subjection of the separate individuals to the division of labor and can only be removed by the abolition of private property and of labor itself." [67]

"Economic conditions had first transformed the mass of the people of the country into workers. The domination of capital has created for this mass a common situation, common interests. This mass is thus already a class as against capital, *but not yet for itself.* In this struggle, of which we have noted only a few phases, this mass becomes united, and constitutes itself as a class for itself. The interests it defends become class interests. But the struggle of class against class is a political struggle." [68]

The context of Marx's view of class and of the functional necessity of conflict to the preservation of class was formed in his earliest essays. The following passage, published in 1844, is indicative of the relationship that conscious conflict held to class consciousness in Marx's mind.

"For a popular revolution and the emancipation of a particular class of civil society to coincide, for one class to represent the whole of society, another class must concentrate in itself all the evils of society, a particular class must embody and represent a general obstacle and limitation. A particular social sphere must be regarded as the notorious crime of the whole society, so that emancipation from this sphere appears as general emancipation. For one class to be the liberating class par excellence, it is essential that another class should be openly the oppressing class." [69]

For Marx, consciousness is absolutely essential to true class. It is not enough that a group of individuals occupy the same objective position in the economic structure of society. There must be subjective awareness. It is the crucial condition of class and of its historic role in economic and political conflict. Marx's views on this may be inferred from his negative comments on the peasantry in France. "The small peasants form a vast mass, the members of which live in similar conditions, but without entering into manifold relations with one another. Their mode of production isolates them from one another, instead of bringing them into mutual intercourse . . . Insofar as millions of families live under economic conditions of existence that divide their mode of life, their interests and their culture from those of other classes, and put them into hostile contrast to the latter, they form a class. Insofar as there is merely a local interconnection among these small peasants, and the identity of their interests begets no unity, no national union, and no political organization, they do not form a class." [70]

Marx never discounted the importance of creating, or helping to create, a sense of class. This was a part of the mission of Communists, of those who would be the vanguard of the proletariat's emergence on the world stage. His analytical system can never be really separated from his vivid sense of man's *making* history. But the fact remains that in Marx's mind there had to be the substance and logic of industrialism and of the dialectic of history manifesting itself through iron development, for this calculated vanguarding to be other than chimerical. For Marx, social class is what the nation was to Hegel, the truest repository of history.

Social class is also, plainly, the dominating, even exclusive, category of the Marxian explanation of the larger problem of social stratification. Is there in Marx even a faint understanding of the kind of multiplicity of patterns of power, economic strata, and status systems in nineteenth-century Europe that Tocqueville had emphasized and that Weber and Simmel were to stress in their fundamental departures from the Marxian view? Can one sense even a dim awareness in Marx of class fragmentation, of status mobility, status invasion and status anxieties, the study of which was to prove the really original contribution of European sociology in the nineteenth century? Here and there, yes. A fragment in a letter, a contemptuous parenthetical aside, a passing jeer at the landed class. But that is all. What is central and constitutive for Marx in the society around him is not the fragmentation but the congealing of class ties; not the dislocation of social status and political power from economic class, but the ever firmer uniting of these three elements.

There is rich irony in the fact that the reasons why social class has never attained anything like the importance in capitalism that Marx ascribed to it flow from the very factors—citizenship, moral ideals of equality, religion, and education—that Marx and his followers relegated to subordinate and reflected status in history. For Marx all struggles within the state, "the struggle between democracy, aristocracy, and monarchy, the struggle for the franchise, etc. etc. are merely the illusory forms in which the real struggles of the different classes are fought out among one another . . ." [71] That nationalism, rather than class, would achieve major appeal to the mass of twentieth-century workers; that the spread of administrative bureaucracy into social and economic areas would itself negate conflict and struggle in those areas; that reform movements, commonly engineered by the bourgeoisie, in the areas of civil and social rights would become ascendant; that, of all forces, education would prove to be the major force of sterilization; that *institutional* rather than class conflicts would attain ascendancy in modern history— conflict between state and economy, between religion and economy, and so on—that the whole sway of economic forces might be drastically lessened from the in fact historically rare importance these held in Marx's day: all of this was inconceivable to Marx, as it has been, for the most part, to his followers.

But in a sense this is of negligible importance. For whatever its intellectual omissions, Marxism became, before the nineteenth century was out, and remains even today, the single most influential idea system in European history since the rise of Christianity. There is irony here, too. For it was Marx's proud boast that he had put ideas in their proper, subordinate, status and had shown that ideas were but the pale reflection of the true dynamic forces of history. That his own ideas should have become, almost independently of the forces they sought to describe, among the key determinants of the modern world—in Asia, Africa, Latin America, as well as in Europe—is a fact sufficient to mark their greatness measured in strictly historical terms.

Even apart from their direct political and "religious" influence, Marxist ideas have had almost undisputed influence in theoretical treatments of social stratification until two or three decades ago. Vague though the Marxist formulation of class was, it maintained a tenacious hold upon the study of stratification. Only within the past few years has the Marxist model of society begun to be supplanted in empirical studies by more imaginative, more flexible, and more relevant insights—insights that have closer relation to the intuitions and impressions of Tocqueville than to what may be found in the Marxian canon. But it would take a rash soul to say that the influence of Marx is altogether gone. He has been, so to speak, the Ptolemy of the subject for a hundred years now, and although his writ is no longer magisterial, no Copernicus has yet come onto the field. We can say only that the reflection-neutralizing, attention-narcotizing icons of Proletarian and Capitalist have, at long last, largely vanished from the altars of Western intellectuals. In Schumpeter's vivid phrase, Marxist rosaries are no longer being fingered.

Marx's influence on the theory of stratification has been strikingly like that of Darwin on the ideas of evolution and natural selection. In each instance we have an impressive s̄ʷoring up of eighteenth-century ideas. The initial manner of statement in both theories had the effect of persuading readers of an originality and break with tradition that did not in fact exist. In precisely the same way that Darwin's ideas are deeply rooted in eighteenth-century ideas of development, so Marx's ideas on the nature of social stratification are rooted in eighteenth-century analyses of inequality. If Darwin had his Lyell, Marx had his Rousseau (*vide* the *Discourse on the Origin of Inequality*). That Darwin's statement of continuous and cumulative variation in genetic change has had a degree of acceptance in biology that Marx's statement of dialectical change in society has not had in sociology is not the point. The point is simply that the prestige of one in the study of biological evolution has been precisely paralleled in the prestige of the other in the study of social stratification, and that in each we are dealing with ideas that have deep eighteenth-century roots.

Class as Gesellschaft—Tönnies

The conceptual unity that Marx gave to social class did not last even in Germany except in the ranks of the politically committed. The discrepancies between the modern order and the Marxist conception of that order were too great to be contained in a theory that aspired to coalesce all the complex elements of power, status, and wealth into one simple theory of social class.

What we see in the generation of sociological thought following Marx in Germany is the gradual disengagement of each of these elements from the others and the formation of new and more complex theories of stratification of which Max Weber's was to prove the most notable and to be by far the most influential on subsequent sociological thought. It was, however, Tönnies' fertile typology of *Gemeinschaft* and *Gesellschaft* that prepared the way.

Whereas Marx with his progressive philosophy of history treated social class as organizational and dynamic in modern society, it was inevitable that Tönnies would see the matter very differently. Class struggle, far from driving Western society into a new and eventually higher form of organization, could only, for Tönnies, lead to a fatal widening of disorganization, one in which the very doom of culture was involved. What Tönnies has to say in the following passage is sufficiently indicative of his view that, not class emancipation, but final disintegration of *Gemeinschaft* will be the major consequence of class struggle.

"City life and *Gesellschaft* doom the common people to decay and death; in vain they struggle to attain power through their own multitude, and it seems to them that they can use their power only for a revolution if they want to free themselves from their fate. The masses become conscious of this social position through the education in schools and through newspapers. They proceed from class consciousness to class struggle. This class struggle may destroy society and the state which it is its purpose to reform. The entire culture has been transformed into a civilization of state and *Gesellschaft,* and this transformation means the doom of culture itself if none of its scattered seeds remain alive and again bring forth the essence and idea of *Gemeinschaft,* thus secretly fostering a new culture amidst the decaying one." [72]

It is not the *Kulturpessimismus* of this passage that is the clue to Tönnies' view of stratification so much as it is the clear implication that *Gesellschaft* is no more capable of containing a coherent, unified, and culturally important social class than it is of including a social community. As we have observed, for Tönnies the essence of modernism—that is, *Gesellschaft*—is the attenuation of traditional social and moral relationships, with consequent depersonalization of society, loss of communal identification, and ever greater impact upon man of the forces of political law and egoistic economism. The view of class that we find in Tönnies is strikingly like that of Tocqueville: more nearly a category or level than a social group possessed of self-awareness or cultural identity. Although there is little to be found on stratification in Tönnies' major work, *Community and Society,* it is not difficult to infer from this volume a view of the subject that matches perfectly what he was to write at greater length in later years. Class in the politically, socially, and culturally unified sense in which Marx used the word simply does not exist for Tönnies in modern society. It did once—in the form of the "social estates" (Stände), which were, in traditional society, manifestations of *Gemeinschaft* quite as much as were kindred and local community. But the distinction between social estate and social class is as sharp as that between *Gemeinschaft* and *Gesellschaft;* it is a distinction enforced by the direction of modern history. The quotations which follow are taken from an article Tönnies wrote many years after publication of *Community and Society*, but like almost everything else he ever wrote these might easily have come from the pages of that volume.

"The terms 'estate' and 'class' are synonyms which are often used interchangeably. But scientifically we want to distinguish these terms in the sense that estates are conceived as *communal* and classes as *societal* collectives. Another distinction between them consists in the greater rigidity of estates as against the often extreme fluidity of classes. Classes are more frequently determined by environmental conditions, which as a rule remain the same for generations, but which become more changeable in the course of social development and which cause individuals and families to rise or fall to a higher or lower class. It follows, on the other hand, that as an estate becomes more identical with a class, the more it disintegrates, i.e., the more the mobility of its members increases." [73]

Estates are at once more diversified and more inclusive of the social and spiritual lives of their members. More diversified in the sense that there are cultural and religious ties as well as those of birth and occupation. Class, however, is the product of a society in which contractual and pecuniary values predominate. Estates encompass the moral and intellectual lives of individuals. Like Tocqueville, Tönnies finds the social roots of such values as dignity, honor, and nobility in the medieval estates, and sees the gradual disintegration of these values under the influence of *Gesellschaft*.

In modern history a conflict between estate and class is endemic. "The estates have been superseded more and more by the awareness of belonging to a 'class.' A class is intent upon developing effective power through the strength of the mass, i.e., through the large number of those who belong to this collective; it depends to a lesser extent on the skills of the individuals. This is true of collectives of every sort. But the farmers, the craftsmen, the civil servants, and the academicians still feel themselves to be occupational estates even today." [74]

The individualistic and pecuniary character of capitalism has had the effect of weakening all modes of social differentiation that are not strictly related to wealth. A form of social isolation develops, though it is partially offset by the new sense of identification and connection arising from the economic division of labor. "The worker is characterized mainly by the fact that he has little money, hence no capital. But frequently he has this much in common with the merchant and the entrepreneur that he is a stranger. As such, he is not bound as a rule to his employer, either by a bond of kinship, of home, of occupation, or yet by any bond of religion which, in any case, diminishes in importance under these conditions. But all these people are dependent on one another: the retail merchant upon the customer; the customer upon the retailer who acts frequently also as a creditor; above all the entrepreneur upon the worker, and the worker upon the entrepreneur." [75]

Estates in modern life are to be seen chiefly in those areas—the professions—where the contractual-economic factor continues to be subordinated: in the clergy, the academic professions, the military, and law and medicine. Even in other areas, however, the spirit of "estate" dies hard. We can observe a strong effort, through trade associations and chambers of commerce, to regain at least a little of the "estate" flavor of the past, to combine the communal and the societal.

"The decisive characteristic of class is class consciousness, just as that of the estate is status-consciousness among members of an estate." [76] Is there a true class conflict, as Marx had argued? There is, but Tönnies is careful to point out that the widening of political suffrage has helped intensify, and remains the context of, this struggle. That is, it is the formation of parties along with mass electorates that has been a powerful means of creating the sense of class conflict that Marx thought was inherent in classes. Tönnies is skeptical, however, of the extent to which the poor develop common political interests. Class sentiment is slow in developing, for the persistence of the "estate" concept of status and the impersonal economic connection of higher and lower groups often cause the poor to vote as they think the wealthy desire them to.

Further mitigating the conflict of classes are the conflicts that take place within a single class—most notably within the capitalist class— "between creditor and debtor, between people in urban and rural areas, between advocates of tariff protection and those who champion free trade, between producers and consumers, between monopolists and those engaged in free competition . . . Thus, there are many economic contrasts and struggles which are more or less sharply reflected in political life. But these contrasts and struggles are obscured by the class struggle, if this has found room to develop, as has been the case increasingly during the last one hundred years. The class struggle itself must be recognized as developing and subject to continuous change." [77]

CLASS VERSUS STATUS—WEBER

The distinction between political power, economic class, and social status is brought to full theoretical explicitness in Weber's work. Weber sees contemporary power in terms that are only incidentally connected with the role of classes and social-status strata. For Weber it is bureaucracy on the one hand and the political party on the other which have largely inherited the political component that once lay in the hierarchical structure of estate or rank. With the increasing assimilation of social conflicts in the framework of the constitutional state, political parties have become the heirs, so to speak, of contending social forces that in earlier times were not only outside the king's jurisdiction, but often formidable rivals to it. Parties, Weber points out, began as personal followings in the Middle Ages—witness the Guelphs and the Ghibellines—and they largely retained this character until the advent of mass democracy in the nineteenth century. To a considerable extent pre-nineteenth-century parties were also closely welded to kinship—great families—and to aristocracy.[78] Unlike the modern connotation of party, which is of a kind of para-political organization, "officially unofficial, unofficially official," the earlier form of party was, in fact, an offshoot of traditional society, a part of the regular hierarchy. Thus, apart from the upper classes in eighteenth-century England, parties in politics are scarcely imaginable.

The breakup of the old order changed this. Modern forms of party "stand in sharp contrast to this idyllic state in which circles of notables and, above all, members of Parliament rule. These modern forms are the children of democracy, of mass franchise, of the necessity to woo and organize the masses, and develop the utmost unity of direction and the strictest discipline." [79] It is not necessary to repeat what has already been said of Weber's theory of power. All I wish to do here is emphasize the fact that in dealing with the problem of stratification in modern society, the first, crucial step taken by Weber, thus allying himself with Tocqueville rather than with Marx, was to deal with power as something that must be distinguished from social class. Political parties, as Weber put it in a memorable phrase, "live in a house of power." [80]

Weber's second step follows both Tocqueville and Tönnies: it is the strict limitation of class to the economic sphere. "The genuine place of 'classes' is within the economic order, the place of 'status groups' is within the social order. . . ." This does not mean hermetic insulation of three elements. In any individual case, "parties may represent interests determined through 'class situation' or 'status situation' and they may recruit their following respectively from one or the other." But, Weber emphasizes, they need be neither purely "class" nor purely "status" parties. They can have, and modern politics shows them increasingly to have, a virtually independent status.[81]

For the separate elements of class, status, and party to have been released in modern times, more than the negative force of fragmentation is involved. There must also have been created through the centuries an environing structure in which these are subordinate to the larger structure. Most of us today would see this as a result of the process of politicization in modern European history. Weber's word for it is "societalization." Diversification has been possible only through "a comprehensive societalization and especially a political framework of communal action within which they operate." [82]

If the political party has inherited most of the political functions of medieval orders, it is class alone that today dominates in the economic sphere just as the status group does in the social sphere. Class has, plainly, a very different significance in Weber from anything to be found in Marx. "In our terminology 'classes' are not communities; they merely represent possible, and frequent, bases of communal action. We may speak of a 'class' when (1) a number of people have in common a specific causal component of their life chances, insofar as (2) this component is represented exclusively by economic interest in the possession of goods and opportunities of income and (3) is represented under the conditions of the commodity or labor markets." [83]

For Weber, class rests thus entirely on economic interest. Even so, he recognized that the concept of "class interest" is an ambiguous one: "it is ambiguous as soon as one understands by it something other than the factual direction of interests following with a certain probability from the class situation for a certain 'average' of those people subjected to the class situation." For, there are many and diverse interests and motivations that enter the individual's mind in modern society, and since by its nature class is *not* communal (which Weber defines as governed by the feeling of the actors that they belong together), the rise of communal action from a common class situation is by no means a certain or universal phenomenon. Neither, for that matter, is a societal action (rationally motivated adjustment of interests).

"To treat 'class' conceptually as having the same value as 'community' leads to distortion. That men in the same class situation regularly react in mass actions to such tangible situations as economic ones in the direction of those interests that are most adequate to their very number is an important and, after all, simple fact for the understanding of historical events. Above all, this fact must not lead to that kind of pseudo-scientific operation with the concepts of 'class' and 'class interests' so frequently found these days, and which has found its most classic expression in the statement of a talented author, that the individual may be in error concerning his interests but that the 'class' is 'infallible' about its interests." [84] Such is Weber's reply to the Marxists!

"The great shift which has been going on continuously in the past, and up to our times, may be summarized, although at the cost of some precision: the struggle in which class situations are effective has progressively shifted from consumption credit toward, first, competitive struggles in the commodity market and, then, toward price wars on the labor market. The 'class struggles' of antiquity—to the extent that they were genuine class struggles and not struggles between status groups—were initially carried on by indebted peasants, and perhaps also by artisans threatened by debt bondage and struggling against urban creditors . . . The propertyless of antiquity and of the Middle Ages protested against monopolies, preemption, forestalling, and the withholding of goods from the market in order to raise prices. Today the central issue is the determination of the prices of labor." [85]

The third element in the modern stratification picture is the status group. This is, for Weber, as distinct from class as each is from the political party. Between the status group and a given social class there can be, of course, liaisons, persistences of common interest, but the differences are nonetheless crucial.

"In contrast to classes, status groups are normally communities. They are, however, often of an amorphous kind. In contrast to the purely economically determined 'class situation' we wish to designate as 'status situation' every typical component of the life fate of men that is determined by a specific, positive or negative, social estimation of *honor*." [86]

Tocqueville, it will be remembered, had made the idea of honor central in his treatment of traditional European society, and his own history of the value was set in the context of the decline of social hierarchy and the emergence of more individualized, autonomous notions of honor in modern democracy. Weber is close to Tocqueville, though he goes beyond him, looking to the ways in which honor and desire for community have *combined* in modern society. He finds this in style of life.

Status lines *may* be linked with those of class and party, but normally they are not, and for the most part status "stands in sharp opposition to the pretensions of property." [87] The basis of the social system lies in the incorporation of honor and in its rigorous identification with a life style. "In content, status honor is normally expressed by the fact that above all else a specific *style of life* can be expected from all those who wish to belong to the circle. Linked with this expectation are restrictions on 'social' intercourse (that is, intercourse which is not subservient to economic or any other of business's 'functional' purposes). These restrictions may confine normal marriages to within the status circle and may lead to complete endogamous closure." [88]

It is in the United States that status groups of the modern type are most clearly to be seen. There the absence or disappearance of the kind of society still to be seen in Europe leads to a stringent emphasis on fashion. Only certain neighborhoods, certain modes of dress, certain kinds of cultural tastes will be accepted at any given time in society. There is strict submission to fashion. "This submission to fashion also exists among men in America to a degree unknown in Germany. Such submission is considered to be an indication of the fact that a given man *pretends* to qualify as a gentleman. This submission decides, at least *prima facie,* that he will be treated as such . . . The development of status is essentially a question of stratification resting on usurpation. Such usurpation is the normal origin of all status honor." [89]

Where status considerations have been realized to their full extent, status groups harden into a closed caste. "Social distinctions are then guaranteed honor not merely by conventions and laws but also by rituals." For the most part, however, "caste" of this sort arises only where there are underlying differences which are held to be ethnic. Dignity is closely related to honor. "Only with the negatively privileged status groups does the 'sense of dignity' take a specific deviation. A sense of dignity is the precipitation in individuals of social honor and of contentional demands which a positively privileged status group raises for the deportment of its members." [90]

Such is the picture of stratification in contemporary society that Weber presents. I have stressed its close relation to Tocqueville's earlier analysis, but it would be unjust if we did not emphasize two important aspects of Weber that are not to be found in Tocqueville. The first is methodological. What Weber does is convert the concepts of power, class, and status into a framework of analysis flexible enough to be used as a comparative perspective in the study of all societies. In Tocqueville the three elements are not only largely implicit, but they are confined to his empirical observation of the United States and Western Europe. They are, thus, more nearly historical than sociological in temper. The second element follows from the first. The concept of status is employed by Weber on a world-wide scale and is made the point of departure of study of specific institutions: particularly religion. Thus, for Weber, the concept of status group becomes an indispensable means of analyzing ancient Judaism, the formation of caste in India, and the rise of the Junkers in modern Prussia. Status becomes a tool of analysis, an explicit framework of observation, through which matters as diverse as religion, economy, education, and political behavior are illuminated. From Weber more than any other sociologist has come contemporary sociology's varied use of status and status group in the analysis of human behavior. Down until the nineteen-thirties. Marx's monolithic and unwieldy vision of class tended to dominate the study of stratification. No doubt what proved necessary to end the spell of Marx in modern sociology was not so much the accumulation of new data as the political spectacle of Stalin's Russia and consequent ideological disaffection. But the result, however gained, was the same: the gradual supersession of "class" by "status" as the key concept in sociological studies of stratification. Today, as a sociological concept, class is dead.

THE AUTONOMIZATION OF STATUS—SIMMEL

There are two quite distinct principles of social organization posited by Simmel which, taken together, go far to explain, or to provide a theoretical setting for, the view of status that had its origin in Tocqueville and received its most creative statement in Weber. The first of these principles is *autonomization;* the second is *objectification.* That the referent of each of these principles is by no means limited by Simmel to the sphere of stratification does not affect the relevance of both to the concept of status in modern society.

Autonomization, for Simmel, is a basic principle of social development, one through which the disengagement or separation of elements previously united is achieved in an institution or a social form. Such elements "become autonomous in the sense that they are no longer inseparable from the objects which they formed and thereby made available to our purposes. They come to play freely in themselves and for their own sake; they produce or make use of materials that exclusively serve their own operation or realization." [91] Prime examples of "autonomization" that Simmel advances are cognition and law. Originally, cognition was but a means by which man engaged in the struggle for existence; it was for primordial man inextricably involved in the strategy of adaptation to environment. But with the advance of culture, cognition increasingly became its own end and reason for being. With the autonomization of cognition went the development of culture. Similarly the histories of logical systems, forms, rhythms, art, and music show the degree to which elements originally locked with attributes of other systems become autonomous. Law is an equally obvious example of the same process. Originally a phase of religion or kinship, it gradually attained autonomous force and prestige.

The same is true of social status. The modern history of European society reveals the degree to which status, formerly embedded in, inseparable from, a system of property or of power, has taken on an autonomous character in modern Europe. Status has become disengaged from class or government in exactly the same way that cognition became disengaged from the struggle for existence. It has attained, in short, existential autonomy.

The second and equally illuminating principle is that which Simmel calls objectification. The whole modern tendency of culture, for Simmel, is to become ever more "objective" to man; or putting it reversely, ever less intimately or "subjectively" a part of man. To be sure, much of the essence and extent of modern political freedom is bound up with this objectification, for only by objectifying the varied offices, positions, and ranks which compose a social order does it become possible for individuals of diverse background to occupy them. It is, however, this process of objectification of rank and political position, of entrepreneurship and citizenship, of war and education, that makes status so relative and so fluctuant, so mobile and diverse; for status remains to a large extent personal while matters of economy and power have become lodged in objective and *impersonal* structures. Historically, the "transition from the subjectivistic relationship of domination to an objective formation and fixation is effected by the purely quantitative expansion of the sphere of domination." With this expansion we find more and more areas of life in which "not the person, but the position, so to speak, is the superordinate element. The *a priori* elements of the relationship are no longer the individuals with their characteristics, out of which the social relation develops, but, rather, these relations themselves, as objective forms, as 'positions,' empty spaces and contours (as it were) which must merely be 'filled' by individuals." [92]

The tension between subjective and objective which is the key to the modern scene, sociologically viewed, is illustrated for Simmel, as it had been for Tocqueville, in the master-servant relation. "In the condition of domestic servants—at least on the whole, in contemporary central Europe—it is still the total individual, so to speak, who enters the subordination. Subordination has not yet attained the objectivity of an objectively, clearly circumscribed service. From this circumstance derive the chief inadequacies inherent in the institution of domestic service." [93]

In traditional society a special mode of objectivity resulted from the patriarchal structure of the household: in it, servants worked for, not the master or the mistress, but for the corporate family. Here the house itself had "an absolute value," one served by the housewife in her way, by the servants in another. But the case is different at the present time. "The contemporary position of the servant who shares his master's house, particularly in the large cities, has lost the first of these two kinds of objectivity, without having yet attained the second. The total personality of the servant is no longer claimed by the objective idea of the 'house'; and yet, in view of the general way in which his services are requested, it cannot really separate itself from it." [94]

Simmel also uses the contrasting relationship of officer and common soldier in situations of combat and of garrison as an example. In combat, though discipline is merciless, there is nevertheless close fellowship between officers and troops. They know each other as individuals, as comrades indeed, in a way that is denied them under peacetime conditions. "During peacetime, the army remains arrested in the position of a means which does not attain its purposes; it is, therefore, inevitable for its technical structure to grow into a psychologically ultimate aim, so that super-subordination, on which the technique of the organization is based, stands in the foreground of consciousness." [95]

The problem of the relation between personal and mere positional superiority branches out, Simmel emphasizes, into two important sociological forms. These are the familiar horns of aristocracy and equality in human affairs. What Simmel calls "dominion by the best" is an ancient dream of man and "suitably expresses the inner and ideal relation among men in an external relation." [96] This is the reason, he suggests, why "artists are so often aristocratically inclined. For the attitude of the artist is based upon the assumption that the inner significance of things adequately reveals itself in their appearance, if only this appearance is seen correctly and completely. The separation of the world from its value, of appearance from its significance, is the anti-artistic disposition . . . Thus, the psychological and historical connection between the aristocratic and artistic conceptions of life may, at least in part, be based on the fact that only an aristocratic order equips the inner value relations among men with a visible form, with their esthetic symbol, so to speak." [97]

But aristocracy in this pure sense is sociologically impossible, for "men rarely are satisfied with the superiority of even the best among them, because they do not wish any superiority at all or, at least, none in which they cannot themselves participate." Furthermore, the possession of power tends to demoralize, even power that was originally acquired in a legitimate manner. If it does not demoralize the individual who holds it, it does the class or organization. Hence the judgment, abstractly reached, that "general equality represents the *lesser* evil." [98] "But since, as a rule, the question of greater or lesser evil can be decided only by personal valuation, the same pessimistic mood may also lead to the exactly opposite conviction. One can argue that, in large as in small groups, there must be *some* government, and that, therefore, it is better that unsuited persons govern than that nobody does."

It is "the very idea of *aristocracies* that they can be only relatively small." This does not merely follow from the dominance of aristocracy over the masses. There is an intrinsic and absolute limit, irrespective of its relation to the rest of society. "If it is to be effective as a whole, the aristocratic group must be 'surveyable' by every single member of it. Each element must still be personally acquainted with every other. Relations by blood and marriage must be ramified and traceable throughout the whole group." [99] When aristocracy lets itself assimilate fresh blood, it is usually doomed. "Where an aristocracy yields to democratic and centrifugal tendencies which usually accompany the transition to very large communities, it becomes entangled in deadly conflicts with its own life principle." [100] This principle is as relevant to aristocracies of manufacture (the guilds) and of education (the universities) as it is to conventional ones.

There is no question that equality has for Simmel, as it had for Tocqueville, a chimerical and elusive nature that makes it forever the gall of mankind, the stuff of frustration and defeat.

"Typically speaking, nobody is satisfied with the position he occupies in regard to his fellow creatures; everybody wishes to attain one which is, in some sense, more favorable. Thus, if the majority which got the worst of a situation feel a desire for a heightened style of life, the expression which most easily suggests itself to them will be the wish to have, and be, the same as the upper ten thousand. Equality with the superior is the first objective which offers itself to the impulse of one's own elevation. This is shown in any kind of small circle, in school classes, groups of merchants, or bureaucratic hierarchies. It is one of the reasons why the resentment of the proletarian usually does not turn against the highest classes, but against the bourgeois. For it is the bourgeois whom the proletarian sees immediately above himself, and who represents to him that rung of the ladder of fortune which he must climb first and on which, therefore, his consciousness and his desire for elevation momentarily concentrate." [101]

6 THE SACRED

THE RECOVERY OF THE SACRED

No other single concept is as suggestive of the unique role held by sociology among the social sciences in the nineteenth century, or as reflective of its underlying premises about the nature of man and society, as the concept of the sacred. I use this word to refer to the totality of myth, ritual, sacrament, dogma, and the mores in human behavior; to the whole area of individual motivation and social organization that transcends the utilitarian or rational and draws its vitality from what Weber called charisma and Simmel piety. What gives distinctiveness to sociology's incorporation of the religio-sacred is not the analytical and descriptive attention such men as Durkheim and Weber gave to religious phenomena. It is rather the utilization of the religio-sacred as a perspective for the understanding of ostensibly non-religious phenomena such as authority, status, community, and personality.

We look in vain in economics, political science, and psychology for anything comparable. In these disciplines doctrines of economic man, secular sovereignty, contract, competition, instinct, and self-interest were the essential and sufficing pillars of social analysis. What need was there to appeal to myth and ritual in the understanding of political and economic behavior when there were processes as fundamental and universal as self-interest and competition to draw on? Ethnology is, of course, a partial exception to what I have just written. But ethnology's interest in the religio-sacred was confined almost entirely to primitive culture, to what were widely supposed to be the early stages of the evolution of religion, or else to so-called "survivals" of primitive belief in modern society, such as folk tales and legends which were held to be fossilized remains of primitive consciousness, without significant effect upon the progress of culture. The religio-sacred cannot be said to have in ethnology—at least not in the nineteenth century—methodological significance in the study of the functional requirements of a social organization or of personality and its relation to society.

But the religio-sacred has all of this significance in sociology. From Tocqueville's analysis of the relation between dogma and intellect, through Fustel de Coulanges' depiction of the rise and fall of the classical city-state, down to Weber's theory of charisma, Simmel's concept of piety, and Durkheim's momentous contrast between the sacred and the profane, the main line of sociology reveals a fascination with the analytical uses of the religio-sacred that is unmatched in any other social science. The typology of the sacred-secular has the same methodological significance that we find in community-society, status-class, and authority-power. It is a conceptual framework of analysis by which not only the nature of religion but the nature of society, economy, and state is illuminated in fresh ways. The religio-sacred, far from being mere superstructure or illusion, is engrained in society; it cannot be consigned to the lumber room of history, for, as Durkheim was to write, "there is something eternal in religion."

There is humor and irony in sociology's rediscovery of religion. Had not the Age of Reason and the Enlightenment proved the expendability of institutional religion and the irrelevance to reason of all the timeworn properties of religion: dogmatic passion and "enthusiasm" at one extreme; liturgy, ritual, and sacrament at the other? The tenor of even the religious writings of the seventeenth and eighteenth centuries had been to rationalize religion, to seek to make it as spare of liturgical trappings and dogmatic belief as possible. The immense vogue of natural law and individualistic rationalism is as apparent in religious thought as elsewhere in these two centuries. And these centuries had been preceded by the Renaissance, which was, if not anti-religious, certainly not Christian in its dominant inspiration.

When we come to the Enlightenment, especially in France, it is fair to say that amid all the diversities of opinion and value in that complex age, there was one conviction on which all the *philosophes* found unanimity: disdain for revealed or institutionalized religion of any kind. In this, of course, the *philosophes* were echoing the sentiments of secular rationalists of all ages, from Democritus and Lucretius in the ancient world down to Bertrand Russell in our own.

If there is any single view of the nature and source of religion that has characterized the critical rationalist tradition, from Lucretius to Russell, it is that all religion emanates from suspension of reason, from absence of science or true knowledge, from, in short, superstition. Nowhere in European history has this view been more influentially and brilliantly expressed than in the French Enlightenment at the end of the eighteenth century. In such works as Voltaire's *Dictionary,* Helvetius' *Treatise on Man,* La Mettrie's *Man a Machine,* Condorcet's *Outline of an Historical View of the Progress of the Human Mind,* and Holbach's *System of Nature* the conviction is apparent that religion, most especially Christianity, is a bundle of superstitions required only by the ignorant and irrational. Holbach, in *Common Sense,* spoke for nearly all the philosophers of reason when he wrote: "Let men's minds be filled with true ideas; let their reason be cultivated; let justice govern them; and there will be no need of opposing to the passions such a feeble barrier as the fear of the gods." [1] What, after all, was the prime purpose of the great *Encyclopedia* but the routing of the forces of superstition and the emancipation of those who had lived under its thralldom?

Few in that age doubted that reason alone is the rock on which true morality is founded. The essential task was the discovery of natural law. But, asked Helvetius, in his *Treatise on Man,* "Who can perceive natural law through the mysterious cloud with which the sacerdotal power surrounds it? This law, they say, is the canvas of all religions. Be it so; but the priests have embroidered so many mysteries on this canvas that the embroidery entirely covers the ground. Whoever reads history will find that the virtue of the people diminishes in proportion as their superstition increases. By what means can a superstitious man be instructed in his duty? How in the night of error and ignorance can he perceive the path of justice?" [2]

There were, to be sure, differences among the *philosophes,* but they were united by the conviction that revealed religion is a collection of superstitions supportable only so long as man remains ignorant of the truths vouchsafed by modern science and philosophy. The *philosophes* did not see religion as a force proceeding from the very nature of the soul or, for that matter, from the nature of society. They saw religion solely as a set of intellectual propositions on the universe and on man; and since these were manifestly false propositions, their eventual liquidation could be confidently prophesied (and helped along!) through the propagation of faith in reason.

The Revolution added, especially in its spectacular de-Christianization decrees in 1793–1794, emphasis that not the most sanguine of secular philosophers could have dreamed of. In retrospect this abortive episode in the Revolution has its elements of the comic: the solemn exorcisement of Christian worship in any of its forms; banishment of its symbolism; prohibition of its nomenclature; inauguration of a new calendar, with the inscribed superstitions of the old forever to be erased from memory; devout worship of the Spirit of Reason in several of the public squares of France; public announcements in the stilted form of religious apostrophe, and so on. But however short-lived and futile these efforts proved to be, there was nothing in the whole course of the Revolution, save possibly the Terror, that matched the de-Christianization decrees for sheer impact upon the conservative and religious mind of the rest of Europe. It can hardly be doubted that the thrill of horror they aroused had much to do with stimulating the immense reaction to rationalist secularism in the nineteenth century.

Not that the secular tradition diminished, either in volume or intensity. In the works of Bentham and Marx, to name but the two mightiest of the descendants of the *philosophes,* there is precisely the same hatred of religion that we find in the works of Holbach and Helvetius, the same disdain for religion considered as a fruitful category or perspective in explanations of society and human behavior.

In his early writings, Bentham had contented himself with attack on revealed religion. He had been, Halévy tells us, "a free thinker in the eighteenth century at Lord Lansdowne's, in a circle whose incredulity scandalized Priestley." [3] Then, however, his free thought had been, like that of his aristocratic companions there, based largely upon contempt for plebeian credulities and superstitions. Like some of the French philosophers, he took refuge in a rationalized Christianity, one purged of all but the simplest precepts, one that claimed the sanction of natural law. But by 1822 Bentham had repudiated even natural religion. Religion in any form was, he thought, harmful "not only to the believer himself, but also to others through him." Quite apart from its intellectual absurdities, religion creates "in the heart of society factitious antipathies between men who believe and men who do not believe, between men who practise religion and men who do not practise, or again between men who practise it in one way and men who practise it in another." [4] And any possible theoretical need of religion as an analytical tool in the understanding of human behavior was absurd. For was there not a hedonistic calculus to draw upon, one that reduced the science of behavior to a few simple propositions infinitely extendable? For Bentham there was in religion and its properties nothing that could possibly illuminate the science of man.

Nor did Marx find any conceptual utility in religion, any essence that made it functional to human association. This is not to say that Marx and Engels were uninterested in religion. Christianity, especially in its earliest history, fascinated them; Engels particularly was struck by the analogy between early Christianity, in its seizure of the mind of the ancient world, beginning with the lower classes, and modern Communism. But this is a far cry from regarding religion as necessary to man, taken either individually or collectively, or from acceptance of the sacred as a fundamental variable in the interpretation of the development of society. For Marx all that was fundamental in the science of society proceeded from the material and especially the economic sphere.

Religion, Marx tells us, is rooted in social oppression. For Marx religion has its source in man's alienation from himself of powers which he projects into the supernatural. Both alienation and religion are for Marx rooted in social oppression: *"Religious* distress is at the same time the *expression* of real distress and the *protest* against real distress. Religion is the sigh of the oppressed creature, the heart of a heartless world, just as it is the spirit of an unspiritual situation. It is the *opium* of the people." So Marx wrote in *Toward the Critique of Hegel's Philosophy of Right.*[5]

This gives us insight into a view of religion that goes beyond what the Enlightenment had said about the matter. For Marx religion is, to be sure, superstition, but to stop at this is to limit religion to a merely intellectual dimension: to abstract belief. It leaves the impression, as we have seen in the *philosophes,* that religion may be dislodged simply by new, rational beliefs. Marx's sense of the matter is more profound. Merely changing beliefs is not enough. The transformation of an entire social order is required, for belief is rooted deeply in the social relations of men.

Religion, writes Marx, "is the self-consciousness and self-feeling of man, who either has not yet found himself or has already lost himself again. But *man* is no abstract being, squatting outside the world. Man is the *world of man,* the state, society. This state, this society produce religion, *a perverted world consciousness,* because they are *a perverted world.* Religion is the general theory of that world, its encyclopedic compendium . . . its enthusiasm, its moral sanction, its solemn completion, its universal ground for consolation and justification. It is *the fantastic realization* of the human essence because the *human essence* has no true reality." [6]

Marx believed, with Ludwig Feuerbach, that what man gives to

God, in the form of worship, he takes from himself. That is, man is persuaded through suffering or through false teaching to project what is his to a supernatural being. But Marx's celebrated indictment of Feuerbach proceeded from a conviction that what is fundamental is not the religious forms—against which Feuerbach had urged revolt—but the economic forms of existence. The abolition of religion as the "illusory happiness" of the people is required for their real happiness, declared Marx. But before religion can be abolished the conditions which nurture it must be done away with. "The demand to give up the illusions about its condition is the demand to give up a condition which needs illusion." [7]

THE SACRED AND SECULAR

In the main line of sociological thought, however, religion is far from illusion—or, if illusion, a functionally necessary one and not likely to disappear through changes in material or social conditions. "There is," Durkheim was to write in his *Elementary Forms of Religious Life,* "something eternal in religion which is destined to survive all the particular symbols in which religious thought has successively enveloped itself. There can be no society which does not feel the need of upholding and reaffirming at regular intervals the collective sentiments and the collective ideas which make its unity and its personality." [8]

Far from being a mere bundle of beliefs, subject, as the Enlightenment had thought, to the exterminative action of education and science, religion is ineradicably built into the very nature of mental and social life. It has the same degree of constitutive and causal efficacy that political and economic forces have. On such propositions Comte, Tocqueville, Weber, Durkheim, and Simmel stood firmly, thus presenting still another front in sociology's revolt against the century's individualistic rationalism.

To say this is not to imply that there was any greater degree of personal *commitment* to religion among the sociologists than, say, among the utilitarians. Durkheim, whose *Elementary Forms* is perhaps the most impressive demonstration ever written of the functional indispensability of religion to society, was a rigorous agnostic. So, undoubtedly, were Weber and Simmel, even if less rigorous. Tocqueville was a believer and, nominally at least, Catholic, but so skeptical of all but the minimum essentials of Christianity and so critical of clericalism that he can hardly be thought of as a religionary. And although Comte's Positivism was to become a form of religion in his mind, it is one that makes society the Grand Being, and draws its dogmas from Positivism conceived as science. In short, sociology's methodological stress on religion as a key variable in the study of society has nothing to do with personal religious commitment. It has everything to do with the profoundly altered conception of the nature of religion that we see rising, along with ideas of community and authority, at the beginning of the century.

Sociology's theoretical concern with religion is a part of the groundswell of interest in religious phenomena that engulfs much of nineteenth-century thought. Not often is it realized by historians of modern thought that the nineteenth century is, so far as religious writing is concerned, one of the two or three richest in the whole history of Western Europe. I have in mind here not the oft-cited waves of tractarianism, revivalism, and evangelism which swept over Europe and America alike, resulting in the formation of more cults, faiths, schisms, and churches than any century since perhaps the sixteenth, but, rather, the eruption of philosophical, humanistic, and literary preoccupation with religion.

Side by side with the individualistic rationalism and secularism of the century went a concern with matters of faith and liturgy that produced some of the foremost theologians in the history of Christianity. More to the point for our purpose, however, is the succession of works, beginning with Chateaubriand's widely read *The Genius of Christianity* in 1802, that was to capture the minds of lay philosophers and historians, turning their analytical interests to religion and creating an ambience of *regard* for religion and its properties that had not been seen in centuries. In this succession of religious works are to be found Lamennais's profound and influential *Essay on Indifference,* Balmes' *Protestantism and Catholicity Compared in Their Effects on European Civilization* (both of which went through many printings and translations in the first half of the century), and Feuerbach's *The Essence of Christianity.* The latter, unlike the other three, was hardly a celebration of Christianity, but few works have ever explored more deeply the doctrinal and liturgical mysteries of Christianity. More important, it reflected a dedication to the importance of religion in society that was to influence a continuous succession of theologians, culminating in our own day with Martin Buber.

What these and other religious works written in the early part of the century succeeded in doing was to rekindle an interest in the role of religion in human thought and society. We see this interest in many places: in the writings of Coleridge and Southey in England, of Hegel in

Germany, and Saint-Simon and Comte in France. Diverse as are the premises and ideas of these men, there is a common acceptance of the necessity of some kind of religion in society; any society, whether constructed according to the middle-class norms of a Hegel or the Positivist specifications of a Comte.

In his *Philosophy of Right* Hegel made religion an autonomous area of social existence, like family, corporation, and social class. Religion, for Hegel, is not limited to belief and faith. It is one of his all-important "circles of association." Religion has a purpose and external organization of its own. "The practice of its worship consists in ritual and doctrinal instruction, and for this purpose possessions and property are required, as well as individuals dedicated to the service of the flock. There thus arises a relation between the state and the church. In the nature of the case, the state discharges a duty by affording every assistance and protection to the church in the furtherance of its religious ends; and, in addition, since religion is an integrating factor in the state, implanting a sense of unity in the depths of men's minds, the state should require all its citizens to belong to a church . . ." [9] In a host of ways Hegel emphasized the crucial role of religion in social order and individual thought. Rationalist he was, but in a profoundly different sense from the rationalists who had preceded him in Germany.

When we turn to Comte it is often hard to remember that we are reading the works not of a theologian but of a self-proclaimed scientist. The religious vein in Comte is a deep one, by no means confined to the pages of *The Positive Polity,* which he wrote late in his life. Even in the *Essays,* written while he was still in his young manhood, there is an appreciation of the necessity of a "spiritual power" in society that contrasts strikingly with the views of the *philosophes*—whom, on this as well as on other grounds, Comte castigates. In one of the essays Comte tells us that all the present dislocations of society are traceable to the spiritual disorganization of Europe that began with the Reformation, when the fabric of Christian unity was rent by the doctrines of Luther and Calvin. The medieval world, Comte writes, was characterized by a strict division between the spiritual and secular powers, a division that held the power of the kings in check on the one hand and, on the other, gave autonomous and secure context to the moral laws of the church. What is necessary today, Comte writes in the *Essays,* is revival of "a spiritual authority that is distinct and independent of the temporal power." [10] Such a spiritual authority will alone be capable of arresting the moral ravages of secularism caused by the "metaphysical dogmas" of the Enlightenment.

It is in *The Positive Polity,* however, that Comte's "religious sociology" is brought to fullest intensity and scope. There we are told that every durable association of men must always require a religion. The glory of the Middle Ages lay in the organic fusion of religion with the rest of society. Christianity has become outmoded by Positivism but this does not mean that religion is extinct. On the contrary, Positivism, born of the scientific temper, will itself become the new religion of man, a religion in which the Grand Being is society. Comte's religion of Positivism has been well characterized as "Catholicism minus Christianity," and few readers of *The Positive Polity* will miss an influence on his mind that began with his devoutly Catholic (and royalist) parents. We are given in this work detailed accounts of the doctrines of the new religion of Positivism and also of the liturgy, the sacraments, the rituals, and even the vestments to be worn by the priests of Positivism, who are, at one and the same time, the scientists.

All of this might be regarded as but the messianic creed of a secular prophet were it not for the fact that in the process of arguing the case for religion in society Comte provides us with some extraordinarily perceptive insights into the relation of religious dogma to personality, of ritual to the integration of family, community, and state, and of faith to moral consensus.[11] Stripped of the Positivist polemics which form the contexts of the insights, they fall clearly in the stream of philosophical awareness of the relation between religion and society that begins with a Chateaubriand and ends with a Durkheim or a Weber.

As we look at the religious writing that appeared in every part of Europe in reaction to the secularism of Enlightenment and Revolution, four fundamental perspectives may be seen, all of them relevant to the special view of religion that the sociologists were to take.

First, religion is necessary to society, not merely in an abstract moral sense, but as an indispensable mechanism of integration of human beings and as a realm of unifying symbols of allegiance and faith. Beginning with Burke's momentous doctrine of prejudice and Chateaubriand's emphasis upon the ritual essence of Christianity, there is a repudiation of the rationalist view that religion is reducible to belief and logical proposition. In the same way that communal bonds are necessary to social order, sacred values are necessary to moral consensus. No social system can survive in terms of a Benthamite calculus of pleasures and pains. So wrote men as different in other respects as Coleridge, Bonald, and Hegel. Apart from motivations and incentives that are non-rational, and that draw their imperativeness from the sacredness with which they are regarded, ordinary relations of contract, habit, or command will dissolve into dust. The error of the Enlightenment had lain in supposing that the sacred is no more than a transient delusion, that men may live within a world of secular values founded on reason and interest.

Second, religion is a key element and a primary sphere of consideration in understanding history and social change. All that establishes its symbolic and integrative importance in social order establishes also its primary role as the sphere within which the most fundamental types of social change will have their origin, or, if not origin, the context within which material changes are transmuted into motivations and values that have wide urgency. It is in these terms indeed that we can account for the preoccupation with Protestantism in the writings of the religious conservatives and romantics. Protestantism, to such men as Bonald, Lamennais, and Balmes, represented, in its emphasis upon individual faith and its depreciation of ritual and liturgy, a destructive force in European history. This is a theme that lights up much nineteenth-century writing. We find it in Burke, who saw a fateful affinity between religious dissent and commercialism and democratic leveling; in Lamennais, who traced modern "indifference" back to the separation of Protestants from Catholic community; and in Chateaubriand, who made Protestantism the essential cause of what he regarded as the decline of cultural values in the modern world. The Spanish Catholic Balmes, in his *Protestantism and Catholicity Compared in Their Effects on European Civilization,* made Protestantism a prime cause not only of unrestrained commercialism but also of modern political despotism.

Third, religion is more than faith, doctrine, and precept. It is also rite and ceremony, community and authority, hierarchy and organization. In his *Theory of Authority* Bonald had declared religion coterminous with the state as a system of duties and rights. For Lamennais, the beginnings of modern disintegration and alienation are to be found in the separation of men from the *authority* as well as the community of religion. The charm and influence of Chateaubriand's *Genius of Christianity* for even secular minds lay in its detailed elaboration of the "mysteries" and the rituals as well as the esthetic values of Christianity. Chateaubriand holds up boldly the *mysteries* of Christianity. "There is nothing beautiful, pleasing or grand in life but that which is more or less mysterious. The most wonderful sentiments are those which produce impressions difficult to be explained. . . . Considering the natural propensity of man to the mysterious, it cannot appear surprising that the religions of all nations should have had their impenetrable secrets." [12] It is Christianity as mystery that leads to his heavy emphasis on the sacred and all those aspects—sacrifices, rituals, ceremonies, and feast days—which make religion primarily a community of symbol and act rather than a thing of reason and logic. It is from the underlying mystery of religion that he works his way to the vital historical relationship of Christianity to the art, music, and literature of Europe. It is the communal character of faith—expressed, he tells us, by liturgy and vestment and sacrament, and symbolized by the bells of the church—that is its most enduring feature. The power of religion to stimulate, to reinforce, and to protect individuals lies not primarily in the *ideas* of religion but in the rites and mysteries through which unattached man becomes conscious of a sense of membership in society. The sacraments and rites of birth, marriage, and death bespeak the affinity of religion, correctly regarded, with family and society.

Fourth, in their desire to re-establish the majesty of religion in thought, the conservatives made it the origin of all fundamental ideas in human thought and belief. There is a long section in Bonald in which he seeks to show the origin of language and the categories of thought in primitive man's contemplation of God. How else, he asks, can the evolutionary antinomy of thought and speech, of idea and word, be resolved except within the realm of the divine?[13] From religious society derive all other forms of society; from religious loyalties all other forms of loyalty; and from religious ideas all other ideas. Not in the finite individual are ideas and values originally born, declared Lamennais, for the individual is but a chimera, "the shadow of a dream." [14] The fault of individualism is not merely moral but metaphysical. Only in those contexts which man regards as divine, that is, as imperative in their sacredness, could the major ideas of mankind have arisen in the first instance.

These are the perspectives, briefly stated, which appear relevant to the rise of what I have called the analytical perspective of the sacred. The polemical and evangelical character of these perspectives is plain enough in the writings of the religious romantics and conservatives. So is it in the works of Comte and Hegel. What we must now turn to is the gradual transformation of context from polemic to intellectual analysis, and the utilization of these perspectives for purposes of understanding rather than of evangelism.

DOGMA AND DEMOCRACY—TOCQUEVILLE

For Tocqueville, religion is the ultimate source of man's conceptions of physical and social reality. "There is hardly any human action," he writes, "however particular it may be, that does not originate in some very general idea men have conceived of the Deity, of his relation to mankind, of the nature of their own souls, and of their duties to their fellow creatures. Nor can anything prevent these ideas from being the common spring from which all the rest emanates." [15]

Religion is, Tocqueville declares, as natural to the human mind as hope, and it is equally inextinguishable. "Men cannot abandon their religious faith without a kind of aberration of intellect and a sort of violent distortion of their true nature; they are invincibly brought back to more pious sentiments. Unbelief is an accident, and faith is the only permanent state of mankind. If we consider religious institutions merely in a human point of view, they may be said to derive an inexhaustible element of strength from man himself, since they belong to one of the constituent principles of human nature." [16]

The major function of religion in society is that it furnishes a framework of belief, one that enables individuals to internalize external diversity into intellectual order. Religion is integrative, and its sudden loss can lead to social disorganization and also to political despotism. "When the religion of a people is destroyed, doubt gets hold of the higher powers of the intellect and half paralyzes all the others. Every man accustoms himself to having only confused and changing notions on the subjects most interesting to his fellow creatures and himself. . . . Such a condition cannot but enervate the soul, relax the springs of the will, and prepare the people for servitude . . . When there is no longer any principle of authority in religion any more than in politics, men are speedily frightened at the aspect of this unbounded independence. The constant agitation of all surrounding things alarms and exhausts them. As everything is at sea in the sphere of the mind, they determine at least that the mechanism of society shall be firm and fixed; and as they cannot resume their ancient belief, they assume a master." [17]

Religion, then, is a structure of belief, and far from being, as the Enlightenment almost universally conceived it, an impediment to man's reason, it provides the sinews of reason. Apart from it, reason lies in a vacuum, inchoate and impotent.

At the heart of religion and of all things sacred is *dogma*. Dogma, Tocqueville tells us, is as indispensable to individual mind as it is to the structure of society. It is the steel spring of thought. Tocqueville would have agreed with Cardinal Newman's epigram, that "men will die for a dogma who will not even stir for a conclusion."

"In order that society should exist and, *a fortiori,* that a society should prosper, it is necessary that the minds of all the citizens should be rallied and held together by certain predominant ideas; and this cannot be the case unless each of them sometimes draws his opinions from the common source and consents to accept certain matters of belief already formed.

"If I now consider man in his isolated capacity, I find that dogmatic belief is not less indispensable to him in order to live alone than it is to enable him to cooperate with his fellows. If man were forced to demonstrate for himself all the truths of which he makes daily use, his task would never end. He would exhaust his strength in preparatory demonstrations without ever advancing beyond them . . . There is no philosopher in the world so great but that he believes a million things on the faith of other people and accepts a great many more truths than he demonstrates." [18]

Here, plainly, Tocqueville has in mind Burke's celebrated defense of prejudice and of the "latent wisdom" that dwells in prejudice. Burke had argued that it is harmful "to cast away the coat of prejudice, and to leave nothing but the naked reason; because prejudice, with its reason, has a motive to give action to that reason, and an affection which will give it permanence. Prejudice is of ready application in the emergency; it previously engages the mind in a steady course of wisdom and virtue, and does not leave the man hesitating in the moment of decision, skeptical, puzzled, and unresolved. Prejudice renders a man's virtue his habit; and not a series of unconnected acts. Through just prejudice, his duty becomes a party of his nature." [19]

But democracy has a dissolving influence upon dogma, at least those types of dogma that do not spring from itself. Equality of condition predisposes men to "entertain a sort of instinctive incredulity of the supernatural and a very lofty and often exaggerated opinion of human understanding." [20] Social equalitarianism induces a disinclination to respect any authority that does not proceed clearly from the mass of the people. Men therefore "commonly seek for the sources of truth in themselves or in those who are like themselves. This would be enough to prove that at such periods no new religion could be established, and that all schemes for such a purpose would be not only impious but absurd and irrational." [21]

But skepticism toward supernatural powers does not mean total skepticism. Such is the need for sacred belief in man that under equalitarianism he will endow the mass and mass opinion with what he takes from the supernatural. In America, Tocqueville tells us, "religion itself holds sway . . . much less as a doctrine of revelation than as a commonly received opinion." [22] More important, public opinion becomes a new form of religion. No matter what the specific nature of laws may be that men live under, "in ages of equality, it may be foreseen that faith in public opinion will become for them a species of religion, and the majority its ministering prophet." There is, hence, a kind of democratic pantheism to be seen. "Among the different systems by whose aid philosophy endeavors to explain the universe I believe pantheism to be one of those most fitted to seduce the human mind in democratic times." [23]

Since it is in democracy that public opinion and love of affluence are strongest, a genuine religion is more important to freedom there than in monarchy or aristocracy. "The greatest advantage of religion is that it inspires diametrically contrary principles." [24]

It is not only religious faith that is functionally necessary to democracy but also the symbolic and liturgical appurtenances of religion. Nothing, Tocqueville notes, is ordinarily more repugnant to men in a democracy than subjection to forms. "Men living at such times are impatient of figures; in their eyes, symbols appear to be puerile artifices used to conceal or to set off truths that should more naturally be bared to the light of day; they are unmoved by ceremonial observances and are disposed to attach only a secondary importance to the details of public worship." But forms are necessary, for they "fix the human mind in the contemplation of abstract truths and aid it in embracing them warmly and holding them with firmness." [25]

In the United States, Tocqueville notes, there is, even among Roman Catholics, less devotion to religious form alone than anywhere in Europe. "I have seen no country in which Christianity is clothed with fewer forms, figures, and observances than in the United States, or where it presents more distinct, simple, and general notions to the mind . . . There are no Roman Catholic priests who show less taste for the minute individual observances, for extraordinary or peculiar means of salvation, or who cling more to the spirit and less to the letter of the law than the Roman Catholic priests of the United States." [26]

Tocqueville is much interested in the role of Catholicism in the United States. He is struck by two apparent tendencies in the relation of Americans to the Catholic Church. On the one hand, American Catholics seem to him to lapse more easily into loss of faith than their European counterparts: that is, to be *in* but not *of* Catholicism. On the other hand, significant numbers of Protestants become converts to Catholicism.

"If you consider Catholicism within its own organization, it seems to be losing; if you consider it from outside, it seems to be gaining. Nor is this difficult to explain. The men of our days are naturally little disposed to believe; but as soon as they have any religion, they immediately find in themselves a latent instinct that urges them unconsciously towards Catholicism. Many of the doctrines and practices of the Roman Catholic Church astonish them, but they feel a secret admiration for its discipline, and its great unity attracts them. If Catholicism could at length withdraw itself from the political animosities to which it has given rise, I have hardly any doubt but that the same spirit of the age which appears to be so opposed to it would become so favorable as to admit its great and sudden advancement." [27]

Tocqueville's visit to the United States coincided with an extraordinary outburst of religious sectarianism. New faiths were arising almost daily in one form or another, usually by processes of branching off or grafting on. With the sectarian temper went a frenzy for evangelism that had, Tocqueville thought, a peculiar relation to politics. Writing of the religious missionaries he encountered in the frontier regions, he notes that "religious zeal is perpetually warmed in the United States by the fires of patriotism. These men do not act exclusively from a consideration of a future life; eternity is only one motive of their devotion to the cause. If you converse with these missionaries of Christian civilization you will be surprised to hear them speak so often of the goods of this world, and to meet a politician where you expected to find a priest." [28]

He is struck by interrelation between material affluence and the spawning of religious fanatics. "Although the desire of acquiring the good things of this world is the prevailing passion of the American people, certain momentary outbreaks occur when their souls seem suddenly to burst the bonds of matter by which they are restrained and to soar impetuously to heaven." [29] In the United States one meets with a form of "fanatical and almost wild spiritualism" that scarcely exists in Europe. The impulse toward spiritual objects is irresistible in the long run. No matter how long it may be repressed by material devotions, the time will come when this spiritual impulse must seek outlet. And the more intense the feeling of material pressures, the greater and more abandoned the mode of outlet.[30]

The relation between religious membership and political affiliation invites Tocqueville's contrast between Catholicism and Protestantism. To most minds of that time it appeared certain that Catholicism was less adapted by creed and structure to political democracy than was Protestantism. But Tocqueville sees the matter differently, and in no way is his reaction to the Enlightenment sharper than in his demonstration of the opposite thesis. He observes first that in the United States there is a close affinity between the overwhelming majority of Roman Catholics and that political party which is the most equalitarian and democratic. "Most Catholics are poor, and they have no chance of taking part in the government unless it opens to all citizens. They constitute a minority, and all rights must be respected in order to ensure to them the free exercise of their own privileges." [31]

But there is an even more fundamental reason, one arising out of the very nature of Catholic theology. "In the Catholic Church the religious community is composed of only two elements: the priest and the people. The priest alone rises above the rank of his flock, and all below him are equal. On doctrinal points the Catholic faith places all human capacities upon the same level; it subjects the wise and the ignorant, the man of genius and the vulgar crowd, to the details of the same creed; it imposes the same observances upon the rich and the needy; it inflicts the same austerities upon the strong and the weak; it listens to no compromise with mortal man, but reducing all the human race to the same standard, it confounds all the distinctions of society at the foot of the same altar, even as they are confounded in the sight of God." [32]

Protestantism on the other hand "tends to make men independent more than to render them equal." [33] There is also, Tocqueville notes, the Protestant love of wealth and privilege that exists side by side with spiritual conviction. It is of the Anglo-Saxon Puritans in America that Tocqueville writes in the following passage: "Men sacrifice for a religious opinion their friends, their family, and their country; one can consider them devoted to the pursuit of intellectual goals which they came to purchase at so high a price. One sees them, however, seeking with almost equal eagerness material wealth and moral satisfaction; heaven in the world beyond, and well-being and liberty in this one." [34]

We must mention finally Tocqueville's discussion of the fateful relation between religion and power. Nothing, he contends, is more necessary to the preservation of liberty in a democracy than absolute separation of religion from state and its politics. And nothing is more difficult to do, given the twin intensities of passion accorded each.

The philosophers of the Enlightenment, Tocqueville writes, had thought that religious passion would decay with modernism. "Religious zeal, said they, must necessarily fail the more generally liberty is established and knowledge diffused. Unfortunately the facts by no means accord with their theory." [35] The spread of political freedom has, if the United States is an example, only intensified the passion for religion. It is separation of church and state alone that can keep these like passions apart, and Tocqueville notes with approval the zealous effort of most members of the American clergy to remain clear of politics or public office. When a religion "connects itself with a government, it must adopt maxims which are applicable only to certain nations. Thus, in forming an alliance with a political power, religion augments its authority over a few and forfeits the hope of reigning over all." The church cannot participate in the power of the state "without being the object of a portion of that animosity which the latter excites." [36]

There is also the danger that derives from seeking to harmonize the universal and eternal propositions of religion with the inevitably mutable conditions of democracy. "In proportion as a nation assumes a democratic condition of society and as communities display democratic propensities, it becomes more and more dangerous to connect religion with political institutions; for the time is coming when authority will be bandied from hand to hand, when political theories will succeed one another, and when men, laws, and constitutions will disappear or be modified from day to day, and this is not for a season only, but unceasingly. Agitation and mutability are inherent in the nature of democratic republics, just as stagnation and sleepiness are the law of absolute monarchies." [37]

In Europe, unlike America, Christianity has for centuries been closely linked with the political powers. "Now these powers are in decay, and it is, as it were, buried under their ruins." The price of the long alliance is that at the present time Christianity is dealt with by unbelievers as a political rather than a religious body. "The unbelievers of Europe attack the Christians as their political opponents rather than as their religious adversaries; they hate the Christian religion as the opinion of a party much more than as an error of belief; and they reject the clergy less because they are the representatives of the Deity than because they are the allies of government." [38]

THE SACRED AS PERSPECTIVE—
FUSTEL DE COULANGES

In Fustel de Coulanges's *The Ancient City* we find the first clearly analytical use of the perspective of the sacred in the interpretation of social organization and institutional change. Not the least part of Fustel's significance lies in the fact that he was one of Durkheim's most influential teachers. Given the prominence that the concept of the sacred holds in *The Ancient City,* and undoubtedly also in Fustel's lectures at the École Normale, which Durkheim attended after he enrolled in 1879, one would not have to look further for the impulse that was to result in Durkheim's own use of the concept. Fustel was himself rationalist in conviction; there is no evidence in his work of religious belief, much less of any desire to espouse or propose. He draws a sharp distinction between human motivations within the ancient city-states of Greece and Rome and those of the modern world. "Man has not, in our day, the way of thinking that he had twenty-five centuries ago; and this is why he is no longer governed as he was governed then." [39] The underlying thesis of the book is that modern man is secular and rationalist in mind to a degree that ancient man was not, and only by recognition of this may we get at the roots of institutional history.

Fustel gives to the sacred and its contrast with the secular the same analytical significance that Maine had given to status and contract. For him the fundamental, clarifying perspective is not legal but religious. "Examine the institutions of the ancients without thinking of their religious notions, and you find them obscure, whimsical, and inexplicable." [40] Why, he goes on, were social classes composed as they were, whence came the absolute authority of the house father, the peculiar severity of communal law, and the absence, in the earliest phases, of any notion of individuality or freedom? Why, later, did this whole social structure disintegrate? The answer to these questions lies, Fustel tells us, solely in the realm of religion.

"A comparison of beliefs and laws shows that a primitive religion constituted the Greek and Roman family, established marriage and paternal authority, fixed the order of relationship, and consecrated the right of property and the right of inheritance. This same religion, after having enlarged and extended the family, formed a still larger association, the city, and reigned in it as it had reigned in the family. From it came all the institutions, as well as all the private law, of the ancients. It was from this that the city received all its principles, its rules, its usages, and its magistracies. But, in the course of time, this ancient religion became modified or effaced, and private law and political institutions were modified with it. Then came a series of revolutions, and social changes regularly followed the development of knowledge." [41] The study of the city-state and its disintegration is "a witness and an example of the intimate relation which always exists between men's ideas and their social state."

This is the theme. What follows is a detailed analysis of, first, the structure of the ancient community, its kinship system, social classes, religion, and polity, and, then, the succession of changes or revolutions by which the community disappeared, to become absorbed by political empire. And central in his entire analysis is the significance that Fustel gives to the sacred and what happened to it. It is this that makes his treatment of the subject unique among the multitude of studies that, in Fustel's age, were directed to ancient law and polity. Fustel endows religion with exactly the same causal primacy that in Marx went to property; in Maine, law; and, in Buckle, physical environment.

The ancient community derived its nature and authority from the sacred fire. "This fire ceased to glow upon the altar only when the entire family had perished; an extinguished hearth, an extinguished family, were synonymous expressions among the ancients." The sacredness of the domestic fire made for a distinction among persons qualified to tend it, among elements that could feed the fire; that is, types of wood and other fuel. For it was "a religious precept that this fire must always remain pure." The fire was something divine; men adored it and offered it worship. "In misfortune man betook himself to his sacred fire, and heaped reproaches on it; in good fortune he returned it thanks. . . . The sacred fire was the Providence of the family." [42]

From the original, exclusive sacredness of the domestic fire emerged gradually more complex manifestations of religion. What was sacred, in contrast to what was unclean or merely material, began to extend from the fire alone to other elements and beings. Thus the altar on which the fire burned became personified as Vesta. Deceased members of the family, who had worshiped at the same fire, became, many of them, the Lares, gradually made indistinguishable from heroes and demons. Eventually, Fustel tells us, the original essence of the sacred fire is transmuted and diversified into the numberless spirits of land, family, and community.

It was religion alone that could have accounted for the absoluteness of paternal authority and for the equal absoluteness of the autonomy possessed by each family in the government of its affairs. Fustel deals one by one with alternative explanations of the authority of the family—natural generation, affection, force, property—and finds each inadequate. "The members of the ancient family were united by something more powerful than birth, affection, or physical strength; this was the religion of the sacred fire and of dead ancestors. This caused the family to form a single body, both in this life and in the next. The ancient family was a religious rather than a natural association." [43]

Every element of ancient family structure—its indissolubility, its corporateness in law, the *patria potestas,* the principle of agnation, and the inviolability of its threshold—that makes it difficult to understand in modern terms can be accounted for solely by the absolute authority of the sacred in men's minds. Marriage was but the religious induction of the female from one family into another: from worship of one sacred fire to a new one, in preparation for which she must be made pure, divorced from all associations with her former worship. Hence the strictness of the agnatic principle.

What is true of the beginning of the family is equally true of the larger associations that surrounded the family. "In the beginning the family lived isolated, and man knew only the domestic gods . . . Above the family was formed the phratry with its god . . . Then came the tribe, and the god of the tribe . . . Finally came the city, and men conceived a god whose providence embraced this entire city . . . ; a hierarchy of creeds, and a hierarchy of association. The religious idea was, among the ancients, the inspiring breath and organizer of society." [44]

Equally decisive is religion with respect to the nature of social class in the ancient community. The momentous distinction between patrician and plebeian had nothing to do with inequality of property ownership, for there were in time wealthy plebeians and impoverished patricians. The distinction between the two classes—once as absolute in Greece and Rome as among the castes of modern India—derived solely from the fact that the patricians possessed the sacred fire and the plebeians did not; for them it was forbidden. "One word characterizes these plebeians —they were without a hearth; they did not possess, in the beginning at least, any domestic altars." Without the sacred fire they were without the rites of marriage, without security of property. "For the plebeians there was no law, no justice, since the law was the decision of religion, and the procedure was a body of rites." [45]

"We see how many classes in the primitive age of the cities were superposed one above another. At the head was the aristocracy of family chiefs, those whom the official language of Rome called *patres,* whom the clients called *reges.* . . . Below were the younger branches of the families; still lower were the clients; and lowest were the plebs. This distinction of classes came from religion."

But, Fustel observes, none of these social arrangements could be permanent. They carried "the germ of disease and death, which was inequality. Many men had an interest in destroying a social organization that had no benefits for them." [46]

We cannot here follow Fustel in his treatment of the three revolutions which, over a period of many centuries, transformed the nature and relation of the social classes and with them the structure of the family and the community. It suffices to say that in the first revolution the aristocracy made itself supreme over king; in the second, the clients revolted, to become, as it were, the middle class of the ancient city; and in the third, the plebeians at last achieved membership in the city. And with this final extension of citizenship the ancient community was no more. The key factor in each of the three revolutions was religion and class rights to participate in it. Thus when the plebeians triumphed, it was in terms, first, of the communal divinities they were allowed to worship, with proper place provided for the worship. "The plebeian celebrated the religious festivals of his quarter, and of his burgh, as the patrician celebrated the sacrifices of his gens and of his curio. The plebeian had a religion." [47] Afterward came political benefits.

"This was the last conquest of the lower orders; they had nothing more to wish for. The patricians had lost even their religious superiority. Nothing distinguished them now from the plebs; the name patrician was now only a souvenir. The old principle upon which the Roman city, like all ancient cities, had been founded, had disappeared." [48]

The Ancient City is more, however, than an analysis of a social organization and its distintegration. It is, throughout, a sociology of knowledge and belief. Fustel is concerned with "the intimate relation which always exists between men's ideas and their social state." It was belief in the sacred properties of certain aspects of the environment that led to a distinctive social system. And it is, equally, the distintegration of this social system that results in profound changes of belief.

"The primitive religion, whose symbols were the immovable stone of the hearth and the ancestral tomb—a religion which had established the ancient family, and had afterwards organized the city—changed with time, and grew old. The human mind increased in strength, and adopted new beliefs. Men began to have an idea of immaterial nature; the notion of the human soul became more definite, and almost at the same time that of a divine intelligence sprang up in their minds." [49]

Here Fustel is dealing with secularization as it affected men's ideas of nature and man. First was the transformation of beliefs in deities into an awareness of physical nature so great that the identities of the gods, including the Lares and Penates, dissolved into nothingness. Next, the public hearth of the city "was insensibly drawn into the discredit into which the domestic fire had fallen." Even the divinities of nature changed their character. Having begun by being domestic, then communal deities, they became syncretized into one being. "The mind was oppressed with the multitude of divinities, and felt the need of reducing their number," first to a few, then to one all-embracing being, God.

"Thus an intellectual revolution took place slowly and obscurely. Even the priests made no opposition, for as long as the sacrifices continued to be offered on designated days, it seemed to them that the ancient religion was preserved. Ideas might change and faith perish, provided the rites received no attack. It happened, therefore, without the practices being modified, that the beliefs were transformed, and that the domestic and municipal religion lost all influence over the minds of men." [50]

It is precisely in these circumstances that we witness, through Fustel's eyes, the birth of Greek rationalism. There were, first, the physical philosophers who, having seen the efficacy of the gods destroyed, looked to such elements as fire, water, and the earth itself for primal potency. Then, a century or two later, came the moral philosophers, who carried secularism to morality and polity. "They moved, as Plato says, what before had been immovable. They placed the rule of religious sentiment, and that of politics, in the human conscience, and not in the customs of ancestors, in immutable tradition." [51] For the knowledge of sacred custom they substituted the secular arts of rhetoric, reasoning, and made challenge of the verities the essence of individual reason.

"When reflection had thus been once wakened, man no longer wished to believe without giving a reason for his belief, or to be governed without discussion of his institutions and values. He doubted the justice of old laws, and other principles dawned upon his mind . . . The authority of the old institutions perished with the authority of the national gods, and the habit of free examination became established in men's homes and in the public squares." [52]

Rarely has the problem of the rise of Greek rationalism in the Golden Age been presented as illuminatingly as by Fustel. It was certainly not his primary intent, when he commenced *The Ancient City,* to offer an explanation of the great fifth century B.C. But this result followed inevitably from his analysis of the role of the sacred in Greek society, its relation to social organization, and what happened when the sacred became, through revolution, war, and trade, secularized. Fustel shows us that just as the basic categories of early Greek and Roman thought were formed in the ambience of the sacred, so the later questions asked by rationalists were questions that sprang from secularization.

Fustel concludes his book with the following passage: "We have written the history of a belief. It was established, and human society was constituted. It was modified, and society underwent a series of revolutions. It disappeared, and society changed its character. Such was the law of ancient times." [53]

THE SACRED AND PROFANE—DURKHEIM

From Fustel de Coulanges to his student, Durkheim, is but a short step. Durkheim's distinction between the sacred and the profane, and his linking of the sacred to the social are but a broadening and systematization of what Fustel had confined to the classical city-state.

Of all concepts and perspectives in Durkheim the sacred is the most striking and, given the age in which he lived, the most radical. His use of the sacred to explain the cohesive nature of society, the constraint that society exercises upon man, the origins of culture and even of human thought must surely rank as one of the boldest contributions of a positivist non-believer. The fact that Durkheim defines the sacred as the apotheosis or transfiguration of society does not mean that it is for him a merely derivative or secondary force. Quite the contrary. The differentiation between the sacred and the profane is, Durkheim tells us, the most fundamental differentiation in all human thought.

Like Tocqueville, Durkheim declares religion to be the origin of not merely all basic ideas but of the framework of human thought. "If philosophy and the sciences were born of religion, it is because religion began by taking the place of the sciences and philosophy. But it has been less frequently noticed that religion has not confined itself to enriching the human intellect, formed beforehand, with a certain number of ideas; it has contributed to forming the intellect itself. Men owe to it not only a good part of the substance of their knowledge, but also the form in which this knowledge has been elaborated." [54]

We need not repeat what has already been said about the specific ways in which Durkheim explains such mental categories as mass, time, and space. That such categories are, in Durkheim's terms, fundamentally social in origin is incontestable. But we should miss much of the special character that Durkheim gives the social if we did not observe that these categories reflect also the sacred. For the sacred and the social are, at bottom, inseparable: distinguishable but not separable. The sacred, we are justified in saying, is the social carried to the highest possible point of categorical imperative in the lives of individuals and, when carried to this point, it lies in a domain of its own.

"The division of the world into two domains, the one containing all that is sacred, the other all that is profane, is the distinctive trait of religious thought; the beliefs, myths, dogmas, and legends are either representations or systems of representations which express the nature of sacred things, the virtues and powers which are attributed to them, or their relations with each other and with profane things. But, by sacred things, one must not understand simply those personal beings which are called gods or spirits; a rock, a tree, a spring, a pebble, a piece of wood, a house, in a word, anything can be sacred. A rite can have this character, in fact, the rite does not exist which does not have it to a certain degree." [55]

Sacred things have a natural superiority to profane things—superior in dignity and power—and particularly is this true in their relation to man himself. Man looks up to them, immolates himself to them, in one degree or other. Sometimes man's relation to the sacred is one of awe, or love, even of measureless dread; other times his relation to sacred objects is one of ease and pleasure. Even before his gods, man is not always in a state of expressed inferiority, for he may joke with and about them, he may beat the fetish which has caused him mishap. But the superiority of sacred things is assumed nevertheless.

The distinction between sacred and profane is absolute. "In all the history of human thought there exists no other example of two categories of things so profoundly differentiated or so radically opposed to one another. The traditional opposition of good and bad is nothing beside this; for the good and the bad are only two opposed species of the same class, namely morals, just as sickness and health are two different aspects of the same order of facts, life, while the sacred and the profane have always and everywhere been conceived by the human mind as two distinct classes, two worlds between which there is nothing in common." [56]

The absoluteness and universality of the contrast does not mean that things and beings cannot pass from one sphere to the other. The manner of this passage, however, highlights the separateness of the two kingdoms. Purifying rites, as in initiation or eucharistic ceremonies, are required for a person or a thing to pass from the profane state to the sacred. By contrast, the passage of things from sacred to profane is more often the consequence of erosion of values, a dislocation of deities and entities resulting from the entrance of new manifestations of the sacred, new religions, or by the spread of skepticism.

The erosion and disappearance of one set of sacred observances are invariably followed by the appearance of new entities or things or states to which sacred status is granted. This is often the fate even of intellectual and social systems that begin in the most utilitarian or rationalistic circumstances, even those that dedicate themselves to the overthrow of some existing system of sacred values in the name of critical reason. Durkheim cites the fate of rationalism during the Revolution, when it was transformed into public worship of the Goddess of Reason and into the establishment of new commemorative festivals.

It is in his methodological application of the sacred that we see, just as we did with respect to community, its full possibilities. Contract is a striking example. We have already noted Durkhiem's insistence that contract cannot be explained in the individualistic terms of interest or reason, that it rests upon pre-contractual foundations derived ultimately from community. But the power of contract is a reflection also of the sacred; the capacity of a society to sanctify the relation in a way that it does not sanctify other relationships. The medium is language.

"There is something in words that is real, natural, and living and they can be endowed with a sacred force, thanks to which they compel and bind those who pronounce them. It is enough for them to be pronounced in ritual form and in ritual conditions. They take on a sacred quality by that very act. One means of giving them this sacred character is the oath, or invocation of a divine being. Through this invocation, the divine being becomes the guarantor of the promise exchanged. Thereby the promise, as soon as exchanged in this way . . . becomes compulsive, under threat of sacred penalties of known gravity . . . This, then, seems to be the origin of contracts made in all due and solemn formality . . . The juridical formula is only a substitute for sacred formalities and rites." [57]

The solemn, ritual contract has been succeeded in most human affairs by the consensual contract which ordinarily is attended by little in the way of solemnity or ritual. But the notion of "irrevocability of will" remains essential to contract in any form—a notion incapable of explanation in utilitarian terms—and this notion requires the continuation of the idea of a higher power giving sanctification to the agreement. "Had it not been for the existence of the contract by solemn ritual, there would have been no notion of the contract by mutual consent. Nor would there have been any idea that the word of honor, which is fugitive and can be revoked by anyone, could thus be secured and given substance." [58]

The perspective of the sacred is equally applicable to the institution of property. Whence comes the notion of the right and sanctity of property? Not, certainly, from instinct or sense of self-interest, for this could result only in desire for aggrandizement, not in a respect for the property of others so deep that it ranks among man's most deeply embedded values.

"The sacredness diffused in things, which withheld them from any profane appropriation, was conducted by means of a certain definite ritual either to the threshold or to the periphery of the field. It there established something like a girdle of sanctity or sacred encircling mound, protecting the domain from any trespass by outsiders. To cross this zone and enter the little island insulated from the rest of the land by ritual was reserved to those alone who had carried out the rites, that is, those who had contracted especial bonds with the sacred beings, the original owners of the soil. By degrees, this sacredness residing in the things themselves passed into the persons: they no longer possessed this quality, except indirectly, because they were subject to persons who themselves were sacred. Property, from being collective, became individual." [59]

Let us see now how the idea of the sacred—and with it the communal—becomes the basis of Durkheim's interpretation of the character of religion. He rejects the view that religion is identified by belief in gods or transcendent spirits. Nor can religion be made synonymous with magic in its origins.

Religious beliefs "are always common to a determined group, which makes profession of adhering to them and of practicing the rites connected with them. They are not merely received individually by all the members of the group; they are something belonging to the group, and they make its unit. The individuals which compose it feel themselves united to each other by the simple fact that they have a common faith. A society whose members are united by the fact that they think in the same way in regard to the sacred world and its relations with the profane world, and by the fact that they translate these common ideas into common practice is what is called a church. In all history we do not find a single religion without a church." [60]

The essence of religion is the *sacred community* of believers, the indispensable feeling of collective oneness in worship and faith. To the possible objection that religion is also, demonstrably, a matter of individual faith, of personal cult, Durkheim replies that "these individual cults are not distinct and autonomous religious systems, but merely aspects of the common religion of the whole church, of which the individuals are the members . . . In a word, it is the church of which he is a member which teaches the individual that these personal gods are, what their function is, how he should enter into relations with them, and how he should honour them." To suppose that religion is, as Protestants and secularists alike have argued, something basically individual "misunderstands the fundamental conditions of religious life." [61]

Durkheim is as critical of rationalist explanations of religion as any religious conservative could be. "The theorists who have undertaken to explain religion in rational terms have generally seen it before all else a system of ideas, corresponding to some predetermined object. This object has been conceived in a multitude of ways: nature, the infinite, the unknowable, the ideal, etc.; these differences matter little." In such theories, conceptions and beliefs are considered the essential elements. Religious rites, from this point of view, appear to be "only an external translation, contingent and material, of these internal states which alone pass as having any intrinsic value." [62]

But, Durkheim notes shrewdly, this appraisal of religion made by outsiders is very different from the appraisal made by those who are within the compass of religion, those who are committed to it. For them, the essence of religion is *not what it says about things, external or internal, but what it does toward making action possible, life endurable.* "The believer who has communicated with his god is not merely a man who sees new truths of which the unbeliever is ignorant; he is a man who is *stronger*. He feels within him more force, either to endure the trials of existence, or to conquer them." [63] The first article of belief, where belief is explicit, may well be belief in salvation, but this idea could never in itself have the transforming meaning, the profound human sustenance that it has, apart from the place of this belief in a community of acts, of observances, of rites.

It is, therefore, the *cult* that is fundamental. Anyone who has ever "really practised a religion knows very well that it is the cult which gives rise to those impressions of joy, of interior peace, of serenity, of enthusiasm, which are, for the believer, an experimental proof of his beliefs. The cult is not simply a system of signs by which the faith is outwardly translated; it is a collection of the means by which this is created and recreated periodically." [64]

Durkheim concludes the long passage of which the above is a part by declaring: "Our entire study rests on the postulate that the unanimous sentiment of the believers of all times cannot be purely illusory." [65] The sociology of religion must begin, in short, with religion as it is practiced, as it is experienced, as it *is* indeed, so far as objective observations can convey it. From Durkheim's point of view, critical rationalists who have sought to dismiss religion as simply a tissue of superstitions, expendable once men are correctly informed, are as much in error as theologians who have endeavored to express the nature of religion in terms of creed and dogma. Religion is *sacred community*—or it is nothing but a precarious assemblage of impressions and words, lacking power to integrate and transfigure.

Every cult presents a double aspect: one negative, the other positive. The two aspects are in practice inseparable; they are nonetheless to be distinguished. Both aspects of the cult flow from the all-important separation of the sacred and profane. "A whole group of rites has the object of realizing this state of separation which is essential. Since their function is to prevent undue mixings and to keep one of these two domains from encroaching upon the other, they are only able to impose abstentious or negative acts. Therefore, we propose to give the name negative cult to the system formed by these special rites. They do not prescribe certain acts to the faithful, but confine themselves to forbidding certain ways of acting; so they all take the form of interdictions, or as is commonly said by ethnographers, of *taboos*." [66] The function of the negative cult is that of freeing man from contamination, or possible contamination, by the profane in order that he may be put in position to achieve the sacred; hence, the value placed upon acts, often extreme, of self-abasement, self-denial, of rigorous asceticism.

But "whatever the importance of the negative cult may be . . . it does not contain its reason for existence in itself, it introduces one to the religious life, but it supposes this more than it constitutes it. If it orders the worshiper to flee from the profane world, it is to bring him near to the sacred world. Men have never thought that their duties toward religious forces might be reduced to a simple abstinence from all commerce; they have always believed that they upheld positive and bilateral relations with them, whose regulation and organization are the function of a group of ritual practices. To this special system of rites we give the name of positive cult." [67]

In the positive cult is effected the relationship of god and man that is, Durkheim emphasizes, *reciprocal*. Unlike such observers as Robertson Smith, who had found the cult's chief function that of uniting men, Durkheim calls witness to the fact that the cult is as important to the gods as the men themselves. For (and here we are back at the essence of Durkheim's entire system of sociology) the gods are but manifestations or personifications of *society*. "We now see the real reason why the gods cannot do without their worshipers any more than these can do without their gods; it is because society, of which the gods are only a symbolic expression, cannot do without individuals any more than these can do without society. Here we touch the solid rock upon which all the cults are built and which has caused their persistence ever since human societies have existed." [68]

The sacred cult is cellular to religion, and it is constitutive to society as a whole. Without the cult, Durkheim tells us, society would weaken. The first effect of religious ceremonies is to put the group's members into action, "to multiply the relations between them and to make them more intimate with one another. By this very fact, the content of their consciousness is changed." Ordinarily, in utilitarian or "profane" activities, there is a strong tendency for individualism, even divisiveness, to operate among men, thus weakening the web of society. But when the cult is in being, when ritual observances are celebrated, men's thoughts "are centered upon their common beliefs, their common traditions, the memory of their ancestors, the collective idea of which they are the incarnation; in a word, upon social things . . . The spark of social being which each bears within him necessarily participates in this collective renovation. The individual soul is regenerated, too, by being dipped again in the sources from which its life came; consequently, it feels itself stronger, more fully master of itself, less dependent upon physical necessities." [69]

Here, then, are the terms within which religious rites become crucial to the sociologist. Rites are the *visible* manifestations of the communion of spirits, of the consensus of ideas and faiths. Sacrifice and imitation are two essential rites: the first, through some mode of transubstantiation, to bridge the gap between profane and sacred in symbolic way; the second, by focusing upon an ideal conception, be it totem or god, to supply the means whereby men may emulate and thus be lifted up spiritually and morally. The idea or category of cause has its origin in the human mind through performance and use of the imitative rites. Beyond these two types of rite—that is, sacrificial and imitative—are two other types, which Durkheim calls "representative" and "piacular."

Representative rites have for their primary function the commemorating of the group's continuity with past and future, the representing, through sacred observances, the links that each living member has with both ancestors and posterity. It is thus that the totemic identification with an animal or a plant is born. Continuity and remembrance are the primary integrative functions, but out of these representative rites come, in time, esthetic and recreational activities—dramatic pageants and games—which give added purpose to them. It is in the gradual disengagement of these latter purposes from the original religious matrix that we witness one important phase of the secularization of culture. Of them, Durkheim writes: "Not only do they employ the same processes as the real drama, but they also pursue an end of the same sort: being foreign to all utilitarian ends, they make men forget the real world and transport them into another where their imagination is more at ease; they distract. They sometimes even go so far as to have the outward appearance of a recreation: the assistants may be seen laughing and amusing themselves openly." [70]

With piacular rites, something else is introduced: the notion of sadness, of fear, of tragedy. All of the other rites—sacrificial, imitative, and representative—have this in common: "they are all performed in a state of confidence, joy, and even enthusiasm." But there are those that are not, those in which the spirit of unease, of latent pessimism, of apprehension, is present. These Durkheim summarizes under the heading of piaculum; that is, expiation, the ritual cleansing of man from his sins or his affronts to the sacred powers. "Every misfortune, everything of evil omen, everything that inspires sentiments of sorrow or fear necessitates a piaculum, and is therefore called piacular. So this word seems very well adapted for designating the rites which are celebrated by those in a state of uneasiness or sadness." [71]

Between the joyful and the piacular rites there is, of course, deep affinity. The two poles of religious life correspond to the two states between which any society must of necessity oscillate. "Between the propitiously sacred and the unpropitiously sacred there is the same contrast as between the states of collective well-being and ill-being. But since both are equally collective, there is, between the mythological constructions symbolizing them, an intimate kinship of nature. The sentiments held in common vary from extreme dejection to extreme joy, from painful irritation to ecstatic enthusiasm, but in any case there is a communion of minds and a mutual comfort resulting from this communion." [72]

Only in man's oscillation between sorrow and joy is he made human. So, with the oscillation between ritual states of spiritual deliverance and spiritual abasement: each is necessary to the other, both to religion and to society. The sense of sin (enforced by piacular rites) is as important to social integration as the committing of crimes (in due proportion) which alone can cause the mobilization of moral values that is the warp of society and of human conscience.

We may summarize by saying that precisely as religion is made by Durkheim into a manifestation of society and its crucial phases, society in turn is made to depend upon a non-rational, supra-individual state of mind that can only be called religious. Between the two, religion and society, there is a functional interplay. It is only because society attains, through sacred-making processes, a limitless majesty over man that his own distinctive qualities of personality and mind are possible. This includes man's most profoundly rational as well as his deepest emotional qualities.

Charisma and Calling—Weber

No sociologist either before or since has equaled the scope and diversity of Weber's interest in religion. It is possible here only to hint at the vastness of his canvas, which included the religions of the ancient world, of Asia, the Near East, as well as of medieval and modern Europe. His analyses of the variant social structures of religion, of the origins and nature of prophecy, of the relation of religion to social and economic institutions, and of the role of religion in social change remain even today unsurpassed. It is difficult indeed to find anything sociological in the contemporary study of religion that was not contributed in one degree or another by Weber.

Our concern is not, however, with Weber's sociology of religion but with his use of the religio-sacred as a perspective in the study of society. Just as Weber advanced the study of religion by taking to it the social concepts of status, authority, and community, so did he advance the study of society by application of religious concepts. The most powerful single doctrine in the sociological study of religion in Weber's Germany was that of Marx, for whom types of religion were but reflections of types of society. The greatness of Weber lies in his reversal of Marx through empirical and logical demonstration that types of society may, equally, be shown to be reflections of types of religion. We shall, in this section, confine ourselves to but two of Weber's demonstrations, each of continuing fertility in sociological analysis. The first is his concept of charisma; the second is his epochal interpretation of the rise of European capitalism.

Too many treatments of charisma stop with its manifestation as a type of authority or influence inhering in a few notable lawgivers or culture heroes in history: in Moses, Buddha, Jesus, Caesar, Cromwell, and Napoleon; individuals whose genius consisted in possession of some spark of leadership, divine or at least supra-rational in the regard of followers. Charisma is thus made to be a force inseparable from the great man rather than a type or a condition of social organization. Its logical relation to Durkheim's concept of the sacred or Simmel's use of piety is accordingly lost or minimized. Instead of a sociological state it becomes something more nearly psychological or at least biographical.

Charisma may not have quite the scope and diversity that Durkheim gives to the sacred, but it is not necessary to read very far into Weber to see that, if not explicitly, certainly by implication, it comes very close. Durkheim, let us remember, did little in the way of exploring the existential *sources* of the sacred. He was content to take the two great categories of sacred and profane as fundamental and irreducible and follow their significance to human behavior and society. With Weber, however, the case is different. He is interested in both the source and the institutionalization of charisma.

There are two very different aspects of charisma: first, the conditions of its origin (which, for Weber, is a recurrent process in the history of civilization) and, second, the passage of charisma into the structures and codes of society. The first leads him (as the sacred only partially led Durkheim) to consideration of great individuals in history: that is, to charismatic leaders such as Jesus or Caesar. The second, which is equally important in Weber's work, leads him into detailed analysis of what he calls the "routinization" of charisma: that is, its hereditary incorporation into families, offices, castes, races, and communities; even, one is justified in saying, into things: rocks, trees, deserts, rivers, and seas to which charisma has been attached by its place in some momentous event in the life of a divine or deeply revered leader.

There is no question but that Weber would have ascribed charisma to the Christian cross, for example, as readily as Durkheim would have placed it in the realm of the sacred. And, as one reads Durkheim's remarks on the great moral leaders of history (in his *Moral Education*), there is as little doubt that Durkheim would have agreed that the sacredness of the cross among Christians is the result solely of its connection with the life of the charismatic (or "sacred-endowing") person of Jesus.

In one respect only is there significant difference between Weber and Durkheim, and that has to do with the relevance of their respective concepts to social change. Weber's interest in change, especially "mutational" change, was far deeper than Durkheim's, and it is hardly strange therefore that he would be more impressed by the change-producing consequences of charisma in the form of the impact of the charismatic leader upon a tradition- or bureaucracy-dominated society. But, again, one has only to read Durkheim on the "deviance" of moral leaders such as Buddha or Jesus to realize that he was hardly blind to this aspect.

Let us turn now to the nature of charisma, dealing first with its origin and second with its transference to social organization through the process of routinization. Charisma, Weber writes, refers to "a certain quality of an individual personality by virtue of which he is set apart from ordinary men and treated as endowed with supernatural, superhuman, or at least specifically exceptional powers or qualities. These are such as are not accessible to the ordinary person, but are regarded as of divine origin or as exemplary, and on the basis of them the individual concerned is treated as a leader." [73] In primitive culture this kind of deference is given to prophets, to military and political leaders, and to those of surpassing wisdom or healing power. The decisive element in our recognition of charisma is the extent and depth of its acceptance by those who follow or revere the individual concerned. We identify the charisma of Jesus or Caesar not by the substantive character of what either said or did but by the supra-rational, supra-utilitarian attachment of followers to each.

It must not be supposed, however, that charisma inheres only in the great and "good" figures of history. Charisma includes, Weber tells us, "the state of a 'berserker' whose spells of maniac passion have, apparently wrongly, sometimes been attributed to the use of drugs. . . . It includes the 'shaman,' the kind of magician who in the pure type is subject to epileptoid seizures as a means of falling into trances . . . Finally, it includes the type of intellectual such as Kurt Eisner, who is carried away with his own demagogic success. Sociological analysis, which must abstain from value judgments, will treat all these on the same level as the men who, according to conventional judgments, are the 'greatest' heroes, prophets, and saviours." [74] In short, charisma may be found in every sphere and at every level of society. Its essence is simply possession of—or belief in possession of—supra-rational qualities by an individual that are variously deemed prophetic, sacred, and transcendental.

Although the true charismatic individual is not dependent upon followers for his own knowledge of his sacred essence (this comes to him by signs from a god or other supernatural force), attraction of followers is crucial. "The corporate group which is subject to charismatic authority is based on an emotional form of communal relationship." [75] There are no "officials," no administrative hierarchy, but only disciples, believers, followers: those of commitment and zeal rather than of employment or service. Charismatic authority is "specifically outside the realm of everyday routine and the profane sphere. In this respect it is sharply opposed both to rational, and particularly bureaucratic, authority, and to traditional authority, whether in its patriarchal, patrimonial, or any other form." [76] Considered in its pristine shape, charismatic authority is, then, as anti-traditional as it is anti-economic or anti-utilitarian, for "charismatic authority repudiates the past, and is in this sense a specifically revolutionary force." [77]

If there were no more to charisma than this, it would represent only a partial approximation of Durkheim's concept of the sacred. It could be regarded as a specialized form of the sacred but no more, for its manifestations are historically spasmodic and revolutionary rather than a stable and continuing part of society. Above all, thus defined, it is inseparable from a *person,* be he a Jesus or a Hitler, a shaman or a berserker, and from the intimate relationship that exists between such an individual and his followers. Charismatic, as a concept, would largely be irrelevant to that vast area of the sacred in society that is institutionalized and passes down from generation to generation in the form of dogma, ritual, law, and sacrament. As Weber writes, "in its pure form charismatic authority may be said to exist only in the process of originating." [78]

But there is much more to charisma than its pure, original form. There is the whole domain of what Weber calls the "routinization of charisma," and here we have something that is precisely analogous to the immense body of ritual and dogma, sacrament and symbol, and hierarchy and laity that comprises the sacred. When the original charismatic individual dies, the subtle but powerful processes of transference commence.

There is, first, the transference of charisma to other persons, the result of which is "a process of traditionalization in favor of which the purely personal character of leadership is eliminated." Now, charisma becomes attached to position rather than to person, and through oracles or through selection by the original charismatic leader, or through rituals of purification and preparation, the charisma is transferred to a line of successors. Especially prominent is "hereditary charisma" in which "recognition is no longer paid to the charismatic qualities of the individual, but to the legitimacy of the position he has acquired by heriditary succession. This may lead in the direction of either traditionalization or of legalization . . . Personal charisma may be totally absent." [79] Once charisma becomes distinguished from the original charismatic individual, it may become an attribute of kinship, of specialized roles and offices, of classes or castes, of locale even of material objects.

What is essential is that each be in some way connected with the life of the original charismatic leader—his charisma transferred, as it were, to them—or else be connected with the life of some one of his legitimate (and therefore charismatic) successors. Inevitably periods of preparation for office become important, as do the ceremonies by which those who later join the mystic communality become members in spirit. Hence the charismatic essence of ritual and of the various precepts and injunctions which form the code by which the fellowship of the charisma is continued and reinforced.

As the process of routinization extends itself through the generations, it cannot help but become traditionalized. As Bendix has written: "In this process a special affinity emerges between charisma and tradition. Though in its pure form the revolutionary implications of charisma are quite incompatible with tradition, both types of domination depend upon a belief in concrete persons whose authority is regarded as sacred and to whom followers or subjects feel bound in religious reverence and duty. As tradition gains, the appeal to charisma is used no longer to oppose everyday routine with an extraordinary message and power but rather as a legitimation of 'acquired rights' in the possession of wealth or social tradition." [80]

It is thus that charisma, in the sense of the sacred, becomes a major part of social and political systems as well as of religions proper. Weber cites caste in India as the classical case of hereditary charisma. "All occupational qualifications, and in particular all the qualifications for positions of authority and power, have there come to be regarded as strictly bound to the inheritance of charisma." [81] Gradually a different relation between charisma and economic matters develops. The immediate effect of charisma is, as we have seen, revolutionary; there is a millennial repudiation of wealth and material possession. "But in case the process of routinization leads in the direction of traditionalism, its ultimate effect may be exactly the reverse." There is then "sacred wealth" in contrast to profane, as when, through ritual means, ordinary money becomes alms. Structures of power are distinguished, some being sacred or charismatic by virtue of origin, others merely secular or profane. Weber's analysis of feudalism is in the context of the charismatic, as is, of course, his treatment of types of kinship. "It is not impossible, as in the case of Napoleon, for the strictest type of bureaucracy to issue directly from a charismatic movement; or, if not that, all sorts of praebendal and feudal types of organization." [82]

Even in the modern rise of democracy there is a charismatic element. "A charismatic principle which originally was primarily directed to the legitimization of authority may be subject to interpretation or development in an anti-authoritarian direction. This is true because the validity of charismatic authority rests entirely on recognition by those subject to it, conditioned as this is by 'proof' of its genuineness. When the organization of the corporate group undergoes a process of progressive rationalization, it is readily possible that, instead of recognition being treated as a consequence of legitimacy, it is treated as the basis of legitimacy. Legitimacy, that is, becomes 'democratic.' " [83]

The upshot of modern European history for Weber has been to diminish the sway of charisma and to lessen the number of occasions on which charismatic authority and relationships might prevail. Rationalization, the master process of European history for Weber, has caused this. There is a useful comparison here with Durkheim. The latter saw in the rising incidence of anomie in modern Europe evidence of a long-run decline in sacred values, a decline caused by individualism and secularization. The individual's relation to the sacred has become (perhaps only temporarily) more tenuous under the influence of modern doctrines of materialism and skepticism. With Weber, however, it is not so much loss of membership as it is organizational hypertrophy, in the form of bureaucratization of culture and life, that must be seen as the immediate source of the decline of charisma. Bureaucracy. Weber thought, was forming a crust over society that might become too thick to permit occasional eruptions of charismatic individuals such as the history of the past revealed. And the whole temper of scientific, rational, modernism would be increasingly alien to the formation of the contexts of belief, or suspension of disbelief, in which alone charismatic power may take form. Had Weber lived until the rise to power of Hitler, he would surely have modified this view. For despite (and perhaps because of) the heavy layer of bureaucracy over German society, it was all too possible for an individual who combined in his person the charismatic traits of the prophet, shaman, and berserker to achieve the power to shake a society as few charismatic individuals in history have been privileged to do.

Durkheim's sense of the inevitability and externality of the sacred is a surer guide in this respect than Weber's more historical view of the rise and fall, the waxing and waning, of charisma. For all their common affinity with the religio-sacred, there is one major difference between Weber's and Durkheim's conceptions of the sacred. For Durkheim the sacred has its origins in collective society; it is an emergent of the irresistible need men feel for reaffirming the values underlying association. But for Weber, despite a clear conception of the omnipresence and the insistent importance of "routinized charisma" in collective association, it is fair to say that the image of charisma remains personal and historically spasmodic.

The second and perhaps most forceful of Weber's uses of the religio-sacred in the analysis of society is to be found in his notable *The Protestant Ethic and the Spirit of Capitalism*. Few works of modern social science have had the impact or have stimulated the amount of research or aroused the controversy that this one has. It has been honored by countless articles, reviews, and books "disproving" its thesis. Not often, however, have the critics kept steadily in mind the limits that Weber himself placed on the argument and implications of the book. *The Protestant Ethic* does *not*—and this point cannot be overemphasized—declare capitalism to be the result of either Protestantism generally or Calvinism specifically. Weber was much too sophisticated a methodologist to have made such a claim for any element, material or immaterial. What he does in this remarkable book is succinctly summarized as follows:

"One of the fundamental elements of the spirit of modern capitalism, and not only of that but of all modern culture: rational conduct on the basis of the idea of the calling, was born—that is what this discussion has sought to demonstrate—from the spirit of Christian asceticism." [84] Does Weber deny in this book the influence of money, of trade, of technology, political centralization, legal rationalization, secularism, luxury, and the many other elements that have been singly and severally advanced to explain the rise of capitalism in the West? He does not. All of these, in varying degrees, have been essential.

But Weber was living at a time when the historical school of economics and, above all, the Marxists were in effect denying the influence of any but material, and specifically technological, forces in the transition of Western society from a feudal-agrarian to a capitalist-industrialist economy. Had not Marx shown that religion is but an illusion, a veil of fantasy through which the real forces of history might be seen, but no more involved in propositions of functional or causal significance than the superstitions of children? For Marx the essential motive power of history and the specific cause of the rise of European capitalism lie in technology, or rather in mutations of technology which translate themselves into intolerable conflicts within the social system.

It is a mark not only of the unique role of sociology among the social sciences but of Weber's own intrepidity of mind that he challenged this whole view. But in doing so he did not make the mistake of substituting the religious factor for the technological as the mainspring of historical change. He did not, like the Marxists, deal with essentially unanswerable questions of absolute origin or seek certainty in a single-factor theory. Weber's words here are illuminating.

"The following study may thus perhaps in a modest way form a contribution to the understanding of the manner in which ideas become effective forces in history . . . For we are merely attempting to clarify the part which religious forces have played in forming the developing web of our specifically worldly modern culture, in the complex interaction of innumerable different historical factors. We are thus inquiring only to what extent certain characteristic features of this culture can be imputed to the influence of the Reformation. . . .

"On the other hand, however, we have no intention whatever of maintaining such a foolish and doctrinaire thesis as that the spirit of capitalism (in the provisional sense of the term explained above) could only have arisen as the result of certain effects of the Reformation, or even that capitalism as an economic system is a creation of the Reformation. In itself, the fact that certain important forms of capitalistic business organization are known to be considerably older than the Reformation is a sufficient refutation of such a claim. On the contrary, *we only wish to ascertain whether and to what extent religious forces have taken part in the qualitative and the quantitative expansion of that spirit over the world.*" [85]

Weber had a profoundly historical sense of individual motivation in social change, or, more accurately, a keen sense of the importance of putting all propositions concerning change into a form that would have demonstrable relevance to the reigning values, incentives, and structures of meaning in a given age. That changes in technology affected the rise of capitalism was incontestable. The question was, however, in what areas of culture might the all-important clues be found to explain the conversion or translation of technological change to a realm of human consciousness and behavior in which the deepest motivations and compulsions of individuals were involved. By itself, the technological was insufficient, and so was the purely utilitarian or material, for countless examples are to be found in history where technological mutation fails to infuse itself into the social consciousness of a people and to generate change in an entire social order.

The age in which capitalism arose was one in which religious and moral questions were deeply evocative; far more so than in the modern age; more so even than at the height of the Middle Ages when religion was so universally present in the cultural order and in men's minds, and still relatively unchallenged by the convulsive doctrinal disputes that the Reformation brought. No age has ever existed in which religious matters were brought to a higher pitch of intensity than in the age immediately following Luther and Calvin. What political ideology has been since the French Revolution, and especially since the rise of Communist zealotry in the late nineteenth and twentieth centuries, religious ideology was in the seventeenth and much of the eighteenth centuries. Such was assuredly the case in an age that spawned preachers and missionaries to an extent not seen since the centuries of early Christianization of Western Europe.

Knowing this, Weber looked to the role of the religious factor in fashioning the larger temper of mind of which the capitalist spirit is a signal part. To repeat, it is not capitalism as a whole that Weber seeks to "explain" by reference to Calvinism but rather a certain capitalist temper in which work, wealth, and profit could become not merely tolerated and enjoyed (this is a timeless and universal attitude) but actually made into something ethically compelling, morally sovereign. In the following passage Weber gives us the kernel of the problem that fascinated him. The passage is set in a larger discussion of the paradox of the presence of a manifest capitalist spirit in the uncapitalist (in the institutional and material sense) backwoods circumstances of eighteenth-century America and, conversely, the lack of such a spirit in affluent, bourgeois Florence of the early modern era.

"Now, how could activity, which was at best ethically tolerated, turn into a calling in the sense of Benjamin Franklin? The fact to be explained historically is that in the most highly capitalistic center of that time, in Florence of the fourteenth and fifteenth centuries, the money and capital market of all the great political Powers, this attitude was considered ethically unjustifiable, or at best to be tolerated. But in the backwoods small bourgeois circumstances of Pennsylvania in the eighteenth century, where business threatened for simple lack of money to fall back into barter, where there was hardly a sign of large enterprise, where only the earliest beginnings of banking were to be found, the same thing was considered the essence of moral conduct, even commanded in the name of duty. *To speak here of a reflection of material conditions in the ideal superstructure would be patent nonsense.* What was the background of ideas which could account for the sort of activity apparently directed toward profit alone as a calling to which the individual feels himself to have an ethical obligation? For it was this idea which gave the way of the new entrepreneur its ethical foundation and justification." [86]

Reduced to its essential substance, this idea was, of course, the Calvinist idea of the calling: that in his undeviating pursuit of wealth, or rather capital, in his devotion to the precepts of personal frugality, in his consecration to those material activities by which grace is alone manifested—in these as well as in his direct and unmediated faith in God—the individual is serving God and fulfilling a calling not the less divine for its orientation toward economic matters. Let us grant readily that in this proposition alone there are difficulties with some of the main aspects of Weber's thesis. Leo Strauss has argued that "the maximum that Weber could reasonably have claimed to have proved is, then, that a corruption or degeneration of Calvin's theology led to the emergence of the capitalist spirit. Only by means of this decisive qualification can his thesis be brought into even approximate harmony with the facts to which he refers . . . Tawney rightly pointed out that the capitalist Puritanism studied by Weber was late Puritanism or that it was the Puritanism that had already made its peace with 'the world.' " [87]

This may be true, and it was perhaps inevitable that Weber would, once he began citing from the practical ethics of early Calvinist preachers, ascribe to their injunctions a degree of causal primacy that is foreign to his declared intent in the book: which, to repeat, is to show that "one of the fundamental elements of the spirit of capitalism . . . was born from the spirit of Christian asceticism." [88] Who, after all, is not carried away to some extent by the momentum of a major idea? And Weber's was indeed a major idea.

To seek the causes of the change of a social system (capitalism) not in itself—which was what so many others, under the spell of the idea of continuity, were doing—but rather in a separate system (Protestantism) was itself a noteworthy accomplishment, given the universality of evolutionary and endogenous theories of change in Weber's day. To insist, further, that if change in society is to be brought down from the level of panoramic generality to the area in which actual motivations to behavior are formed, it must be in terms of the values that hold most evocative meaning at the time of the change: this too was a major contribution. And, finally, to put the entire matter of the study of the rise of capitalism in a genuinely comparative context was unique in that day of still commanding unilinear developmentalism, with the "comparative method" most commonly understood to be simply a means of illustrating stages of evolution in a single progression, as in Marx and in Spencer.

Weber did not himself think he had exhausted the subject with his religious perspective. Toward the end of the book he tells us: "The next task would be . . . to show the significance of ascetic rationalism, which has only been touched in the foregoing sketch, for the content of practical social ethics, thus for the types of organization and the functions of social groups from the conventicle to the state. Then its relations to humanistic rationalism, its ideals of life and cultural influences; further to the development of philosophical and scientific empiricism. Then its historical development from the medieval beginnings of worldly asceticism to its dissolution into pure utilitarianism would have to be traced out through all the areas of ascetic religion. Only then could the quantitative cultural influence of ascetic Protestantism in its relation to the other plastic elements of modern culture be estimated." [89]

And in the final paragraph of the book, he writes: "Modern man is in general, even with the best will, unable to give religious ideas a significance for culture and national character which they deserve. But it is, of course, not my aim to substitute for a one-sided materialistic an equally one-sided spiritualistic causal interpretation of culture and of history. Each is equally possible, but each, if it does not serve as the preparation, but as the conclusion of an investigation, accomplishes equally little in the interest of historical truth." [90]

THE FUNCTION OF PIETY—SIMMEL

Piety has substantially the same denotation in Simmel that the sacred has in Durkheim and charisma in Weber. Like these two concepts, piety represents a conviction that full understanding of social phenomena is impossible save in terms of a recognition of the unalterable, irreducible role of the religious impulse.

In his general treatment of the scope and method of sociology Simmel makes plain that the social and the religious are closely linked. There he calls attention to the fact that "members of a Social-Democratic labor union may exhibit the same traits in their common and mutual behavior" as are found in a specifically religious organization. His basic argument, to be sure, in this discussion is directed to students of religion: to remind them "that religious behavior does not exclusively depend on religious contents, but that it is a generally human form of behavior which is realized under the stimulus not only of transcendental objects but also of other motivations";[91] motivations deriving from community, authority, and status. But there is no question that for Simmel this is a two-way street, and it is in his account of the nature of piety that this becomes clear.

There are, Simmel tells us, "autonomous religious values" in all durable social states and relations. It is indeed only with the aid of these autonomous religious values, embedded as they are in social relations, that the "basic religious mood acquires a certain form, whose transcendental gradations and objectivation unfold the objects of religion in their general meaning." In short, it is not a crude relation here between the "social" and the "religious" that Simmel is defending; it is rather an insistence that in the social itself, as a very part of its essence, there is a religious factor.[92]

"The relation of a devoted child to his parents, of an ardent patriot to his fatherland or a similarly enthusiastic cosmopolitan to mankind; the relation of a worker to his class, which is pressing onward, or of a nobleman conscious of his rank to the aristocracy; the relation of the vanquished to his conqueror, or of the good soldier to his army—all these relations with their infinitely manifold contents can indeed have a general tenor as far as their psychic aspect is concerned—which must be called a religious key." [93]

In these relations—as in man's relation to God and to church and to clergy—there is a "strange mixture of selfless devotion and desire, of humility and elation, of sensual immediacy and spiritual abstraction." It is precisely these emotional elements, Simmel argues, that compose what we commonly call the religious frame of mind. "For the very fact that they are religious gives them a flavor distinguishing them from relations based on sheer egoism or pure suggestion or mere outward or moral powers." [94] Here, plainly, is the same repudiation of the utilitarian, individualist-rationalist philosophy that we have seen in the sociological tradition from Comte and Tocqueville on. It is at this point in the discussion that Simmel identifies the concept of piety.

"This particular emotional frame of mind can perhaps, generally speaking, be defined as *piety*. Piety is an emotion of the soul which turns into religion whenever it projects itself into specific forms. Here it should be noted that *pietas* means the pious attitude towards both man and God. Piety, which is religiosity in a quasi-fluid state, will not necessarily have to coalesce into a stable form of behavior vis-à-vis the gods; i.e., into religion." [95]

As there are for Weber charismatic individuals, so there are, for Simmel, "pious men who do not turn their piety toward any god, that is, to that phenomenon which is the very object of piety; they are religious natures without a religion." [96] Such men may endow "non-religious" objects or relationships with a religious character. "We call it 'religious' because the autonomous object, which sprang from it of itself, exists as an object of the religion in existence, as the bacilli culture of impulses, moods, and need which grow under those conditions out of the empirical, social matter." [97]

Without piety and without the religious faith that piety evokes, society would be impossible. On this point Simmel stands squarely in the main tradition of sociology. The following passage is a succinct summary of his view of the role of religion in society.

"So far nobody has inquired beyond the individual meaning of this religious faith, into its purely social significance; but I am sure that without it society as we know it could not exist. Our unswerving faith in a human being or collective, beyond all proof, often against all proof, is one of the strong bonds by which society is held together. Submissive obedience is often not based on positive knowledge of the right and superiority of the other one, nor is it rooted in love and suggestion, but rather in that 'faith' in the power, the merit, the irresistibility and goodness of the other one—a faith which is not merely a theoretical hypothesis, but a very particular spiritual phenomenon operating among men." [98]

7 ALIENATION

THE MEANING OF ALIENATION

There is nothing strange in the fact that intimations of moral break-down and social estrangement are to be found in the very same writings in the nineteenth century that produced the vision of community. Both states of mind tend to arise from common soil, and have in fact done this throughout history. Any social order—be it post-Peloponnesian Athens, the Rome of St. Augustine, or France after the Revolution—that is seized by convulsive change, dislocation of values, and spiritual uncertainty inevitably invites preoccupation with community on the one hand and breakdown or alienation on the other.

Alienation is, quite as much as community, one of the major perspectives in nineteenth-century thought—in literature, philosophy, religion, as well as in sociology. Tocqueville, Burckhardt, Dostoevski, Kierkegaard, Weber—to draw from a wide range—all saw past, present, and future in ways that would have been generally incomprehensible to the Enlightenment, indeed to the whole Age of Reason. It is the special genius of much nineteenth-century thought that it could see possibilities of social decay and individual estrangement in the very conditions that to most of the Enlightenment had promised, for the first time in history, man's emergence into the light of true freedom and rational order.

I mean by the idea of alienation something that goes considerably beyond what is contained in the Marxist use of the word, which use is, to be sure, the principal channel by which the word itself has reached twentieth-century writing. Marx's view of man's relation to the social order has, as I shall emphasize later in this chapter, more in common, generally, with that of the Enlightenment than it does with what such men as Tocqueville, Weber, Durkheim, and Simmel had in mind: these are the

264

minds more nearly responsible for the *content* of the twentieth-century use of the word "alienation."

By alienation I mean something that goes beyond mere disaffection with a surrounding social scene. Repudiation, even categorical repudiation, of a social system, such as capitalism, need not be a reflection of the alienated mind, any more than revolutionary action is. Thus the Enlightenment would not, I think, qualify as an alienated age in any sense that has currency today, yet its opposition to the institutional order that prevailed was almost total. But, whatever their contempt for Christian and feudal values, the majority of the *philosophes* had a view of natural man, a faith in humanity and in the possibilities of reason, once reason was cleansed of its institution-caused imperfections, which, in their union, made for the kind of faith that Carl Becker has so notably described for us.

There are, I suggest, two fundamental and distinguishable perspectives of alienation to be found in nineteenth-century sociological thought. The first rests on an alienated view of the individual, the second on an alienated view of society.

In the first perspective we see modern man as uprooted, alone, without secure status, cut off from community or any system of clear moral purpose. Estrangement is sovereign: estrangement from others, from work, from place, and even from self. Far from possessing within himself the resources of reason and stability, man feels these resources threatened and himself metaphysically beleaguered, as it were. Suffering from, rather than rejoicing in, the liberation that history has given him, the individual is unable to establish the resistances necessary to living with the world and with himself. Gone, in this view, is the historic rationalist conviction of the self-sustaining nature of the individual. The price of individual liberation from tradition may be, we learn, loss of individuality—to be seen in suicide, unreason, robotization, and other forms of pathological deviation from the norm of personality. Renaissance secularism had taken from man his divine nature, but it left him his dignity. Now, it is thought, the forces of modernism threaten even man's dignity, diminishing him in spirit and influence. Loss of community isolates man, and the mounting pressure of vast institutions and organizations, far from shoring up his being, only intensifies the alienative process: by fragmenting him into the mechanical roles he is forced to play, none of them touching his innermost self but all of them separating man from this self, leaving him, so to speak, existentially missing in action.

The second perspective is closely related to the first, but the emphasis is different. The emphasis here is on society, the people, the general will. In this perspective, modern society is inaccessible because of its remoteness, formidable from its heavy structures of organization, meaningless from its impersonal complexity. The cultural order, once engaged in, now seems aloof, devoid of what Burke called the "inns and resting places" of the human spirit. The whole democratic-industrial order, the advent of which was being, and would continue to be, celebrated by apostles of modernism from Bentham to Lenin, from Manchester to Moscow, is seen in this perspective as one in which the essential springs of culture are threatened and in which political authority, far from expressing itself through the dreamed-of general will, exists in a spectrum that has plebiscitarianism at one extreme and centralized bureaucracy at the other. Mass opinion succeeds the discipline of taste and judgment; the harsh and stunting disciplines of the factory succeed the rhythms of countryside; rationalization of society degenerates into regimentation; and the primary values of European culture—honor, loyalty, friendship—are seen as withering away under the dead weight of objectification.

THE INVERSION OF PROGRESS

Alienation, considered as a sociological temper, is the antithesis of the idea of progress and of rationalist individualism: antithesis and also inversion, for the conclusions regarding man and society reached by the alienated sociologists rest upon an inversion of the selfsame premises that supported the idea of progress and of individualism.

For two centuries the dominant philosophy of history in Western Europe had been progressive. There were exceptions, to be sure. Even within the French Enlightenment—so often treated as the scene of universal optimism—there were doubts now and then about what could be expected in the long-run future. But as against the views of the majority of philosophical rationalists, reaching from Bacon and Descartes at the beginning of the seventeenth century through Condorcet and Bentham in the late eighteenth, to Marx and Spencer in the nineteenth, these occasional doubts are negligible. Fontenelle had written in 1688: "Men will never degenerate, and there will be no end to the growth and development of human wisdom." [1] In the next century this conclusion was taken from the area of knowledge, to which alone Fontenelle gave it relevance, and transferred to the larger and amorphous area of institutions, laws, and human happiness. "The great inequality of mind observable in mankind . . . only depends on the different education they receive," wrote Helvetius,[2] and the work of reform and education could thus seem liberative to man's thought and goodness: liberative from the chains of error and superstition. "And how admirably calculated is this picture of the human race," wrote Condorcet, "free from all these chains, secure from the dominion of chance, as from that of the enemies of its progress, and advancing with firm and sure steps towards the attainment of truth, virtue, and happiness, to present to the philosopher a spectacle which shall console him for the errors, the crimes, the injustice, with which the earth is still polluted, and whose victim he often is! It is in the contemplation of this picture that he receives the reward of his efforts towards the progress of reason and the defense of liberty." [3] Such is Condorcet's famous summary of the tenth and, he thought, imminent stage of man's final progress from barbarism to knowledge, democracy, and happiness.

In the nineteenth century, Auguste Comte declared that "amelioration is as unquestionable as the development from which it proceeds." Progress for Comte is the fundamental law of social dynamics.[4] Marx, with equal confidence, referred to laws of development of society, "working with iron necessity towards inevitable results." Marx never doubted the inevitability of progress for all nations toward socialism.[5] And Herbert Spencer wrote: "Progress, therefore, is not an accident, but a necessity. . . . As surely as the tree becomes bulky when it stands alone . . . so surely must the human faculties be moulded into complete fitness for the social state; so surely must the things we call evil and immorality disappear; so surely must man become perfect." [6]

It was only too easy, given this faith in progress and given also the more fundamental faith in the unity and irreversibility of historical development, to conclude that such phenomena as industrialism, technology, urbanism, and rationalization were the infallible stigmata of beneficence and that in the further development and diffusion of these phenomena lay the greatest hope of the future. Whatever the sizable differences among Comte, Marx, and Spencer, there was no disagreement on this point. In their historical ethics, past equaled bad, present good, and the future best. Belief in the law of progressive development made this certain for them and, of course, for many others in the Century of Great Hope.

But while progress may epitomize the dominant temper of the nineteenth century, it is not the whole story. Alongside it, in its shadow indeed, is another view of the nature and possible end of Western development; one that, from identical premises of what was evolving—mass democracy, technology, rationalism, secularism, and so on—derived opposite conclusions: not political freedom, but tyranny imposed by the mass; not individual autonomy, but morbid isolation; not rationalism of mind, but rationalization of spirit; not secular release, but sterile disenchantment.

What we see, beginning with the conservatives in their general distrust of modernism, is the tragic view of life set in time perspective. It is a view that draws its melancholy forecast of the future, not from extraneous or fortuitous factors, but from the very substance of history, from the very forces that the rationalists had hailed as promising liberation and the new empire of reason. In this view history is conceived as being periodically seized by deep moral crises which do not—as the thinkers of inexorable progress argued—automatically resolve themselves but remain instead to haunt and mock man's hopes of secular salvation.

We may take Bonald as the exemplar of the conservative distrust of modern European development. "We are approaching a great phase in the social development of the world. The Revolution which, like all revolutions, was both religious and political, was the result of the general laws governing the preservation of societies, and is to be compared to a terrible and salutary crisis, by means of which nature roots out from the social body those vicious principles which the weakness of authority had allowed to creep in and restores to it its health and pristine vigour." [7]

Will this crisis be the basis of a regenerated Europe, one that will return to its essential foundations of family, corporation, church, and social class and expunge from itself the toxic elements of individualism and secularism? Bonald thinks there is a possibility, but only that. The recognized horror of the Revolution and the restoration of political authority suggests at least the possibility that "the atheistic dogma of the religious and political sovereignty of man . . . that principle of every revolution and germ of all the evils which afflict society" [8] will be banished by other European governments in which it has taken root. Hence the relentless advocacy by conservatives of authority: religious, family, economic, political.

But there is no certainty. The germs of defeat and corruption are already in the European body, spread by the infection in France. "Anarchy has been dethroned and the armies of atheism are defeated; but the precedent lives on after these successes and the principles survive the precedent. A generation has grown up which hates authority and is ignorant of its duties, and which will transmit to succeeding generations the fatal tradition of so many accepted errors and the noxious memory of so many crimes which remain unpunished. The causes of disorder, which always subsist at the heart of society, will sooner or later reproduce their terrible effects unless the authority vested in the different societies substitutes its unlimited powers of preservation for this thorough system of destruction. . . . That spirit of pride and revolt which, curbed but never destroyed, and ever present in society because it is always alive in man, will wage an internecine and stubborn war until the end, in the bosom of society as well as in the heart of man." [9]

All of this, be it emphasized, is the consequence of no passing insanity, no simple plot of subversion. It is bred deeply in modern European history. "Until the sixteenth century the life of Europe had been based on the two great principles of monarchy and the Christian religion. . . . A great schism in religion occurred in the sixteenth century and a great cleavage in politics was the inevitable result." From both came ever-increasing centralization on the one hand and moral anarchy on the other. "So the struggle began in Europe and will never perhaps be concluded." [10]

Central to the alienated view of history is the sense of indwelling and tragic conflict between good and evil; a conflict that to the conservatives was manifest in the struggle between the old and the new orders, with defeat of the old almost foreordained. Thus Carlyle wrote of the "deep-lying struggle in the whole fabric of society; a boundless grinding collision of the New with the Old." Like Burke, from whom he had learned most of his canons of right and wrong, Carlyle saw the French Revolution as but one embodiment of what Burke had called "a hollow murmuring underground"; one threatening "a general earthquake in the political world." The French Revolution, Carlyle tells us, "was not the parent of the mighty movement but its offspring." All that the apostles of progress had promised could be seen turning upon itself, defeating humanitarian hopes. Political rationalism, Carlyle writes, has taken the form of a widespread "mighty interest in mere political arrangements." He speaks of a "new trade" that has grown up, that of code-making in the abstract, and, almost in the words that Weber was to use at the end of the century, writes of the "dark features" which bespeak a "faith in mechanism," one calculated to grind the heroic into the merely cog-like and mechanical. It was from exactly this diagnosis of his age that Carlyle turned increasingly to the veneration, the near worship of the charismatic figures of history. The Great Man was Carlyle's despairing hope for an age in which somehow the promise of European history had become subverted.

Later, Burckhardt wrote: "I have no hope at all for the future. It is possible that a few half endurable decades may still be granted to us, a sort of Roman imperial time. I am of the opinion that democrats and proletarians must submit to an increasingly harsh despotism, even if they make the wildest efforts, for this fine century is designed for anything rather than true democracy." [11] And in a letter he went even further. "For a long time I have been aware that we are driving toward the alternative of complete democracy or absolute despotism without law and right. This despotic regime will not be practiced any longer by dynasties. They are too soft and kind-hearted. The new tyrannies will be in the hands of military commandos who will call themselves republican. I am still reluctant to imagine a world, the rulers of which, will be completely indifferent to law, well-being, profitable labor, industry, credit, etc., and will govern with absolute brutality." [12]

As we shall see, there is more than a faint touch of this pessimism regarding the future in Tocqueville, Weber, and Durkheim, more than a faint suspicion that the future of the West holds a time of troubles that will take its departure from forces that were being hailed as progressive in the nineteenth century.

THE INVERSION OF INDIVIDUALISM

Just as sociological alienation is the antithesis and inversion of progress, so is it the antithesis and inversion of individualism. Stretching from Bacon and Descartes in the seventeenth century to Shaftesbury, Condillac, and Rousseau in the eighteenth, and Marx and Spencer in the nineteenth, was an image of human nature compounded of three essential elements: innateness, potential goodness, and long-run indestructibility. The first led to an emphasis, whether "Cartesian" or "Newtonian," on the proposition that what is fundamental and decisive in man proceeds from what is *within* man—from instinct, sensation, the inner drives of self-interest or altruism—rather than from the social structure and from conventional morality. The second held, though with the occasional misgivings that we find in a Voltaire or a Diderot, that, once the external corrupters of faith and reason had been removed from the environment—priestcraft, feudalism, ignorance—the goodness (or, at worst, the neutrality) inherent in man and humanity would come to the surface. The third proposition, flowing in large part from the first two, said that, given man's innate possession of reason and moral sentiments, the effects of evil institutions are but temporary, that whatever the debasement of man as priest, as soldier, as peasant, or as nobleman, man *as man* would retain, through all the vicissitudes of history, his essential durability.

From Bacon's *Essays* and *Novum Organum* to Bentham's *Fragment on Government* the rationalist tradition had given profound emphasis to the goals of intellectual release, of separation, from established tradition and community. Why should there not have been this emphasis? What could seem more ephemeral than the long succession of monarchies, classes, and priestly codes that were the stuff of ordinary history —conventional history? And, correspondingly, what could seem more stable and enduring than man, natural man, with his indestructible instincts—passions or sentiments as they were commonly called in the eighteenth century—and, of course, his never-doubted innate capacity for reason? It was indeed the prime task of what the Age of Reason called, variously, "natural," "conjectural," or "hypothetical" history (in contrast to conventional historiography) to lay bare the reality of natural man and the natural order, "to lay the facts aside," as Rousseau expressed it in a frequently misunderstood phrase, and devote attention to what was timeless and universal. It was not the institutional order that interested the great philosophers of the seventeenth and eighteenth centuries, except in a polemic and pejorative sense, but the natural order. To cut through the underbrush of what *appeared* to be and find what *was,* this was the chosen task of the rationalists in the eighteenth century, a task that gives unity to such otherwise different works as *The Social Contract, The Wealth of Nations* and *A Fragment on Government.*

It is plain enough to us, and has been frequently noted, that what the rationalists unconsciously did was endow nature and natural man with attributes distilled from certain preferred spheres of the surrounding social order. In the same way that Luther and Calvin had conceived their pure and artless man of faith on the basis of the best models already formed by the long Catholic tradition, proposing only that the "excrescences" of Christianity be extirpated—Papacy, sacraments, monasteries, ecclesiastical courts—so the rationalists of the eighteenth century chose to see in man, natural man, a distillation of the best qualities of the inherited institutional order.

Nineteenth-century philosophers, beginning with Lamennais and Comte, were fond of noting that the moral qualities with which Rousseau had constructed his natural man of probity and reason were, far from being innate in human beings, the results of centuries of civilization and, more specifically, of a civility, a decorum, that had its roots in the conventions of Christianity and feudalism, not in nature.

In the same way that the rationalist image of man was unconsciously distilled from the manners and sentiments of human beings formed by a traditional social order, so was the rationalist image of the good society. For Voltaire, as Charles Frankel has written, "the works of the mind must in the end constitute the touchstone of an age because they made up in the end most of what remained when the age had passed. Voltaire's belief in progress ultimately rested upon this conviction that the arts and sciences had the greatest power of survival . . . Voltaire did not, of course, expect progress to end in a millennium: men would continue to be men, and calamities would continue to afflict them in all ages. But industry and the art of reason would steadily improve, evils and prejudices would be gradually mitigated, and philosophy, becoming more widespread, would bring men some consolation." [13] That there was perhaps a vital relation between the *culture* that Voltaire admired in the age of Louis XIV and the *institutions* that existed with it was a point that he, as an Enlightener, was less likely to brood upon than was, say, Tocqueville in the following century.

The same is true of what is perhaps the most famous of the images of the good society to emerge from the Enlightenment: the General Will, stated most brilliantly and persuasively by Rousseau, but by no means confined to him. The General Will is no mere technique for achieving rational society; it *is* rational society for Rousseau. And it will prevail, will be brought up to the surface, Rousseau thought, exactly as the real being of rational man will emerge, once fettering superstitions and prejudices are removed and a propitious environment created. What is true of the individual is true of that natural community formed by the interaction of men's wills and interests that had once existed but been corrupted by all the social ills flowing from inequality and special interest. Banish from society the artificial and baneful ties of social class, religion, guild, and other forms of "partial association," and for the first time a scene will be created in which the natural community will be recovered, in which the real will of the people, the *general* will, may emerge. The General Will, Rousseau tells us in a celebrated passage, "is always in the right, but the judgment which guides it is not always enlightened." [14] Hence the eternal necessity of protecting the people in their commonalty as in their individuality from the prejudicial influence of traditional institutions. In England this was precisely the ground of Bentham's hatred of church, university, borough, the patriarchal family, and other forms of traditional unity. Man in his reality is not made by institutions; institutions are made by man and they are therefore expendable.

But no sooner had this theory been stated by the *philosophes* and by the leaders of the Revolution in France than the reaction began to take place. "The disease of the Western world" is Comte's memorable epithet for individualism. The immediate occasion of Comte's phrase is what he calls the "moral disorganization" that is daily invading the consensus of society. To individualism and all its adjuncts—equality, rights, popular sovereignty—Comte hurls the contemptuous phrase, "metaphysical dogmas." Apart from institutions and close, corporate communities, Comte argues, man will be not merely helpless and fearful, he will not even be able to realize his essential humanity. This is the social psychology that underlies the whole of his *Positive Polity*.

Lamennais, whose *Essay on Indifference* we have already noted as one of the masterpieces of religious thought in the early part of the century and whose whole life—even after his excommunication from the Church—was devoted to work in behalf of causes that he thought would offset social atomism and its evil twin, political centralization, put the matter eloquently and movingly in a short piece on suicide: "As man moves away from order, anguish presses around him. He is the king of his own misery, a degraded sovereign in revolt against himself, without duties, without bonds, without society. Alone, in the midst of the universe, he runs, or seeks to run, into nothingness." [15]

For Comte and for Lamennais, and for all indeed who had been touched by the conservative vision of tradition, community, and membership, the movement of modern, democratic, rationalized, secular society appeared to have as its destination a form of social emptiness that the individual would not be able to tolerate in the long run, an emptiness that would magnify political power and desolate culture. Comte thought that Positivism would be the antidote to the disease of individualism, and his *Positive Polity* is written to this end with all the assurance and wealth of argument that we would find in a medieval treatise on God, man, and society. There were many in the nineteenth century who thought that by one device or another—religious revival, utopianism, reform, democracy, science and education, or the spirit of secular brotherhood—the tendencies toward moral disorganization, social alienation, and magnification of political power that had emerged with the two revolutions could be offset. Marx thought all that was needed was the abolition of private property; James Mill, the eradication of religion; Herbert Spencer, the spread of education. But when we turn to Tocqueville, Weber, Durkheim, and Simmel, we find an alienation that is too deep to be cured by belief in such secular pieties.

THE DIMINUTION OF MAN—TOCQUEVILLE

What is the picture of culture and human character that Tocqueville gives us in his treatise on democracy? Tocqueville accepts the reality and inevitability of the democratic and secular revolutions. He does not, like the conservatives, reject the ideological elements of equality and individual rights, and he is not haunted, as was Comte, by the specter of social and moral disorganization. Nor does he, like Lamennais, spend his life in search of a substitute for the church. Tocqueville is much too dispassionate and aloof an observer for his picture of democratic man to be in monochrome. He does not seek to hide the manifest facts of intellectual buoyancy, cultural release, passionate commitment to democratic cause, and withal the sense of human justice that he found wherever he turned in the United States. Such indeed is the praise that Tocqueville gives to American democracy that European conservatives—Le Play among them—found his picture intolerably optimistic.

Optimism is not, however, the word we would use today for the spirit of Tocqueville's picture. Lights there may be in it, but there are also shadows that reflect a somberness of mood that grows steadily in his *Democracy in America*. Nearly a decade intervened between his visit to the United States and the publication of the second volume, and in that time, it is plain, a good deal happened to his assessment of democracy. And, taking the work as a whole, it is hard to resist the conclusion that Tocqueville reserved his greatest interpretive skill for the shadows. Try as he might, he could not conquer the feeling that in the achievement of equalitarian justice, American democracy (and this, he thought, would apply *a fortiori* to democracies elsewhere) had run the risk of eroding away the social and cultural bases of human greatness: that is, the diversity, the variety, the hierarchy of society and culture on which individual greatness must rest. He is frank about his troubled indecision, and is willing, he says in a concluding passage, to defer to the view that perhaps only God is privileged to take.

"When I survey this countless multitude of beings, shaped in each other's likeness, amid whom nothing rises and nothing falls, the sight of such universal uniformity saddens and chills me and I am tempted to regret that state of society which has ceased to be. . . . Such is not the case with that Almighty and Eternal Being whose gaze necessarily includes the whole of created things and who surveys distinctly, though all at once, mankind and man . . . What appears to me to be man's decline is, to His eye, advancement; what afflicts me is acceptable to Him. A state of equality is perhaps less elevated but it is more just: and its justice constitutes its greatness and its beauty." [16]

To those who fondly imagine that it is possible to have, by some historical miracle, a society dedicated to equalitarian democracy and also, at the same time, to a cultural or intellectual aristocracy, Tocqueville writes:

"I find that a great number of my contemporaries undertake to make a selection from among the institutions, the opinions, and the ideas that originated in the aristocratic constitution of society as it was; a portion of these elements they would willingly relinquish, but they would keep the remainder and transplant them into their new world. I fear that such men are wasting their time and their strength in virtuous but unprofitable efforts." [17]

But if God may take comfort in equalitarian justice at the expense of men great in mind and character, Tocqueville cannot. Nothing is more vivid in his pages, read today, than the sense of the deterioration of the nobility and greatness of man: man in his relation to the universe and man in his relation to his fellows. Amid mild and humane laws there is little energy of character. Violence and cruelty are checked, but there are few instances of exalted heroism and of virtues of the highest, brightest, and purest temper. Ignorance is banished, information diffused, but men of great learning are not found and genius becomes rare. There is abundance in the arts but little perfection. The bond of humanity is strengthened, but the ties of race, rank, and country are weakened.[18]

And what of the likelihood in the future of those occasional intellectual revolutions which have thus far in mankind's history furnished the real motive power of man's progress?

"We live at a time that has witnessed the most rapid changes of opinion in the minds of men; nevertheless it may be that the leading opinions of society will before long be more settled than they have been for several centuries in our history; that time has not yet come, but it may perhaps be approaching. As I examine more closely the natural wants and tendencies of democratic nations, I grow persuaded that if ever social equality is generally and permanently established in the world, great intellectual and political revolutions will become more difficult and less frequent than is supposed . . .

"It is believed by some that modern society will be always changing its aspect; for myself, I fear that it will ultimately be too invariably fixed in the same institutions, the same prejudices, the same manners, so that mankind will be stopped and circumscribed; that the mind will swing backwards and forwards forever without begetting fresh ideas; that man will waste his strength in bootless and solitary trifling, and, though in continual motion, that humanity will cease to advance." [19]

Crucial to Tocqueville's envisagement of democratic individualism is his conviction that the meaning of the individual has paradoxically and tragically diminished. First, by secularization, itself the result of the application of abstract reason to values formerly sanctified by religion. Second, by the immense sway of public opinion, the tyranny of the invisible majority. Third, by the effects of division of labor which have made man the mere creature of the machine. Fourth, by separation from the ties of community. Added to these, there is, he believes, a loosening of moral values. Such values as honor and loyalty, having lost their social roots, tend to lose their historic importance in the social order.

Secularization, Tocqueville tells us, has been a constant process since the Protestant Reformation, leading to a weakening of the dogmas by which men live and, in time, to a trivialization of the themes of culture. The Protestant reformers "subjected some of the dogmas of the ancient faith to the scrutiny of private judgment . . . In the seventeenth century Bacon, in the natural sciences, and Descartes, in philosophy, properly so-called, abolished received formulas, destroyed the empire of tradition, and overthrew the authority of the schools. The philosophers of the eighteenth century, generalizing at length on the same principle, undertook to submit to the private judgment of each man all the objects of his belief." [20] But this, we are told, instead of enhancing man and magnifying the role of his individual reason, has actually diminished it. Reason is like happiness: make it the exclusive goal and we cannot achieve it. Take from reason the supports (barriers, the Enlightenment had argued) given it by tradition, revelation, and hierarchy, and in time reason itself is diminished. This, clearly, is the argument that underscores all of the early chapters of the second volume of *Democracy in America*.

Individual reason leads in time to its own trivialization. There accrues slowly but relentlessly a sterilization of the trust that reason requires, even where it is sovereign in men's allegiances. For, as men "perceive that they succeed in resolving without assistance all the little difficulties which their practical life presents, they readily conclude that everything in the world may be explained, and that nothing in it transcends the limits of the understanding. Thus they fall to denying what they cannot comprehend; which leaves them but little faith for whatever is extraordinary and an almost insurmountable distaste for whatever is supernatural. As it is on their own testimony that they are accustomed to rely, they like to discern the object which engages their attention with extreme clearness; they therefore strip off as much as possible all that covers it; they rid themselves of whatever separates them from it, they remove whatever conceals it from sight, in order to view it more closely and in the broad light of day. This disposition soon leads them to condemn forms, which they regard as useless and inconvenient veils placed between them and the truth." [21] True culture, true intellect demands, in addition to a secure place for reflection and pure speculation (which democrats characteristically disparage), a respect for intellectual authority, a belief in the reality of great, rare individuals and in the urgency and elevation of noble themes. It demands acceptance of at least some form of revelation, and it requires at least some degree of enchantment, of willingness to believe that forces greater than man's finite reason ultimately rule the universe.

These Tocqueville finds largely lacking in democracy. Theory and philosophy are despised or neglected, making for a utilitarian devotion to technique that must, in the end, dry up the springs even of science. Worship of the phantoms of the majority and of public opinion makes true independence of mind impossible. "I know of no country in which there is so little independence of mind and real freedom of discussion as in America . . . If America has not as yet had any great writers, the reason is given in these facts; there can be no literary genius without freedom of opinion, and freedom of opinion does not exist in America." [22] Love of equality makes for a suspicion of the brighter and abler, and induces as much hostility to the thought of an intellectual aristocracy as to that of a political aristocracy.

There are other reasons for the man's deterioration. Large and noble themes are jettisoned in the general preoccupation with the useful, the finite, and the average. Literary tragedies in the Greek, or even in the Elizabethan sense, are impossible in a democracy because the general view of the nature of man does not permit sufficient exaltation of virtues in great men to permit the required emphasis upon the flaws of character by which the great are destroyed. There is also the disappearance of the enchanted view of life and the universe. The religion of secular progress robs men of veneration for the past and for that crucial realm of values and meanings which lies between pure mythology and the empirical. Aristocracy tends to be more favorable to poetry than to democracy. "In democratic communities, where men are all insignificant and very much alike, each man instantly sees all his fellows when he surveys himself. The poets of democratic ages, therefore, can never take any man in particular as the subject of a piece; for an object of slender importance, which is distinctly seen on all sides, will never lend itself to an ideal conception." [23]

The tragic paradox of democracy, Tocqueville feels, lies in the fact that a system of government dedicated ostensibly to the individual ends up by diminishing his stature and latitude. The individual is lost or overwhelmed amid the sheer number of his equals. "Whenever social conditions are equal, public opinion presses with enormous weight upon the mind of each individual; it surrounds, directs, and oppresses him; and this arises from the very constitution of society much more than from its political laws. As men grow more alike, each man feels himself weaker in regard to all the rest; as he discerns nothing by which he is considerably raised above them or distinguished from them, he mistrusts himself as soon as they assail him . . . he is instantly overwhelmed by the sense of his own insignificance and weakness." [24]

Tocqueville sees a decline indeed from earlier levels of individuality in America. "In that immense crowd which throngs the avenues to power in the United States, I found very few men who displayed that manly candor and masculine independence of opinion which frequently distinguished the Americans in former times, and which constitutes the leading feature in distinguished characters wherever they may be found. It seems at first sight as if all the minds of the Americans were formed upon one model, so accurately do they follow the same route." [25]

This deterioration in quality of leadership is in direct proportion to the deterioration in culture and morality. "In New England, where education and liberty are the daughters of morality and religion, where society has acquired age and stability enough to enable it to form principles and hold fixed habits, the common people are accustomed to respect intellectual and moral superiority and to submit to it without complaint. . . . But as we descend to the South, to those states in which the constitution of society is more recent and less strong, where instruction is less general and the principles of morality, religion, and liberty are less happily combined, we perceive that talents and virtues become more rare among those who are in authority.

"Lastly, when we arrive at the new Southwestern states, in which the constitution of society dates but from yesterday and presents only an agglomeration of adventurers and speculators, we are amazed at the persons who are invested with public authority, and we are led to ask by what force, independent of legislation and of the men who direct it, the state can be protected and society made to flourish." [26]

There is also the vaunted new economic system, born of individualist and rationalist division of property and reinforced by liberal prescriptions of individual ownership, contract, and social mobility. But with its undoubted diffusion of wealth, the new system has brought ills. Thus, "the diffusion of property has lessened the distance which separated the rich from the poor; but it would seem that, the nearer they draw to each other, the greater is their mutual hatred and the more vehement the envy and the dread with which they resist each other's claims to power; the idea of right does not exist for either party, and force affords to both the only argument for the present and the only guarantee for the future." [27] Arising from all of this and especially from the diffusion of property is the lowered regard for private property. All seek profits and wealth but few, Tocqueville concluded, respect property as an institution, as the necessary foundation of individuality.

More tragic, in Tocqueville's judgment, is the degradation of the worker under the economic specialization and division of labor that accompany democracy. "When a workman is unceasingly and exclusively engaged in the fabrication of one thing, he ultimately does his work with singular dexterity; but at the same time he loses the general faculty of applying his mind to the direction of the work. He every day becomes more adroit and less industrious; so that it may be said of him that in proportion as the workman improves, the man is degraded. What can be expected of a man who has spent twenty years of his life in making heads for pins? And to what can that mighty human intelligence which has so often stirred the world be applied in him except it be to investigate the best method of making pins' heads? . . . In proportion as the principle of the division of labor is more extensively applied, the workman becomes more weak, more narrow-minded, and more dependent. The art advances, the artisan recedes." [28]

Tocqueville's words are here applied to an industrial craft, but in various parts of his work it is clear that he saw the tyranny of craft and technique as extending throughout the modern system—in the preference for applied science over theoretical, and for business affairs over philosophy and reflection. Technicism is, he thought, one manifestation of modern man's separation from the roots of culture.

The whole populace becomes attracted in time to the spirit of commercialism. We see it in what Tocqueville calls "the trade of literature." From democracy the commercial classes acquire the taste for letters, but they promptly introduce a "trading spirit" into literature.

"In aristocracies readers are fastidious and few in number; in democracies they are far more numerous and far less difficult to please. The consequence is that among aristocratic nations no one can hope to succeed without great exertion, and this exertion may earn great fame, but can never procure much money; while among democratic nations a writer may flatter himself that he will obtain at a cheap rate a moderate reputation and a large fortune. For this purpose he need not be admired; it is enough that he is liked.

"The ever increasing crowd of readers and their continual craving for something new ensure the sale of books that nobody much esteems.

"In democratic times the public frequently treat authors as kings do their courtiers; they enrich and despise them. What more is needed by venal souls who are born in courts or are worthy to live there?

"Democratic literature is always infested with a tribe of writers who look upon letters as a mere trade; and for some few great authors who adorn it, you may reckon thousands of idea-mongers." [29]

We see the cankering spirit of commercialism even more fundamentally and perhaps ruinously, Tocqueville thinks, in its impact upon agriculture and the rural way of life. Agriculture is suited only to those who already have great wealth or to those whose ingrained poverty bids them to seek a bare subsistence. But in democracy the spirit of trade and commerce induces agriculturalists to use land merely as a springboard to something else. "It seldom happens that an American farmer settles for good upon the land he occupies; especially in the districts of the Far West, he brings land into tillage in order to sell it again, and not to farm it . . . Every year a swarm of people from the North arrive in Southern states and settle in the parts where the cotton plant and sugar cane grow. These men cultivate the soil in order to make it produce in a few years enough to enrich them . . . Thus the Americans carry their business-like qualities into agriculture, and their trading passions are displayed in that as in other pursuits." [30]

It is this trading spirit, this pervasive commercialism, of democracy that makes for, Tocqueville believes, an endemic disease manifested by the recurrent panics to which democratic economies are subject. Since all or most are in commerce rather than in agriculture, the slightest shock puts them in jeopardy. "I believe that the return of these commercial panics is an endemic disease of the democratic nations in our age. It may be rendered less dangerous, but it cannot be cured, because it does not originate in accidental circumstances, but in the temperament of these nations." [31]

Democracy has corrosive effects on consensus in society. "Aristocracy had made a chain of all the members of the community, from the peasant to the king; democracy breaks that chain and severs every link of it . . . Thus, not only does democracy make every man forget his ancestors, but it hides his descendants and separates his contemporaries from him; it throws him back forever upon himself alone and threatens in the end to confine him entirely within the solitude of his own heart." [32]

In the long run, Tocqueville argues, individualism becomes selfishness. "Individualism is a mature and calm feeling, which disposes each member of the community to sever himself from the mass of his fellows and to draw apart with his family and his friends, so that after he has thus formed a little circle of his own, he willingly leaves society at large to itself . . . Individualism at first only saps the virtue of public life; but in the long run it attacks and destroys all others and is at length absorbed in downright selfishness. Selfishness is a vice as old as the world, which does not belong to one form of society more than to another; individualism is of democratic origin, and it threatens to spread in the same ratio as the equality of condition." [33]

And what of equality, the very cornerstone of democracy? Here too Tocqueville finds the dark underside. "When all the privileges of birth and fortune are abolished, when all professions are accessible to all, and a man's own energies may place him at the top of any one of them, an easy and unbounded career seems open to his ambition and he will readily persuade himself that he is born to no common destiny. But this is an erroneous notion, which is corrected by daily experience. The same equality that allows every citizen to conceive these lofty hopes renders all the citizens less able to realize them; it circumscribes their powers on every side, while it gives freer scope to their desires . . . They have swept away the privileges of some of their fellow creatures which stood in their way, but they have opened the door to universal competition; the barrier has changed its shape rather than its position . . ." [34]

Equality can be, especially in turbulent times, the cause of vices which further diminish the moral nature of man. "When equality of conditions succeeds a protracted conflict between the different classes of which the older society was composed, envy, hatred, and uncharitableness, pride and exaggerated self-confidence seize upon the human heart, and plant their way in it for a time. This, independently of equality itself, tends powerfully to divide men, to lead them to mistrust the judgment of one another, and to seek the light of truth nowhere but in themselves. Everyone then attempts to be his own sufficient guide and makes it his boast to form his own opinions on all subjects. Men are no longer bound together by ideas but by interests; and it would seem as if human opinions were reduced to a sort of intellectual dust, scattered on every side, unable to collect, unable to cohere." [35]

Moral values also suffer the erosions of democratic processes. Most of these values, at least in the form in which they have reached the modern world, are feudal in origin; certainly in context and supporting tissue. Trust, responsibility, allegiance, service, honor—all, Tocqueville notes, as we know them, had their origin in the Middle Ages. Then the sense of collective or abstract power was weak. Close personal relations were the cement of society, and, given the character of these, moral values founded upon trust and decorum were indispensable. Honor was the feudal counterpart of modern patriotism. The word has remained, but its meaning and its function have changed drastically in democratic society.

"Thus, the laws of honor will be less peculiar and less multifarious among a democratic people than in an aristocracy. They will also be more obscure, and this is a necessary consequence of what goes before; for as the distinguishing marks of honor are less numerous and less peculiar, it must often be difficult to distinguish them." [36]

In feudal times moral values had an immediacy and a clarity in day-to-day life that were the result of the concreteness and relative stability of the human relationship within which they were set. "This can never be the case in America, where all men are in constant motion and where society, transformed daily by its own operations, changes its opinions together with its wants. In such a country men have glimpses of the rules of honor, but they seldom have time to fix attention upon them." [37] A few loose notions of traditional honor "are to be found scattered among the opinions of the Americans, but these traditional opinions are few in number, they have but little root in the country and but little power. They are like a religion which has still some temples left standing, though men have ceased to believe in it." [38]

The decline of aristocracy has still another moral effect: that of reducing respect for *quality* as contrasted with achievement. He quotes Pascal: "It is a great advantage to be a man of quality, since it brings one man as forward at eighteen or twenty as another man would be at fifty, which is a clear gain of thirty years." [39] In democracy, where the number of prizes is perforce limited and the way to them opened to all, advancement is necessarily retarded and increasingly made a matter of carefully prescribed, universally imposed rules and regulations. Tocqueville remarks on the similarity of democratic development in this respect with what has long existed in China, where, given the multiplicity of examinations for every post, "a lofty ambition breathes with difficulty." In democracy, where all candidates are regarded by definition as alike, and since it is difficult to make a choice without infringing the principle of equality, there is, first, a tendency "to make them all advance at the same rate and submit to the same trials." This applies not only to politics and political office but to all aspects of culture.

"Thus in proportion as men become more alike and the principle of equality is more peaceably and deeply infused into the institutions and manners of the country, the rules for advancement become more inflexible, advancement itself slower, the difficulty of arriving quickly at a certain height far greater. From hatred of privilege and from the embarrassment of choosing, all men are at last forced, whatever may be their standard, to pass the same ordeal; all are indiscriminately subjected to a multitude of petty preliminary exercises, in which their youth is wasted and their imagination quenched, so that they despair of ever fully attaining what is held out to them; and when at length they are in a condition to perform any extraordinary acts, the taste for such things has forsaken them." [40]

Hence, Tocqueville concludes, the paradox that while equality leads to fewer and fewer men of lofty ambition and forces ambition for the most part to remain within narrow limits, it is nevertheless true "that once it gets beyond that, hardly any limits can be assigned to it . . . So that when once an ambitious man has the power in his grasp, there is nothing he may not dare; and when it is gone from him, he meditates the overthrow of the state to regain it. This gives to great political ambition a character of revolutionary violence, which it seldom exhibits to an equal degree in aristocratic communities." [41]

In democracy is also to be found an exaggerated taste for physical gratifications and a devotion to the present that tends to make for equal disregard of past and future. When these are combined with the worship of success in place of fame and of competitive achievement in place of individual ambition, the results are, Tocqueville finds, conducive to a restlessness that breeds melancholy.

"To these causes must be attributed that strange melancholy which often haunts the inhabitants of democratic countries in the midst of their abundance, and that disgust at life which sometimes seizes upon them in the midst of calm and easy circumstances. Complaints are made in France that the number of suicides increases; in America suicide is rare, but insanity is said to be more common than anywhere else. These are all different symptoms of the same disease. . . . In democratic times enjoyments are more intense than in the ages of aristocracy, and the number of those who partake in them is vastly larger; but, on the other hand, it must be admitted that man's hopes and desires are oftener blasted, the soul is more stricken and perturbed, and care itself more keen." [42]

For Tocqueville, therefore, democracy, with all its triumphs and all its inevitability as a historical force, has an inescapable tide of cultural desolation in it, a tendency toward desiccation of the values on which both personal character and legitimate government must ultimately rest. Democracy and individualism are in relentless conflict with their own premises; each threatens to destroy what it most needs—institutional and moral props that originated in pre-democratic, pre-individualistic society. In democracy "man is exalted by precept but degraded in practice." The success of democracy rests upon preservation somehow of the image of man born of aristocratic society, but a whole host of forces are at work to make this impossible.

In 1848 Tocqueville asked: "Shall we ever, as we are assured by other prophets, perhaps as delusive as their predecessors, shall we ever attain a more complete and more far-reaching social transformation than our fathers foresaw and desired, and that we ourselves are able to foresee; or are we not destined simply to end in a condition of intermittent anarchy, the well-known chronic and incurable complaint of old peoples? As for me, I am unable to say; I do not know when this long voyage will be ended; I am weary of seeing the shore in each successive mirage, and I often ask myself whether the *terra firma* we are seeking does really exist, and whether we are not doomed to rove upon the seas forever!" [43]

THE ALIENATION OF LABOR—MARX

It is ironic that although Marx is the medium through which the *word* alienation has reached contemporary thought, the *meaning* that alienation has bears very little relation to that which Marx gave it. The irony is extended when we realize that present-day meanings of alienation stem from those—like Tocqueville and Weber—who made no use of the word itself and whose views of the nature of man, society, and history were in almost diametric opposition to the views of Marx.

A number of Marxists or neo-Marxists of the present, post-Stalinist generation have sought to make alienation a key concept of Marx's thought. As Daniel Bell has written, these students "see in the idea of alienation a more sophisticated radical critique of contemporary society than the simplified and stilted Marxist analysis of class." But as Bell wisely emphasizes, this "is *not* the 'historical Marx'. . . . Marx had repudiated the idea of alienation divorced from his specific economic analysis of property relations under capitalism, and, in so doing, had closed off a road which would have given us a broader and more useful analysis of society and personality than the Marxist dogmatics which did prevail. While one may be sympathetic to the idea of alienation, it is only further myth-making to read this concept back as the central theme of Marx." [44]

To begin with, Marx was not an alienated mind in the sense that Tocqueville was. To make Marx's revolutionary attitude toward the social system around him synonymous with alienation is to miss altogether the intervening philosophy of history, which was, in its way, as optimistic as anything spawned by Manchester liberals of the age. Marx—I refer to the mature, the "historical" Marx—saw the individual in subjection to capitalism, his nature temporarily warped by the "fetishism of commodities." Marx saw society as characterized by the grinding down of the working class under the iron logic of surplus value, but he saw this not as betokening an increasingly bleak and hopeless future, but rather as the first step toward the *emancipation* of man. He saw the ills of his time, not as portents of any proletarianization of man's soul and spirit, not as betokening the garrison-like future that such men as Burckhardt and Weber envisioned, but as hardly more than a short-lived time of troubles that would soon terminate magnificently in revolution and, then, pass into the promised land of socialism. The authentic Marx, we must agree with Bell, is the Marx reflected in all the literature on Marxism down to a decade ago: the confident, ruggedly optimistic prophet of secular redemption, the sworn enemy of all traditional institutions, the believer in progress, in democracy to be fulfilled by economic revolution, even the individualist! It is Marx the heir of the Enlightenment, the philosopher of the general will (transferred to the working class), the skeptic of all states of mind and relationships not rooted directly in man's economic position who is the essential Marx.

For Tocqueville, as we have seen, the dislocations of modern society are deeply rooted in the modern human scheme. They are, in his view, a part of the tragic essence of political history. They are not likely to be offset by democracy or secular welfare, or by revolution. Human alienation and social dislocation will become steadily more fundamental.

How very different is Marx's view. For Marx, the stigmata of mass society are transient: a part of bourgeois society, but not of democracy, secularism, equality, or industrialism. The same economic progression that carried man from slavery to feudalism and then to capitalism will also carry him across history's final step—to communism—a step for which capitalism and bourgeois democracy have prepared the way. There is not a hint in Marx's writings—or in those of his followers, that the kind of uncertainties and fears about the future that tortured Tocqueville, Burckhardt, Weber, and others in the century ever bothered Marx. Like any apostle of capitalism or bourgeois democracy, Marx had boundless confidence in the fundamental stability of Western society. Such a statement may at first sight seem odd, but it accords perfectly with the view that beneath the superstructure of capitalism lay certain iron laws of organization—manifest in technology, the factory, political administration, and trade—which would guarantee the essential structure of society, no matter what happened during the coming revolution. The new society was already well formed within the womb of the old. For three generations socialists were to reflect Marx's own confidence and optimism through their characteristic deprecation of problems of organization, personality, and power. Marx had all the certainty of a Bentham or a Spencer in his conviction that the important sinews of society are founded on the impersonal harmony of economic interests, not on community, tradition, or ethical values.

He had the same confidence in human nature and its indestructibility. Granted that Marx could write in *Capital:* "individuals are dealt with only in so far as they are the personifications of economic categories, embodiments of particular class relations and class interests." [45] One cannot, however, conclude from this or from analogous statements that he ever confused these methodological or analytical representations with the existential reality of man. We speak often of Marx's "social" conception of the nature of human personality, contrasting it with the conception of man that is to be seen in the writings of the classical economists of his day. But it would be a mistake to assume from this that Marx's view of the nature of man is social in the sense that we find in, say, Durkheim—or even in Weber and Simmel. For all Marx's historical sense of social organizations and of the shifting manifestations of human types—slave, serf, proletarian, and so on—there is nevertheless an unwavering acceptance of the stability and reality of the human being. The root is man!

It is tempting to compare Marx's proletarian with Calvin's man of God. In each there is to be seen man's relation to an elect; an elect (be it religious or economic) composed, basically, of self-sufficing individuals who form, as it were, an "invisible community." Inexorable processes will make this "community" someday visible and eternal. Whatever his trials and torments, the true believer—Calvinist or proletarian—will be buoyed up by the knowledge that iron laws must lead to his eventual emancipation from this vale of sorrow and his residence in the realm of the righteous. The proletarian has, in short, a kind of heroic stature and indestructibility of spirit that Calvin would have recognized and, *mutatis mutandis,* approved.

But if there is a Puritan dimension to Marx's proletarian, there is even more strikingly one born of the Enlightenment. Marx, as I have said, is a latter-day *philosophe.* In the Enlightenment it is Rousseau— the Rousseau of the epic *Discourse on the Origin of Inequality*—who forms the clearest prototype to Marx. The similarities between Marx's view of man under capitalism and Rousseau's view of man under the institutions of traditional society are striking. Both views take for granted man's natural (but alienated) goodness and the basic indestructibility of his reason and his character. Both begin with an aboriginal condition in which man was in full possession of all his powers and faculties, of his *self,* so to speak. For Rousseau this is the state of nature; for Marx, primitive communism. Both see the beginning of man's subjection in the rise of private property and the institutions created to safeguard it. Both see class inequality as the hallmark of the oppressive social system around them. Finally, and much to the point here, each sees man's loss of freedom lodged in the transference to others, in the development of civil society, of the autonomy that man had once known.

What could be more "Marxian" in the early pages of the Rousseau's *Discourse* than the picture of primitive man enjoying the fruits of his own labor, serving as his own hunter, his own fisherman, living a life springing from his own resources rather than one dictated by those to whom man had alienated, so to speak, his natural rights and powers. Far from living in fear of the elements, Rousseau's man of nature enjoyed all the trust and confidence that could spring from one who was his own priest, his own philosopher. All of this is changed when, as the result of the establishment of private property and the ensuing development of political, social, and religious institutions, man becomes tyrannized by forces which were once his own, forces now objectified in external institutions which keep him in subjection.

Marx's view of what happened to man in the long evolution of society from idyllic primitive communism is hardly different. He is as impressed as Rousseau by man's subjection to institutions, seeing in them not indispensable supports to mind and character, as Tocqueville had, but as causes of the fragmentation of man's existence. The action of capitalist institutions is politically tyrannical but morally and psychologically superficial. That is, man's nature remains the same underneath, and when the capitalist deathknell has sounded, human beings will step forth, once again able to lead the kind of whole, unfragmented lives they had known before the rise of private property.

How strong Rousseau's influence was on Marx's view of human nature and its relation to society may be inferred from the following passage that Marx and Engels wrote in *The German Ideology:* "In communist society, where nobody has one exclusive sphere of activity but each can become accomplished in any branch he wishes, society regulates the general production and thus makes it possible for me to do one thing today and another tomorrow, to hunt in the morning, fish in the afternoon, rear cattle in the evening, criticize after dinner, just as I have a mind, without ever becoming hunter, fisherman, shepherd, or critic." [46] Or take the following passage from Engels' *Anti-Dühring:* "In time to come there will no longer be any professional porters or architects . . . The man who for half an hour gives instructions as an architect will also act as a porter for a period, until his activity as an architect is once again required." [47]

The point of this is clear enough. Precisely as Rousseau had seen the establishment of the general will as the means whereby men could be liberated from the fragmenting, corrupting influence of institutions, Marx saw socialism as this means. In both cases what is involved psychologically is the restoration to man of elements of his nature, his inner being, that had been taken from him by religious, economic, and political institutions. "Every emancipation is a restoration of the human world and of human relationships to man himself," wrote Marx. "Human emancipation will only be complete when the real, individual man has absorbed in himself the abstract citizen, when as an individual man, in his everyday life, in his work, and in his relationships, he has become a *social being* and when he has recognized and organized his own powers (*forces propres*) . . ." [48] In Marx, as in Rousseau, there is the assumption that underneath the effects of civil institutions the fundamental health and stability of human nature remains—remains good, as it remains viable. Communist man is Marx's rendering of the eighteenth century's natural man.

These two essential perspectives in Marx—the beneficence of what is truly modern in society and the underlying stability of the human spirit, both perspectives drawn from the Enlightenment—form the context of the difference that we find between his conception of alienation and that of Tocqueville. Marx's conception, even in its earliest statements, is eminently individualistic: far from lamenting the loss of man's ties with institutions, it seeks the return to man of what has falsely been given to external society—to religion, to state, and to economy, especially to the latter. The youthful Marx may have been concerned with man's relations to all institutions, but once he threw himself into the workers' movement, he transferred to economy alone the theoretical interest that he had previously given to other parts of society.

Marx, as we know, took the word alienation from Hegel and, more directly, from the "left Hegelians." For Hegel, as Bell has written: "Alienation, in its original connotation, was the radical dissociation of the 'self' into both actor and thing, into a *subject* that strives to control its own fate, and an *object* which is manipulated by others." [49] In Hegel's strict and rigorous usage alienation is not, it must be emphasized, a mere finite state, least of all the transient consequence of a stage of social development. It is, on the contrary, deeply embedded in man's nature; it is ontological and metaphysical. Because of it, absolute freedom—which Hegel defined as "that voyage into the open where nothing is below us or above us, and we stand in solitude with ourselves alone" [50]—is probably forever unattainable. Always there will be some degree of dissociation of the self, manifest in thought and life. Hegel could write criticisms of certain developments in the nineteenth century that placed him clearly with both philosophical conservatives and with sociologists, but his conception of alienation has almost nothing to do with these social criticisms. Alienation is a state deeply and ineradicably buried in the nature of man's self and its effort to achieve communication with the world.

It is the mark of the "left Hegelians," however, that what had been ontological in Hegel is made increasingly sociological. Thus Feuerbach, whom Marx credited with having carried the concept of alienation for the first time to the empirical world, treated it as an essentially religious condition; as arising, that is, from man's loss of self to the tyranny of religion. In Feuerbach there is a fusion of Hegelian ontology with the Enlightenment's onslaught against institutional religion, especially Christianity. For Feuerbach, the prime cause of man's alienation lay in his subjection to the forms and superstitions of traditional religion. Feuerbach did not limit himself to the forms; he included the very concept of God among those things which must be extirpated if man's identity was to be returned to him, if his alienated self was to be restored to pristine wholeness.

For Marx, however, this missed the real point. Economics was prior to religion in setting the context of alienation. In the same way that Feuerbach had reduced Hegel's view of alienation to something expressible in terms of religion, Marx reduced it still further to something expressible in terms of private property and labor. In the separation of man from the fruits of his labor lies the Marxian essence of alienation.

"In what does this alienation consist? First that the work is *external* to the worker, that it is not a part of his nature, that consequently he does not fulfill himself in his work but denies himself, has a feeling of misery, not of well-being, does not develop freely a physical and mental energy, but is physically exhausted and mentally debased. The worker, therefore, feels himself at home only during his leisure, whereas at work he feels homeless. His work is not voluntary but imposed, *forced labor.* It is not the satisfaction of a need, but only a *means* for satisfying other needs. Its alien character is clearly shown by the fact that as soon as there is no physical or other compulsion it is avoided like the plague. Finally, the alienated character of work for the worker appears in the fact that it is not his work but work for someone else, that in work he does not belong to himself but to another person." [51]

Marx deals with alienation in work much as he (and before him Feuerbach) had earlier dealt with religion. Alienation consists of the individual letting something of himself go outside of himself, thus to become an external influence or authority. The tyranny imposed by capitalism is the objectified tyranny of something that rightfully belongs within the worker. "Just as in religion the spontaneous action of human fantasy, of the human brain and heart, reacts independently, that is, as an alien activity of gods or devils, upon the individual, so the activity of the worker is not his spontaneous activity. It is another's activity, and a loss of his own spontaneity." [52]

There is no better and more succinct statement of what Marx meant by alienation than the following: "The object produced by labor, its product, now stands opposed to it as an *alien being,* as a *power independent* of the producer. The product of labor is labor which has been embodied in a thing, and turned into a physical thing; this product is an objectification of labor. The performance of work is at the same time its objectification. This performance appears, in the sphere of political economy, as a *vitiation* of the worker, objectification as a *loss* and as *servitude to the object,* and appropriation as alienation." [53]

Such statements, taken from Marx's early writings, have a clear relation to his later, mature work. What, from one point of view, might be regarded as the attenuation of alienation, as a concept, in his system, may, from another point of view, be regarded as socialist devotion to what alone causes (or, better, *represents*) alienation: capitalism. With Hegel, Marx says that man is alienated: that is, his true self is dissociated. This is stage one of Marx's development. Stage two is reached in his agreement with Feuerbach that such alienation is not ontological but historical-institutional. The third stage is reached in Marx when, repudiating Feuerbach as well as Hegel, he declares alienation to be reducible to private property: to man's alienation from himself of an essential faculty, work. Having reached this decision, he gave himself exclusively to the analysis and condemnation of capitalism. The following passage is taken from *Capital* but is nevertheless rooted in early reflections:

"Within the capitalist system all methods for raising the social productiveness of labor are brought about at the cost of the individual laborer; all means for the development of production transform themselves into means of domination over, and exploitation of, the producers; they mutilate the laborer into a fragment of a man, degrade him to the level of an appendage of a machine, destroy every remnant of charm in his work, and turn it into a hated toil; they estrange him from the intellectual potentialities of the labor process in the same proportion as science is incorporated in it as an independent power; they distort the conditions under which he works, subject him during the labor process to a despotism the more hateful for its meanness, they drag his wife and child beneath the wheels of the juggernaut of capital." [54]

But while there is an affinity between this passage and the tortured view of division of labor that we have seen in Tocqueville, the affinity does not extend below the surface. What matters is the context. For Marx all of this fragmentation, this soul-destroying discipline, this degradation of man, is a function simply of capitalism, of private ownership of the means of production in society. "Religion, the family, the State, law, morality, science, art, etc. are only particular forms of production and come under its general law. The positive abolition of private property, as the appropriation of human life, is thus the positive abolition of all alienation, and thus the return of man from religion, the family, the State, etc., to his human, that is, social life." [55] But this is in a different universe from Tocqueville's envisagement of the degradation of the laborer in *the system of production itself,* in division of labor, and in technology. Who actually owns the means of production would have been, for Tocqueville, irrelevant when compared to the larger forces making for the subjection of man.

For Marx and his followers, however, there were no forces—spiritual or institutional—that were larger than the system of capitalism Abolish this, substitute socialism and, eventually, communism, and you have completed the work of destroying all that presently separates man from freedom and from his true self.

"When society," wrote Engels, "by taking possession of all means of production and managing them on a planned basis, has freed itself and all of its members from the bondage in which they are at present held by means of production which they themselves have produced but which now confront them as irresistible, alien power; when consequently man no longer proposes but also disposes—only then will the last alien power which is now reflected in religion vanish. And with it will also vanish the religious reflection itself, for the simple reason that there will be nothing left to reflect." [56]

That alienation might be a state of mind under socialism, that socialism indeed might be regarded as but a more intensified stage of the bureaucratization of the human spirit that mass democracy and machine industrialism presently represent, with the individual left ever more isolated from the sources of cultural identity, ever more lost in routine and technology, and with the will of the people ever more diverted from itself by the operation of "rational" and "progressive" forces in history—all of this is utterly foreign to Marxism. It is not foreign, however, to Weber, to Durkheim, and to Simmel.

THE NEMESIS OF RATIONALISM—WEBER

In Weber we find a temper of mind very close to Tocqueville. There is striking similarity between the perspectives and the conclusions of the two men regarding the course of Western history. In Weber no more than in Tocqueville is there preview of a future made bright by the forces of rationalism, democracy, and secularism. The melancholy that tinctures Weber's greatest essays is Tocquevillian in nature.

In Weber's lifetime socialism held much the same contextual significance that democracy had for Tocqueville. Just as France was alive, in the 1830s, with the doctrines and counter-doctrines of democratic equalitarianism, thus shaping Tocqueville's envisagement of the American scene, so was Germany alive, from 1890 to the outbreak of World War I, with the doctrines and counter-doctrines of socialism, chiefly Marxian. To many of the greatest minds of that day socialism appeared as liberating and beneficent as it did inevitable. But not to

Weber. Inevitable perhaps, given the structure and development of capitalism, but not beneficent. Socialism, far from being the antithesis of capitalism for Weber, is instead its malign intensification. What does it matter, Weber asks in effect, quite as Tocqueville had asked of democracy, if ownership passes from the few to the many if the fundamental forces of modern society—bureaucracy, rationalization of values, alienation from community and culture—continue? It is Weber's view that capitalism and socialism are both manifestations of a far more fundamental force in Western society. This force is rationalization: the conversion of social values and relationships from the primary, communal, and traditional shapes they once held to the larger, impersonal, and bureaucratized shapes of modern life.

As we cannot fail to detect in Tocqueville a strong preference for aristocracy and in Tönnies a ruling affection for *Gemeinschaft,* neither can we fail to detect in Weber, throughout his life and work, a haunted preoccupation with the traditional values that were being jettisoned, as it seemed, by the rulers of the new society. It is useful to remember that Weber's serious work as a sociologist had begun when, as a young man, he had gone to East Prussia to find out, among other things, why the peasant workers there were so zealously seeking wage contracts in place of the more secure status relationships they had inherited from their forefathers.

It was undoubtedly this experience that led him eventually to the conclusion that rationalization—of labor-management relationships, of government, religion, and culture in general—was a tidal force in modern history that must sweep everything before it. Rationalization serves Weber precisely as equalitarianism serves Tocqueville. In each we see a historical tendency that can be understood only in terms of what happens to traditional society—to values of culture and community that had once given men a feeling of close relatedness and of personal identity. The drive toward equality that Tocqueville had been able to find in European history, going all the way back to the breakup of the Middle Ages, affecting culture, values, authority, and human character, is matched by the drive toward rationalization that Weber finds.

Weber, comparative scientist that he was, does more with rationalization than to leave it simply as a unique process in modern Europe. Rationalization becomes, in his hands, a far-reaching methodological concept, neutrally applicable to patterns of culture and thought in all civilizations. He uses rationalization to illuminate processes involved in the history of religion in the ancient world, in music, art, warfare, authority, and economy. He does not therefore restrict concern with rationalization, as Tocqueville did equalitarianism, to the West alone. But this, while true, is nevertheless incidental to the central point that it was in the contrast between Western medieval traditionalism and modern society that Weber first obtained his image of what rationalization as a process was. No matter how "value-free" his treatment of rationalization is, there is simply no question that the moral *evaluation* of rationalization in Weber's mind was cast ultimately in the same perspective in which Tocqueville had cast his evaluation of equality and individualization.

In the same way that Tocqueville's alienation may be seen as an inversion of individualism—leading him to take man's deterioration as the long-run consequence of release from institutions—Weber's alienation springs from an inversion of rationalism. Tocqueville saw the future in a spread of atomized masses surmounted by absolute, if providential, power. Weber, in no disagreement with this perspective, puts the future in the complementary terms of a reduction of all values, all relationships, all culture to a monolithic, secular, and utilitarian bureaucracy. Rationalization, having removed the traditional, the patriarchal, the communal, the "enchanted," along with the irrational, the personally exploitative, the superstitious, becomes, in the end, its own nemesis.

There is thus the same note of tragic paradox in Weber's mind that lies in Tocqueville's. From being a force of "progress"—the indispensable means of liberating man from the tyrannies of the past—rationalization becomes eventually the seedbed of a tyranny greater, more penetrating, more lasting, than anything previously known in history. Rationalization is no mere process of politics; it is not limited in its effects to political bureaucracy. It has affected all culture, even the human mind, as it has affected the structure of modern economy and state. So long as the process of rationalization had something to feed on—that is, the structure of traditional society and culture that was formed during the Middle Ages—it was a generally creative and liberating process. But with the gradual diminution and desiccation of this structure, with man's increasing disenchantment with the values of this structure, rationalization threatens now to become, not creative and liberating, but mechanizing, regimenting, and, ultimately, reason-destroying.

"The fate of our times is characterized by rationalization and intellectualization and, above all, by the 'disenchantment of the world.' Precisely the ultimate and most sublime values have retreated from public life either into the transcendental realm of mystic life or into the brotherliness of direct and personal relations. It is not accidental that our greatest art is intimate and not monumental, nor is it accidental that today only within the smallest and most intimate circles, in personal human situations, in *pianissimo,* that something is pulsating that corresponds to the prophetic *pneuma,* which in former times swept through the great communities like a firebrand, welding them together. If we attempt to force and to 'invent' a monumental style of art, such miserable monstrosities are produced as the many monuments of the last twenty years. If one tries intellectually to construct new religions without a new and genuine prophecy, then, in an inner sense, something similar will result, but with still worse effects. And academic prophecy, finally, will create only fanatical sects but never a genuine community." [57]

There is a striking resemblance between this view of modern culture and that found in Weber's contemporary, George Sorel. Without sentimentality, both men saw the relentless transformation of European culture from one based upon action rooted in personal *feeling*—belief, hope, love, joy, hate, cruelty—to one based increasingly upon impersonality; upon a leaching out of feeling, along with personal dominion, from the management of life. It was this grim conclusion that drove Sorel into the search for a "myth" that, like Christianity in imperial Rome, might be the means of restoring hope and faith—and also action.[58] Weber, we need not doubt, would have regarded such a search as more nearly the betrayal than the fulfillment of destiny.

Weber, like Tocqueville, sees a change taking place even in the character of man, one resulting from his modern role of being almost totally governed, managed, dealt with custodially, in ever-widening areas of life and, more crucially, in ever smaller and more personal details. But the genius of Weber is that of Tocqueville: knowing this, he still did not set himself, as did so many in his time, blindly against the forces of modernism, of progress. He could see, as Tocqueville had, magnificent accomplishments of equalitarianism and rationalization in modern European history: the liberation of man from contexts whose very personality and intimacy had been, too often, their tyranny, from values whose very sacredness had been the measure of their suffocating effect upon life and creativeness. Both men could see the iron necessity of these movements; a historical necessity that doctrinaire radicalism and liberalism superfluously joined and clamantly extolled. As we find some of the richest odes to capitalism in Marx, so do we find some of the richest odes to equalitarianism in Tocqueville and to rationalization in Weber.

It is a further mark of the intellectual greatness of both Tocqueville and Weber that they chose to pursue the lonely course of uncompromising principle rather than the easier and soul-warming one of abnegation to either traditionalism or modernism. Does Weber, for all his despair with the consequences of rationalization, urge return to the past, to those aspects of the present that are least modern? Plainly, not! No more than Tocqueville, who sided, let us not forget, with the revolutionaries, not with the disciples of reaction, in 1848. Each recognized that there is an irreversible quality to history in its large dimension and that while it is the duty of the intellectual to face history rigorously and harshly, to call it what it is, tyrannous or vulgar or both, and not abase oneself to it, it is equally the intellectual's duty to refrain from narcotic retreats to the false gods of archaism. Weber was preoccupied by the relation of religion to the world that was being created by science and bureaucracy. His own torment with modernism made him charitable to those who, finding it intolerable, returned to the historic faiths.

"To the person who cannot bear the fate of the times like a man, one must say: may he rather return silently, without the usual publicity build-up of renegades, but simply and plainly. The arms of the old churches are opened widely and compassionately for him. After all, they do not make it hard for him. One way or another he has to bring his 'intellectual sacrifice'—that is inevitable. If he can really do it, we shall not rebuke him. For such an intellectual sacrifice in favor of an unconditional religious devotion is ethically quite a different matter than the evasion of the plain duty of intellectual integrity, which sets in if one lacks the courage to clarify one's own ultimate standpoint and rather facilitates this duty by feeble relative judgments. *In my eyes, such religious return stands higher than the academic prophecy, which does not clearly realize that in the lecture rooms of the university no other virtue holds but plain intellectual integrity.* Integrity, however, compels us to state that for the many who today tarry for new prophets and saviors, the situation is the same as resounds in the beautiful Edomite watchman's song of the period of exile that has been included among Isaiah's oracles:

> 'He calleth to me out of Seir, Watchman,
> what of the night? The watchman said,
> The morning cometh, and also the night:
> if ye will enquire, enquire ye: return,
> come.'

"The people to whom this was said has enquired and tarried for more than two millennia, and we are shaken when we realize its fate.

From this we want to draw the lesson that nothing is gained by yearning and tarrying alone, and we shall act differently. We shall set to work and meet the 'demands of the day,' in human relations as well as in our vocation. This, however, is plain and simple, if each finds and obeys the demon who holds the fibers of his very life." [59]

In our day, not even Albert Camus could have said this more poignantly, more compellingly. Alienation is not, after all, a mode of anchoritic renunciation; it is a special form of insight.

But for those intellectuals who, instead of returning frankly and honestly to the great faiths, making the genuine "intellectual sacrifice," play instead with trappings and symbols of religion, Weber had nothing but contempt. "Never as yet has a new prophecy emerged (and I repeat deliberately this image which has offended some) by way of the need of some modern intellectuals to furnish their souls with, so to speak, guaranteed genuine antiques. In doing so, they happen to remember that religion has belonged among such antiques, and of things religion is what they do not possess. By way of substitute, however, they play at decorating a sort of domestic chapel with small sacred images from all over the world, or they produce surrogates through all sorts of psychic experiences to which they ascribe the dignity of mystic holiness, which they peddle in the book market. This is plain humbug or self-deception." [60]

It is not *dis*organization any more than it is catastrophe that Weber fears, but, rather, *over*organization, a future sterilized of the informal and the use-and-wont contexts within which personality takes on the stuff of resistance to mass-mindedness and cultural uniformity. The rationalization that made democracy and capitalism triumph over the social systems which preceded them will, if not freshly inspired, bring about a society in which democracy and capitalism themselves will not survive, in which only caricatures of these systems will exist, with man converted from his modern Faustian character to a demon-ridden creature of apathy and fear.

In the final, eloquent pages of his *The Protestant Ethic and the Spirit of Capitalism* Weber implies that the other side of asceticism (the motive force of capitalist work) may be an alienation from the things that asceticism brings with it. "Since asceticism undertook to remodel the world and to work out its ideals in the world, material goods have gained an increasing and finally an inexorable power over the lives of men as at no previous period in history. Today the spirit of religious asceticism—whether finally, who knows?—has escaped from the cage.

But victorious capitalism, since it rests on mechanical foundations, needs its support no longer. The rosy blush of its laughing heir, the Enlightenment, seems also to be irretrievably fading, and the idea of duty in one's calling prowls about in our lives like the ghost of dead religious beliefs. Where the fulfillment of the calling cannot directly be related to the highest spiritual and cultural values, or when, on the other hand, it need not be felt simply as economic compulsion, the individual generally abandons the attempt to justify it at all. In the field of its highest development, in the United States, the pursuit of wealth, stripped of its religious and ethical meaning, tends to become associated with purely mundane passions, which often actually give it the character of sport.

"No one knows who will live in this cage in the future, or whether at the end of this tremendous development entirely new prophets will arise, or there will be a great rebirth of old ideas and ideals or, if neither, mechanized petrification embellished with a sort of convulsive self-importance. For of the last stage of this cultural development, it might well be truly said: 'Specialists without spirit, sensualists without heart; this nullity imagines that it has obtained a level of civilization never before achieved!' " [61]

Weber took much the same view of the self-sterilizing qualities in education and of the ominous prospect of a "meritocracy" that in the long run would be as prejudicial to equality and liberty as earlier aristocracies founded on religion, property, or war. He thought that the rationalization of education, the increasing dependence of government and society on the technical skills and knowledge vouchsafed by education, would make for a new stratum of privilege and power with the diploma succeeding the coat of arms.

"The development of the diploma from universities, and business and engineering colleges, and the universal clamor for the creation of educational certificates in all fields make for the formation of a privileged stratum in bureaus and offices. Such certificates support their holders' claims for intermarriages with notable families (in business offices people naturally hope for preferment with regard to the chief's daughter), claims to be admitted into the circles that adhere to 'codes of honor,' claims for a 'respectable' remuneration rather than remuneration for work well done, claims for assured advancement and old-age insurance, and, above all, claims to monopolize social and economically advantageous positions. When we hear from all sides the demand for an introduction of regular curricula and special examinations, the reason behind it is, of course, not a suddenly awakened 'thirst for education' but the desire for restricting the supply for these positions and their monopolization by the owners of educational certificates. Today the 'examination' is the universal means of this monopolization, and therefore examinations irresistibly advance." [62]

This, it will be recalled, was Tocqueville's premonition of the long-run consequence of a social system predicated upon the ethic of equality in which recognition of quality must be subordinated to the mechanism of identical examinations and hurdles for all in their efforts to rise, thus holding the swiftest back to the speed of the slowest.

Throughout Western society, but especially in Germany, Weber could see the gradual rise of a new form of patrimonialism based upon civil service and extending itself to all areas of society: social security, education, the professions, business, and government. It would be the patrimonialism of bureaucracy. His words on this are eloquent and passionate:

"It is horrible to think that the world could one day be filled with nothing but those little cogs, little men clinging to little jobs and striving towards the bigger ones—a state of affairs which is to be seen once more, as in the Egyptian records, playing an ever-increasing part in the spirit of our present administrative system, and especially of its offspring, the students. This passion for bureaucracy . . . is enough to drive one to despair. It is as if in politics . . . we were deliberately to become men who need 'order' and nothing but order, become nervous and cowardly if for one moment this order wavers, and helpless if they are torn away from their total incorporation in it. That the world should know no men but these: it is in such an evolution that we are already caught up, and the great question is, therefore, not how we can promote and hasten it, but what can we oppose to this machinery in order to keep a portion of mankind free from this parceling-out of the soul, from this supreme mastery of the bureaucratic way of life." [63]

Such for Weber is the indwelling canker in the vaunted system of administrative meritocracy and universal education that had been, ever since the French Enlightenment, the royal road to secular salvation.

And what, finally, of the spirit in which modernism was brought to birth and eventual triumph? Weber writes in words that could hardly have been strengthened by even the author of that nineteenth-century dirge, *The City of Dreadful Night*. They form the closing section of his *Politics as Vocation*:

"Not summer's bloom lies ahead of us, but rather a polar night of icy darkness and hardness. When this night shall have slowly receded, who of those for whom Spring apparently has bloomed so luxuriously will be alive? And what will have become of all of you by then? Will you be bitter or banausic? Will you simply and dully accept world and occupation? Or will the third and by no means the least frequent possibility be your lot: mystic flight from reality for those who are gifted for it, or—as is both frequent and unpleasant—for those who belabor themselves to follow this fashion?" [64]

ISOLATION AND ANOMIE—DURKHEIM

The specter of modern man's isolation from traditional society hovers over all of Durkheim's work, giving theme to his analyses of division of labor and suicide and background for his relentless emphasis on social solidarity. It is not the diminution of the meaning of man, as it was for Tocqueville, that marks Durkheim's perception of alienation, for it is his constant argument that in modern society the meaning of the individual has soared beyond all possible sustenance. Nor does Durkheim, like Weber, see the inversion of rationalism; he is too much the positivist for that. But what he does see all around him—in confutation of the hopes of the Enlightenment and its utilitarian successors—is release from community and tradition that results in despair and insupportable aloneness. Not self-discovery but self-fear, not confident optimism but excessive melancholy and anxiety: these, for Durkheim, are the consequences of the modern history of individualism. The essence of modernism is, in short, devitalization of that sense of society which alone can maintain individuality. This has been the major result of industrialism, mass democracy, and secularism.

What is in fact characteristic of our development, Durkheim suggested, is that it has successively destroyed all the established social contexts; one after another they have been banished either by the slow erosion of time or by violent revolution, and in such fashion that nothing has been developed to replace them.[65]

Comte's obsession with individualism as "the disease of the Western world" is no less vivid in Durkheim. His unremitting emphasis upon authority as constitutive of both social order and personality has for its obverse side a recognition of strong currents of dislocation of authority in his day, currents that weakened morality and society and left the individual ever more exposed to circumstance and fate.

Human personality necessarily presupposes a stable social order.

"If this dissolves, if we no longer feel it in existence and action about and above us, whatever is social in us is deprived of all objective foundation. All that remains is an artificial combination of illusory images, a phantasmagoria vanishing at the least reflection; that is, nothing which can be a goal for our action. Yet this social man is the essence of civilized man; he is the masterpiece of existence. Thus we are bereft of reasons for existence; for the only life to which we could cling no longer corresponds to anything actual; the only existence still based upon reality no longer meets our needs." [66]

For Durkheim it is not what excessive individualism *produces,* but individualism itself that is the cause of suicidal currents in society and of all the other manifestations of disorganization and alienation. For individualism by its very nature is separation from the norms and communities that are the sinews of man's spiritual nature. While it is not true that man must have a *supra*-mundane, much less a deistic, end to give meaning to his individuality and nerve to his life, there is this much truth in it: social man, in contrast to physical man, does require something authoritative, something that transcends man and enforces his sense of being. It is different with respect to physical life. In it "man can act reasonably without thought of transcendental purposes . . . Insofar as he has no other needs, he is therefore self-sufficient and can live happily with no other objective than living." But this is not the case with man in society, that is, civilized man. He has many ideas, feelings, and practices unrelated to organic needs. The functions of art, morality, religion, political faith, and science itself are not to repair organic exhaustion nor to provide sound functioning of the organs, but to arouse in us the sentiments of sympathy and solidarity drawing us toward others. It is "society which, fashioning us in its image, fills us with religious, political, and moral beliefs that control our actions. To play our social role we have striven to extend our intelligence, and it is still society that has supplied us with tools for this development by transmitting to us its trust fund of knowledge." [67]

But what, tragically, has happened to society in modern Europe, under the impacts of revolution, industrialism, and the whole succession of secularizing, atomizing forces of modernism has been to make it ever more difficult "to play our social role." A host of passages in Durkheim's works supports the conclusion that in his mind the cohesive and stabilizing forces of European society were undergoing disintegration. This, after all, is the larger shape of his theory of suicide, for suicide is taken by Durkheim as the index of something very deep in the social constitution: that is, "the general unrest of contemporary societies." In moderate degree suicide is normal, but in contemporary civilization "the exceptionally high number of voluntary deaths manifests the state of deep disturbance from which civilized societies are suffering, and bears witness to its gravity." And it is precisely in those sectors of society that are most "modern," most "progressive"—Protestant, urban, industrial, and secular—that suicide rates are highest.

He refers to the "currents of depression and disillusionment emanating from no particular individual but expressing society's state of disintegration." [68] Such currents "reflect the relaxation of social bonds, a sort of collective asthenia, or social malaise, just as individual sadness, when chronic, in its way reflects the poor organic state of the individual." Such currents are collective; that is, social. And because they are social "they have, by virtue of their origin, an authority which they impose upon the individual and they drive him vigorously on the way to which he is already inclined by the state of moral distress directly aroused in him by the disintegration of society." [69] Admittedly, a certain incidence of suicide, like a certain incidence of crime, is inseparable from the conditions which also produce high culture—the arts, letters, and the liberal professions. But what suicide has come to mark in our society, Durkheim concludes, "is not the increasing brilliancy of our civilization, but a state of crisis and perturbation not to be prolonged with impunity." [70]

Durkheim's melancholy does not rest on the incidence of suicide alone. In his *Division of Labor* he had noted the virtually inverse relation between the development of culture and human happiness. States of boredom, anxiety, and despair are relatively unknown in primitive or simple society, he observed, for their common causes are largely absent. In civilization they mount and, with them, endemic unhappiness. We should not conclude, Durkheim emphasizes, that progress causes these states. More likely they are concomitant. "But this concomitance is sufficient to prove that progress does not greatly increase our happiness, since the latter decreases, and in very grave proportions, at the very moment when the division of labor is developing with an energy and rapidity never known before." [71]

Durkheim's attitude toward happiness has little in common with the reigning notions of his day. Far from seeing in happiness the proper goal of individual and social energies, he deprecates it. "Too cheerful a morality is a loose morality; it is appropriate only to decadent peoples and is found only among them . . . From certain indications it even seems that the tendency to a sort of melancholy develops as we rise in the scale of social types." There is a kind of functional necessity in sadness, as there is in crime. "Man could not live if he were impervious to sadness. Many sorrows can be endured only by being embraced, and the pleasure taken in them naturally has a somewhat melancholy character. So, melancholy is morbid only when it occupies too much place in life; but it is equally morbid for it to be wholly excluded from life." [72] One can imagine such a sentiment coming from Tocqueville or Weber but not from Mill or Spencer.

Historical periods like ours, Durkheim observes, are necessarily filled with anxiety and pessimism. For our objectives are Faustian in scope. "What could be more disillusioning than to proceed toward a terminal point that is nonexistent, since it recedes in the same measure that one advances? . . . This is why historical periods like ours, which have known the malady of infinite aspiration, are necessarily touched with pessimism. Pessimism always accompanies unlimited aspirations. Goethe's Faust may be regarded as representing *par excellence* this view of the infinite. And it is not without reason that the poet has portrayed him as laboring in continual anguish." This is precisely the condition that had led Tocqueville to see increasing frustration and unhappiness as the consequence of democracy, and it is the background that Durkheim sees for the general breakdown in social and moral discipline around him. That he regarded this breakdown as critical is plain enough. "Indeed, history records no crisis as serious as that in which European societies have been involved for more than a century. Collective discipline in its traditional form has lost its authority, as the divergent tendencies troubling the public conscience and the resulting general anxiety demonstrate." [73]

There are still other ways of assaying the intensity of the modern malaise that has gripped European society: through the proliferation of philosophical systems based on skepticism and materialism. Durkheim compares the modern age in this respect with periods of decadence in Hellenistic Greece and Imperial Rome when, similarly, belief systems arose that reflected loss of faith and membership in society.

"The formation of such great systems is . . . an indication that the current pessimism has reached a degree of abnormal intensity which is due to some disturbances of the social organism. We well know how these systems have recently multiplied. To form a true idea of their number and importance is it not enough to consider the philosophies avowedly of this nature, such as those of Schopenhauer, Hartmann, etc.? We must also consider all the others which derive from the same spirit under

different names. The anarchist, the esthete, the mystic, the socialist revolutionary, even if they do not despair of the future, have in common with
the pessimist a single sentiment of hatred and disgust for the existing
order, a single craving to destroy or to escape from reality. Collective
melancholy would not have penetrated consciousness so far if it had not
undergone a morbid development . . ." [74]

Such is Durkheim's reaction to an age that others in his day—secularists, individualists, Protestants, progressives alike—were hailing as
the onset or at least the harbinger of a new order, a new freedom, a new
morality. Durkheim's is clearly an alienated view of modern culture. He
is too much the child of modernism himself, too deeply devoted to science and to liberal democracy, to seek refuge in any of the traditional-
isms that a vain and reactionary politics sought to impose upon France
—and Europe in general. But unlike a great many of his fellow rationalists, fellow liberals, and fellow democrats, he knew that no stable order
could be built *directly* on the intellectual pillars of modernism; that until
the values of science and liberal democracy were rooted in *social* contexts as secure and binding as the contexts in which religion and kinship
had once been rooted, and endowed with the *moral* authority, the *sacredness,* that these more ancient institutions had once known, European
society would continue in the state of crisis that would subvert each and
every political remedy that the reformers put forward.

Durkheim's reaction to the sanguine atmosphere of moral progress
in his time was, thus, as complete as his reaction to individualism and
biologism. His concepts of the collective conscience, of the eternal cult,
of anomie, and of the functional role of discipline are predicated indeed
upon this moral reaction, and we may properly conclude by saying that
to overlook the moral in Durkheim's thought is tantamount to overlook-
ing the social. Moral and social are but two faces of the same coin.

As alienation is a temper in Tocqueville and Weber that permitted
original analyses of history, the social order, and personality, so is it
equally fruitful in Durkheim. It is a fair statement—and in methodological
terms an important one—that his alienated view of Western progress
preceded his empirical study of suicide. From this view came an insight
into not only the incidence of suicide but personality and its roots in
moral and social community.

THE TYRANNY OF OBJECTIVISM—SIMMEL

"The deepest problems of modern life," wrote Simmel in his notable essay on metropolis, "derive from the claim of the individual to preserve the autonomy and individuality of his existence in the face of overwhelming social forces, of historical heritage, of external culture, and of the technique of life. The fight with nature which primitive man has to wage for his *bodily* existence attains in this modern form its latest transformation." [75]

For Simmel the most paradoxical of the bequests left by modern rationalist individualism is the inability of man to preserve a sense of the wholeness and identity of self against the very currents which had been supposed to be the prime means of both liberating and emphasizing this wholeness and identity of self. The eighteenth century, he writes, had called upon man to "free himself of all the historical bonds" in society, thus to permit the unhampered development of the nature in man thought by rationalists to be common and good. Then, in the nineteenth century, occurred the functional specialization that makes "each individual incomparable to another, and each of them indispensable to the highest possible extent." Everything promised the release of individual identity in a way not known before in history.

But instead of this release of the whole individual, we see in metropolitan life the progressive fragmenting of the individual self into routinized roles, and a blunting, first, of recognition of others, then, of one's own self. Eighteenth-century philosophers, Simmel tells us, foresaw man's release in terms only of aggregates and contexts with which they were familiar—towns, villages; rarely, cities—and the result was a "release" conditioned unconsciously by psychological factors persisting from traditional society. They did not, that is, anticipate man's release from his European character. But the actuality of release must be seen in that form of life which is increasingly the natural habitat of modern man —the metropolis. And here what is released is not man's wholeness, but rather a "highly personal subjectivity" against a background of "a structure of the highest impersonality." It is as though the atom of human identity had been split, with the "social" aspect lost in the external and objective forces of metropolitan society and the "personal" fleeing ever more deeply into a buried, incommunicable subjectivity.

In Simmel, alienation is a kind of epistemological perspective, one that is as emotion-free as his treatments of the dyad and triad or his analyses of secrecy and of the stranger. I do not suggest that he was lacking in moral awareness. Far from it. We have only to read his moving reactions to what was happening to liberal culture in Europe to be aware of Simmel's ethical consciousness. But where Weber's reflections on rationalization are often set in a spiritual melancholy—an aspect of felt disenchantment—and Durkheim's reflections on individual alienation arise within his deep conviction of endemic social disorganization in Europe, we find neither of these in Simmel. Alienation is, for him, almost solely methodological; it is a means of fresh analysis of human personality and its relation to the world rather than the basis of any kind of spiritual or ethical evaluation.

"I see," he wrote in his *Sociology of Religion,* "the most capacious and far-reaching collision between society and individual, not in the aspect of particular interests but in the general form of the individual life. Society aspires to totality and organic unity, each of its members constituting but a component part. The individual as part of the society has to fulfill special functions and employ all his strength; he is expected to modify his skills so that he will become the best-qualified performer of these functions. But this role is opposed by man's bent toward unity and totality as an expression of his own individuality." [76]

This does not mean, of course, that alienation is a constant and unvarying state in human history. The "collision between society and individual" has contrasting periods of relative dormancy and febrility. Our age, with its magnification of power, its ever sharper dichotomy between the objective and subjective, and its proliferation of moral antinomies, is, Simmel thought, a breeding ground for these collisions of self and society. In the Middle Ages, on the other hand, the sense of alienation was not dominant. How could it have been, with "corporations and communities like so many intersecting circles forming a net out of which only the hardiest of souls could find his way"? In his treatment of authority Simmel emphasized the essentially "personal" character of authority in the medieval system. All powers were personal, including the king's, and so were all rights. Modern history for Simmel is an account of the splitting of the "personal" into the *objective* social—reflected in the spreading impersonality and remoteness of authority, work, religion, and architecture—and the *subjective* social, to be found in man's retreat into the purely private, cut off from society by thickening layers of "reserve." Whether in Simmel's occasional forays into political history, his recapitulation of Western philosophy, or his treatment of secrecy, the stranger, and money, this is the historical canvas on which he paints his conception of the soul of modern man.

One detects in Simmel a certain zest in living in an alienated epoch, for it is in such an epoch, he writes, that the powers of human impression and sensibility are at their sharpest. The loosening of social and moral bonds makes this possible. His essay on "The Ruin" has, as he makes evident in the following passage, implications for the social and cultural "ruin" that characterizes ages of decadence. In the physical ruin of an edifice or a monument we see "purpose and accident, nature and spirit, past and present resolve the tension of their contrasts—or, rather, preserving this tension, they yet lead to a unity of external image and internal effect. It is as though a segment of existence must collapse before it can become unresistant to all currents and powers coming from all corners of reality. Perhaps this is the reason for our general fascination with decay and decadence, a fascination which goes beyond what is merely negative and degrading. The rich and many-sided culture, the unlimited *impressionability,* and the understanding open to everything, which are characteristic of decadent epochs, do signify this coming together of all contradictory strivings. An equalizing justice connects the uninhibited unity of all things that grow apart and against one another with the decay of those men and the works of men which now can only yield, but can no longer create and maintain their own forms out of their own strength." [77]

It is this sensitivity to alienation, set in emotional and moral aloofness, that makes possible the innumerable insights in Simmel's work into the microscopic estrangements and alienations that are to be found in even the most durable relationships of love, faithfulness, and gratitude. A trace of strangeness, he tells us, "enters the most intimate of relationships. In the stage of first passion, erotic relations strongly reject any thought of generalization: the lovers think that there has never been a love like theirs; that nothing can be compared either to the person loved or to the feelings for that person. An estrangement—whether as cause or as consequence it is difficult to decide—usually comes at the moment when this feeling of uniqueness vanishes from the relationship. A certain skepticism in regard to its value, in itself and for them, attaches to the very thought that in their relation, after all, they carry out only a generally human destiny; . . ." [78]

Who but Simmel could have written the following passage which opens his essay, "The Stranger"?

"If wandering is the liberation from every given point in space, and thus the conceptional opposite to fixation at such a point, the sociological form of the 'stranger' presents the unity, as it were, of these two characteristics. This phenomenon too, however, reveals that spatial relations are only the condition, on the one hand, and the symbol, on the other, of human relations. The stranger is thus being discussed here, not in the sense often touched upon in the past, as the wanderer who comes today and goes tomorrow, but rather as the person who comes today and stays tomorrow. He is, so to speak, the *potential* wanderer: although he has not moved on, he has not quite overcome the freedom of coming and going. He is fixed within a particular spatial group, or within a group whose boundaries are similar to spatial boundaries. But his position in this group is determined, essentially, by the fact that he has not belonged to it from the beginning, that he imports qualities into it, which do not and cannot stem from the group itself." [79]

Such a passage is almost paradigmatic so far as Simmel's view of modern society is concerned. For the essence of modernism for Simmel is metropolis, and in metropolis every man tends to be something of a stranger: the potential wanderer, *in* but not really *of* his society.

The direction of history is toward metropolis, which for Simmel is the structure of modernism, performing for his thought the role that democracy does for Tocqueville, capitalism for Marx, and bureaucracy for Weber. "The psychological basis of the metropolitan type of individuality consists in the *intensification of nervous stimulation* which results from the swift and uninterrupted change of outer and inner stimuli." Everywhere in metropolis there is "deep contrast with small-town and rural life with reference to the sensory foundations of psychic life." Metropolis exacts from man a different amount of consciousness than does the rural setting, where the rhythms of life and mental images flow more slowly and more evenly. "Precisely in this connection the sophisticated character of the metropolitan psychic life becomes understandable—as over against small-town life which rests upon deeply felt and emotional relationships." [80] The latter are emotional relationships; they are rooted in the unconscious layers of the psyche and grow most readily in the kind of contexts that ruralism affords. "The intellect, however, has its locus in the transparent, conscious, higher layers of the psyche; it is the most adaptable of our inner forces." Given the incessant stimuli of metropolitan life, rural-like emotional response would be perilous; incessant exposure of feelings to excitation would disorient them. Hence the intellect takes command in metropolitan life in a way that is unknown in the small town, where feeling and emotion can be safely presented to the external world.

Metropolis, Simmel tells us, is the culture of the mind, not the heart. He refers frequently to this dichotomy. The modern metropolitan mind becomes therefore ever more calculating, precise, and regimented.

"Through the calculative nature of money, a new precision, a certainty in the definition of identities and differences, an unambiguousness in agreements and arrangements has been brought about in the relations of life elements—just as externally this precision has been effected by the universal diffusion of pocket watches." [81]

But a tension arises. The same factors that lead to a regimentation of the mind and a blunting of its sense of individuality lead also to a withdrawal from the outer world, a retreat into the blasé attitude. "There is perhaps no psychic phenomenon which has been so unconditionally reserved to the metropolis as has been the blasé attitude. The blasé attitude results first from the rapidly changing and closely compressed contrasting stimulations of the nerves. From this, the enhancement of metropolitan intellectuality, also, seems originally to stem. Therefore, stupid people who are not intellectually alive in the first place are not exactly blasé." [82]

From the same pressure comes the individual's protective reserve, which is also a means of seclusion from stimuli, of withdrawal from excitements too frequent and too intense to support specific and appropriate response to each and every one. "As a result of this reserve, we frequently do not even know by sight those who have been our neighbors for years. And it is this reserve which, in the eyes of the small-town people, makes us appear to be cold and heartless. Indeed, if I do not deceive myself, the inner aspect of this outer reserve is not only indifference; more often than we are aware, it is a slight aversion, a mutual strangeness and repulsion, which will break into hatred and fight at the moment of a closer contact, however caused." [83]

Reserve, considered as a mood of alienation, has had, Simmel reminds us, a creative role in the development of the Western mind from its beginnings in Athens. In one of the most perceptive passages of this essay, he points out that behind the cultural efflorescence of Athens in the fifth century B.C. lay the struggle "against the constant inner and outer pressure of a de-individualizing small town. This produced a tense atmosphere in which the weaker individuals were suppressed and those of stronger natures were incited to prove themselves in the most passionate manner. This is precisely why it was that there blossomed in Athens what must be called, without defining it exactly, "the general human character" in the intellectual development of our species." [84]

What is true of alienation is equally true of social conflict. Simmel, drawing from the same conceptual resources that can deal with alienation as a creative force in culture, puts conflict in a positive light. Conflict has an indispensable value to the structure of the group. Any group "in order to attain a determinate shape, needs some quantitative ratio of harmony and disharmony, of association and competition, of favorable and unfavorable tendencies." A perfectly harmonious and centripetal association could show no vitality or change. "The society of saints which Dante sees in the Rose of Paradise . . . is without any change and development; whereas the holy assembly of Church Fathers in Raphael's *Disputa* shows if not actual conflict, at least a considerable differentiation of moods and directions of thought, whence flow all the vitality and the really organic structure of that group." [85]

We are reminded momentarily here of Durkheim's treatment of the functional indispensability of crime and of the inevitability of moral deviation (he also uses the example of a hypothetical society of saints to prove his point), but the parallel will not long stand up. Everything in Durkheim tends toward the deprecation of conflict and anomie. His theoretical system hardly admits conflict as functional to the social order. After all, the "good" that is done by crime consists only in the instant mobilization of the forces of consensus and in the emphasizing, by the breach, of the norms of rectitude and solidarity.

It is very different with Simmel. In his thought, a degree of conflict is absolutely essential to human relations, just as a degree of alienation is essential to man's awareness of himself as an individual. Even, he writes, within the dyad—the marital relationship, for example—a certain amount "of discord, inner divergence, and outer controversy is organically tied up with the very elements that ultimately hold the group together; it cannot be separated from the unity of the sociological structure." [86] What is true of conflict within the group is equally true of opposition from outside that is directed toward the group as a whole. The Hindu caste system, for instance, rests not only on communal forces within but upon the mutual repulsion of the castes.

Conflict and opposition may not have any direct or visible role in the maintenance of the group's unity, but "it may yet achieve an inner balance (sometimes even on the part of *both* partners to the relation), may exert a quieting influence, produce a feeling of virtual power, and thus save relationships whose continuance often puzzles the observer. In such cases, opposition is an element in the relation itself; it is intrinsically interwoven with the other reasons for the relation's existence. It is not only a *means* for preserving the relation but one of the concrete functions which actually constitute it." [87]

It is in these terms that Simmel remains analytically neutral with respect to processes which to other sociologists formed the very character of disorganization and evil. Alienation and social conflict can have positive, functional value to society and to individuality. It is in this sense that alienation for Simmel is a kind of methodology by which ever more minute aspects of the social order are brought into view.

But while alienation can be creative, it can also produce opposite consequences. Simmel became increasingly preoccupied by what he regarded as the gulf between external culture and the individual soul. He writes: "If, for instance, we view the immense culture which for the last hundred years has been embodied in things and in knowledge, in institutions and in comforts, and if we compare all this with the cultural progress of the individual during the same period—at least in high status groups—a frightful disproportion in growth between the two becomes evident. Indeed, at some points we notice a retrogression in the culture of the individual with reference to spirituality, delicacy, and idealism." [88]

Simmel characterizes the whole development of modern culture as manifesting the preponderance of what he calls "the objective spirit" over "the subjective spirit." Because of this preponderance it becomes increasingly difficult for the individual to know himself as himself; he sees himself increasingly as a mere part of the external, objective culture. "The individual has become a mere cog in an enormous organization of things and powers which tear from his hands all progress, spirituality, and value in order to transform them from their subjective form into the form of a purely objective life. It needs merely to be pointed out that metropolis is the genuine arena of this culture which outgrows all personal life. Here in buildings and educational institutions, in the wonders and comforts of space-conquering technology, in the formations of community life, and in the visible institutions of the state, is offered such an overwhelming fullness of crystallized and impersonalized spirit that the personality, so to speak, cannot maintain itself under its impact." [89]

What is the function of the metropolis? It provides, Simmel tells us, the essential arena for the most fateful struggle that man is involved in. "The external and internal history of our time takes its course within the struggle and in the changing entanglements of these two ways of defining the individual's role in the whole of society." The two ways are, of course, the eighteenth century's relentless insistence upon liberation from the ties of community and the nineteenth century's desire to achieve individuality without the supporting bonds and norms of close social relationship.

"Metropolis reveals itself as one of those great historical formations in which opposing streams which enclose life unfold, as well as join one another with equal right. However, in this process the currents of life, whether their individual phenomena touch us sympathetically or antipathetically, entirely transcend the sphere for which the judge's attitude is appropriate. Since such forces of life have grown into the roots and into the crown of the whole of the historical life in which we, in our fleeting existence, as a cell, belong only as a part, it is not our task either to accuse or to pardon, but only to understand." [90]

Most of what is fundamental in the perspectives of alienation we find in Tocqueville, Marx, Durkheim, and in Weber is epitomized in Simmel's vision of metropolis. Metropolis, as Simmel limns it, is at once analytical and encapsulating, past and present, collective and individual. Tocqueville gives us a picture of man's diminution of stature, Marx of his conversion to commodity, Durkheim of human isolation, Weber of the nemesis of rationality. Simmel's vision of metropolis contains all of these, but goes beyond them in its sense of their involvement in the nature of the social process, in the very nature of man. Community and alienation are, for Simmel, but the two poles of man's eternal identity.

PART THREE

EPILOGUE

Do we exaggerate in referring to the period 1830–1900 as a golden age in sociology?

Troeltsch, in his *Historismus und Seine Probleme,*[1] suggests that in all such ages there is to be found a clear transition from a social order characterized primarily by communal-traditional ties to one in which secular norms and rationalist individualism are dominant. Troeltsch is making use, of course, of the typology of *Gemeinschaft* and *Gesellschaft.* But he adds to it something important that is not in Tönnics. What is ultimately and crucially required in such an age, Troeltsch writes, is a spark that is ignited during that very brief period when the two social orders are of almost equal power in the loyalties they inspire and the incentives they arouse in reflective minds. As Troeltsch describes the process, it is not the transition as such that is precipitative; it is the confrontation, so to speak, of the two orders: the old one moribund, and the new one not yet wholly grown. Out of such confrontation comes friction—to be seen in the problems, often agonizing, that become transmuted into the moral philosophy, the art, and the science of the age—and out of the friction comes the flame of creativity manifest in new insights, new perspectives, and new ideas.

We cannot be sure of a golden age until we see what follows. History reveals many conflicts of what F. J. Teggart calls "idea systems" in history, but only a few, relatively, result in the long-term consequences to thought and culture that permit the adjective "golden" to be relevantly applied. We must find in such an age ideas and perspectives which, although precipitated by a historically defined set of circumstances, prove seminal so far as later thought is concerned. Thus, we properly speak of the Greek fifth century B.C. as a golden age in philosophy and drama because, quite apart from the fascinating institutional conditions of the time and the manifest fermentation of thought, the ideas that came forth from Socrates and, then, Plato and Aristotle were to form the essence of the Western philosophical tradition. To try to imagine what we know as Western philosophy apart from perspectives drawn originally from Socrates and his followers would be impossible. The same applies to the drama that took form under Aeschylus, Sophocles, and Euripides in the same period. Its essential problems were those of spirit and conscience precipitated by the conflict of two powerful and, for a time, almost equally evocative, social and moral orders: the one a reflection of sacred tradition, the other of individual release.

We can hardly claim for the period we have treated in this book the dimension and luster of a Greek fifth century B.C. But there are major and minor golden ages. What is of importance to the historian or sociologist is the texture, not the size, of the tapestry. Put in the terms we have just used, it seems clear that the period we have described, with its half-dozen titans, has every claim to being called a golden age. Its contextual frame was the conflict between two social orders: the feudal-traditional and the democratic-capitalist. Plainly, the conflict, the friction, between these two orders produced a spark of creativity—not only among social scientists, but among philosophers, theologians, and artists.

And the visions and the ideas that were ignited! Would anyone deny that the sociological ideas which emerged in the brief period between Tocqueville and Weber have been other than determinative of the way we, a century later, continue to see the social world about us? Would anyone wish to estimate what would be left in contemporary sociological analysis if we stripped from it such constitutive ideas as community, authority, status, the sacred, alienation—and all of the related ideas and perspectives that flow from them? How many of us even *perceive* the society around us—quite apart from interpreting it—except through the perceptual filters of these ideas and perspectives?

What happens to the intellectual processes that go into the making of a creative age? I am not speaking of the great broad ideas themselves, which go on for generations and even centuries, but of the mental operations by which the ideas come into being in the first place. What prevents them from becoming ritualized, even fossilized? Not, surely, the amassment of data, for, as the long history of science only too plainly shows, men can go on for centuries gathering data, finding "evidence" for ideas that remain fixed. It was not primarily new data but new concepts that marked the passage from the Ptolemaic to the Copernican world view.

It is instructive to quote here a passage from the too-little-known work of the late John Livingston Lowes, *Convention and Revolt in Poetry,* a small volume that says much about the processes involved in social as well as poetic change.

"Out of the seeming chaos . . . of poetic conventions, emerge two weighty and paradoxical facts, which have influenced the development of poetry from its beginnings, and are potent still today: the plasticity of conventions, while the life still runs in their veins; and their tendency (if

I may change the figure) to harden into empty shells, like abandoned chrysalids when the informing life has flown. And through these two opposing characteristics of convention, it comes about that art moves from stage to stage by two divergent paths: on the one hand, by moulding the still ductile forms; on the other, by shattering the empty shells—the way of constructive acceptance, and the way of revolt." [2]

It is hardly an exaggeration to say that for two generations now, sociology, in both Europe and America, has followed the way of "constructive acceptance." With every technique at our disposal, with every methodological refinement conceivable, we have been "moulding the still ductile forms" bequeathed to us by such minds as Tocqueville, Marx, Tönnies, Weber, Simmel, and Durkheim. And the results have been extraordinary: to be seen not merely in sociological hypothesis and conclusion but in the fertilizing effects of sociological perspective upon other disciplines. And nowhere today are the results of application of sociological insight to be seen more vividly than in the study of the new nations, which are undergoing, *mutatis mutandis,* the same revolution that Western society experienced a century ago. The scientific study of the new, modernizing societies rests squarely upon the central concepts of sociology: most notably those of Tönnies, Weber, and Durkheim.

Does this suggest any possible limits to the utility of sociological theory? I have suggested that the key ideas of sociology are, in an almost literal sense, conceptualizations of elements crucially involved in the two revolutions. It was the intoxicating feeling of participating in or at least watching from the philosophical sidelines, these revolutions that provided impetus to the sociological tradition—from Comte to Weber.

We have reached the point today, however (I am speaking, of course, only of the West), when the word *revolution* begins to have a hollow sound. On every side, to be sure, we continue to ring changes on it with respect to technology, education, civil rights, suburbanism, international relations, morality, and so on. No doubt there is some degree of applicability of "revolution" to every aspect of culture in every age. But it must be admitted that much clarity and evocativeness have eroded away in the past few decades. For, like it or not, the two revolutions, in any concrete sense of the word, have been accomplished. We *are* urban, democratic, industrial, bureaucratic, rationalized, large scale, formal, secular, and technological. That many of us are uncomfortable amid the results of the two revolutions—uneasy, perplexed, even nostalgic—does not affect the matter. And, despite our occasional, quixotic tilting at windmills, the results of the revolutions are fixed. They are irreversible.

It thus becomes ever more difficult to squeeze creative juices out of the classic antitheses that, for a hundred years, have provided theoretical structure for sociology. Community-society, authority-power, status-class, and sacred-secular all have vitality so long as the substantive equivalents have reality and relevance. It is like the distinction between state and society or between rural and urban: good so long as substantive referents are still existent, still imperative in their reality, but of diminishing significance, even illusory, once they are gone. The tidal movements of change that up until now have given significance to these antitheses and their numberless corollaries have all too clearly reached a stage of completeness—a stage of mere expansion rather than of continuing development—that cuts much of the empirical ground out from under the antitheses. It becomes ever more difficult to extract new essence, new hypothesis, new conclusion, from them. Distinctions become ever more tenuous, examples ever more repetitive, vital subject matter ever more elusive.

It would be absurd to imply that the sociological tradition, as we have known it for a century, is therefore valueless. There is no more reason why the ideas of a Max Weber in the social sciences should become sterile than that the images and forms of a Milton should lose their power or the Newtonian laws their majesty. There will always be something fresh to be gained by the reader first brought to the pages of Weber or Simmel. But this is not the point. What matters is the continuing viability of a *tradition* or, rather, of the concepts which form it. It is well to remember that while Milton himself retained his power for all subsequent generations, there came a time when the Miltonic tradition was anything but vivid and evocative; when imitation (we may say replication) took command, when the mere "moulding of still ductile forms" produced ritualism and inanition. The history of science is filled with identical instances. Quantification of result and multiplication of instance are no more vitalizing in the sciences than they are in the arts.

The process of "moulding of still ductile forms" cannot go on forever. Sooner or later the process of revolt, of abandonment of "chrysalids" of concept and method, takes place. Perhaps it is taking place in our own day before our unseeing eyes, with some thus far mute, inglorious Weber or Durkheim even now encapsulating stray hypotheses and random observations into a new idea system for sociology: one as different from that which we inherited from the titans of 1830–1900 as theirs was from the idea system of the Enlightenment.

If such a new idea system does appear, to give new life and impetus to the realities of contemporary Western society, it will not be the consequence of methodology, much less of computers, of mass data gathering and retrieval, or of problem definition however rigorous, or research design however aseptic. It will be the consequence, rather, of intellectual processes which the scientist shares with the artist: iconic imagination, aggressive intuition, each given discipline by reason and root by reality. So it has always been and so it is now in those contemporary intellectual areas of most intense creativity. Foremost is the passion for reality—reality not obstructed by the layers of conventionalization, but reality that is direct and unmediated.

What the distinguished mathematician Marston Morse has written is an appropriate note on which to conclude a book about Tocqueville, Marx, Weber, and Durkheim:

"The creative scientist lives in 'the wildness of logic' where reason is the handmaiden and not the master. I shun all monuments that are coldly legible. I prefer the world where the images turn their faces in every direction, like the masks of Picasso. It is the hour before the break of day when science turns in the womb, and, waiting, I am sorry that there is between us no sign and no language except by mirrors of necessity. I am grateful for the poets who suspect the twilight zone."

"The more I study the interrelations of the arts the more I am convinced that every man is in part an artist. Certainly as an artist he shapes his own life, and moves and touches other lives. I believe that it is only as an artist that man knows reality. Reality is what he loves, and if his love is lost it is his sorrow." [3]

BALMES, JAIME LUCIANO (1810–1848). Spanish, Catholic conservative. *Protestantism and Catholicism Compared in Their Effects on European Civilization* (1842–1844).

BONALD, LOUIS GABRIEL AMBROISE, VICOMTE DE (1754–1840). Leading philosopher of French post-Revolutionary traditionalism. *Theory of Political and Religious Authority in Civil Society* (1796); *Primitive Legislation* (1802).

BURCKHARDT, JACOB CHRISTOPH (1818–1897). Swiss historian. *The Culture of the Renaissance in Italy* (1860); *Cultural History of Greece* (1898–1902).

BURKE, EDMUND (1729–1797). Founder of modern British conservatism. *A Vindication of Natural Society* (1756); *Thoughts on the Causes of the Present Discontents* (1770); *Reflections on the Revolution in France* (1790).

CHATEAUBRIAND, FRANÇOIS AUGUSTE RENÉ, VICOMTE DE (1768–1848). French Catholic romantic. *Historical, Political and Moral Essay on Revolutions* (1797); *Genius of Christianity* (1802).

COLERIDGE, SAMUEL TAYLOR (1772–1834). English poet, critic, philosopher. *On the Constitution of the Church and State* (1830).

COMTE, ISIDORE AUGUSTE MARIE FRANÇOIS XAVIER (1798–1857). French Positivist and sociologist. *The Positive Philosophy* (1830–1842); *The Positive Polity* (1851–1854).

CONDORCET, MARIE JEAN ANTOINE NICHOLAS CARITAT, MARQUIS DE (1743–1794). French *philosophe* and revolutionary. *Outline of a Historical Picture of the Progress of the Human Mind* (1795).

DURKHEIM, ÉMILE (1858–1917). French sociologist. *The Division of Labor in Society* (1893); *The Rules of Sociological Method* (1895); *Suicide* (1897); *The Elementary Forms of Religious Life* (1912); *Moral Education* (1925); *Professional Ethics and Civic Morals* (1957).

ENGELS, FRIEDRICH (1820–1895). German, with Karl Marx founder of "scientific" socialism. *The Condition of the Working Class in English* (1845); *Herr Eugen Dühring's Revolution in Science* (1878); *The Origin of the Family, Private Property, and the State* (1884); *Ludwig Feuerbach and the End of Classical German Philosophy* (1888).

FUSTEL DE COULANGES, NUMA-DENYS (1830–1889). French historian. *The Ancient City* (1864); *History of Political Institutions in France* (1875).

GIERKE, OTTO VON (1844–1921). German jurist and historian. *German Law of Associations* (1868–1913); *German Private Law* (1895–1917); *Johannes Althusius and the Development of Natural Rights Political Theory* (1880).

HALLER, KARL LUDWIG VON (1768–1854). Swiss-German conservative, jurist and historian. *The Restoration of the Social Sciences* (1816–1834).

HEGEL, GEORG WILHELM FRIEDRICH (1770–1831). German philosopher. *Phenomenology of Mind* (1807); *Philosophy of Right* (1821); *Philosophy of History* (1837).

HELVETIUS, CLAUDE ADRIEN (1715–1771). French *philosophe*. *On Mind* (1758); *On Man, His Intellectual Faculties and Education* (1772).

LAMENNAIS, HUGUES FÉLICITÉ ROBERT DE (1782–1854). French religious and social philosopher. *Essay on Indifference* (1817); *Words of a Believer* (1834); *On the Past and Future of the People* (1841).

LE PLAY, PIERRE GUILLAUME FRÉDÉRIC (1806–1882). French mining engineer and sociologist. *The European Workers* (1855); *Social Reform in France* (1864); *The Organization of the Family* (1871); *The Essential Constitution of Humanity* (1881).

MAINE, SIR HENRY JAMES SUMNER (1822–1888). English jurist and historian. *Ancient Law* (1861); *Village Communities* (1871); *Early History of Institutions* (1875); *Early Law and Custom* (1883).

MAISTRE, COMTE JOSEPH MARIE DE (1753–1821). Leader of post-Revolutionary French traditionalists. *Considerations on France* (1796); *Essay on the Generative Principle of Political Constitutions* (1814).

MARX, KARL (1818–1883). German philosopher, economist, sociologist; founder, with Engels, of "scientific" socialism. *On the Jewish Question* (1844); *Contribution to the Critique of Hegel's Philosophy of Right* (1844); *The German Ideology* (1846); *Manifesto of the Communist Party* (1848); *The Class Struggle in France* (1850); *Eighteenth Brumaire of Louis Napoleon* (1852); *Critique of Political Economy* (1859); *Capital* (1867).

MICHELS, ROBERT (1876–1936). Italian economist and sociologist. *Political Parties: A Sociological Study of the Oligarchical Tendencies in Modern Democracy* (1911).

RIEHL, WILHELM HEINRICH (1823–1897). German historian and sociologist. *The Natural History of Peoples* (1851–1864).

ROUSSEAU, JEAN-JACQUES (1712–1778). French *philosophe*. *Discourse on the Arts and Sciences* (1750); *Discourse on the Origin of Inequality* (1755); *The Social Contract* (1762); *Émile* (1762).

SAINT-SIMON, CLAUDE-HENRI DE ROUVROY, COMTE DE (1760–1825). French philosopher and utopian. *On the Reorganization of European Society* (1814); *The New Christianity* (1825).

SIMMEL, GEORG (1858–1918). German philosopher and sociologist. *The Problems of Philosophy of History* (1892); *Philosophy of Money* (1900); *Sociology* (1908).

SPENCER, HERBERT (1820–1903). English philosopher and sociologist. *Social Statics* (1850); *Principles of Sociology* (1876–1896); *Man versus the State* (1884).

TAINE, HIPPOLYTE-ADOLPHE (1828–1893). French philosopher, critic, historian. *The Origins of Modern France* (1876–1893).

TOCQUEVILLE, ALEXIS CHARLES HENRI MAURICE CLEREL DE (1805–1859). French historian and sociologist. *Democracy in America* (1835–1840); *The Old Regime and the Revolution* (1856); *Recollections* (1893).

TÖNNIES, FERDINAND (1855–1936). German philosopher and sociologist. *Community and Society* (1887); *Sociological Studies and Criticisms* (1925–1929).

TROELTSCH, ERNST (1865–1923). German historian and sociologist. *The Significance of Protestantism in the Modern World* (1911); *Social Teachings of the Christian Church* (1912); *History and Its Problems* (1924).

WEBER, MAX (1864–1920). German historian, economist, sociologist. *The Status of Rural Workers in East Germany* (1892); *The Protestant Ethic and the Spirit of Capitalism* (1904–1905); *Economy and Society* (although not published in this form until 1921, most of the sections were written by Weber 1910–1914); *Sociology of Religion* (1920–1921, but based upon pieces which, in many instances, go back to the beginning of the century); *Politics as a Vocation* (1919); *Science as a Vocation* (1919).

NOTES

CHAPTER 1 THE UNIT-IDEAS OF SOCIOLOGY

1. *The Great Chain of Being* (Cambridge: Harvard University Press, 1942), 3.
2. *Système de Politique Positive* (4th ed.; Paris: 1912), III, 605. For a detailed account of the influence of conservatism on nineteenth-century thought see my "Conservatism and Sociology," *American Journal of Sociology* (September 1952).
3. It is one of the many merits of Raymond Williams' excellent *Culture and Society: 1780–1950* (Garden City: Doubleday Anchor Books, 1960) that it emphasizes and documents the literary impact of medievalism in the nineteenth century. For the social impact see my "DeBonald and the Concept of the Social Group," *Journal of the History of Ideas* (June 1944), 315–331, especially pp. 320 f.
4. The half-dozen paragraphs which follow are taken from my "Sociology as an Art Form," *Pacific Sociological Review* (Fall 1962).

CHAPTER 2 THE TWO REVOLUTIONS

1. *The Age of Revolution* (New York: Mentor Books, 1964), 17 f. See also Raymond Williams, *op. cit.*, xi–xviii.
2. Cited by Williams, *op. cit.*, 25.
3. Williams, 26.
4. Williams, 15.
5. Williams, 16.
6. *Manifesto of the Communist Party* in Lewis S. Feuer ed., *Marx and Engels: Basic Writings on Politics and Philosophy* (Garden City: Doubleday Anchor Books, 1959), 9.
7. See Asa Briggs "The Language of 'Class' in Early Nineteenth Century England" in *Essays in Labour History*, Asa Briggs and John Saville, eds. (London: Macmillan and Co., 1960), 47.
8. Lewis Namier, *England in the Age of the American Revolution* (2nd ed.; New York: St Martin's Press, 1961), preface.
9. Cited by Briggs, *op. cit.*, 48.
10. Alexis de Tocqueville, *Journeys to England and Ireland*, George Lawrence and K. P. Mayer, trans., K. P. Mayer, ed. (New Haven: Yale University Press, 1958), 107 f.
11. "On Authority" in Feuer, *op. cit.*, 483.
12. Carlyle, "Signs of the Times," Williams, *op. cit.*, 79.
13. *Ibid.*, 79 f.
14. *Democracy in America*, Phillips Bradley, ed. (New York: Alfred Knopf, 1945), II, 159.

15. Leo Strauss, *Natural Right and History* (Chicago: University of Chicago Press, 1953), 57. Professor Strauss could, however, have extended his insight to cover other major ideas in Western history, starting perhaps with the effects of the Peloponnesian Wars on Greek political philosophy in the fourth century B.C.

16. *Words Ancient and Modern,* cited by Williams, *op. cit.,* xii.

17. *The Old Regime and the French Revolution,* Stuart Gilbert, trans. (Garden City: Doubleday Anchor Books, 1955), 12 f. Burke had written in 1790: "all circumstances taken together, the French Revolution is the most astonishing that has hitherto happened in the world."

18. *Confessions of Jean Jacques Rousseau* (Boston: The Bibliophilist Society, 1933), II, 141.

19. *The Social Contract and Discourses,* G. D. H. Cole, trans. and ed. (New York: E. P. Dutton and Company, 1950), 297 f.

20. An excellent recent treatment of the social aspects of the Revolution is Norman Hampson, *A Social History of the French Revolution* (London: Routledge and Kegan Paul, 1963). See also Franklin F. Ford's distinguished article "The Revolutionary-Napoleonic Era: How Much of a Watershed?" *American Historical Review* (October 1963), 18–29. Professor Ford writes: "The most important change of all occurred in the social structure and, equally important, in the way men conceived of social structure." For the detailed institutional histories of the Revolution (which contain the real essence of its impact upon the old order), it is still necessary to go back to the remarkable group of works done in France at the turn of the century, only a few of which can be mentioned in the following pages. On the laws which destroyed the *corporations* and *communautes,* the best of all studies remain Étienne Martin Saint-Léon, *Histoire des corporations de métiers* (Paris: 1898) and Roger Saleilles, *De la Personalité juridique* (Paris: 1910).

21. The best study of the impact of the Revolution on kinship in France remains Marcel Rouquet, *Evolution du droit de famille vers l'individualisme* (Paris: 1909).

22. See Philippe Sagnac, *La Législation civile de la Révolution Française* (Paris: 1898).

23. Antonin Debidour, *Histoire des rapports de l'église et de l'état.* 2nd ed. (Paris: 1911).

24. G. Lowes Dickinson, *Revolution and Reaction in Modern France* (London: 1892), 54.

25. Cited in Charles Guignebert, *A Short History of the French People,* F. Richmond, trans. (New York: 1930), II, 265.

26. Cited by Paul Janet, "La Propriété pendant la Revolution Française," *Revue des Deux Mondes* (1877), 328.

27. Cited by John Morley in his biography of Rousseau (London: 1915), II, 132.

28. Robert R. Palmer, *Twelve Who Ruled* (Princeton: Princeton University Press, 1941), 311.

29. Cited by Palmer, *op. cit.,* 276.

30. *Democracy and the Organization of Political Parties* (London: 1902), I, 48.

31. *The Works of Edmund Burke* (New York: Harper and Brothers, 1837), I, 524 f.

CHAPTER 3 COMMUNITY

1. *Social Contract, op. cit.,* 13 f.

2. *Discourse on the Origin of Inequality, op. cit.,* 244, 254.

3. Cited by Lewis Mumford, *The City in History* (New York: Harcourt, Brace & World, 1961), 454.

4. The classic work on Bentham remains Halévy's *Growth of Philosophical Radicalism* in which this aspect of Bentham's thought and its powerful impact upon his followers is dealt with in rich detail. See also Gertrude Himmelfarb's fasci-

nating essay "The Haunted House of Jeremy Bentham" in *Ideas in History: Essays in Honor of Louis Gottschalk* (Durham, N. C.: Duke University Press, 1965).

5. *Works*, I, 498.
6. *Works*, I, 518.
7. Williams, *op. cit.*, 106.
8. Cited by May Morris, *William Morris: Artist, Writer, Socialist* (Oxford: Basil Blackwell, 1936), I, 145.
9. See the *Système de politique positive*, I, 361 f. Comte's view of individualist and democratic rights as "metaphysical" is a continuous one from his early *Essays* until the end of his life. It was Burke who first pronounced the Revolution's cherished natural rights as "metaphysical." "The pretended rights of these theorists are all extremes; and in proportion as they are metaphysically true, they are morally and politically false." *Works*, I, 482.
10. *Système*, II, 181.
11. *Système*, II, especially 185 ff.
12. *Les Ouvriers Européens* was published in 1855; the second and greatly expanded edition, which I have used, in 1877–1879. Shortly after its publication, the French *Académie des Sciences* awarded it a prize and recommended that a society be founded to carry forward Le Play's method. To this end the *Société d'Économie Sociale* was founded in 1856. If Le Play's comparative study of the family has any single inspiration it is Bonald's remarkable essay "De la famille agricole et de la famille industrielle," *Oeuvres Complètes* (Paris: 1859–1864, II, 238 ff.), first published in 1818, in which he uses the family as a point of departure for a study of the contrasting effects of traditionalism and modernism.
13. Dorothy Herbertson, *The Life of Fréderic Le Play*, Victor Branford and Alexander Farquharson, eds. (first published independently in 1950 by the Le Play House Press; reprinted as Section Two of Volume 38, *The Sociological Review* [1946], 112).
14. *Les Ouvriers Européens*, I, *passim*.
15. The best summary of Le Play's study of family and other communal groups is his own in *La Réforme sociale* (Paris, 1864) which bears the subtitle: "deduite de l'observation comparée des peuples européens."
16. My summary of this aspect of Le Play's study is drawn from Dorothy Herbertson's excellent treatment. *Op. cit.*, 114 f.
17. See *La Réforme sociale*, II, especially chs. 42, 46, and 47. See also *Les Ouvriers*, II, 217 f.; III, 38 f. and 355–372; and V, 33 ff.
18. *Communist Manifesto* in Feuer, *op. cit.*, 29.
19. "The British Rule in India," Feuer, 476.
20. *Ibid.*, 480.
21. *Ibid.*, 480.
22. *Karl Marx: Early Writings*, T. B. Bottomore, trans. and ed. (New York: McGraw-Hill, 1964), 28 f.
23. "On Social Conditions in Russia," Feuer, *op. cit.*, 472.
24. See Proudhon's *Solution du problème social*, his *Idée générale*, and *La Pornacratie*. I have dealt with Proudhon's traditionalist roots in my article on Bonald. *Op. cit.*, 326.
25. Ferdinand Tönnies *Gemeinschaft und Gesellschaft*, 1887; 8 Auflage (Leipzig: 1935). All succeeding references will be to *Community and Society*, Charles Loomis, trans. and ed. (New York: Harper Torchbook, 1963).
26. *Community and Society*, 192.
27. *Ibid.*, 64 f. Italics mine. In Bonald's essay on rural and urban society, previously referred to, we find strikingly comparable wording: "l'agriculture qui disperse les hommes dans les campagnes, *les unit sans les rapprocher*"; whereas "le commerce qui les entasse dans les villes, *les rapproche sans les unir*," Bonald, *Oeuvres*, II, 239.
28. Tönnies, *op. cit.*, 165.
29. *Ibid.*, 166.

30. *Ibid.*, 202.
31. *The Theory of Social and Economic Organization*, A. M. Henderson and Talcot Parsons, trans.; Talcott Parsons, ed. (New York: Oxford University Press, 1947), 137.
32. *Ibid.*, 137 f.
33. *Ibid.*, 139.
34. See *The City*, Don Martindale and Gertrude Neuwirth, trans. and ed. (Glencoe: The Free Press, 1958). It is no disservice to Weber's greatness to observe that this book rests on Tönnies's typology.
35. *The Elementary Forms of Religious Life*, Joseph Ward Swain, trans. (London: George Allen S. Unwin, 1915), 418.
36. *The Division of Labor in Society*, George Simpson, trans. (New York: The Macmillan Company, 1933), 277.
37. See *Suicide: A Study in Sociology*, John A. Spaulding and George Simpson, trans. (New York: The Free Press of Glencoe, 1951), 373 f. This was first published in 1897, four years after the *Division of Labor*. In his second edition of the *Division of Labor*, Durkheim added a new preface elaborating these remarks.
38. *The Rules of Sociological Method*, Sarah A. Solovay and John H. Mueller, trans.; George E. G. Catlin, ed. (Chicago: University of Chicago Press, 1938; New York: The Free Press of Glencoe, 1950), especially Ch. 2.
39. *Division of Labor*, 399.
40. *Moral Education: A Study in the Theory and Application of the Sociology of Education*, Everett K. Wilson and Herman Schnurer, trans. (New York: The Free Press of Glencoe, 1961), 87.
41. *Division of Labor*, 399 f.
42. *Moral Education*, 53.
43. *Ibid.*, 80.
44. *Ibid.*, 120.
45. See Otto von Gierke, *Natural Law and the Theory of Society, 1500–1800*, Ernest Barker, trans. (Cambridge: The Cambridge University Press, 1934); Elie Halévy, *The Growth of Philosophical Radicalism*, as cited. These two works remain the best treatments of this vein of thought.
46. *Division of Labor*, 203 f.
47. *Suicide*, 36 f.
48. *Ibid.*, 35.
49. *Ibid.*, 37.
50. *Ibid.*, 299.
51. *Ibid.*, Bk. 2, Ch. 2.
52. *Ibid.*, 254.
53. *Ibid.*, Bk. 2, Ch. 4.
54. *Ibid.*, 300.
55. *Elementary Forms of Religious Life*, 347.
56. *Suicide*, 213.
57. *Elementary Forms of Religious Life*, 17 f.
58. *Sociology of Religion*, trans. from the German of Curt Rosenthal (New York: The Philosophical Library, 1959), 50.
59. *Conflict and the Web of Group Affiliation*, Kurt H. Wolff and Reinhard Bendix, trans., foreword by Everett C. Hughes (New York: The Free Press of Glencoe, 1955), 149.
60. *Ibid.*, 149.
61. *Ibid.*, 150 f.
62. *Philosophie des Geldes* (Leipzig: 1900). Nicholas J. Spykman, *The Social Theory of George Simmel* (Chicago: University of Chicago Press, 1925), has an excellent synopsis of this much-neglected work.
63. *Sociology of Religion*, 10.
64. *The Sociology of George Simmel*, Kurt H. Wolff, trans. and ed. (New York: The Free Press of Glencoe, 1964), Part IV.

65. *Ibid.*, 311 f.
66. *Ibid.*, 312.
67. *Ibid.*, 313.
68. *Ibid.*, 316.
69. *Ibid.*, 317 f.
70. *Ibid.*, 325.
71. *Ibid.*, 325 f.
72. *Ibid.*, 326 f.
73. *Ibid.*, 328.
74. *Ibid.*, 328.
75. *Ibid.*, 333 f.
76. *Ibid.*, 334 f.
77. *Ibid.*, 336.
78. *Ibid.*, 361; 345–376.

CHAPTER 4 AUTHORITY

1. *Democracy in America*, II, 314.
2. *The Letters of Jacob Burckhardt*, Alexander Dru, trans. and ed. (London: Routledge and Kegan Paul, 1955), 147. "There is nothing more wretched under the sun . . . than a government from under whose nose any club of political intriguers can steal the executive power, and that is left to tremble before 'liberalism,' enthusiasm, boors, and village magnates. I know too much history to expect anything from the masses but a future tyranny, which will mean the end of history" (p. 94).
3. See my "The French Revolution and the Rise of Sociology in France," *American Journal of Sociology* (September 1943), 156–164. It may be said with no exaggeration that Tocqueville, Marx, Le Play, Durkheim, Weber, Simmel, Michels, and Mosca—the prime figures in the development of the sociology of power—all wrote as though the Jacobins were looking over their shoulders.
4. *The Positive Philosophy*, Harriet Martineau, trans. (London: George Bell & Sons, 1896), II, 161.
5. *Works, op. cit.*, 543.
6. Bonald, *Oeuvres complètes* (Paris: 1864), I, 355–358. Also II, 357.
7. *Philosophy of Right*, T. M. Knox, trans. (Oxford: Clarendon Press, 1942), 292.
8. *Ibid.*, 290 f.
9. *The Organization of Labor*, Gouveneur Emerson, trans. (Philadelphia: 1872), 252; *La Réforme sociale, op. cit.*, III, 590.
10. *Democracy in America*, II, 298, 303, and Bk. 2, Ch. 7, *passim*.
11. *Solution du problème social*, 86 and *Idée générale*, 116 f.
12. See my article on Lamennais and the rise of social pluralism in the *Journal of Politics* (November 1948).
13. "L'Avenir," *Oeuvres complètes* (Brussels: 1839), II, 440.
14. See the discussion of the physiocrats' love of centralized despotism and their hatred of intermediate groups in François Oliver-Martin, "Le Declin et la Supression des Corps en France au XVIIIe Siècle" in *L'Organisation corporative du moyen âge à la fin de l'ancien régime* (Louvain: University of Louvain, 1937), 156.
15. See my "The Politics of Social Pluralism," *Journal of Politics*, X, 764–786.
16. *Works, op. cit.*, 504.
17. *Ibid.*, 504 f.
18. *Ibid.*, 505.
19. *Positive Philosophy*, II, 180 f.
20. *The Old Regime*, 140.
21. *Ibid.*, 140.
22. *Ibid.*, 146
23. *Ibid.*, 147.
24. *Ibid.*, 147.

25. *Democracy in America*, I, 10.
26. *Ibid.*, II, 298.
27. *Ibid.*, II, 298.
28. *Ibid*, II, 299 f.
29. *Ibid.*, II, 300 f.
30. *Ibid.*, II, 302.
31. *Ibid.*, I, 265. It is interesting to observe, however, that in the notebooks Tocqueville kept during his stay in the United States, no such characterization is to be found, though there are several references to public opinion. See *Journey to America*, George Lawrence, trans.; J. P. Mayer, ed. (New Haven: Yale University Press, 1960), *passim*. It has to be remembered constantly, as one reads *Democracy in America*, that its author did indeed, while there, see "more than America" and that it was, as he explicitly tells us, "the image of democracy" that he sought. See I, 14.
32. *Democracy in America*, II, 194.
33. *Ibid.*, 194.
34. *Ibid.*, II, 27.
35. *Ibid.*, II, 266.
36. *Ibid.*, II, 266.
37. *Ibid.*, II, 274.
38. *Ibid.*, II, 277 f.
39. *Ibid.*, II, 278.
40. *Ibid.*, I, 208.
41. *Ibid.*, II, 307.
42. *Ibid.*, II, 310. Tocqueville would have been only amused by the myth, sedulously cultivated by the American business class starting in the 1880s that it thrived under and desired *laissez-faire*.
43. *Ibid.*, II, 313.
44. *Ibid.*, II, 313.
45. *Ibid.*, II, Chs. 1 and 2.
46. *Ibid.*, II, 319.
47. *Ibid.*, I, 192 f. and II, Chs. 5, 6, 7. In his notebooks, *op. cit.*, 212, Tocqueville wrote: "The power of association has reached its highest degree in America. Associations are made for purposes of trade, and for political, literary, and religious interests. It is never by recourse to higher authority that one seeks success, but by an appeal to individual powers working in concert." Tocqueville thought American temperance societies were "the last word in the way of an association."
48. *Democracy in America*, II, 118.
49. *Ibid.*, II, 108.
50. *Ibid.*, II, 110.
51. *Basic Writings, op. cit.*, 29.
52. *Ibid.*, 106.
53. *Early Writings, op. cit.*, 31.
54. *Ibid.*, 13.
55. *Ibid.*, 14.
56. *Ibid.*, 15.
57. *Ibid.*, 15.
58. *Ibid.*, 26.
59. *Selected Writings in Sociology and Social Philosophy*, T. B. Bottomore, trans.; T. B. Bottomore and Maximilien Rubel, eds. (New York: McGraw-Hill Book Company, 1956), 218.
60. *Early Writings*, 16.
61. *Selected Writings*, 244.
62. *Ibid.*, 237 f.
63. *Ibid.*, 238.
64. *Basic Writings*, 363.
65. *Ibid.*, 28 f. Marx's insight into *l'idée Napoléonienne*, though limited by its strict economic perspective and therefore less revealing than what Michels

was to write a generation later, is nevertheless penetrating. For Marx there are, in fact, *four* aspects of the Napoleonic Idea: (1) the enslavement of peasant under the guise of his liberation, (2) strong and unlimited government in order to hold the urban proletariat in harness, (3) a "well groomed bureaucracy, large in size," and (4) domination of clergy as an instrument of government. See *Basic Writings*, 341–344.

66. *Ibid.*, 336 f.
67. *The State and Revolution* (New York: Vanguard Press, 1929), 205.
68. *Basic Writings*, 483.
69. *The Theory of Social and Economic Organization, op. cit.*, 341.
70. *Ibid.*, 333 f.
71. *From Max Weber: Essays in Sociology*, H. H. Gerth and C. Wright Mills, trans. and eds. (New York: Oxford University Press, 1946), 253.
72. *The Theory of Social and Economic Organization*, 363 f.
73. *Community and Society, op. cit.*, 226.
74. *Essays*, 196.
75. *Ibid.*, 196–203.
76. *Ibid.*, 76. Like Tocqueville, however, and almost in Tocqueville's words, Weber writes: "Bureaucratic organization has usually come into power on the basis of a levelling of economic and social difference . . . Bureaucracy inevitably accompanies modern *mass democracy* in contrast to democratic self-government of small, homogeneous units" (p. 224).
77. Translated by Eden and Cedar Paul (New York: The Free Press, 1949). The book was first published in journal form in 1908; in German in 1911; and in English, 1915. Michels' indebtedness to Tocqueville and Weber should not blind us to its striking originality.
78. *Ibid.*, 189.
79. *Ibid.*, 386.
80. *Ibid*, 372 f.
81. *Ibid.*, 32 f.
82. *Ibid.*, 408.
83. *The Division of Labor, op cit.*, Preface.
84. *Moral Education, op. cit.*, 31 f.
85. *Ibid.*, 35 f.
86. *Professional Ethics and Civic Morals*, Cornelia Brookfield, trans. (London: Routledge and Kegan Paul, 1957), 14.
87. *Ibid.*, 14.
88. *Moral Education*, 46.
89. *Ibid.*, 54.
90. *Ibid.*, 54.
91. *Division of Labor*, 36 f.
92. *Ibid.*, 110.
93. *Moral Education*, 44.
94. *Suicide*, 371.
95. *Ibid.*, 372 f.
96. *Ibid.*, 373 f.
97. *Suicide*, 389.
98. *Ibid.*, 376.
99. *Ibid.*, 380.
100. *Ibid.*, 380. This is the proposal (at which charges of "medieval corporatism" were flung by some of Durkheim's critics) that he expanded into the long Preface to the second edition of *The Division of Labor* which was published in 1902, five years after the appearance of *Suicide*.
101. *Suicide*, 383.
102. *Ibid.*, 388.
103. *Ibid.*, 388.
104. *Ibid.*, 389.
105. *Professional Ethics*, 45.

106. *Ibid.*, 79.
107. *Division of Labor*, 195.
108. *Professional Ethics*, 60.
109. *Ibid.*, 61.
110. *Ibid.*, 62 f.
111. *Ibid.*, 63.
112. *The Sociology of Georg Simmel, op. cit.*, 299 f.
113. *Ibid.*, 299.
114. *Ibid.*, 299.
115. *Ibid.*, 370 f.
116. *Ibid.*, 375.
117. *Ibid.*, 183 f.
118. *Ibid.*, 33.
119. *Ibid.*, 181.
120. *Ibid.*, 182.
121. *Ibid.*, 183.
122. *Ibid.*, 187.
123. *Ibid.*, 198.
124. *Ibid.*, 201 f.
125. *Ibid.*, 203.
126. *Ibid.*, 206.
127. *Ibid.*, 217.
128. *Ibid.*, 218.
129. *Ibid.*, 219.
130. *Ibid.*, 226 f.
131. *Ibid.*, 233 f.
132. *Ibid.*, 252.
133. *Ibid.*, 253 f.
134. *Ibid.*, 263.
135. *Ibid.*, 273.
136. *Ibid.*, 274 f.
137. *Ibid.*, 276.
138. *Ibid.*, 277
139. *Ibid.*, 275.

CHAPTER 5 STATUS

1. See A. L. Rowse, *The England of Elizabeth; The Structure of Society* (London: Macmillan, 1951), Ch. 6 for a superb account of social class in the age and of men's passionate devotion to rank and lineage.
2. See my *Community and Power* (New York: Oxford University Press, 1962), 138 f.
3. Quoted by Asa Briggs, *op. cit.*, 43 f.
4. *Ibid.*, 43 f.
5. Ostorgorski, *op. cit.*, I, 47–8.
6. Raymond Williams, *op. cit.*, xiii. Burke's views on status turbulence are perhaps predictable but worth noting. Of the French Revolutionaries, he writes: "The next generation of the nobility will resemble the artificers and clowns, and money-jobbers, usurers, and Jews, who will be always their fellows, sometimes their masters. Believe me, Sir, those who attempt to level never equalize. In all societies, consisting of various descriptions of citizens, some description must be uppermost. The levellers therefore only change and prevent the natural order of things. . . ." (*op. cit.*, 476). Elsewhere he writes bitterly of the business class which "felt with resentment an inferiority, the grounds of which they did not acknowledge. . . . They struck at the nobility through crown and church. . . . The monied interest is in its nature more ready for any adventure, and its possessors more disposed to new enterprises of any kind. . . . It is therefore the kind of wealth which will be resorted to by all who wish for change" (504).

And, finally, Burke refers to the alliance of the business class in France with the "cabal" of the *philosophes* whom he calls political men of letters (a phrase Tocqueville was to employ in his *The Old Regime* where there is analogous discussion). Burke writes: "Writers, especially when they act in a body, and with one direction, have great influence on the public mind; the alliance therefore of these writers with the monied interest had no small effect in removing the popular odium and envy which attended that species of wealth" (505).

7. *Democracy in America, op. cit.,* I, 5. The central thesis of Tocqueville's later work, *The Old Regime and the French Revolution,* is substantially an expansion of this proposition plus his related demonstration of the roots of administrative centralization in the old order.
8. *Ibid.,* 6.
9. *Ibid.,* II, 252.
10. *Ibid.,* 252 f.
11. *Ibid.,* I, 47. See also his *Journey to America, op. cit.,* 19 and *passim.*
12. *Democracy in America,* I, 248.
13. *Ibid.,* II, 154.
14. *Ibid.,* II, 154 n.
15. *Ibid.,* II, 155.
16. *Ibid.,* II, 160.
17. *Ibid.,* II, 160.
18. *Ibid.,* II, 128.
19. *Ibid.,* II, 129.
20. *Ibid.,* II, 228. See *Journey to America,* 69 f.
21. *Democracy in America,* II, 138.
22. *The Old Regime,* xiii.
23. *Democracy in America,* II, 168.
24. *Ibid.,* II, 169.
25. *Ibid.,* II, 172.
26. *Ibid.,* II, 173.
27. *Ibid.,* II, 173.
28. *Ibid.,* II, 173 f.
29. *Ibid.,* II, Ch. 5. As I point out below, both Weber and Simmel were to continue Tocqueville's special interest in the relations of masters and servants.
30. *Ibid.,* II, 178.
31. *Ibid.,* II, 178 f.
32. *Ibid.,* II, 179.
33. *Ibid.,* II, 183 f.
34. *Ibid.,* II, 184 f.
35. *Ibid.,* II, 185.
36. *Ibid.,* II, 181.
37. *Ibid.,* II, 182.
38. *Ibid.,* II, 183.
39. *Ibid.,* II, 166. There are numerous references in *Journey to America* to the Negroes and their contrasting status in South and North. A long final chapter in Volume I of *Democracy in America* is devoted to the three races—Caucasian, Negro, and Indian—and their respective positions in American society.
40. *Ibid.,* II, 256.
41. *Ibid.,* I, 378.
42. *Ibid.,* I, 379.
43. *Ibid.,* I, 373 f.
44. *Ibid.,* I, 375.
45. *Ibid.,* I, 375.
46. *Ibid.,* I, 358.
47. *Ibid.,* I, 358.
48. *Ibid.,* I, 359.
49. Le Play, *The Organization of Labor,* Gouveneur Emerson, trans. (Philadelphia: 1872), 275.

50. *Ibid.*, 276.
51. *Ibid.*, 278.
52. Hippolyte Taine, *The Modern Regime*, John Durand, trans. (London: 1891), I, 250.
53. *Ibid.*, I, 252 f.
54. *Ibid.*, I, 256.
55. *Ibid.*, I, 257 f.
56. *Division of Labor*, 379.
57. *Basic Writings, op. cit.*, 8.
58. *Ibid.*, 12.
59. *Ibid.*, 291.
60. *Ibid.*, 256 f.
61. *Ibid.*, 9.
62. *Ibid.*, 43.
63. *Ibid.*, 44.
64. *Selected Writings, op. cit.*, 78.
65. *Basic Writings*, 12 f.
66. *Ibid.*, 14.
67. Quoted in Reinhard Bendix and Seymour M. Lipset, eds., *Class Status and Power* (Glencoe, Ill.: The Free Press, 1953), 31.
68. *Ibid.*, 31.
69. *Selected Writings*, 180.
70. *Ibid.*, 188 f.
71. *Basic Writings*, 255.
72. *Community and Society*, 231.
73. Cited by Bendix and Lipset, *op. cit.*, 50.
74. *Ibid.*, 56.
75. *Ibid.*, 59.
76. *Ibid.*, 61.
77. *Ibid.*, 63.
78. *Essays in Sociology, op. cit.*, 99.
79. *Ibid.*, 102.
80. *Ibid.*, 194. See *The Theory of Social and Economic Organization, op. cit.*, 424–429.
81. *Essays*, 194 f.
82. *Ibid.*, 195.
83. *Ibid.*, 181.
84. *Ibid.*, 183, 184 f.
85. *Ibid.*, 185 f.
86. *Ibid.*, 186 f. *Theory of Social and Economic Organization*, 428 f.
87. *Essays*, 187.
88. *Ibid.*, 187 f.
89. *Ibid.*, 188.
90. *Ibid.*, 189 f.
91. *The Sociology of Georg Simmel, op. cit.*, 41.
92. *Ibid.*, 293.
93. *Ibid.*, 265.
94. *Ibid.*, 266.
95. *Ibid.*, 266.
96. *Ibid.*, 296.
97. *Ibid.*, 296.
98. *Ibid.*, 297.
99. *Ibid.*, 90.
100. *Ibid.*, 91.
101. *Ibid.*, 275.

CHAPTER 6 THE SACRED

1. Quoted by Irving Horowitz, *Claude Helvetius: Philosopher of Democracy and Enlightenment* (New York: Paine-Whitman, 1954), 50.
2. *Ibid.,* 56.
3. Halévy, *op. cit.,* 291.
4. *Ibid.,* 293.
5. *Basic Writings, op. cit.,* 263.
6. *Ibid.,* 262 f.
7. *Ibid.,* 263.
8. *The Elementary Forms of Religious Life, op. cit.,* 427.
9. *Philosophy of Right, op. cit.,* 168.
10. The citation is from the first of Comte's *Essays* (which are appended to Volume IV of *The Positive Polity, op. cit.*). Similar judgments are to be found in *The Positive Philosophy* and in the text of *The Positive Polity.* Comte's rationalism, it should never be forgotten, was set in a deeply religious frame of mind.
11. *The Positive Polity.* See the long discussion of the social and integrative aspects of religion in Volume II.
12. *The Genius of Christianity,* Charles I. White, trans. (Baltimore: 1856), 51–53.
13. *Oeuvres complètes, op. cit.,* 1066 f. Without the thought, Bonald argues, man cannot have devised the word; but without the word, he could not have held the thought. The paradox is resolved only in divine will.
14. From a fragment published posthumously in *Revue de Métaphysique et de Morale VI,* 718. Lamennais's full indictment of secular individualism is in his *Esquisse d'une philosophie* (Paris: 1840). See especially II, 7 f.
15. *Democracy in America, op. cit.,* II, 20.
16. *Ibid.,* I, 310.
17. *Ibid.,* II, 21 f.
18. *Ibid.,* II, 8.
19. Burke, *Works, op. cit.,* I, 494.
20. *Democracy in America,* II, 9.
21. *Ibid.,* II, 9.
22. *Ibid.,* 10 f.
23. *Ibid.,* II, 11 and 32.
24. *Ibid.,* II, 22.
25. *Ibid.,* II, 25.
26. *Ibid.,* II, 27.
27. *Ibid.,* II, 29.
28. *Ibid.,* I, 306. See *Journey to America, op. cit.,* 344 f. and *passim.* Tocqueville's notebooks reveal an interest in religion in America that is second only to his interest in political democracy. He was fascinated by all aspects of it.
29. *Democracy in America,* II, 134.
30. *Ibid.,* II, 135.
31. *Ibid.,* I, 301.
32. *Ibid.,* I, 301.
33. *Ibid.,* I, 300.
34. *Ibid.,* I, 43.
35. *Ibid.,* I, 308.
36. *Ibid.,* I, 310.
37. *Ibid.,* I, 311.
38. *Ibid.,* I, 314.
39. *The Ancient City: A Study on the Religion, Laws, and Institutions of Greece and Rome,* Willard Small, trans. (Boston: 1873), 11. The book was first published in 1864, in Paris.
40. *Ibid.,* 11.
41. *Ibid.,* 12.

42. *Ibid.*, 29, 132.
43. *Ibid.*, 51 f.
44. *Ibid.*, 175.
45. *Ibid.*, 311.
46. *Ibid.*, 313.
47. *Ibid.*, 381.
48. *Ibid.*, 409.
49. *Ibid.*, 471.
50. *Ibid.*, 472, 473 f.
51. *Ibid.*, 475.
52. *Ibid.*, 475 f.
53. *Ibid.*, 529.
54. *The Elementary Forms of Religious Life*, 9.
55. *Ibid.*, 37.
56. *Ibid.*, 38 f.
57. *Professional Ethics, op. cit.*, 182.
58. *Ibid.*, 194.
59. *Ibid.*, 171.
60. *The Elementary Forms of Religious Life*, 44.
61. *Ibid.*, 425 f.
62. *Ibid.*, 416.
63. *Ibid.*, 416.
64. *Ibid.*, 417.
65. *Ibid.*, 417.
66. *Ibid.*, 299 f.
67. *Ibid.*, 326.
68. *Ibid.*, 347.
69. *Ibid.*, 348 f.
70. *Ibid.*, 380.
71. *Ibid.*, 389.
72. *Ibid.*, 413 f.
73. *The Theory of Social and Economic Organization, op. cit.*, 358 f.
74. *Ibid.*, 359.
75. *Ibid.*, 360.
76. *Ibid.*, 361.
77. *Ibid.*, 362.
78. *Ibid.*, 364.
79. *Ibid.*, 366.
80. Reinhard Bendix, *Max Weber: An Intellectual Portrait* (Garden City: Doubleday and Company, 1960), 307.
81. *The Theory of Social and Economic Organization*, 372.
82. *Ibid.*, 383.
83. *Ibid.*, 386.
84. *The Protestant Ethic and the Spirit of Capitalism*, Talcott Parsons, trans. (New York: Charles Scribner's Sons, 1958), 180.
85. *Ibid.*, 90 f. Italics added.
86. *Ibid.*, 74 f. Italics added.
87. Leo Strauss, *op. cit.*, 59 f., 61.
88. *The Protestant Ethic*, 180.
89. *Ibid.*, 182 f.
90. *Ibid.*, 183.
91. *The Sociology of Georg Simmel, op. cit.*, 15.
92. *The Sociology of Religion*, 23.
93. *Ibid.*, 23.
94. *Ibid.*, 24.
95. *Ibid.*, 24.
96. *Ibid.*, 25.
97. *Ibid.*, 25.
98. *Ibid.*, 33 f.

CHAPTER 7 ALIENATION

1. "A Digression on the Ancients and Moderns" in Frederick J. Teggart, ed., *The Idea of Progress: A Collection of Readings* (Berkeley: University of California Press, 1929), 125.
2. "On the Mind," in Teggart, *op. cit.*, 194.
3. "Progress of the Human Mind," in Teggart, 276.
4. *The Positive Philosophy, op. cit.*, II, Bk. 4, Ch. 6.
5. *Basic Writings, op. cit.*, 135.
6. *Social Statics; or, The Conditions Essential to Human Happiness Specified, and the First of Them Developed* (New York: 1886). See Ch. 2, titled "The Evanescence of Evil."
7. Cited in *Catholic Political Thought, 1789–1848*, Bela Menczer, ed. (London: Burnes Oates, 1952), 81.
8. *Ibid.*, 82.
9. *Ibid.*, 81 f.
10. *Ibid.*, 84.
11. Cited by Albert Salomon, *The Tyranny of Progress* (New York: The Noonday Press, 1955), 6.
12. *Ibid.*, 7.
13. Cited in Charles Frankel, *The Faith of Reason* (New York: Columbia University Press, 1948), 111 f.
14. *The Social Contract, op. cit.*, 34.
15. *Oeuvres complètes, op. cit.*, I, 151. I am indebted to César Graña for this revealing passage. See his excellent *Bohemian versus Bourgeois* (New York: Basic Books, 1964), Ch. 2.
16. *Democracy in America, op. cit.*, II, 332 f.
17. *Ibid.*, II, 333.
18. *Ibid.*, II, 332.
19. *Ibid.*, II, 262 f.
20. *Ibid.*, II, 5.
21. *Ibid.*, II, 4.
22. *Ibid.*, I, 263, 265.
23. *Ibid.*, II, 73.
24. *Ibid.*, II, 261.
25. *Ibid.*, I, 267. The following note made by Tocqueville while in the United States is profoundly suggestive of the spirit of his later writings on democracy and individuality: "Why, as civilization spreads, do outstanding men become fewer? Why, when attainments are the lot of all, do great intellectual talents become rarer? Why, when there are no longer lower classes, are there no longer upper classes? Why, when knowledge of how to rule reaches the masses, is there a lack of great abilities in the direction of society? America clearly poses these questions. But who can answer them?" *Journey to America, op. cit.*, 160.
26. *Democracy in America*, I, 203 f. It is amusing to read in this connection what Tocqueville thought of Andrew Jackson, who was President during Tocqueville's stay in the United States. He refers to Jackson as a "heartless despot, alone intent on preserving his power. Ambition is his crime and will yet prove his curse.

   "Intrigue is his vocation, and will yet overthrow and confound him. Corruption is his element and will yet react upon him to his utter dismay and confusion. He has been a successful as well as desperate gangster, but the hour of retribution is at hand; he must disgorge his winnings, throw away his false dice, and seek the hermitage, there to blaspheme and execrate his folly, for to repent is not a virtue within the capacity of his heart to obtain" (*Journey to America*, 161). The editor, J. P. Mayer, informs us that Tocqueville wrote this passage in English. There is little doubt that for Tocqueville President Jackson's administration was a preview of the kind of corrupt, equalitarian, centralization that would become more and more common in democratic governments.

27. *Democracy in America,* I, 10.
28. *Ibid.,* II, 158 f.
29. *Ibid.,* II, 61.
30. *Ibid.,* II, 157.
31. *Ibid.,* II, 157.
32. *Ibid.,* II, 99.
33. *Ibid.,* II, 98.
34. *Ibid.,* II, 137.
35. *Ibid.,* II, 7.
36. *Ibid.,* II, 238.
37. *Ibid.,* II, 238 f.
38. *Ibid.,* II, 235.
39. *Ibid.,* II, 245.
40. *Ibid.,* II, 246. This, like so much else in Tocqueville, is virtually identical with what Weber was to conclude about equalitarian meritocracy.
41. *Ibid.,* II, 247.
42. *Ibid.,* II, 139.
43. *The Recollections of Alexis de Tocqueville,* Alexander Teixeira de Mattos, trans.; J. P. Mayer, ed. (London: The Harvill Press, 1948), 73.
44. "The 'Rediscovery' of Alienation," *The Journal of Philosophy,* LVI (November 1959), 935.
45. *Basic Writings, op. cit.,* 136.
46. *Ibid.,* 254.
47. *Anti-Dühring,* Emile Burns, trans. (Moscow: Foreign Language Publishing House, 1954), 278.
48. *Selected Writings,* 236.
49. *Daniel Bell, op. cit.,* 936.
50. *Ibid.,* 936 n.
51. *Selected Writings,* 169 f.
52. *Ibid.,* 170.
53. *Ibid.,* 171.
54. *Capital* (Chicago: Charles H. Kerr Co., 1906–1909), I, 708.
55. *Selected Writings,* 244.
56. *Anti-Dühring,* cited by Bell, *op. cit.,* 944.
57. "Science as Vocation" in *Essays, op. cit.,* 155.
58. Georges Sorel, *Les Illusions du progrès* (Paris: 1908) and *Reflections on Violence,* T. E. Hulme and J. Roth, trans. (Glencoe, Ill.: The Free Press, 1950). Edward Shils' introduction is noteworthy.
59. *Essays,* 155 f.
60. *Ibid.,* 154.
61. *The Protestant Ethic, op. cit.,* 181 f.
62. *Essays,* 241 f. As noted above, Weber's view of "meritocracy" is strikingly similar to Tocqueville's.
63. Cited by J. P. Mayer, *Max Weber and German Politics* (London: Faber and Faber, 1943), 127 f.
64. *Essays,* 128.
65. *Suicide, op. cit.,* 388.
66. *Ibid.,* 213.
67. *Ibid.,* 211 f.
68. *Ibid.,* 391, 214.
69. *Ibid.,* 214.
70. *Ibid.,* 369.
71. *Division of Labor, op. cit.,* 250.
72. *Suicide,* 365 f.
73. *Moral Education, op. cit.,* 40, 101.
74. *Suicide,* 370.
75. *The Sociology of Georg Simmel, op. cit.,* 409.
76. *Sociology of Religion, op. cit.,* 48.

77. "The Ruin," in *Georg Simmel: 1858–1918*, Kurt Wolff, ed. (Columbus, Ohio: The Ohio State University Press, 1959), 266.
78. *The Sociology of Georg Simmel*, 406.
79. *Ibid.*, 402.
80. *Ibid.*, 409 f.
81. *Ibid.*, 412.
82. *Ibid.*, 414.
83. *Ibid.*, 415.
84. *Ibid.*, 418.
85. *Conflict, op. cit.*, 15.
86. *Ibid.*, 18.
87. *Ibid.*, 19.
88. *The Sociology of Georg Simmel*, 421 f.
89. *Ibid.*, 422.
90. *Ibid.*, 423 f.

EPILOGUE

1. Ernst Troeltsch, *Gesammelte Schriften*, Vol. III: *Historismus und Seine Probleme* (Tubingen: 1912–1925), 742, 45 f. and 362 f.
2. *Convention and Revolt in Poetry* (London: Constable and Co., 1919), 34.
3. "Mathematics and the Arts," *Bulletin of the Atomic Scientists*, 15 (February 1959), 58.

ACKNOWLEDGMENTS

Brief sections of this book have appeared in my *Emile Durkheim*, published in 1965. Permission from Prentice-Hall, Englewood Cliffs, New Jersey, to reprint these sections in adapted form is gratefully acknowledged.

For permission to cite from the following books, I thank these publishers: Alexis de Tocqueville, *Democracy in America*, edited by Phillips Bradley, copyright 1945 by Alfred A. Knopf, Inc., New York; Georg Simmel, *Sociology of Religion*, translated by Curt Rosenthal, 1959, Philosophical Library, New York; *Catholic Political Thought, 1789–1848*, edited by Bela Menczer, 1952, Notre Dame University Press and Burns & Oates, Ltd., London; Max Weber, *The Protestant Ethic and the Spirit of Capitalism*, translated by Talcott Parsons, 1958, Charles Scribner's Sons, New York and George Allen & Unwin, Ltd., London; Ferdinand Tönnies, *Community and Society*, translated and edited by Charles Loomis, 1957, The Michigan State University Press, East Lansing; Emile Durkheim, *Elementary Forms of Religious Life*, translated by Joseph Ward Swain, 1915, George Allen & Unwin, Ltd., London; *Max Weber: Essays in Sociology*, translated, edited, and with an introduction by H. H. Gerth and C. Wright Mills, 1946, Oxford University Press, Inc., New York; *Selected Writings in Sociology and Social Philosophy*, translated by T. B. Bottomore and edited, with an introduction and notes, by T. B. Bottomore and Maximilien Rubel, © 1956, and *Karl Marx: Early Writings*, translated and edited by T. B. Bottomore, © 1964, McGraw-Hill Book Co., New York; Arthur O. Lovejoy, *The Great Chain of Being*, 1936, Harvard University Press, Cambridge; Emile Durkheim, *Professional Ethics and Civic Morals*, translated by Cornelia Brookfield, 1957, Routledge & Kegan Paul, Ltd., London; *Georg Simmel: 1858–1918*, edited by Kurt Wolff, © 1959 by Ohio State University Press, Columbus; Robert R. Palmer, *Twelve Who Ruled*, © 1941, Princeton University Press, Princeton; Max Weber, *The Theory of Social and Economic Organization*, translated by A. M. Henderson and Talcott Parsons, 1947, Oxford University Press, New York; Hegel, *Philosophy of Right*, translated with notes by T. M. Knox, 1942, The Clarendon

339

Press, Oxford; Reinhard Bendix, *Max Weber: An Intellectual Portrait,* © 1960 by Reinhard Bendix, Alexis de Tocqueville, *The Old Regime and the French Revolution,* translated by Stuart Gilbert, © 1955 by Doubleday & Company, Inc., Doubleday & Co., New York; Lewis C. Feuer, ed., *Marx and Engels: Basic Writings on Politics and Philosophy,* 1959, Foreign Language Publishing House, Moscow, and Doubleday & Co., New York; Georg Simmel, *Conflict and the Web of Group Affiliation,* translated by Kurt H. Wolff and Reinhard Bendix, with a foreword by Everett C. Hughes, 1955, *Class Status and Power,* ed. by Reinhard Bendix and Seymour M. Lipset, 1953, *The Sociology of Georg Simmel,* translated, edited, and with an introduction by Kurt H. Wolff, 1950, Robert Michels, *Political Parties,* translated by Eden and Cedar Paul, 1949, Emile Durkheim, *Moral Education: A Study in the Theory and Application of the Sociology of Education,* translated by Everett K. Wilson and Herman Schnurer, 1961, Emile Durkheim, *Suicide: A Study in Sociology,* translated by John A. Spaulding and George Simpson, 1951, and Emile Durkheim, *The Division of Labor in Society,* translated with an introduction by George Simpson, 1933, The Free Press of Glencoe, Macmillan Co., New York; Alexis de Tocqueville, *Journeys to England and Ireland,* translated by George Lawrence and K. P. Mayer, edited by J. P. Mayer, 1958, Yale University Press, New Haven; Alexis de Tocqueville, *Journey to America,* translated by George Lawrence, edited by J. P. Mayer, 1960, Yale University Press, New Haven; *The Recollections of Alexis de Tocqueville,* translated by Alexander Teixeira de Mattos, edited by J. P. Mayer, 1948, The Harvill Press, London; and J. P. Mayer, *Max Weber and German Politics,* 1943, Faber and Faber, London.

INDEX